AMERICAN APOCALYPSE

AMERICAN APOCALYPSE

A History of Modern Evangelicalism

MATTHEW AVERY SUTTON

THE BELKNAP PRESS OF HARVARD UNIVERSITY PRESS

Cambridge, Massachusetts | London, England   2014

Library of Congress Cataloging-in-Publication Data

Sutton, Matthew Avery, 1975–
    American apocalypse : a history of modern evangelicalism / Matthew
Avery Sutton.
        pages cm
    Includes biblographical references and index.
    ISBN 978-0-674-04836-2 (alk. paper)
1. Evangelicalism—History.   2. United States—Church history—20th
century.   I. Title.
    BR1640.S88 2014
    277.3'082—dc23
                                                            2014014034

To Kristen

CONTENTS

PREFACE

ERNEST SANDEEN OPENED his groundbreaking book *The Roots of Fundamentalism* (1970) by noting that ever since fundamentalism's "rise to notoriety in the 1920s, scholars have predicted the imminent demise of the movement. The Fundamentalists, to return the favor, have predicted the speedy end of the world. Neither prophecy has so far been fulfilled." How things have changed since he penned those words. While many fundamentalists and evangelicals continue to predict the speedy end of the world, we no longer expect the fundamentalist-orchestrated revival of radical evangelical religion to dissipate anytime soon. Instead, journalists, historians, sociologists, and political scientists have labored to explain its influence on American religious life as well as its staying power.

This book draws on a lively cast of characters and extensive archival research to document the ways an initially obscure group of charismatic preachers and their followers have reshaped American religion, at home and abroad, for over a century. Perceiving the United States as besieged by satanic forces—communism and secularism, family breakdown and government encroachment—Billy Sunday, Charles Fuller, Billy Graham, and many others took to the pulpit and airwaves to explain how biblical end-times prophecy made sense of a world ravaged by global wars, genocide, and the threat of nuclear extinction. Rather than withdraw from their communities to wait for Armageddon, they used what little time was left to warn of the coming Antichrist, save souls, and prepare the United States for God's final judgment. Their work helped define the major issues and controversies of the twentieth century, and they continue to exert a tremendous influence over the American mainstream today.

While I will elaborate on my terms further as the book progresses, a few quick definitions are in order. I use the general term "evangelical" to refer to Christians situated broadly in the Reformed and Wesleyan traditions who over the last few centuries have emphasized the centrality of the Bible, the death and resurrection of Jesus, the necessity of individual conversion, and spreading the faith through missions. I use the more specific term "radical evangelicals" to refer to those from both the Wesleyan holiness and Higher Life Reformed traditions who in the post–Civil War period aggressively integrated apocalyptic ideas into their faith. I shift from "radical evangelicals" to "fundamentalists" to describe the network of white, Anglo-American radical evangelicals who in the 1910s established a distinct, definable, interdenominational apocalyptic movement. By the 1940s, many of the men and women who had built the fundamentalist movement determined that the label "fundamentalist" was doing more harm than good, so they dropped it. They replaced "fundamentalist" with the older, more historic term "evangelical." As this narrative moves into the 1940s and beyond, my language shifts again accordingly.

I also include pentecostals in this study. Pentecostalism, like fundamentalism, grew out of radical evangelicalism in the late nineteenth and early twentieth centuries. Pentecostals' emphasis on the "baptism with the Holy Spirit," an emotional experience that occurred after conversion, usually associated with speaking in tongues and other divine gifts, distinguished them from their fundamentalist peers. While I do not ignore the many differences that separated pentecostals from other fundamentalists, by the early 1940s they had joined together to craft the modern evangelical movement. It is important to take seriously the history that made a pentecostal-fundamentalist alliance possible, as well as the ways that pentecostalism and fundamentalism overlapped in the early decades of the twentieth century.

The majority of this book necessarily focuses on elite white fundamentalists and evangelicals, the men and a small number of women who directed the movement, policed its borders, and crafted its public image. Laypeople read, heard, and interpreted the words, actions, and beliefs of prominent fundamentalists and evangelicals in many different ways. Nevertheless, I have sought to understand and narrate the attitudes and responses of laypeople through their correspondence with religious leaders, with each other, and to magazine editors. The thousands of letters I read erased any doubts I had about how seriously the faithful, laypeople and leaders alike, took their apocalyptic theology and all of its implications. There was little difference between the rhetoric they used in public and the beliefs and ideas they expressed in private. In fact, what the subjects of this book said in confidence about Christ's imminent return was often more decisive, tense, and anxiety-ridden than their public presentations.

This book builds on two generations of excellent scholarship on American fundamentalism and evangelicalism. Looming large in the research on fundamentalism is the work of Ernest Sandeen, George Marsden, and Joel Carpenter. Marsden defined fundamentalism in his now classic *Fundamentalism and American Culture* (1980) as "militantly anti-modernist Protestant evangelicalism." Fundamentalism, he further explained, was a "loose, diverse, and changing federation of co-belligerents united by their fierce opposition to modernist attempts to bring Christianity into line with modern thought." He later offered a simpler definition echoing Jerry Falwell: "a fundamentalist is an evangelical who is angry about something." Fundamentalism, according to Marsden, had deep intellectual roots; but it was also reactionary. The faithful organized in response to perceived threats to the faith.

Sandeen offered a narrower definition that identified millenarianism as fundamentalism's defining doctrine. The "fundamentalist movement possessed a self-conscious identity and structure," he wrote, and "it is millenarianism which gave life and shape" to it. Marsden disagreed with Sandeen's emphasis on millenarianism. "It is doubtful that premillennialism was really the organizing principle" of fundamentalism, he responded, "even in" the fundamentalists' "own thought." In part the difference between their definitions had to do with whom each counted as a fundamentalist. Marsden included many different "anti-modernists" in his study, including churchly, creedal conservatives, while Sandeen did not. Marsden focused on multiple groups who opposed liberal theology; Sandeen focused instead on the self-identified fundamentalists who self-consciously created an alternative to liberal Protestantism. In other words, Marsden focused on the negative—those who opposed theological modernism—while Sandeen focused on the positive, those who created one explicit movement among many that offered an alternative to theological liberalism. Marsden wisely noted that fundamentalism had deeper roots than Sandeen acknowledged; nevertheless, Sandeen correctly identified millennialism as the distinguishing feature of the fundamentalist movement.

Sandeen's book is now over forty years old, and Marsden's is over thirty. While their work was and is excellent, their books reflect the times in which they were written. Both historians hoped to push academics to take fundamentalism and fundamentalists seriously. They more than succeeded in that goal. However, they did their research alongside rather than within the rise of the new social history, and neither focused on issues of race, gender, or class, oversights Marsden has long since acknowledged. My work asks different questions of fundamentalist sources and as a result comes to different conclusions.

My periodization also challenges traditional histories. According to the chronology proposed by Marsden and Joel Carpenter, which has become so ingrained in textbooks that most religious scholars and historians simply assume it is indisputable, fundamentalism emerged in the late nineteenth and early twentieth centuries, peaked in the 1920s, and then disappeared from mainstream culture and life until after World War II. Both historians emphasize the 1925 Scopes trial as a major turning point. "It would be difficult to overestimate the impact of 'the Monkey Trial' at Dayton, Tennessee, in transforming fundamentalism," Marsden writes. "The strength of the movement in the centers of national life waned precipitously." Carpenter's excellent *Revive Us Again* builds on Marsden's work, arguing that "fundamentalists were in many respects determinedly sectarian and isolated from the American cultural mainstream" between the mid-1920s and early

1950s, at which point their separatism gave way to a "reawaking of American fundamentalism."

My reading of the sources tells a different story. First, I place substantial emphasis on World War I, arguing that it served as the central pivot that brought decades of tension between radical evangelicals and their more liberal counterparts to a head. Had it not been for the war, apocalypse-oriented radical evangelicals might have continued to coexist in the major religious denominations. The war pushed the premillennialist-liberal battle beyond questions of theology and on to questions of lived religion. Radical evangelicals and liberals passionately and brutally accused each other of inadequate patriotism and of undermining the American war effort. The social and political ramifications of their debates compelled the creation of a distinct fundamentalist movement.

Second, I argue that historians have exaggerated the significance of the Scopes trial. After all, the symbol of antievolution fundamentalism, William Jennings Bryan, was hardly a fundamentalist and he cared little for individuals' salvation, certainly one of the most, if not the most, fundamental of all fundamentals. The trial did not mark the end of fundamentalist influence and the beginning of retreat; in fact it had little to do with the trajectory of fundamentalism proper at all. What it did inadvertently accomplish was to muddy the meaning of "fundamentalism," which eventually forced fundamentalists to reclaim the "evangelical" name.

Third, while the Marsden-Carpenter rise-fall-rebirth narrative has dominated the way historians tell fundamentalist history, my work emphasizes continuity more than discontinuity. Cultural engagement rather than sectarian isolation remained both a priority and a reality between the late nineteenth century and the present. Fundamentalists' reactions to the 1928 Al Smith presidential campaign and their attacks on the New Deal—to cite but two examples—reveal that they were anything but withdrawn in the aftermath of Scopes. Despite the claims of post–World War II evangelicals such as Carl Henry, fundamentalists never expressed indifference to the world around them nor did they ever lack interest in influencing the broader culture. They never retreated. Fundamentalists and evangelicals have consistently insisted that God has called them to use their talents to occupy, reform, and transform their culture in ways that matched their beliefs and ideologies.

Finally, I do not draw a sharp distinction between the politics and tactics of pre–World War II fundamentalism and postwar evangelicalism. Postwar evangelicals tried to distance themselves from their depression-era predecessors, and historians have generally accepted the narratives of their subjects. However, the priorities of prewar fundamentalists and postwar evangelicals remained far more alike than not. They held remarkably similar views on issues of the state, the economy, women's roles, African-American civil rights, organized labor, and popular culture. The principle change in the postwar era was one of effectiveness, growth in numbers of adherents, and public image. Their ideology and agenda remained consistent.

In sum, as twenty-first-century scholars and journalists try to make sense of fundamentalism and evangelicalism, they need to take seriously the way the apocalyptic sensibilities of their subjects, refined by more than a century of global turmoil, shaped modern American religion. Fundamentalists' and evangelicals' confidence that time was running out defined who they were, how they acted, and how they related to those around them. This conviction inspired their production of a distinct religious culture and a distinct form of Christian cultural engagement that has impacted the world in profound ways. But how evangelical ideas will influence the twenty-first century is not yet clear. While evangelicals' apocalyptic convictions have waned somewhat in the United States, the belief that the end is nigh is rapidly spreading through the Southern Hemisphere. What this means for the future not even the most prescient evangelical prophets can see.

AMERICAN APOCALYPSE

PROLOGUE

ON THURSDAY APRIL 11, 1912, Philip Mauro boarded the Cunard Line steamer *Carpathia* from New York's Pier 54. He planned to spend yet another summer on the Mediterranean relaxing with his family and doing some evangelistic writing. Ever since his conversion to a radical form of evangelical Christianity, the wealthy corporate attorney had used his gifts of persuasion, refined by multiple appearances before the United States Supreme Court, to make the case for faith.[1]

Mauro's summer plans fell apart just after midnight on the fifteenth when the *Carpathia* received an urgent communication from a nearby US-bound ship, the RMS *Titanic*. The *Titanic* had hit an iceberg at 11:40 P.M. and was taking on freezing ocean water. The *Carpathia* abruptly changed course. It turned north and just slightly west to close the sixty miles separating it from the *Titanic*. Somehow Mauro slept through the frenzy of activity. Available workers from all over the vessel descended on the engine room to help the crew shovel as much coal as possible onto the fires. Passenger cabins grew cold, as the captain redirected all of the ship's steam toward powering the vessel. The relatively rapid acceleration of the *Carpathia* put tremendous strain on the engines, causing the entire ship to vibrate. The steamer eventually reached seventeen knots, faster than anyone had imagined it capable. Meanwhile, the rest of the crew hastily erected first aid stations, scattered blankets around the ship, brewed coffee, prepared lifeboats, and organized the ship's doctors. Then they waited.

While Mauro remained asleep, oblivious to the commotion above, small groups of curious passengers crept onto the deck to watch the action. They felt occasional blasts of arctic air, not what they were expecting on a voyage to the beaches of southern Europe. The ship's staff quickly sent them back to their cabins. Those who learned why the *Carpathia* had turned north onto such a dangerous course beset by scores of treacherous icebergs could hardly believe what they heard, that the great *Titanic* was sinking.

At 4:10 A.M. the *Carpathia* came upon the first lifeboat from the *Titanic*. Mauro awoke soon thereafter. "The scene that greeted our eyes when we went on deck . . . is indescribable," Mauro recalled the next day. "All around us in the sea were detached icebergs glistening in the sun. It was a perfect, polar scene, and although it was only yesterday, and although we remained for hours skirting along the ice-field looking for boats and bodies, it seems already like a dream—so unreal and strange does it appear. Surely the hand of God is most manifestly appearing in the affairs of men."[2]

Within hours, the crew had rescued 705 *Titanic* voyagers; the remaining 1,503 men and women perished. Mauro, along with the rest of the *Carpathia*'s passengers, spent the next four days attending to the survivors and then hearing their stories of the tragedy as they returned to New York. For the lay evangelist, the tragic sinking of the *Titanic* could mean only one thing: it represented "an epitome, a miniature, of the great shipwreck that is coming in the fast-approaching day when the Lord shall rise to shake terribly the earth." According to Christians like Mauro, time was running out.[3]

In the late nineteenth and early twentieth centuries a growing number of radical evangelicals—preachers, evangelists, broadcasters, businessmen, Bible-college professors, publishers, and laypeople—began preaching an imminent apocalypse. They came from every part of the country, north, south, east, and west, and represented all economic classes and levels of education. Some were independents but most worshipped in the nation's major denominations, identifying as Baptists, Methodists, Presbyterians, Episcopalians, Congregationalists, and pentecostals. They organized and attended interdenominational Bible and prophecy conferences, swapped pulpits, spoke at each other's schools, wrote for each other's magazines, engaged in lengthy correspondence, built new institutions, established innovative ministries, launched state-of-the-art radio stations, and set up powerful advocacy groups. And they were predominately male and almost all white. They took gender and racial privilege for granted and excluded minorities from their networks, rarely recognizing social and racial injustice.

Radical evangelicals initially worked to resurrect and refashion early-church millennialism, which they applied to the modern world in creative ways. But soon their ambitions and agenda expanded. What started as a revival of millennial thinking evolved into an interdenominational crusade for the total restoration of the "fundamentals" of the faith. Yet even as adherents' work expanded beyond apocalypticism, their conviction that time was running out so shaped the ways in which they understood their lives and their world, so influenced their character and actions, and so defined how they lived and practiced their religion, that it became an identity-forming norm of religious orthodoxy as well as the most distinguishing characteristic of the movement that they eventually dubbed "fundamentalism." Fundamentalism, therefore, is best defined as radical apocalyptic evangelicalism.[4]

Fundamentalists believed that the world was going to end. Imminently. Violently. Tragically. This conviction defined their relationships to those inside and outside of the faith. It conditioned their analysis of politics and of the economy. It impacted how they voted and for whom. It determined their perspectives on social reform, moral crusades, and progressive change. It influenced the curriculum they brought into their schools and their views of American higher education. It defined their evaluation of alternative expressions of Christianity as well as competing religions. It framed their understanding of natural disasters, geopolitical changes, and war. In short, fundamentalists' anticipation of the soon-coming apocalypse made them who they were.[5]

Apocalypticism, however, never functioned in isolation from other factors. Radical evangelicals' cultural and social milieu, along with their race, class, and gender, influenced them as well. The conviction that Armageddon was imminent worked in concert with other ideas and

beliefs, sometimes conscious and sometimes not, in mutually reinforcing ways to structure the ideology and behavior of those who believed
the world was doomed. Apocalypticism provided radical evangelicals
with a framework through which to interpret their lives, their communities, and the future, which in turn often inspired, influenced, and
justified the choices they made. It filled in blanks, rationalized choices,
and connected dots, all the while making options more urgent and compromise unlikely.[6]

While proponents often identified fundamentalism as the "old-time
religion" or as the "conservative" faith, there was very little traditional or
conservative about it. That is, fundamentalists were not trying to conserve something from the past but were instead savvy religious innovators. Fundamentalism provided Christians with a third way between
liberal Protestantism and creedal, churchly conservatism. But they were
never totally monolithic; throughout their history fundamentalists debated and contested various aspects of the faith. At the same time, they
routinely built alliances with churchly conservatives and other religious antimodernists in their effort to combat what they interpreted as
false understandings of Christianity. While the leaders of fundamentalism tried to shape, direct, and control the movement, its influence grew
exponentially, transforming the nature of faith in the United States in
immense and unpredictable ways. It also shaped a new kind of politics,
one infused with absolute moral stakes.

A very practical faith that functioned in powerful ways, fundamentalism gave adherents secret knowledge derived from a careful reading
of ancient scriptures that allowed them to make sense of the chaos they
witnessed around them. Fundamentalists believed that they alone understood the past, the present, and the future, which gave them an unwavering sense of confidence and absolute authority. Theirs was a utopian movement that looked longingly to a glorious future. While God
had destined the rest of humanity to succumb to the Antichrist, tribulation, and then final judgment, the faithful looked forward to eternal
bliss. They even sometimes seemed to find satisfaction in anticipating
the ultimate annihilation of those who ignored or derided their faith.

But this did not mean that fundamentalists were indifferent to the
world around them. In fact just the opposite. Although they felt sure
that the global apocalypse was imminent, it was never too late for the

individual, the nation, or the world to be reborn. Like devout Calvinists who sent missionaries abroad even though they knew that they were powerless to affect anyone's salvation, or orthodox Marxists who challenged the market economy despite believing that capitalism was an inevitable step on the road to the socialist paradise, fundamentalists never let their conviction that God had already determined the future lead them to passivity.

Fundamentalists drew repeatedly on Jesus's parable of the ten pounds to justify their work. In this story, a king called his servants together, entrusted them with his money, and told them to "occupy till I come" (Luke 19:13). When he returned, he rewarded the servants who by trading wisely had significantly increased the king's investment and he condemned the servants who had buried their money, afraid of losing it. Fundamentalists constantly asserted that Christ had called them to "occupy" the earth until he returns by exercising influence in all areas of life. And occupy they have. Fundamentalists' apocalyptic sensibilities instilled in them a sense of determination that demanded constant action. They believed that they had to wield their influence and power as effectively as possible to prepare the world for the end of days. Jesus was coming soon to separate the sheep from the goats, and they wanted to be ready. They also recognized that obedience had its benefits. No matter how dire the circumstances, no matter what challenges they faced, they were certain that they would ultimately prevail. When events worked out as they hoped, they claimed that God had rewarded their faithfulness and their efforts to bring revival. When conditions aligned against them, they trusted that God was moving the world closer to its end. Either way, the Bible's prophecies were coming true and victory was theirs. While they might lose a battle here or there, they were going to gain the world.

Fundamentalists' efforts to "occupy" until Jesus's return took overt social and political forms. The faithful expected the Antichrist to come in the guise of a political leader and they believed that the world would reach its climax in a violent, global war. The political implications of such ideas were unmistakable. Fundamentalist apocalypticism created a very particular ideology and a very particular form of cultural engagement. It fostered in believers a sense of urgency and certainty and a vision of the world defined in absolute terms. While liberal expressions of Protestant Christianity encouraged patience, humility, willingness to compromise, and tolerance on a range of important issues (at least in terms of ideals if not always practices), fundamentalists believed that they were engaged in a zero-sum game of good versus evil. They had no time or regard for incremental change, or for reasoning with those who differed with them, or for mediation, or for gradual reform. They called for drastic and immediate solutions to the problems they saw around them. With time running out, they hoped to shake the world. Their business was that of instant redemption, of immediate transformation. Fundamentalists created a different kind of morally infused American politics, one that challenged the long democratic tradition of pragmatic governance by compromise and consensus. Theirs was a politics of apocalypse.[7]

During the first years of the twentieth century, fundamentalists seemed deeply out of touch with contemporary trends. Their jeremiads and absolutist ideals provided a stark contrast with the optimism of the Progressive Era, and their movement remained relatively small and dispersed. Despite some radical evangelicals' connections with prominent business and political leaders, to many observers fundamentalism represented little more than an obscure faith on the religious fringe. It might have stayed that way had it not been for momentous events at home such as labor strife, growing class and income disparities, debates over immigration, economic depression, and the development of powerful new forms of mass media and entertainment, combined with dramatic events abroad including Zionism, the Bolshevik revolution, the rise and fall of the League of Nations, fascism, and two world wars. Then, with the detonation of atomic bombs over Hiroshima and Nagasaki the entire world suddenly realized that a global cataclysm had become a very real possibility. As Americans encountered a world ravaged by crises, depression, and violence, fundamentalist doomsayers no longer seemed so outrageous. From the start of the Cold War and continuing to this day, we know that the world we live in could disappear quickly and soon. Nuclear weapons, the environmental crisis, overpopulation, global warming, and "rogue" states armed with weapons of mass destruction all remind us of our vulnerability.

Fundamentalists and their evangelical successors told us it would be this way. As a result Americans have taken them increasingly seriously.

Though evangelicals proved vulnerable to excess and routinely misread current events, their apocalyptic thinking put them in a surprisingly advantageous spot. Amid the disjuncture of modern times, apocalypticism often made better sense than competing theologies. Indeed, evangelical apocalypticism helped inspire a new kind of politics without compromise and gave post–World War II Americans—from those residing in church pews to those occupying the White House—a language and an ideology through which to frame their relationships to the rest of the world. From the Cold War to the "war on terror," from the production of nuclear arms to the deployment of killer drones, apocalyptic ideas have surfaced at crucial moments in American history over the past century, capturing fundamentalist promises of terror, destruction, and vindication. In crafting an absolutist, uncompromising, good-versus-evil faith, evangelicals have transformed the lives of countless individuals and established a new form of radical politics.

When Mauro observed on board the *Carpathia* that surely "the hand of God is most manifestly appearing in the affairs of men," he could not have anticipated how that manifestation would affect the trajectory of the United States. While many Americans expected the apocalyptic worldview of those like Mauro to foster complacency, indifference, and apathy, it had the opposite effect. Clutching newspapers in one hand and well-read Bibles in the other, fundamentalists and evangelicals redefined the nature of religion in the United States and its relationship to the broader culture. In anticipating the imminent end of the world, fundamentalists paradoxically transformed it.

1

JESUS IS COMING

JESUS IS COMING.

At least that's what William E. Blackstone assured thousands of anxious Christians in 1878. A wealthy Chicago real estate developer and friend of evangelist Dwight L. Moody, Blackstone felt energized by the chaos he saw around him. The dapper man with bald head and prominent mutton chops believed that the Bible laid out a series of signs that would indicate when the end was nigh. The signs were starting to appear.

Certain that time was running out, Blackstone decided to take up a pen and draft *Jesus Is Coming* to warn as many people as possible about the imminent apocalypse. To illustrate how close the world was to Armageddon, Blackstone cited various signs that touched on almost every aspect of modern life. The precarious states of capitalism and democracy represented one ominous indication that the apocalypse was near. "We believe," he wrote, "if we can rightly read the signs of the times, that the godless, lawless trio of communism, socialism and nihilism" are "preparing the way for Antichrist." Other signs lined up perfectly with the conditions that inspired Mark Twain's novel *The Gilded Age*. Blackstone viewed "oppressing monopolies, systematic [s]peculation and fraud" as important indicators that the days were numbered. Others had to do with moral issues, such as the rising circulation of "obscene literature," which had provoked a series of so-called Comstock laws constraining the publication and sale of such works. The future as Blackstone saw it was bleak. "Surely then this wicked world, which is so radically opposed to God, and under the present control of His arch enemy, is not growing better. On the contrary, judgment, fire and perdition are before it. Perilous times are coming."[1]

Despite Blackstone's expectation of such a dire future, his sentiments did not drive him or his fellow believers to apathy or indifference. "We neither despair, nor fold our hands to sleep," the businessman-theologian explained. "On the contrary, we are filled with a lively hope." Explaining that millennial convictions sparked action rather than ennui, he continued, "Surely this positive conviction of coming doom is a mightier incentive to action than can be the quieting fallacy that things are moving on prosperously and that EVEN THE WORLD IS GETTING BETTER." While critics accused men and women like Blackstone of otherworldliness, their convictions seemed to have the opposite effect. Preparing for Jesus's return fostered intense, relentless engagement with the world around them.[2]

The publication of *Jesus Is Coming* signaled the beginning of a radical new religious movement that eventually transformed the faith of millions in the United States and then the world. By the time of Blackstone's death in 1935, over a million copies of his book had been printed in multiple editions in forty-eight languages, making it one of the most influential religious books of the twentieth century.[3]

Blackstone's gloomy prognostications combined with his call for action appealed to a small but significant group of Americans. Whether driven by innately cynical dispositions, challenging personal circumstances, or simple restlessness, a handful of Christians from all regions, classes, levels of education, and walks of life determined that they were living in a shallow and meaningless age. Grasping newspapers in one hand and the prophetic books of the Bible in the other, they looked for encompassing solutions to their own—and the world's—problems. They found one in the resurrection and reconstruction of an ancient Christian tradition of millennialism. Following the lead of past generations of Christians, they used the Bible to decode history. Their sacred text provided them with secret knowledge of ages past, present, and to come.

Their faith fostered a powerful sense of purpose and personal identity, it helped them make sense of the challenges around them, and it provided them with a triumphant vision of the future. It offered them the promise of transformation and redemption in a world that seemed void of both. It also served as a call to battle rather than as a justification for withdrawal. God had given them much to do and very little time in which to do it. Positive that Jesus was coming soon, they preached revival and engaged directly and aggressively with their culture. Their efforts to remake the world while standing at the eve of Armageddon inspired the rise of a revolutionary new expression of Christianity.

Americans like Blackstone living in the mid- to late nineteenth century faced many disquieting circumstances. The Civil War had claimed six hundred thousand lives and yet the nation remained divided in significant ways. Presidential politics reached an all-time low in 1876 when disputed electoral college votes sparked a constitutional crisis that culminated in the "corrupt bargain" that put Rutherford B. Hayes into the White House. In exchange for the presidency, Republicans brought Reconstruction to an inglorious end, essentially abandoning recently emancipated slaves to their former masters. The government's actions bred increased cynicism about national politics and fostered discord and nascent racism.

The economy had also faltered. It began contracting in 1873 and did not recover for over half a decade. Hungry and frustrated, workers increasingly turned to unions for help, which led to the expansion of groups like the Knights of Labor. Unions proposed alternative ways of organizing the economy and criticized laissez-faire capitalism and abusive labor practices. In 1877 railroad employees working for some of the most powerful, modern corporations in the nation went on strike. They brought rail traffic to a standstill across the country. Various governors called on state militias and then federal troops to crush the uprising, inciting violence. Such events highlighted the mounting class divisions and labor unrest in the United States. Meanwhile, farmers, facing depressed prices, began to organize as well, laying the foundations for the Populist revolt of the 1890s and for the emergence of a new form of protest and dissent.

The development of new technology reshaped the rhythms of daily life and erected novel and unfamiliar patterns of mobility and communication. In 1878, Thomas Edison established the Edison Electric Light Company. Before long, urban Americans no longer based their schedules on the rising and setting of the sun. Railroads spread across the continent and cables established communications networks around the United States and with Europe. Time became something Americans sought to measure, predict, and control. Within a few decades the automobile, film, and then radio would further transform American culture and indeed the environment, both urban and rural, by shrinking time and distance through new modes of transportation and communication. Some Christians saw such technological innovations as evidence that the world must be edging toward Judgment Day.

Controversies over race and ethnicity came to the fore in the late nineteenth century as the population diversified. Millions of immigrants, including record numbers of Catholics and Jews, flooded into the country, raising anxieties among native-born whites as Protestant power began to wane. Many immigrants settled in urban areas, joined by thousands of Americans fleeing the nation's farms. Bustling but dirty and overcrowded, cities took center stage in American political and social life in the early twentieth century along with a growing sense of uprootedness and anomie. The expansion of dense urban populations broke down traditional means of moral surveillance, creating a sense of insecurity and disorder.

In the aftermath of Reconstruction, white and black Americans continued to redefine their relationships to each other. During the late 1800s southern state legislatures put a series of Jim Crow laws into effect, codifying segregation, while de facto segregation continued to characterize much of the North and West. African Americans living at the turn of the century faced innumerable challenges as race and racism shaped Americans' approaches to just about every facet of life from politics to entertainment to religion. White radical evangelicals, like almost all white Christians in this era, most often prioritized race over theology. They made the color line much harder to surmount than any theological boundaries.

Changes abroad influenced Americans' lives and sense of themselves as well. In the race for empire, European and Asian states aggressively worked to expand their power and territories by carving up Africa, the Pacific, and parts of Asia. Meanwhile, the United States did the same, expanding beyond the North American continent in search of new territories in the Caribbean and the Pacific. The world seemed to shrink as different peoples came into closer contact with one another, not as equals but in hierarchies derived from color and religious creed. Understanding the new geopolitical structures that resulted from imperialism, colonization, and nationalism kept busy those who used the Bible to assess the significance of geopolitics. Comparing international news to arcane prophecies required a lot of work and patience.

As Americans approached the end of the century many hoped for a better future for themselves and their world. They celebrated how far the United States had come in fulfilling its "Manifest Destiny" as it stretched from the Atlantic to the Pacific. They believed that democracy and the free market provided the kinds of unlimited opportunities represented in Horatio Alger's popular rags-to-riches stories, and they embraced a new era of scientific innovation, which they hoped would help humans achieve their full potential. But the period between the Civil War and World War I proved deeply unsettling as well. Individuals' lives, like the nation as a whole, remained in flux. While some Americans interpreted change as progress, others believed that it created insecurity. The latter struggled to control the pace and direction of events. In the face of so many challenges, many Americans longed for peace and stability.

Religion served as one source of hope and encouragement for many people. Conservative churchmen appealed to tradition, doctrine, and creeds in their effort to keep humans' lives grounded. Their work offered stability and consistency to countless Christians. Theologically liberal Protestants, meanwhile, sought new ways to apply Christianity to the many questions and issues facing the nation. They adapted religion to a changing population by emphasizing the person and ethics of Jesus over traditional doctrines and creeds. They viewed God as immanent in the world and as working through it rather than transcendent, and they stressed human reason over supernatural revelation. Liberal Protestants interpreted theology as the product of the evolution of ideas rather than as a fixed set of immutable truths. Religion, like humankind, was progressively ascending an evolutionary ladder over time. Some liberal Christians even began to question the nature and authority of the Bible itself. In the late nineteenth century they adopted a literary-critical approach to interpreting the sacred text called higher criticism, which raised serious questions about the authorship, historicity, and dating of certain biblical books. Their conclusions seemed to undermine traditional views of the scripture's accuracy and authority. The Bible, they believed, was great literature that spoke to the human condition rather than a book of scientific or historical truths delivered in propositional form. Nevertheless, the differences between liberals and conservatives were not always clear or distinct. In many cases, liberal-leaning and conservative-leaning men and women worked and fellowshipped together, exchanging ideas and beliefs. This lasted until World War I, when the impact of the global crisis fractured mainstream American Protestantism.[4]

Near the turn of the century some leading theological liberals began to call themselves "modernists." Drawing on the modernist movements in art, literature, and culture, they focused on the process of being Christian. They interrogated their faith with the goal of making it relevant to the contemporary world. In so doing, they abandoned notions of an absolute, objective, external, orthodox religion. Instead they emphasized the practice of believing, of asking questions of themselves and their faith and then embarking on an intellectual journey in search of answers to those questions. The process of embracing faith rather than the ends of defining and claiming it became the substance of modernist Protestantism.[5]

Theological modernism took shape in part through the Social Gospel movement. Social Gospel leaders sought to apply the message of Jesus to current conditions in new ways. For generations evangelicals had integrated social concern with their ministries, but Social Gospelers went a step further by prioritizing activism and good works over doctrine and by reading the latter through the lens of the former. They worked with a broad base of activists and contributed to and drew on the latest social science research as they focused on alleviating the destructive social and environmental conditions that caused so much of the poverty and despair they witnessed around them. Downplaying individual sin, they served Jesus not by preaching the gospel but by transforming their communities. In articulating solutions to the problems they witnessed, they advocated structural over individual solutions, which often called for substantial transformations of American society and the economy. They developed new partnerships, realizing that enacting the types of reforms they envisioned required time, political mobilization, and alliances with the state.

Whether conservative, creedal Christians, innovative liberals and modernists, or something in between, most late nineteenth-century Protestants felt optimistic about the future. They longed for the coming of the millennium, a thousand-year period of peace, prosperity, and righteousness described in the book of Revelation, which they hoped to help inaugurate through their own good works. They believed that the return of Christ would mark the conclusion of the millennium. As a result they identified as "postmillennialists," based on their conviction that the second coming of Christ would occur after the millennium. A few, however, identified as amillennialists; they believed that the millennium was more metaphorical than literal.

While postmillennialists, both conservative and liberal, offered Americans an enthusiastic vision of the future, a group of radical white evangelicals kept a skeptical eye on much of what was occurring around them. Living amid the rise of the modern university system, massive urbanization, political turmoil, and significant Catholic and Jewish immigration, a determined group believed that true Christianity, and perhaps their way of life, was under siege. They feared that churchly conservatives had lost the authentic radicalism of New Testament Christianity and had failed to make faith relevant to the world's changing conditions. They viewed liberal Protestantism and movements like the Social Gospel as troubling distortions of Christianity that had seemingly transformed religion into little more than a shallow nostrum for curing temporal problems.

As radical evangelicals tried to make sense of the changing times, they began to find in the scriptures verses that they had not noticed before, while vague and obscure passages came into sharper focus. Informed by their historical context, their reading of church history, and the work of a few relatively obscure European apocalypticists, they came to the startling conclusion that they were not preparing the world for a godly millennium. Instead, they were living in the end times— the period of history predicted by biblical writers thousands of years earlier that would immediately precede the battle of Armageddon and the second coming of Jesus. Rather than waiting for the kingdom of God to appear through moral reform or personal regeneration, they saw tribulation and death looming on the horizon. For them time was short and humankind was careening toward an inevitable apocalypse. They felt the need to warn the nation and the world that Jesus was coming back. And he was coming soon.

Throughout Western history, various Christians have seen in dramatic social changes hints of the coming apocalypse. The Crusades, the Reformation, and the French Revolution inspired short-lived millennial movements that eventually faded into obscurity. In the United States, groups like the Shakers, the Church of Jesus Christ of Latter-day Saints, and other more mainstream Protestants have at times heralded Christ's coming kingdom. Doomsaying has often walked hand in hand with the Christian faith. What made the apocalyptic movement of Mauro and Blackstone's generation different were the ways in which massive geopolitical changes in the late nineteenth and twentieth century seemed to confirm adherents' hopes, expectations, and predictions. World events appeared to be lining up with biblical prophecy as never before.

Radical evangelicals, despairing of world conditions, crafted a new theology informed by the intellectual currents of their day. They claimed to practice a literal and direct reading of the holy text. In so doing, they sought to differentiate themselves from theological liberals who strove to interpret the text in the light of contemporary thinking. These evangelicals believed that all truth derived from God and that through "common sense" all people could discern that truth. They admired the empirical philosophy of Francis Bacon as well as the Scottish Common Sense Realism of philosophers like Thomas Reid. In a sermon defending the second coming of Christ as the "doctrinal center of the Bible" A. T. Pierson explained, "I like a Biblical theology that does not start with the superficial Aristotelian method of reason, that does not begin with an hypothesis, and then warp the facts and the philosophy to fit the crook of our dogma, but a Baconian system, which first gathers the teachings of the word of God, and then seeks to deduce some general law upon which those facts can be arranged."[6]

However, radical evangelicals could not escape their historical contexts. They treated the Bible like a series of propositions that when properly arranged and classified unveiled the plan of the ages. Their emphasis on scientific accuracy, quantification, classification, and interpretive rigor reflected their own dependence on the same modes of thinking that defined theological modernism. So did their historical consciousness and their obsession with structuring and ordering time. Rather than creating an antimodernist alternative derived from some kind of universal common sense, these believers pioneered a new form of Christianity deeply grounded in and reflective of the modernist intellectual currents of their era. While they came to describe their approach as "conservative" in contrast to modernist methods, there was little that was conservative or traditional about it.[7]

Protestant apocalypticists like Blackstone drew inspiration from the work of theologians in the British Isles. Some evangelists and ministers across the Atlantic, inspired especially by the seeming fulfillment of prophecy in the French Revolution, had been reviving and revising millennial beliefs. During the mid-nineteenth century one strand of millennialists codified their ideas into a theological system called dispensational premillennialism, which emphasized the interrelationships between secular politics, divine history, and the end times. Irishman John Nelson Darby, dispensational premillennialism's greatest early popularizer, introduced North Americans to his beliefs in the 1860s and 1870s during a series of evangelistic tours. His campaign to convince Canadians and Americans that exceedingly dark days loomed ahead initially met with little success. "The condition of the States spiritually— indeed, in every way except money-making—is frightful," he wrote his brother from Toronto. "The common course for Christians is to go to balls, &c." Nevertheless, he found reason to press on. "All through the States the truths are drawing attention. Ministers come here to see what it is." As his influence and ideas spread, he provided American apocalypticists with a palette of ideas from which they could pick and choose.[8]

Darby and his coreligionists believed that God had divided up human history, stretching from the Garden of Eden to the millennial kingdom, into distinct chronological sections called "dispensations." According to their interpretations, God worked with humans in each dispensation in a different way. For example, God's relationship with Adam and Eve, who were created in moral innocence, differed from God's relationship with Moses, through whom God established the law. Things grew a little more complicated for dispensationalists as they analyzed the New Testament. Most believed that the church age, which began in the era of the original apostles and continues to this day, was the great "parenthesis" between Christ's post-Resurrection ascension to heaven and his coming return for his church. The basis for this interpretation was in part a creative reading of the prophet Daniel's references to "seventy weeks" in Daniel 9:22–27 (which they interpreted as seventy "sevens" or 490 years). Darby and his followers believed that the first sixty-nine weeks occurred in the span between the rebuilding of Jerusalem (documented in Ezra and Nehemiah) and Jesus's time. The seventieth week, a seven-year period of trial and tribulation yet to occur, would mark the end of the church age. Looking for signs that this final seven-year week was imminent motivated most of their prophetic analysis.

The system was not without controversy even among adherents. Dispensationalists have never reached total consensus on some of the elements of their theology. They argue, for example, about the number of dispensations and their characteristics. They also debate when the dispensations will unfold in human history. The vast majority of Christians who eventually called themselves fundamentalists joined Darby in settling on a "futurist" interpretation, believing that prophecies of the last days outlined in Daniel, Ezekiel, Matthew, and Revelation would occur in the "seventieth week" in rapid succession just before Christ's return. This contrasted with the more traditional "historicist" position, which held that the fulfillment of prophecy had unfolded over centuries. The most famous American historicist, William Miller, had predicted the return of Christ in the 1840s. He was wrong. When Christ did not return as expected, thousands of his followers felt disillusioned, while newspapers and magazines around the nation mocked them. In the wake of the Miller debacle, the futurist position proved for many American premillennialists to be the safer and more practical option. It provided adherents with an imminent hope of the second coming without forcing them to identify a specific date. Jesus, they determined, was always coming; they had to be ready at all times.

Influenced by dispensationalism, radical evangelicals agreed that at the end of the current age a series of extraordinary events would unfold. Most expected the "rapture" to initiate Daniel's seventieth week.

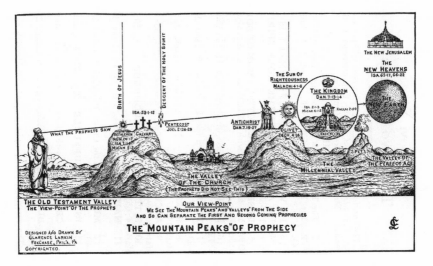

Clarence Larkin, a mechanical engineer, draftsman, and preacher, created dozens of popular charts in the 1910s that masterfully illustrated premillennial ideas. "The 'Mountain Peaks' of Prophecy" shows how the rise of the Antichrist will mark the end of the current "church" age, a great parentheses between the first and second comings of Christ.

Clarence Larkin, "The Mountain Peaks of Prophecy," *Rightly Dividing the Word* (Philadelphia: Fox Chase, 1921), 66.

Identifying and explaining the rapture—a dramatic experience in which all living Christians will mysteriously vanish from the earth and the dead will rise to heaven—was one of Darby's great theological innovations. The word "rapture" does not appear in the Bible and it was not a well-developed biblical concept prior to the nineteenth century. Premillennialists locate the rapture in 1 Thessalonians 4:15–17: "For the Lord himself shall descend from heaven with a shout, with the voice of the archangel, and with the trump of God: and the dead in Christ shall rise first: Then we which are alive and remain shall be caught up together with them in the clouds, to meet the Lord in the air: and so shall we ever be with the Lord." Darby and his followers taught that after the rapture, those left behind would undergo a seven-year tribulation. A new leader—who is actually the Antichrist—will take power in this period, assuming control over a ten-kingdom confederacy established within the boundaries of the old Roman Empire. His reign will be characterized by what the prophet Daniel called a

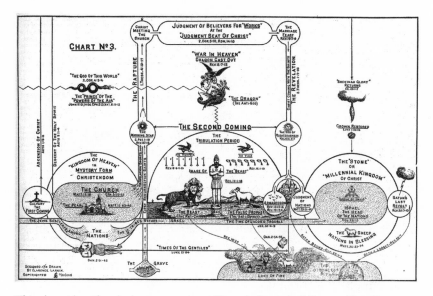

This chart identifies the key events that will mark the end of the age. First, Jesus will rapture all true Christians to heaven, paving the way for the Antichrist to preside over the world during a seven-year tribulation. His reign will end with the second coming of Christ, the battle of Armageddon, the judgment of the nations, and finally the start of the new millennium.

Clarence Larkin, "Chart No. 3," *Dispensational Truth* (New Rochelle, NY: published by the author, 1920).

combination of "iron" and "clay" (Daniel 2:40–43). Premillennialists interpreted this as a mix of totalitarian rule (iron) supported by popular democracy (clay). Although the Antichrist would have unprecedented political control, his confederation would face enemies to the north, south, and east. Radical evangelicals' preoccupation with anticipating who those enemies would be drove them to become serious students of geopolitical developments. Some radical evangelicals, however, believed that the rapture would occur slightly later in the prophetic scheme. Rather than affirming Darby's pretribulation rapture, they anticipated a "mid-trib" or "post-trib" rapture.[9]

Darby also taught that Jews would play a prominent role on the world stage in the last days. His reading of the scriptures convinced him that God planned to restore Jews to Palestine, and that this restoration would serve as a major signal that the end times had begun. Building on Darby's ideas, some American premillennialists saw great significance in Matthew 24:32–33: "Now learn a parable of the fig tree; When his branch is yet tender, and putteth forth leaves, ye know that summer is nigh: So likewise ye, when ye shall see all these things, know that it is near, even at the doors." Interpreting the fig tree as a symbol of the Jewish nation, they believed that in order for the remaining last-days prophecies to be fulfilled, Jews needed to return to Palestine, the land that God had established for them. Without a major Jewish migration, there could be no second coming.

For Blackstone, helping facilitate Jewish restoration to Palestine became a consuming passion. "Do you wonder," he asked readers in *Jesus Is Coming,* "that the great mass of Jews, at the present time, have an abiding faith that they are to be returned to Canaan? . . . Shall we, who have accepted so much greater light, refuse this overwhelming testimony of the Word? God forbid." He called Israel "God's sun dial. If we want to know our place in chronology, our position in the march of events," he wrote, "look at Israel."[10]

Blackstone's theological convictions directly inspired his actions. As he embraced premillennialism he also assumed a leading role in the development of American Zionism. Despite his somewhat controversial theological beliefs, his wealth and connections with prominent Americans provided him with substantial influence. In 1891 he penned the now famous Blackstone Memorial, advocating the creation of a new homeland for Jews in Palestine. It included the signatures of over four hundred prominent Americans, including the chief justice of the Supreme Court, the Speaker of the House of Representatives, future president William McKinley, the editors of the country's major newspapers, including the *New York Times* and *Chicago Tribune,* and corporate barons J. P. Morgan and John D. Rockefeller. Blackstone also presented it to the current president, Benjamin Harrison. In a letter accompanying the petition, Blackstone explained to Harrison that prophecy guaranteed that Jews would return to Palestine. He also cited Genesis 12:3, "I will bless them that bless thee," promising the president that God would favor the United States if the president supported the Zionist cause. In this way Blackstone both predicted the return of Jews to Palestine and worked to make it happen. As a result he has been remembered as one of the fathers of modern Zionism.[11]

The restoration of Israel, however, would not conclude with a happy ending for Jews, at least not according to the prophetic scheme popularized by Blackstone. While premillennialists expect the Antichrist to appear initially as the Jews' savior, they believe that he will soon demand worship from the Jews. Those who refuse will encounter horrific persecution. Meanwhile, the Antichrist will face a series of enemies who seek control of the supposedly vast untapped resources yet to be discovered in Palestine. Near the end of the Antichrist's seven-year reign, he will engage in a series of wars culminating in a great battle at Armageddon, a literal valley in Israel. There Christ and his army of saints will vanquish the Antichrist, inaugurating Jesus's millennial reign on earth.

Darby's audiences initially scoffed at this radical understanding of biblical prophecy. Most American Protestants in the nineteenth century, liberals and conservatives, believed that the world was growing more and more Christian and that the kingdom of God would soon appear on earth in part as a result of their faithful efforts. The return of Christ would follow after the establishment of this millennium. Many even believed that the United States, like ancient Israel, was the vehicle through which God would perfect the world. Such sentiments had animated American Christians since colonial times and had helped inspire the Social Gospel movement.

Darby's premillennial conviction that there would be no period of peace and prosperity until after the battle of Armageddon and the return of Christ presented a direct and somber challenge to this optimistic view. His ideas, adapted and modified in various ways, appealed to a small group of radical evangelicals in the United States and Canada who like Blackstone felt disillusioned by more mainstream understandings of the Christian faith and unsettled by national and international events. It remains unclear why these men and women adopted such a pessimistic expression of faith. They simply described their embrace of apocalypticism as the product of a straightforward reading of the scriptures. Yet premillennialism offered those who for many reasons felt discontented with the status of their lives, their nation, or their world the opportunity to have some control over the future, which they understood to be theirs and theirs alone. Some premillennialists were poor and marginal members of American society who may have been attracted to apocalyptic visions of the coming destruction of their betters. Others were wealthy businessmen who had found tremendous success in this world but nevertheless felt that their achievements rang hollow. Other premillennialists led elite congregations in major cities where they grew disenchanted by the opulence they saw around them. Others still preached premillennialism in small rural churches. But for all of them, regardless of their class status and their personal circumstances, publicizing the message of an end-times tribulation and Jesus's imminent return gradually became a central tenet of their faith. They called it the "blessed hope."

The apocalyptic premillennialism developing in late nineteenth-century North America derived from many different ideas and influences. Americans, Canadians, English, and Irish all shared and debated theologies and beliefs, agreeing on some elements of the premillennial scheme while disagreeing on others. But over time a series of prophecy conferences combined with the rise of a handful of popular publications helped begin to define the parameters of what was emerging in the United States as a distinct interdenominational radical evangelical faith. In the fall of 1878, the same year *Jesus Is Coming* first appeared, a group of the nation's religious leaders convened at the Church of the Holy Trinity in New York City to discuss current and anticipated events in the light of the Bible's prophecies. While Darby's evangelistic tours had helped spark interest in premillennialism, prophecy conferences provided the best opportunity for American believers to organize and to hammer out their ideas. Conferences brought together like-minded individuals from many different regions and denominations committed to integrating faith in a premillennial apocalypse with the Christian life even as they debated what that meant.[12]

When the New York conference opened at 10:00 A.M., the Church of the Holy Trinity was packed. Despite a light rain falling outside, ministers and laypeople converged on Madison Avenue and Forty-Second Street to listen and learn. Speakers included the emerging luminaries of the premillennial movement such as Samuel H. Kellogg, A. J. Gordon, and Nathaniel West, men whom generations of fundamentalists later quoted with reverence. Over one hundred ministers sat on the platform near a placard that read, "Surely I come quickly. Amen. Even so, come Lord Jesus." The promise of the meeting—to make sense of current events through biblical prophecy—had struck a chord.[13]

The 122 men who signed the call for the conference included Presbyterians, Baptists, Episcopalians, Congregationalists, and Methodists. Representing most of the major US denominations, they symbolized the expansive reach of premillennialist ideas. "The diversity of denominational representation," the *Chicago Inter Ocean* noted, "shows the wide range of the upspringing belief, and what a firm hold it is taking upon the churches."[14]

In justifying the purpose of the conference, organizers explained that Christians had long ago lost the truth and meaning of the second coming. They now hoped to recover it. They pledged not to set a specific date for Jesus's return, making sure that they distanced themselves as much as possible from the legacy and false predictions of predecessors like William Miller. Nevertheless, their ideas still provoked controversy. An editorial in the *Congregationalist* summarized the meeting. The author warned that premillennialism "has been . . . insidiously harmful to the spiritual life of the church; easily lapsing into fanatical disorders, warping the judgment, absorbing undue attention, and balefully blighting the influence and power of those who surrender their souls to its strange infatuation." Conference participants' encounters with skepticism from other theologians and ministers simply reinforced their conviction that they had embarked on the right path and that the devil was working to stop them. That they had such a hard time convincing their theological opponents of the truth of their ideas represented for premillennialists "one of the conspicuous signs of the apostasy of the last days." After all, 2 Peter 3:3–4 warned, "There shall come in the last days scoffers, walking after their own lusts, And saying, Where is the promise of his coming?" Using circular logic premillennialists explained first that in the last days a great apostasy away from true theology would occur, and second that since large numbers of people denied that premillennialism was true, the apostasy must be under way. Therefore, they concluded, premillennialism is true and these must be the last days.[15]

The *New York Times* covered the prophecy conference, running favorable stories summarizing the proceedings, while the *Tribune* ran an "extra" that included transcripts of the talks. Numerous other papers around the nation also printed news of the meeting. Trinity's Stephen H. Tyng, Jr., thanked journalists for their "liberal" coverage of the event. He contrasted their attention to the silence of the religious press. The more theologically liberal Christians who ran most religious publications preferred to ignore their fellow believers' growing interest in prophecy. But they could not ignore it for long. "The sounds of the theological war," the *Times* presciently reported, "are already in the air." Conference speakers accurately predicted that opposition to premillennialism would not come from the people in the pews but from established religious leaders, "those in the pulpit—the men who teach theology—and the religious and denominational newspapers." Although the war would not begin in earnest for a few more decades, the New York prophecy conference and the press it garnered marked the public debut of a new expression of American premillennialism. The gauntlet had been thrown. Premillennialism was not just the work of a few evangelists and theologians and a Chicago real estate developer but a new and popular movement that was taking shape in American Christianity.[16]

Despite the positive press premillennialism received in New York in 1878, its influence remained fairly marginal. While some individual premillennialists wielded serious power through their ecclesiastical or social positions, premillennialism had not yet inspired the rise of a distinct apocalyptic movement. Instead, the conviction that Armageddon might be imminent simply functioned as a secondary belief that did not have a clear or substantial impact on American religion as a whole. Nevertheless, premillennialism's influence continued to grow as more and more men and women in many different denominations began to integrate apocalyptic visions into their worldviews. The true believers kept the faith, writing books and pamphlets elaborating on the themes and significance of ideas expressed in *Jesus Is Coming* and preached from the pulpit at the Church of the Holy Trinity.

In 1886 some of premillennialism's leading advocates decided to gather together in Chicago for another conference. Once again the adherents of premillennialism proved to be a diverse lot who understood and applied their apocalyptic faith in varying ways. Nevertheless, meeting together provided them with an opportunity to shape and exchange ideas. The Baptist *Standard* described the significance of the conference. "Pre-Millennial views, whatever may be said of them, have become so widespread in the various denominations . . . that it is folly to ignore this mode of Christian thinking."[17]

Working hard to cultivate a positive image, conference organizers described themselves as careful students of the Bible rather than "idle star-gazers, eratic [sic] time-setters," or "theological adventurers." Their concern over the direction in which American Protestantism was headed united them. Their stated purpose was to "give prominence" to the "neglected truth" of God's millennial plan and to awaken "Christians from slumber." They understood their actions as a declaration of war against what they viewed as the growing religious apostasy of the end times. "This Bible and Prophetic Conference," they proclaimed, "calls attention to the doctrine of 'last things' as a bulwark against the skepticism of modern theology."[18]

In one of the conference's defining lectures, E. P. Goodwin explained in clear and concise language how premillennialism functioned for its adherents. The conviction that Armageddon was imminent would inspire the faithful, he preached, to "open their purses and pour forth treasures with unstinted hand for every form of gospel work. It would send them forth to personal service in comforting the saints and saving the lost. . . . It would fasten their eyes on the promise of the Lord's return, and by day and by night, keep them toiling, praying waiting with ever increasing earnestness and longing till the flash of his glorious coming shall burst athwart the sky." Goodwin's summary echoed the ideas of Blackstone and others. Premillennialism, rather than serving as justification for indifference or apathy, inspired fervent, relentless, intrepid action—now. Premillennialists believed that they could change the world as Judgment Day neared.[19]

Many of the conference participants believed that signs of the nearness of the second coming had started to appear. The "seething, surging, rioting masses of the dangerous classes of the ground tier," A. J. Frost preached, with their "armies marching and countermarching with banners on which are emblazoned dynamite, anarchism, communism, nihilism," indicated the rapid approach of Christ. Americans' growing immorality, he complained, was manifest in "infidel doctrines, cheap fictitious sentimental literature and the decadence of family training." A. T. Pierson associated popular amusements of the era with the debauchery predicted for the end times. "Satan," he preached, "has for centuries stamped five institutions as especially his own—the card table, the horse race, the dance, the stage, and the wine cup. Professing Christians," he warned, "receive his coals in their bosoms and yet expect not to be burned." Darwinian theories of evolution made the list of premillennial signs as well, long before evolutionary theory had made its way into the national conscience. "Science," Pierson preached, "constructs its systems of evolution and leaves out a personal God; spontaneous generation becomes the only creator, natural law the only determining power, and natural selection the only Providence."[20]

The New York and Chicago meetings, along with a few subsequent conferences held in both the North and the South, helped create a loose, disparate, interdenominational premillennial network. Despite the diversity of adherents and the many traditions from which they came, the faithful had begun to identify the key themes that would drive their movement for decades to come: Jesus was coming soon; signs of the end were emerging in popular culture, social movements, politics, and various international events; and the religious apostasy predicted in Revelation—which included the denial of premillennialism—had begun. Christians in turn felt that God had called them not to neglect their duties in this world but to help prepare for the coming judgment; to be wary of state power and global alliances that would serve the devil's agenda; and finally to watch the Jews for signs of their return to Palestine. Facing a grim future, at least in the short term, premillennialists believed they would have to go it alone as they vied for the hearts and minds of the nation. But they never faltered. Theirs was a faith of and in redemption. They believed that while they were living in the shadow of the second coming, they could remake the world.

A series of influential publications codified and reinforced the work accomplished by prophecy conferences. Working alongside Blackstone, some radical evangelicals—both scholarly theologians and laypeople—published books on apocalyptic themes that promoted premillennialism and defined its relevance to the broader world. Others edited small broadsheets that kept the faithful abreast of the growing premillennial movement, which over time gave way to more professional, higher-circulation magazines.[21]

It is impossible to know how many American Christians embraced premillennialism in the late nineteenth and early twentieth centuries since they worshipped in many denominations and organizations. Premillennialism was a conviction and an ideology. It was not a church or a denomination. As a result it is difficult to measure the size of the premillennial movement in the decades before pollsters began asking specific questions about Jesus's imminent return. The best we can do is simply cite the meteoric growth of churches and denominations that claimed premillennialism in their statements of faith—such as the Christian and Missionary Alliance, the Church of God in Christ, the Assemblies of God, and numerous Baptist and Presbyterian groups—and in the post–World War II era the tremendous surge in the number of independent evangelical churches that affirmed premillennialism.

Nevertheless, relatively impressive magazine circulation figures can provide some sense of premillennialism's reach in the first part of the twentieth century. One of the most important vehicles for spreading premillennialism was the *Institute Tie* (founded in 1900), published by Moody Bible Institute (MBI). The institute later changed the title to the *Christian Workers Magazine* and eventually *Moody Monthly.* By the 1930s, it had a monthly circulation of seventy thousand. *King's Business,* marketed as a "Christian family" magazine by the Bible Institute of Los Angeles (BIOLA), began in 1910 and reached a monthly circulation of fifty thousand during the interwar era. Perhaps the most influential religious periodical of the first half of the twentieth century, which evolved alongside the radical evangelicalism it represented, was the venerable *Sunday School Times* (founded shortly after the Civil War). It maintained a weekly readership of approximately eighty thousand. Arno Gaebelein's *Our Hope* (begun in 1894) and later Donald Grey Barnhouse's *Revelation* (begun in 1931) never gained large circulations (peaking at between twelve and fifteen thousand subscribers) but proved popular among the nation's radical evangelical preachers and teachers. Texan John R. Rice's *Sword of the Lord* began with a handful of subscribers in 1934 but quickly grew into the South's leading fundamentalist periodical, with a readership in the thousands and eventually a hundred thousand. The Assemblies of God's *Pentecostal Evangel* (begun in 1913) boasted over 115,000 readers by World War II. Other popular premillennial magazines included J. Frank Norris's *Searchlight,* William Bell Riley's *Pilot,* and Aimee Semple McPherson's *Bridal Call.*[22]

The most important means of spreading premillennialism, however, was a new comprehensive reference work. In 1909 Oxford University Press published the *Scofield Reference Bible,* which subtly introduced millions of readers to the premillennial second coming. Nothing published since has matched its impact on the movement. The editor of this work, Cyrus Ingerson Scofield, a Civil War veteran (he had fought for the

Confederacy), a lawyer, and a bit of a scoundrel, had experienced a dramatic conversion and become a minister. Although he wrote extensively about premillennialism and established a popular correspondence course focused on biblical interpretation, the Scofield Bible was his greatest achievement.

The Bible included Scofield's notes at the bottom of almost every page, which helped readers interpret verses within a dispensational and premillennial framework. Scofield occasionally inserted notes into the text itself as well, blurring the lines between the scriptures and his interpretations. The publication, with millions of copies in circulation, is probably the best-selling book in the history of Oxford University Press. It has been guiding Christians through the intricacies of premillennialism—whether they realize it or not—ever since. Dallas Theological Seminary theologian Lewis Sperry Chafer called it "God's gift to the Church in the last days."[23]

The Scofield Bible was not the only gift God had seemingly prepared for the last days. In 1906 a major interracial, premillennial-infused revival hit Los Angeles. Sure that the New Testament story of Pentecost was reoccurring before their eyes, modern-day "pentecostals" began practicing New Testament gifts of the spirit such as healing, speaking in tongues, and prophesying. These predominantly working-class believers offered a reinvigorated Christianity as an all-encompassing, holistic faith that approximated the experience of the first-century church. They believed that the return of apostolic-era spiritual gifts was proof of the coming of the rapture. Although most other premillennialists believed that spiritual gifts had ceased with the closing of the biblical canon, the explosion of the pentecostal movement, like the publication of the Scofield Bible, made premillennialism tangible to countless Americans.[24]

According to pentecostal tradition, the modern tongues movement began on January 1, 1901, when minister Charles Fox Parham laid his hands in prayer on a student who began babbling in an unknown language. Parham and his disciples followed the student's example by seeking, and then promoting, this miraculous gift, which some believed was a heavenly language and others interpreted as a human dialect unknown to the speaker that missionaries sometimes used to communicate with those who did not understand their language.

A few years after Parham renewed interest in this most exotic gift of the spirit, African-American preacher William J. Seymour, a disciple of Parham, initiated the 1906 Azusa Street revivals in southern California. These meetings, led and supported by an interracial and inter-ethnic group of African Americans, Anglo-Americans, Asians, European immigrants, and Latinos, lasted almost three years and attracted Christians and curiosity seekers from around the country. Because the Azusa leaders believed that the Holy Spirit should control the direction of the meetings, they had no formal, organized service order or explicit leadership. Men and women prayed, preached, exhorted, spoke in tongues, wept, trembled, and convulsed as they believed the spirit dictated. Many participants experienced various gifts of the Holy Spirit. As word of the unique events occurring at the Azusa mission spread, a *Los Angeles Times* reporter broke the story, bringing national attention to the new movement.[25]

Pentecostals took seriously Peter's promise in Acts 2:17–20: "And it shall come to pass in the last days, saith God, I will pour out of my Spirit upon all flesh: and your sons and your daughters shall prophesy, and your young men shall see visions, and your old men shall dream dreams: And on my servants and on my handmaidens I will pour out in those days of my Spirit; and they shall prophesy: And I will shew wonders in heaven above, and signs in the earth beneath; blood, and fire, and vapour of smoke: The sun shall be turned into darkness, and the moon into blood, before that great and notable day of the Lord come." As pentecostals understood this sermon, Peter—quoting the prophet Joel—explicitly linked the outpouring of spiritual gifts with signs of the last days. Pentecostals drew on these verses to demonstrate that their revival heralded the imminent return of Christ. They also used this passage as justification for including women in leading roles at a time when most other premillennialists assigned women to secondary positions in the movement.

The second coming became a prominent theme at the Azusa mission, where participants often delivered messages in tongues that others translated and interpreted. God apparently wanted pentecostals to know that Jesus planned to return soon. During one meeting a teenage participant delivered the message, "Jesus is coming again, Coming again so soon," in words that a visiting missionary recognized as and translated from an African language. Jesus's imminent return, one mission leader observed, was the message "that the Holy Ghost is speaking today through nearly everyone that receives the baptism with the Holy Ghost." Some participants even had visions of the savior himself, who assured them, "I am coming soon." Summing up what had been happening at the mission, Seymour wrote, "O the time is very near. All the testimonies of His coming that have been going on for months are a witness that He is coming soon."[26]

Editors of *Apostolic Faith,* a magazine that served to publicize and document the Azusa revival, printed numerous messages and poems by participants. Many contributors emphasized the imminent second coming. One poem, "The Warfare, The Rapture and Afterwards," warned, "The night is hastening fast, / The morn will soon appear; / The battle strong will not last long; / Our Christ will soon be here." The final section of the poem ominously focused on life "After the Rapture" for those left behind and illustrated the ways in which premillennialists relished having the ultimate revenge on their moral and theological enemies.

A sense of awe creeps o'er
The hearts of men now left.
Wives their husbands cannot find;
Husbands of wives bereft.

Men sleeping side by side—
One left alone to stay;
Two women grinding at the mill—
One quickly caught away.

With faces blanched, men look
Each other in the eye;
Women and children screaming run
And wish that they could die.

Men rush from the saloon
And crowd the place of prayer,
From brothel, race, and gambling hall,
While some still linger there.

The blatant infidel
Now seeks to hide away,
And men who never bowed before
Now settle down to pray.

True picture of the end
Is here in rhyme laid bare,
When Jesus comes to claim His bride
And saints the rapture share.

Brother, heed the warning given,
Let every soul press on;
Get right with God while yet there's time;
Let no man take thy crown.[27]

Pentecostals looked to many of the same signs as other radical evangelicals for evidence of impending Armageddon, but they also boasted of extraordinary experiences that further affirmed their premillennialist convictions. According to one tract an Oregon woman saw written on her kitchen wall, "JESUS IS COMING SOON, GO AND TELL IT," and the same message appeared in fiery letters in the evening sky in Bombay, India. Others still saw religious symbols in the stars; on the moon; in an eclipse in Kentucky; and in a rainbow that circled the sun for hours over Oklahoma City. All of these signs testified to Jesus's imminent return. Pentecostals were under orders; God demanded that they act now.[28]

In the first decades of the twentieth century, pentecostal and non-pentecostal premillennialists generally labored along separate lines. Issues of race, class, and education, as well as pentecostals' less restrictive views of gender, kept them somewhat segregated. But they exchanged ideas and beliefs. And at times their ministries and their revivals overlapped. Eventually they would join forces, but that would take decades of careful work.[29]

As the premillennial movement started to coalesce around the turn of the century, adherents wrestled over its implications. What did it mean to anticipate the second coming of Christ? How did this affect practical Christian duty? What were premillennialists' obligations to the larger world around them? Although Blackstone and others challenged the idea that their faith fostered apathy and indifference, premillennialists found no easy or clear answers.

The implications that some premillennialists drew from their theology at times bordered on the absurd. The *Sunday School Times,* for example, ran an article without any sense of irony about an insurance man who asked his company to take the rapture into consideration as it planned for the future. He explained that while he expected his bosses to be taken to heaven, he admonished that even in their "aerial abode" they might experience "a degree of discomfort, scarcely compatible with perfect bliss," if they did not provide sufficient funds to cover the post-rapture claims of those left behind. Los Angeles evangelist Aimee Semple McPherson publicized plans to build a "Blessed Hope Cemetery." If she died before the rapture, she wanted to be buried in the center of the graveyard. She encouraged her followers to reserve their own burial plots in the cemetery. Those nearest her were the most expensive, since their occupants would rise alongside Aimee, while those farthest away from her tomb were priced lower. There they could all await the blessed hope, the return of Christ, and then rise to the heavens together.[30]

But insurance plans and burial plots were not the primary concerns of premillennialists. After all, they were not simply affirming an abstract doctrine; premillennialism shaped how the faithful engaged with Christians and non-Christians alike. To believe that humankind was careening toward Armageddon, that signs of the last days were embedded in social and political changes, that long-term reform was futile, that global war was inevitable, and that massive numbers of Jews were destined for Palestine had ramifications that extended far beyond the walls of their churches. As the implications of premillennialists' beliefs became increasingly clear, they began to define their relationship to the rest of society.

Making room within the prophetic scheme for action became a necessary and crucial part of crafting a new radical evangelical theology. Early premillennialist Samuel H. Kellogg explained that the common understanding "of premillennialists as a body of enthusiasts waiting for the Lord in ascension robes, hopeless pessimists with neither faith nor interest in the redemption of the nations . . . ought to be abandoned

forever." Instead he asserted that the eager anticipation of the imminent second coming played a vital role in fostering Christian ministry.
Blackstone, in turn, warned the faithful not to become complacent
even as he simultaneously identified the signs of Christ's imminent return. God made it impossible, he wrote, for Christians to identify conclusively "the time" of the church's rapture that they "should, in any
interval, cease to be vigilant." In other words, Kellogg and Blackstone
wanted readers to watch for the end but to work faithfully too. This did
not stop Blackstone, however, from privately and incorrectly predicting
the date of the rapture on multiple occasions.[31]

A few early premillennialists made faith in Jesus's imminent return a
mandate for cultural withdrawal. If the world was teetering on the edge
of apocalypse, these believers wondered, why work for reform, why
participate in politics, why do anything other than evangelize? Darby,
for example, laid out one way for premillennialists to understand their
relationship to the rest of society. Acknowledging that Satan was lord
of the kingdoms of this world, he instructed true Christians to shun
politics. "Everybody says that a citizen of the country, a Christian, should
be interested in the government of the country to which he belongs, and
ought to vote, so as to help to put good men in power. God," Darby
instructed, "says differently." The Christian should give "his vote and
interest to the Man in heaven, whom God has exalted as King of kings,
and Lord of lords."[32]

Scofield reiterated the message of ministers like Darby. His *Rightly
Dividing the Word of Truth,* originally published in the 1880s, significantly
influenced many radical evangelicals. According to Scofield, God had
chosen the Old Testament Jews to rule over an earthly kingdom in a
very specific geographic location in the Middle East. Had they accepted
Jesus as the Messiah, the millennium would have commenced. But when
they rejected him, God turned to the Gentiles, establishing a church
from which to rule over a spiritual kingdom composed of citizens of all
nations. The church then represented a spiritual entity established for a
spiritual purpose.

Scofield believed that the church had not lived up to its calling. Instead of focusing exclusively on preaching the gospel before the return
of Christ, Christians had sought to reform the world, as had the Old
Testament Jews. Such misguided efforts had corrupted the faith. "The

Judaizing of the Church," he wrote, "has done more to hinder her progress, pervert her mission, and destroy her spirituality, than all other causes combined. Instead of pursuing her appointed path of separation, persecution, world-hatred, poverty, and non-resistance, she has used Jewish Scripture to justify her in lowering her purpose to the civilization of the world, the acquisition of wealth," and "the invocation of God's blessing upon the conflicts of armies." While many premillennialists did not recognize the strict distinction between Old Testament Israel and the New Testament church made by rigid dispensationalists like Scofield, they still took his conclusions seriously. For Scofield, social reform, militarism, nationalism, and the pursuit of money represented the antitheses of true Christianity.[33]

Premillennialists' call to separate from the world appeared in many books and tracts in the late nineteenth and early twentieth centuries. The faithful made a clear distinction between evangelism and reform, and they rejected liberal Protestants' effort to craft a social gospel that applied faith to contemporary cultural and political problems. Instead, they believed that conversion remained the only hope for humankind. "Gigantic is the misconception," wrote Nathaniel West, "to dream that God has given the Church . . . to build the Christian State up to a Kingdom of Christ, or to reform the world." "The Church," I. M. Haldeman explained, "is not to try to tinker and patch up a world system which God has doomed, and which the Son of God will sweep away at his coming. The Church is not to be occupied with political issues, with social reforms, with so-called 'civic' righteousness." Unlike many conservative and liberal Protestants who had faith in the righteousness of American imperialism and in the nation's mission to reshape the world in its image, most premillennialists believed that the idea that the United States was some kind of Christian nation was absurd.[34]

The separatist social ethic laid out by Darby, Scofield, and others has long dominated the story of early premillennialism. Cultural withdrawal seemed to be the most logical outcome of apocalyptic theology and some of the movement's founding fathers advocated it. But separatism was not the only approach. Many premillennialists—probably even a majority—around the turn of the century refused to draw a strict line between faith and action. Rejecting the evangelism/reform dichotomy, they began to find creative ways to integrate their hope in the second coming with social activism. While they rejected the Social Gospel, they crafted a form of engaged premillennialism, a radical evangelical creed that blended what they called the old-time religion with work on a slate of specific issues. They breathed new life into apocalypticism, shaping it into a powerful creed that inspired vigorous and vigilant action.

Nobody integrated faith with cultural engagement better than the people associated with Dwight L. Moody's various Chicago-based ministries. The most popular evangelist of the Gilded Age, Moody adopted premillennialism in the 1870s. "I look on this world as a wrecked vessel," he famously declared. "God has given me a life-boat, and said to me, 'Moody, save all you can.'" Nevertheless, he believed that social reform and Christian mission did not to have to be mutually exclusive.[35]

The evangelicals associated with MBI developed and embodied their founder's message. They named the MBI periodical the *Christian Workers Magazine,* which highlighted their emphasis on "work" as a substantial component of Christian ministry. Articles routinely profiled the efforts of Moody students to clean up political corruption, shut down vice districts, and reduce the consumption of alcohol in the Windy City. The magazine constantly implored readers to support downtown missions and wrote positively of churches' efforts to serve the poor and to partner with conservative labor unions. Yet editors never wavered from their premillennial convictions, explaining that with regard to such problems as labor-capital conflicts, urban slums, government corruption, diseased milk supplies, tuberculosis, bad schools, and juvenile delinquency, the churches should not compromise their "testimony to the Gospel" by entering "into politics." "Regenerated members of the church," they nevertheless insisted, "should exert their individual influence as citizens and members of society to bring about these betterments." In other words, Moody leaders distinguished between Christians acting corporately as Christians, which they rejected, and Christians acting as individual citizens, which they encouraged. Until the rapture, they explained, "it is our duty to stand in our lot and bear our testimony, not only by our lips but by our lives, which means our acts, political and otherwise, while our souls wait for the Lord."[36]

James Gray best represented the blend of premillennialism and social reform under way in Chicago. In a 1900 sermon delivered from the pulpit of the Chicago Avenue Church (later renamed the Moody Church), he set out to define the relationship between radical evangelicalism and civil government. In direct opposition to the ideas espoused by Darby, he called on each individual Christian to register to vote and to exercise the franchise, to study the important political issues of the day, and most important, to exert "his influence by example, by word of mouth, and the use of other means to awaken among his neighbors and fellow-citizens a revival of civil righteousness." Peering out at the congregation through small frameless eyeglasses, he called on fellow believers to put people into office to "execute the laws, close the dram shops, exterminate the gambling hells, sanctify one day in seven as a day of rest, and make in every way for the betterment of the poorer classes." On another occasion he listed "faithful jury duty, intelligent voting, the exercise of the citizen's right of petition, and even the holding of office where necessary and compatible with other duties" as "sound and consistent principles of Christian living." A few years after preaching in the Chicago Avenue Church, Gray became dean of MBI. There he helped train what amounted to more evangelical teachers, preachers, and evangelists than anyone else of his generation. He instructed them to work for the betterment of society while clinging to the hope of the second coming.[37]

Gray was not alone in his conviction that Christians needed to do what they could to influence society. Evangelist and minister A. C. Dixon, whose gentle demeanor belied his ironclad convictions, criticized those Christians who did not participate in politics. Jesus, he explained, "had much to do with politics." Kentucky-born minister and firebrand William Bell Riley also integrated ministry with activism. He answered the question, "Should ministers have anything to do with politics?" with, "I vote with a vengeance, and I fight for sobriety with all the ability that is in me. . . . The life of Christ has changed the politics of the centuries." Southern evangelist Bob Jones acknowledged that the true Christian will not "work as a mere reformer, for he knows there can be no permanent reform until Christ comes again." However, "he cannot be indifferent to the sins and evils which he sees on every hand. . . . He is in accord with the Spirit's ministry when he reproves, rebukes and exhorts." Jones cited Prohibition, white slavery, gambling, "and every other form of vice" as legitimate targets for Christian work.

J. Wilbur Chapman pledged not to allow anyone "to go beyond" him "in seeking to ameliorate the condition of the suffering and present a cure which may help to solve the problems which are on every side to be settled." George Müller, the famous German evangelist, missionary, reformer, and committed premillennialist, taught that "instead of indulging in inactivity and listlessness on account of the evil state of things around us, we should pray and work, and work and pray, as if it were in our power to stem the torrent of abounding iniquity."[38]

Despite such sentiments, radical evangelicals for the most part had not yet developed a coherent political philosophy. In the late nineteenth century they admonished followers to exercise the franchise, but they did not have a unified vision for national politics. The first generations of premillennialists most often voted along regional lines— those in the North and West leaned Republican, while those in or from the South most often sided with the Democrats. They all generally agreed that party politics was corrupt and they expressed only limited enthusiasm about national leaders. They also consistently denounced socialism as a sign of last days evil.

In the historic 1896 presidential campaign some radical evangelicals rallied behind Democratic presidential contender and populist William Jennings Bryan, while others supported the probusiness ideals of the Republican candidate, devout Methodist William McKinley. The explicit Protestant faith of McKinley and then his successor, Theodore Roosevelt, reassured the faithful that the country was in relatively good hands. However, they saw the GOP's selection of William Howard Taft in 1908 in an entirely different light. Businessman Lyman Stewart, an active member of the Republican Party dating back to his days in the Union army, had never been comfortable with Taft. "While I am in sympathy with Mr. Taft politically," he explained to a friend, "as a Unitarian he is an enemy of the cross of Christ." Meanwhile in a sermon on the signs of the times, evangelist French Oliver lamented, "when a man like W. H. Taft, who denies the Deity of Jesus Christ, can be elected to the presidency of our country, it shows that something is radically wrong with the voters of the nation." Not pulling any punches, he concluded, "any number of church members crucified Jesus Christ at the polls when they voted for a Unitarian president." Premillennialists saw no contradiction in their expectation that the Antichrist was coming soon to rule the earth and that they should have a Christian in the White House.[39]

The 1912 campaign drew more substantial attention from premillennialists. Taft, whose religious convictions continued to trouble the faithful, wanted to serve a second term. Meanwhile Theodore Roosevelt, back from an African safari, challenged the incumbent and tried to reclaim the Republican nomination. When party leaders refused to support the former president, he bolted the GOP and organized the new Progressive Party (dubbed the "Bull Moose" party). Roosevelt's 1912 campaign fared little better than Taft's in the eyes of radical evangelicals. Delegates attending the Bull Moose convention sang a traditional hymn but replaced Jesus's name with the candidate's. The *New York Times*—apparently no fan of T. R.—criticized the activists by quoting 2 Peter's admonition against false prophets. Premillennialists also felt troubled by Roosevelt's claim to be "standing at Armageddon" and promise to battle for the Lord. They quickly corrected him on the meaning of Armageddon.[40]

The Democrats, buoyed by dissension in the GOP ranks, settled on Woodrow Wilson, a devout Presbyterian, to serve as their nominee. Most radical evangelicals remained silent on the Princeton academic. He was a southerner and a Democrat, which made northern and western evangelicals reluctant to support him. But despite premillennialists' concerns about growing state power as a sign of the end times, they did not connect the progressive politics espoused by any of the major candidates to the supposed threat of socialism, nor did their sermons and books link faith to a particular party. At least not yet.

Following Wilson's 1912 victory radical evangelicals made clear how pleased they were with the results. In a smart and witty editorial, *Christian Workers* praised the fact that the president-elect, vice president–elect Thomas R. Marshall, and new secretary of state William Jennings Bryan—all Presbyterians—could work harmoniously together after a difficult primary campaign, demonstrating "what Calvinism can accomplish even in a Democratic heart." The editorial concluded by expressing hope "that the next four years has been politically predestined," again playing on Presbyterians' Calvinist theology, "to mark an epoch in the well-being of our native land." Stewart was also pleased. "The people," he explained to a friend, "particularly the progressive republicans, are

very well satisfied with his course thus far. It is a great satisfaction to
have three such men as Wilson, Marshall and Bryan at the very head of
our government."[41]

Despite the interest garnered by the 1912 election, reform-oriented
premillennialists put far more emphasis on moral campaigns than on
national politics. They generally believed that they could improve their
communities in the short term even though they did not expect to
have a long-term impact. A few, however, developed a radical theory,
convinced that the actions of Christians could in fact speed or slow the
coming apocalypse. Riley, for example, was asked what role Christians
played in the timing of the second coming. He gave a startling answer.
"We have already given proof to the world that we can delay it! I do
believe we can hasten it. I think there is a divine program, but human
instrumentalities are involved in the question." The idea that humans
can affect God's chronology was for most Protestants theologically suspect. And yet a significant number of premillennialists adopted this position, which further justified their seeming schizophrenia. They could
preach both the imminent second coming and the necessity of social
action, Armageddon and revival. They warned sinners of God's impending judgment and simultaneously called on Christians to work to
hold off that judgment. For many premillennialists, the uncertainty of
the timing of the rapture meant simply that they had an obligation to
evangelize as quickly and aggressively as possible. But for others like
Riley, such convictions gave them a broader mandate to improve their
communities.[42]

In the early twentieth century evangelist Billy Sunday best exemplified the developing paradox of premillennialism: the call to exercise
influence in politics and culture as aggressively as possible while preparing the world for the oncoming apocalypse. The wiry, Iowa-born
preacher had little formal education. He became a professional baseball
player in 1883 and gained fame as a gutsy base runner for the Chicago
White Stockings. A few years later, he converted to Christianity and
abandoned the ballpark for the revival tent. He would no longer be
stealing bases from other teams but souls from the devil. During one of
his first campaigns, the *Chicago Tribune* called him "shy." That was not
a characterization that would last. By the early twentieth century, Sunday's revivals filled the largest auditoriums in the country's greatest

cities. In part his success—like that of most revivalists in American history—derived from his style. He was a common guy, a man of the people. He described himself as "proud" to be from the "corn rows of Iowa." "The mal-odors of the barnyard are on my feet," he boasted, "I have greased my hair with goose-grease; I have blackened my shoes with a cob; I have wiped my proboscis with a gunny sack; I have drunk coffee out of my saucer and eaten peas with a knife. . . . I am a graduate from the University of Poverty and Hard Knocks." Sunday's language and style reflected his antielitist sensibilities. "When I began to preach," he explained, "I wrote sermons with sentences so long that they'd make a Greek professor's jaw squeak for a week after he said one of them: but I soon found that that didn't get any results. So I loaded my gospel gun with rough-on-rats, ipecac, dynamite and barbed wire, and the gang's been hunting a hole ever since."[43]

The evangelist's use of vernacular language sparked controversy. One article in a Christian magazine complained of his "happy-go-lucky air of equality with his Master. . . . Instead of stealing hushed and awe-struck to the garment hem of God," the author lamented, "the evange-list bolts into the divine presence like a gossipy neighbor 'dropping around' for a chat." The city council of Wheeling, West Virginia, even passed an ordinance aimed squarely at Sunday. It imposed a fine on any-one who "in a public address should use vile or vulgar language." One councilman explained that they did it to curb "the vocabulary of 'Billy' Sunday," who was planning a revival in the city. But the *Atlanta Consti-tution* praised the evangelist's form. "He brings the Scripture down" to his audience's "level; he talks to them in the vernacular; he exhorts them in the style of vigorous directness common to the baseball dia-mond and the street; he translates the Bible into the slang of the day and paraphrases the sacred text with a freedom that is startling in its realism." Sunday's populist impulses encouraged some radical evangeli-cals to connect better with the public, while they embarrassed others.[44]

While Sunday rarely dwelt on the more complicated elements of Christian theology, he identified the second coming of Christ as "the emphatic doctrine of the New Testament." "Many have an idea the world will grow better and better until the coming of the millennium," he preached. "You hear that stuff preached, but the Bible does not teach any such trash." He also believed that it was imminent. "The present

Few revivalists have been as popular as former baseball player Billy Sunday. His masterful blend of premillennialism with political engagement and American patriotism set precedents for subsequent generations of fundamentalists and evangelicals who sought to transform their culture.

crisis points toward the close of the times of the Gentiles. The modernists in our pulpits, and the socialists and radicals in our government, are
forerunners of some calamity spiritually and materially." Nor was he a
fan of the Social Gospel. "All men's schemes of reconstruction must be
subsidiary to the second coming of our Lord." Yet time and again Sunday plunged into reform work of all kinds. In popularizing the form of
premillennial cultural engagement advocated by Riley, Chapman, Gray,
Dixon, and many others, this brusque, hypermasculine evangelist helped
shape the way radical evangelicals understood their relationship to the
broader culture. They saw through his work the value in creating a faith
that entwined an urgent conviction that time was running out with a
belief in the possibility of instant redemption.[45]

As the premillennial movement coalesced, its leaders debated its many
implications. While a few millennialist pioneers advocated cultural
withdrawal, most radical evangelicals recognized that they could better
accomplish their goal of making disciples of all nations in the context of
a culture that shared their values. The biblical prophets had determined
that the nations of the world would eventually unite behind the Antichrist, but most premillennialists believed that this did not release them
from their obligations to society. When Jesus returned, they insisted, he
had better find them engaged in Christian work. Although the prophets
had set in stone the events leading up to Armageddon, the timing of those
events was not necessarily foreordained. The faithful could hold back the
apocalypse. Therefore, they simultaneously predicted the imminent destruction of the world while trying to reform their own communities.

As premillennialists worked through the social and political implications
of their theology, they never took their eyes off of the international situation. They constantly scanned the horizon for evidence of the end
times' approach, trusting that Jesus had told them exactly what to expect.
According to Matthew 24:3–8, as Jesus sat on the Mount of Olives his
disciples asked him, "What *shall be* the sign of thy coming, and of the end
of the world? And Jesus answered and said unto them, Take heed that no
man deceive you. . . . And ye shall hear of wars and rumours of wars: see
that ye be not troubled: for all *these things* must come to pass, but the end
is not yet. For nation shall rise against nation, and kingdom against king-

dom: and there shall be famines, and pestilences, and earthquakes, in divers places. All these *are* the beginning of sorrows."

Wars and rumors of wars. Many premillennialists in the early twentieth century obsessed over these words. Yet to most other Bible readers of the period they seemed hopelessly out-of-date and contrary to the spirit of the era. During the first decade of the new century, progressive idealists in the United States and abroad organized dozens of peace movements. Some even sought to remake international relations along new lines, for example steel baron Andrew Carnegie financed the creation of a Peace Palace at The Hague and then established the Church Peace Union (later called the Carnegie Endowment for International Peace). Millions of Americans and Europeans, most often working through their churches and religious organizations, hoped, prayed, and labored to make the brutal warfare of the nineteenth century a thing of the past. According to many mainstream Protestants, such work could help usher in the kingdom of God.

Premillennialists knew better. Minister R. A. Torrey remained skeptical of what he saw in the peace movements. "All our present peace plans," he noted in 1913, "will end in the most awful wars and conflicts this old world ever saw." New York evangelist Arno C. Gaebelein fretted about the future as well. "Never before," he preached, "have been the signs of the times so numerous and ominous as in the beginning of 1913. The sky indeed is red and lowering. Foul weather is coming for this poor world. The clouds are gathering on every side. The storm is brewing." A few months later his magazine ran an article warning that "probably the Antichrist is alive and is being trained for his Satanic mission."[46]

In February 1914, a group of influential premillennialists decided to convene again. It had been years since the last major prophecy conference and a new generation of leaders was maturing. They gathered at MBI, a less impressive venue than the historic Manhattan church where prophecy experts had met decades earlier. The shift represented, in part, the way premillennialism was slowly moving from a theological conviction easily integrated within mainstream American religious life into one that was inspiring a new spiritual and political movement independent of traditional churches and denominations.

The conference functioned in part to consolidate the growing, diverse, interdenominational premillennial movement. This did not mean, however, that radical evangelicals saw every issue in the same light. Adherents continued to disagree over many particulars of theology as well as its application to their lives and their cultures. Participants included many of the men who would soon shape the fundamentalist movement. James M. Gray, William Bell Riley, C. I. Scofield, and Arno Gaebelein all preached. To hearten the faithful, organizers put together a symposium on "how I became a premillennialist," inviting prominent leaders to share their conversion stories. No one had been born or raised a premillennialist, at least not yet. Theirs was a new faith that had to be explicitly and consciously accepted. Conference leaders also published a list of "some exponents of premillennialism." They cited Clement of Rome, Ignatius of Antioch, St. Francis of Assisi, Martin Luther, John Calvin, Isaac Newton, Cotton and Increase Mather, C. I. Scofield, and Dwight Moody as their theological forbearers.[47]

Premillennialists claimed this intellectual heritage somewhat disingenuously. Although they defended premillennialism as the historic faith, most leaders—at least in private—recognized that most Christians throughout time would not recognize it. Dallas Theological Seminary founder Lewis Sperry Chafer, in a letter to MBI professor Wilbur Smith, tried to explain and justify the "recovery" of premillennialism. He believed that the true faith had vanished in the Middle Ages and the Protestant Reformation had only partially rediscovered it. "The Reformers recovered vital truth in the field of Soteriology [the theology of salvation], but they did not go one step in other fields," he explained, "especially Ecclesiology and Eschatology, and their successors made the mistake of petrifying the Reformation findings into a system of theology which could not be lessened or increased." Indirectly admitting that premillennialism was a new phenomenon, he continued, "therefore, the door was closed for further study and it was many years before a man like J. N. Darby got free from these bondages and presented the Pauline doctrine of the Church." Chafer knew that premillennialism had never been as important in church history as he and his colleagues now claimed. Premillennialists maintained, however, that they alone were engaged in the restoration of the ancient faith.[48]

The MBI prophecy conference took place at a time when much of the world remained at peace. Participants, however, knew that the calm

Prophecy conferences provided valuable venues for premillennialists to share ideas and craft strategies. The apocalyptic prophecies heralded at this 1914 Moody Bible Institute conference, photographed by C. I. Scofield, seemed to be validated just a few months later by the start of World War I.

Permission: Photo by C. I. Scofield, Courtesy of the Moody Bible Institute Archives, Historical Collections.

could not last. In his conference address Riley denounced the hypocrisy of nations that signed international peace treaties while simultaneously expanding their militaries. Such actions served as a primary example of the truth of Jesus's words on the Mount of Olives, but certainly not the only one. The minister cited significant geopolitical changes, especially widespread talk of a coming one-world government and the growing Zionist movement as additional signs. Religious apostasy and the substitution of Darwinian theories for what he saw as unassailable scientific "truth" about the nature of creation rounded out Riley's reasons for proclaiming the imminence of Christ's coming. Gaebelein saw similar evidence of the last days. "There has never been a time in the history of the Church," he preached, when biblical predictions "are being fulfilled so universally and completely, as in our own times."[49]

The radical evangelicals who had revived and adapted an ancient form of Christian millennialism in the late nineteenth and early twentieth centuries believed that history was nearing its end. As they worked out the implications of their theology, they found creative ways to integrate their faith in an imminent apocalypse with their yearning to transform their culture. As the world moved toward war, premillennialists realized that they had been right. The world truly stood on the verge of Armageddon. But as radical evangelicals diligently searched the signs of the times for hints of what was to come, they had no idea how dramatically the war was about to transform their fledgling movement.

2

GLOBAL WAR AND CHRISTIAN NATIONALISM

EMERALD CITY DIVINE MARK MATTHEWS loved God and he loved Woodrow Wilson. The tall, lanky, Georgia-born minister, who looked more like a stern plantation overseer than a warm cleric, relished the fact that a fellow southerner, Presbyterian, and Democrat had won the White House. Matthews believed that with Woodrow Wilson at the helm the United States would finally return to the sea of righteousness. During the early decades of the twentieth century, Matthews became one of the most powerful religious leaders in the United States. His Seattle congregation was the largest Presbyterian church in the world, with over ten thousand members at its peak. He played an important role in denominational politics and served as moderator of the General Assembly of the Presbyterian Church U.S.A. In 1924, the *New York Times* named Matthews in a poll of twenty thousand ministers as one of the most influential preachers in the nation.[1]

Like so many radical evangelicals of his generation, Matthews saw troubling signs at home and abroad. As European nations armed for war in the 1910s, the minister shifted from postmillennialism to premillennialism. While he had believed in the power of the Social Gospel to bring to fruition the kingdom of God, he now feared that the world was careening toward an inevitable apocalypse. Yet his growing premillennial sensibilities did nothing to curtail his political engagement. He worked closely with community organizers on a variety of issues and he cultivated relationships with state and national leaders, none more important than Wilson.

Matthews routinely wrote the president with advice and to ask for favors for himself and his friends. He even promised Seattleites that through Wilson he would get congressional pork flowing back to the Pacific Northwest. The president occasionally sought Matthews's opinions as well. Their correspondence demonstrates that Matthews had the ear of the president and that he had no reservations about speaking boldly to men in power.[2]

The Presbyterian's messages to Wilson often strayed far from his expertise as a preacher and community servant. Revealing the ways premillennialism had transformed him, some of Matthews's letters mixed prophecy, politics, and even foreign policy. The cleric believed that the Bible had clearly outlined the United States' responsibilities during World War I. He admonished Wilson not to "discuss peace any more. The infamous forces against which we are contending," he asserted, "must be crushed. We do not want peace until they are crushed. We do not want them to break. We want to strike them down." Then he turned to the Bible to justify his strident, uncompromising militarism. "Prophecy is clear on this question," he insisted. How it was clear he did not say. He concluded his letter by confiding in Wilson that he hoped to "have the privilege of shooting the Kaiser" himself.[3]

World War I represented a major turning point for Matthews and for those like him in the growing premillennial movement. For decades, radical evangelicals had believed that contrary to the claims of creedal conservatives, Social Gospel liberals, and political progressives, humankind was not improving. Although premillennialists did not necessarily rejoice over the outbreak of war, they could not help but find some satisfaction in international turmoil. As the British promised to establish a homeland for Jews in Palestine and Wilson consolidated power in the executive branch, premillennialists knew beyond any doubt that the beginning of the end had commenced. The global cataclysm signaled to them that they had read prophecy accurately and that they could offer a viable, realistic alternative to the rosy religion of Social Gospel optimists. While most radical evangelicals believed that the rapture would occur before the unveiling of the Antichrist, they believed that they would see global developments unfolding as the Bible foretold to set the stage for the seven-year, final tribulation. They used the war to promote their gospel and their movement. Their ability to anticipate conflicts around the rapidly changing world with total confidence and to explain their meaning captured the souls of thousands of Americans. At the same time, World War I forced radical evangelicals to reconcile their beliefs about the future with the realities of their obligations to a nation at war. That premillennialism might seem inimical to good citizenship made the faithful politically and socially vulnerable.

Upon moving into the Oval Office Wilson probably felt the weight of the end times on his shoulders as one crisis after another unfolded. The Mexican Revolution started to spill into the American Southwest, eventually forcing the president to dispatch the US army after Pancho Villa. Problems had begun to mount in Europe as well, where a series of alliances crafted over many decades had produced two major coalitions. The first, the Triple Alliance (or Central Powers), included Germany, Austria-Hungary, and Italy, and the second, the Triple Entente (or Allies), included Great Britain, France, and Russia. The precarious balance of power began to unravel in the Balkan countries of southeastern Europe, where Serbian nationalists hoped to annex Bosnia, a province of the Austro-Hungarian Empire. On June 28, 1914, a Serbian assassinated Archduke Franz Ferdinand, heir to the Austro-Hungarian throne, in the Bosnian capital, Sarajevo. Germany encouraged its alliance partner to respond decisively while Serbia appealed to Russia for help. Russia, in turn, looked to France for support. In late July, Austria-Hungary declared war against Serbia, and before long most of Europe was embroiled in the conflict.[4]

Premillennialists responded to the outbreak of war with cries of vindication. *King's Business* ran a long headline on its cover that juxtaposed "True Biblical Optimism" with "the Shattering of Man's Empty Optimism." Arno Gaebelein, who blended strident apocalypticism with a love for classical piano and the arts, rushed a quick editorial to press in which he quoted his own predictions of war from a few years earlier.

The next month, he elaborated on the significance of the war. "We see in this great European upheaval a vindication of the Word of God concerning the present age," he gloated. "How the Higher Critics have sneered at Bible Prophecy and ridiculed those who have stood up for it! . . . Oh the irony!" Chronicling the careful military preparations that had been under way for years at the same time that "false prophets" had assured "a deluded world that there is peace and safety," premillennialists, he insisted, had seen the war coming and they alone would be capable of truly making sense of its horrors.[5]

Radical evangelicals plunged right into analyzing the changing geopolitical situation. Initially they had more questions than answers since the alliances dividing Europe did not match those they had identified as the major end-times powers. But James Gray knew that coalitions could change quickly. Although "a student of prophecy must not be a prophet," the dean of Moody Bible Institute warned, national boundaries were shifting so fast that the nations could rapidly fall into place for Armageddon. Although premillennial leaders recognized that they could not say for certain how the European war might develop, they believed it was of great importance. "Never before," Southern Baptist leader Victor Masters asserted, "did the world face a situation which seemed so completely to fulfill this prophecy as it does today."[6]

During the war radical evangelicals perfected their prophetic formula. They routinely predicted what was to come while also couching their forecasts in enough disclaimers to ensure that they could not be labeled "false prophets." The formula allowed them to adjust their prognostications to changing events on the ground in creative and innovative ways.

The war especially thrilled William Blackstone, who had spent decades looking for evidence of prophecies' fulfillment. "Does it not seem," he wrote Secretary of State William Jennings Bryan, "that the environment of the world's present conditions exactly fits the prophetic statement in 1 Thess. 5–3 'When they are saying peace and safety, then sudden destruction cometh upon them'?" Then he turned to what he saw as the United States' singular international obligation. "May it be," Blackstone exhorted the nation's chief diplomat, that the United States will serve as "the instrument which God has prepared" to establish a new Jewish state in Israel. A few months later he sent a similar letter to President Wilson.[7]

The war served as an opportunity for premillennialists to win converts by trumpeting the message of the coming apocalypse. "The appalling crisis that has fallen upon Europe," Ford C. Ottman warned, "should sober the thought of Christendom, and awaken new and solemn interest in long-forgotten Bibles. The Prophecy of Daniel and the Book of Revelation are the burning lamps that reveal God's purpose as man's day upon the earth darkens to the end." Movement leaders tried to give all who would listen the tools to interpret those burning lamps. The most influential premillennialist magazines of the early twentieth century, *Our Hope, King's Business,* and *Christian Workers,* ran regular prophecy columns throughout the war. Charles Trumbull noted that when the *Sunday School Times* began to emphasize the second coming of Christ, subscriptions and profits dramatically increased. Prophecy also served as a major feature of the *Searchlight,* a new southern periodical launched during the war by Texas minister and staunch radical evangelical J. Frank Norris. Below the *Searchlight* masthead Norris included the premillennial trope: "Jesus Is Coming." From the very first issue of this paper, he made a concerted effort to build the growing radical evangelical movement in the South, identifying premillennialism as its most distinctive feature.[8]

In addition to preparing the world for the second coming, premillennialists believed that the war served as a means by which God could punish nations for their sins. According to Leonard Newby, the war represented God's chastening of Belgium for atrocities in the Congo; France for infidelity; and Great Britain for squandering its opportunities to Christianize its colonial subjects. Blackstone, meanwhile, believed that England's actions in Asia had angered the Almighty. He wrote the archbishop of Canterbury imploring him to lead the British people in repenting for the "unparalleled sin of the opium crime against China."[9]

Although most premillennialists focused on the faults of other nations, a few lamented the sins of the United States. Businessman A. A. Hyde, who had made a fortune on the development and distribution of Mentholatum Ointment, confronted his own nation's transgressions. "How about our past and present treatment of the original Americans, the Indians?" he asked in *Christian Workers.* "Then think about our century-long exploitation of Mexico. Again, have we dealt justly and wisely with the negro? And how about the Chinese and Japanese in our midst . . . ? Then what of God's chosen race . . . the Jews . . . ?" He attacked America's "aristocracy of wealth" and its mistreatment of the poor, concluding that judgment would likely fall on the United States. Evangelist French Oliver was even more strident in his denunciations. "Hear me, ye pusillanimous peace propagandists!" he preached, "the present European war is a mere Sunday school program, or sham battle compared to what shall yet be seen upon this earth. Poor, proud, vain, rich, arrogant, prayerless, backslidden America! Your partnership with the liquor traffic, and your rejection of Christ shall yet be punished!"[10] Premillennialists believed that at the end of the age, God planned to judge each nation. The war provided a preview of the horror that was to come.

The war gave some radical evangelicals the opportunity to affirm their position that the United States was not a "Christian" nation. While journalists and clerics often lamented that all Christendom was at war, premillennialists insisted that a Christian was a redeemed individual, not a governing entity, a national group, or a state. "There is not, and never has been," Newby explained, "such a company of people as a Christian nation, and never will be until the Lord comes." *King's Business* made a similar point. Editors defined "a Christian nation" as one that as a nation "has accepted Christ as its Saviour and as its Lord" in commerce, in politics, in international relations, "and in all the departments of its life." But "such a nation does not exist on earth, and never has existed, and never will exist until our Lord comes again." Pentecostal leader Stanley Frodsham characterized national pride as an "abomination" and encouraged fellow believers to "renounce their loyalty" to their "former king"—their nation—on joining God's spiritual kingdom. Such sentiments irritated more mainstream Protestants, who more often committed themselves to using the power of the state to Christianize and Americanize the world.[11]

As the war in Europe developed, Wilson pledged the United States to neutrality. His position reaffirmed the long American tradition of keeping free from European entanglements. Furthermore, the conflict had divided the loyalties of the American people. Many US citizens boasted German roots; others had French or British ancestors. Wilson wanted to limit domestic turmoil by not taking sides any earlier than necessary. But what neutrality meant in practice remained far from clear. Should the United States substantially enlarge the military in a show of strength and defense, or would military preparations more easily draw the country into Europe's war? Eventually the president chose expansion. The National Defense Act and Navy Act of 1916 dramatically increased funding for and the size of the US military.

While most premillennialists advocated isolationism, they did not always see eye to eye on specific issues of national defense. *King's Business* editors strongly opposed enlarging the US military. "There was never a more unreasonable or unnecessary war in all history than the present one," they lamented. They questioned why "cool-headed statesmen, brought up in the atmosphere of American traditions, should advocate such schemes for a colossal navy and a colossal army" that would "squander the money that ought to go into schools and reforms and other social improvements" and that would "rob our young men of some of the best years of their life." Then the radical evangelical editors ran a sermon by liberal Protestant Henry Sloane Coffin questioning the influence of big business on the Wilson administration. "The gravest danger to our peace at present," Coffin preached, "lies not in the attack of some foreign power jealous of our wealth, but in our own imperialistic commercialism eager to pre-empt for its selfish advantage the markets of the world." Finally, just one month before Wilson asked Congress for a declaration of war, *King's Business* ran yet another editorial warning of the dangers of expanding the military, asserting "there is no prospect of a great war for America for some years to come." The premillennial crystal ball needed some polishing.[12]

Christian Workers on the other hand called for a significant increase in the size of the United States' armed forces. "We believe the only real protection of our navy against aggression is an army and navy that will command respect if not awaken fear," the editors wrote. This did not mean, however, that their faith in the second coming had waned. "Let us therefore keep looking for the Lord to come, but in the meantime not handicap our government by contributing to a false sentiment about peace, when under existing conditions there can be no peace." Gaebelein lined up with the Chicago-based premillennialists. He believed that American military expansion was justified because "this age will never see universal peace, but wars will continue to the end."[13]

At least one major premillennial leader swam against the tide by praying for US intervention. A. C. Dixon believed that the United States needed to get into the war—and fast. The former pastor of the Moody Church was in a unique position to judge; he now had a front-row seat at the conflict as the pastor of London's Metropolitan Tabernacle. Reacting to the initiation of hostilities, he lamented in a letter to his wife that "terrible fighting" seemed imminent "and thousands of men will doubtless be killed. Terrible is the whole affair." Then he expressed his disappointment about the United States' isolationism. "I wish that the United States would join the Allies and thus help to bring it to an end." As the United States remained on the sidelines, he wrote to his daughter: "The English are beginning to look upon President Wilson's policy as a very shilly-shally affair and I rather share their feelings." Discouraged by the United States' neutrality, he put his trust in his premillennial faith. "Our only hope," he wrote a friend, "and a blessed hope it is, is in the return of our Lord. 'Come, Lord Jesus, come quickly.'"[14]

As the war progressed, neutrality became increasingly difficult for Wilson to navigate. The British cut off supply lines to Germany and the Germans responded with aggressive submarine warfare in the North Atlantic, hoping to knock out Allied shipping. Germany promised to try to spare passenger ships but warned the United States that ocean liners suspected of carrying munitions or other war supplies would be sunk. German officials even placed notices in US papers cautioning Americans not to travel in the North Atlantic or they might inadvertently end up in the crosshairs of a U-boat.

On May 7, 1915, American officials realized their greatest fears when a German submarine torpedoed the *Lusitania,* killing everyone aboard. The British liner carried 128 Americans among its more than one thousand passengers. It also carried war supplies. The sinking of the *Lusitania* had a major effect in the United States, provoking militarists like Teddy Roosevelt to demand that Wilson go to war. Others, such as William Jennings Bryan, had hoped to keep the United States out of war by keeping Americans out of harm's way. When Wilson issued an ultimatum warning Germany to cease U-boat attacks, the secretary of state resigned. In a letter to Mark Matthews, Bryan explained that he had quit in order to organize a fight against "the President, the entire Metropolitan Press, the financial interests, the munitiion [*sic*] manufacturers and the militarists," who, he believed, intended to drive the nation into the conflict.[15]

Most radical evangelicals did not blame the president for the tragedy, nor did they believe that Wilson wanted to go to war. *King's Business* editors "hoped that war between America and Germany will not result from the Lusitania outrage." While they rejoiced that the United States had "a calm and righteous President, and, one who loves peace," they also reveled in the chaos the war brought, using worsening global conditions to heckle their more mainstream counterparts. "We are glad in these days that we are not Post-Millennialists. . . . If we were Post-Millennialists, we could not help being hopeless pessimists."[16]

The debate over war shaped the 1916 presidential campaign. Wilson had the support of the nation's premillennialists, who took comfort in the president's pledge to keep the United States out of the European conflict. Nevertheless, they generally avoided making public commitments to either party and most still voted along regional lines. As the election neared, *King's Business* praised both the Democratic incumbant and the Republican nominee, Charles Evans Hughes. "God has certainly been good to America in the present political campaign," the magazine concluded. "Both of these men are pronounced Christian men. Both of them are sons of ministers of the gospel. Whatever way the election may go we are assured of having a true Christian man in the presidency for the next four years." *Christian Workers*—usually the more political of the major evangelical periodicals—remained mostly quiet on the 1916 election and simply encouraged readers to vote.[17]

The one major radical evangelical leader who had no qualms about jumping directly into the partisan political fray was Mark Matthews. In 1916 he stumped for Wilson from his pulpit and throughout the Pacific Northwest. In a sermon titled "Why Mr. Hughes?"—which he could have more accurately titled "Why Wilson!"—Matthews detailed Wilson's many accomplishments, ranging from the enactment of child labor laws to the establishment of the Federal Reserve to the championing of policies intended to reduce the influence of corporations on government. He carefully avoided attacking the Republican nominee as an individual but railed instead against the "old-time, boodle-loving, convention-day, boss-regime, Republican politicians" who ran the GOP. According to Matthews, Wilson had proven to be one of the most successful presidents in history and deserved reelection.[18]

Immediately after the election, Matthews made sure that the president appreciated his efforts. "I told you I would do my best to carry the State of Washington for you," he telegrammed Wilson. "It is yours. . . . God reigns and the government at Washington is safe." The Democrats could not have been more pleased with Matthews's efforts. "All lovers of the people's causes," Wilson responded, "will rejoice that you felt that you must do it and that you did it with such spirit and enthusiasm." Matthews received a letter from prominent Democrat and secretary of the treasury William Gibbs McAdoo congratulating him "heartily" on his "splendid work" in the campaign and on his role in helping win the Pacific Northwest for Wilson.[19]

After the election Blackstone wrote the president enthusiastically as well. He assured Wilson that he had not only the premillennialist's support but God's as well. He sent the president a copy of his latest apocalyptic tract interpreting the European war in the light of prophecy and he took the opportunity of Wilson's reelection to push the Zionist cause. He believed that God had selected Wilson to help execute the Almighty's plans for bringing about the end of the world.[20]

Reelection gave the president a free hand to deal with the ongoing European crisis and Germany's increasing provocations. In early February 1917 German leaders enacted a strategy of unrestricted submarine warfare, gambling that sinking every ship in the North Atlantic in order to prevent the Allies from resupplying was worth potentially drawing the United States into the conflict. They believed that such an aggressive tactic would secure victory for the Central Powers before the United States could mobilize. Meanwhile, the British intercepted secret dispatches from German foreign secretary Arthur Zimmermann to his representative in Mexico. Zimmermann suggested that if his ambassador could convince the Mexican government to ally with Germany against the United States, then Germany would in turn restore much of the American Southwest to Mexico.

As American outrage over Germany's subterfuge increased, U-boats sank a number of American commercial vessels. Blackstone telegrammed the president again, pleading with him to remain steadfast. "May God," he wrote, "enable you to continue your wise restraint from plunging our nation into the horrors of war." But the president's patience had run out. Despite winning reelection on the slogan "He Kept Us Out of

War!" Wilson was now ready to lead his people to battle. On April 2, 1917, he appeared before Congress. There he solemnly read a list of Germany atrocities and called for a declaration of war. Building to the lines that would define the rest of the war, he demanded that the world "be made safe for democracy. Its peace," he pledged, "must be planted upon the tested foundations of political liberty. We must have no selfish ends to serve. We desire no conquest, no dominion. We seek no indemnities for ourselves, no material compensation for the sacrifices we shall freely make. We are but one of the champions of the rights of mankind."[21]

Premillennialists had mixed responses to Wilson's declaration. Gaebelein, confident that the conflict was setting the stage for the end times, believed that American involvement fulfilled prophecy. "We have often pointed out that while the United States are not directly mentioned in prophecy," he wrote, "as an offshoot of Europe, we would probably be involved in the political upheavals of these last days of the times of the Gentiles. This has now come to pass." But Blackstone had a different take. He still believed that God wanted to spare the United States. He wrote Wilson yet again to reiterate the message he had sent to the president and the secretary of state three years earlier outlining the particular role that the United States seemed destined to play. "Oh, Mr. Wilson," he wrote, "in conformity with the prophecy . . . stand still and see the salvation of God, which He has in store for our peace-loving nation in contrast to the militarist powers, which are facing destruction." Blackstone warned Wilson that the rapture was imminent—probably just weeks away—and encouraged him to "watch and be ready . . . to meet our Lord in the air." He concluded by assuring the president that he was "praying that this may be your experience and that God will provide a fit Successor to guide our nation through the Tribulation Period."[22] Armageddon or not, the United States was at war.

World War I transformed the growing premillennial movement. While the faithful waited for the rapture, they worked to define their obligations to the state. For millennia Christians had debated their rights and responsibilities during times of war and premillennialists proved no different. Since the assassination of Ferdinand, they had wrestled over a series of important issues. If the US government asked them to support American military intervention, how should they respond? Should they serve in the armed forces? Should they kill their enemies? Or was the appropriate Christian response to turn the other cheek? Once Wilson vowed to make the world safe for democracy, the faithful had to take a position on this as well. Was a lasting peace possible? Should Christians support the president's crusade? They knew that the world was careening toward Armageddon, but what role they should play in the growing conflagration proved harder to discern.

Many radical evangelicals preached pacifism. S. Ridout believed that Christians should separate from the wartime spirit by refusing to bear arms, while Scofield bemoaned the United States' dependence on military force. Canadian evangelist Oswald Smith justified his pacifism by explaining that the devil was the ruler of this world. "If Satan," he preached, "is using men and nations as mere pawns on his great chess board . . . then why should God's people identify themselves with uprisings that have been fomented by Satan?" Some radical evangelicals denounced compulsory military service as well. "To try to imagine Peter, James, John and Paul, or other true disciples in the trenches shooting each other," wrote P. A. Klein, "or charging each other with fixed bayonet is a thing I cannot comprehend. And that a law which would create such a state of things can be right is likewise to me unthinkable."[23]

Throughout the war, many if not most pentecostals embraced pacifism. "There is no greater inconsistency extant than for the Church of Jesus Christ to go to war," wrote Frank Bartleman. "Her business is to preach, not murder. . . . War is not God's way for the Church. Ours is a different, opposite calling in this dispensation." He believed that American efforts both in Mexico (tracking Poncho Villa) and in Europe simply reflected the nation's imperial ambitions and greed. "It is all for gold. We are in the game of war. . . . We want the dollar." In reference to American munitions sales, he warned, "chickens come home to roost. And so will much of our ammunition, with interest."[24]

The burgeoning Assemblies of God also took a strong pacifist stance. At their 1917 general convention, denomination leaders affirmed their "unswerving loyalty to the Government of the United States" but then declared, "we cannot conscientiously participate in war and armed resistance which involves the actual destruction of human life, since this is contrary to our view of the clear teachings of the inspired Word of God." In fact, it was the threat of war that helped accelerate the organization of independent pentecostal churches into a new denomination. Assemblies leaders warned their loosely affiliated congregations that they would have to formally join the denomination to have their pacifist claims recognized by the state. This brought numerous churches more directly into the fold. Leaders at the Glad Tidings Assembly of God in New York praised God for "having so graciously anticipated our need and met it for us long before any one of us knew of our need of protection from participation in the works of darkness [the war] in these last days." Radical evangelicals' nonviolent stand often came at a price. Those who defended pacifism during the war faced repercussions in various forms. Nevertheless, many of the faithful remained undaunted.[25]

While one segment of the radical evangelical movement preached consistent nonviolence, another modified its views over the course of the conflict. During American neutrality *King's Business* warned that patriotism was not a Christian virtue and called blind allegiance to country "a thoroughly vicious sentiment" but vacillated on the question of bearing arms. The editors even changed the words of scripture to read: "in Christ Jesus there is neither Jew nor Greek, Barbarian, Scythian, German, Englishman, Russian or American, we are all one in Him." Such radical—and pluralistic—reinterpretations of the Bible echoed ideas that would later be found on the Christian left; not among radical evangelicals. The unfolding violence in Europe particularly troubled the *King's Business* editors. An article titled "Praying and Killing" told the story of a French chapel dug into one of the trenches. While soldiers took communion those by their sides prepared to detonate land mines should the Germans come into range. "To think of some praying while their companions sit ready any moment to send other human beings into eternity, has something horrible to it," the unnamed writer lamented. "How must a God of infinite love feel as He looks down from heaven and sees these antagonists both praying to Him and both ready to kill one another!" The article exemplified the challenges radical evangelicals (and others) faced trying to serve both God and Uncle Sam.[26]

Once Congress declared war, *King's Business* changed its tune. Editors reluctantly supported the draft and then praised the superiority of Christian servicemen whose conviction that heaven awaited them supposedly made them the best soldiers—more willing than those without the "blessed hope" to fight aggressively and to sacrifice their lives on behalf of their country. The evolution of radical evangelicals like those at the Bible Institute of Los Angeles on such important issues raises serious questions about motivation. Premillennialism worked in conjunction with other competing ideologies like nationalism and patriotism to influence the faithful. Sometimes Christians' expectations about the end of the world explicitly directed their choices; at other times premillennialism simply served to validate and reinforce the choices that believers made for other reasons. Yet either way, whether inciting action or justifying decisions already made, apocalypticism provided its advocates with confidence that they were acting righteously and on God's behalf.[27]

Other radical evangelicals never expressed reservations about military service. Those connected to MBI believed that Christians had a duty as citizens to "shoulder" guns for Uncle Sam and criticized pacifists who would not "kill human beings nor shed human blood" but would "enjoy the freedom and prosperity purchased . . . by those who will do both things if necessary." As Christ tarried, Moody's position eventually proved to be the most viable for premillennialists.[28]

As many radical evangelicals debated their obligations to the state, Billy Sunday, the most famous evangelist in the nation, rallied hundreds of thousands of Americans behind the military. Responding immediately to Wilson's request for a declaration of war, he promised that the United States would "back the old Kaiser off the map." According to a *New York Times* reporter he concluded a Manhattan revival service by leaping "up on top of his pulpit" and "wildly waving a flag with both hands while every soul in the audience was on his feet cheering." The journalist called it "a roaring climax to a meeting that had oscillated between patriotism and religion all evening."[29]

Sunday often preached on the imminent second coming of Christ and the rapid fulfillment of biblical prophecy during his revival campaigns, blending classic evangelicalism, nationalism, and premillennialism. He pushed Christians to support the war, and he pushed those who supported the war to embrace the radical evangelical faith. As one critic put it, "he so adroitly combines patriotism and religion as to make it appear that not to become a trail hitter is to declare one's self an enemy of the Stars and Stripes." Sunday saw the world in black and white terms and he had little patience for the nuances and debates that ran in the major Christian periodicals. He criticized pacifists and draft dodgers and encouraged his audiences to support the war in every way possible. "No man can be true to his God," he harangued, "without being true to his country." According to reporters, during his wartime sermons he often "went off at a tangent" to "flay 'Kaiser Bill' and 'his dirty bunch of pretzel-chewing, limburger-eating highbinders.'" When invited to give a benediction before Congress, Sunday concluded, "we pray thee that thou wilt bare thy mighty arm and strike that great pack of hungry, wolf-ish Huns, whose fingers drip with blood and gore." Congressmen broke decorum by responding to the prayer with yells, cheers, and clapping.[30]

Sunday passionately denounced German sympathizers and his dia-tribes occasionally sparked violence. In one Atlanta meeting he threat-ened to punch any man in the crowd who would raise his voice for the kaiser. A couple of weeks later he had to make good on his promise. As Sunday opened one of his characteristic attacks on Germany, W. H. Beuterbaugh made his way to the stage, ready to fight the evangelist. According to reporters at the meeting, once Sunday realized what was happening, he sprung into action. "There was not the slightest sign of fear in Billy's face," explained the *Atlanta Constitution,* "but with the ut-most calmness he crouched into the position assumed by trained fighters and, without waiting for the man to take the aggressive, Billy launched an uppercut." But he missed. "The man ducked and . . . as the evangelist swung round from the force of the lick he had aimed at the stranger's jaw, the man landed a light blow upon Mr. Sunday's cheek. Then recov-ering with the agility of a cat, Billy landed an uppercut which caught the stranger under the neck, bringing him into a clinch." At that point Sunday's aides wrestled the man to the floor amid cries of "get a rope" and "lynch him." The police responded quickly, but not quickly enough to prevent the crowd from roughing up Beuterbaugh as he retreated down the sawdust trail. By the time the would-be assailant made it out of the building his clothes were torn and "his face was swollen from the blows that had been showered upon him by the indignant men."[31]

While few premillennialists resorted to fisticuffs, they all agreed that Germany's liberal theology and embrace of Darwinian theories of human origin had caused the conflagration in Europe. According to

William Bell Riley, Germans' "discrediting of the Word of the Lord left the brute in the ascendant, trampled the very breadth from the body of Christianity, and left the Fatherland the form thereof without its power." R. A. Torrey saw a connection between German academics' pioneering work in higher criticism and Germany's wartime actions. He called it the "land not only of systematized and university-bred and fostered violence, lust, outrage and general deviltry, but the land of systematized and university-bred and fostered falsehood." French Oliver enthusiastically piled on. "The beer-soaked theologians of Germany have done more to preach infidelity in the form of the Higher Criticism into the world during the past forty years than all other educators combined." Cortland Myers agreed. "The Abomination of abominations in the modern religious world is that ripe, rank, rampant, rotten new theology made in Germany," which sparked a "world-tidal wave of barbarism, savagery, and immorality." Dixon's criticism of Germany extended beyond theology. Living in London he saw wartime atrocities firsthand. In a letter to his daughter he explained, "the Germans are waging war like savages. Indeed I feel like begging pardon of wild American Indians for calling them savages." He further lamented that such a highly educated culture had perpetuated this violence. "There has been something radically wrong with their philosophy of science and culture." Billy Sunday put the theological debate into terms laypeople could understand. "If you turned hell upside down," he famously preached, "I'll bet you'd find 'Made in Germany' stamped on the bottom of it." The conflict gave premillennialists a perfect opportunity to link their religious beliefs to the Stars and Stripes and to connect liberal theologies with the nation's wartime enemies.[32]

While premillennialism had its greatest impact among white evangelicals, African-American Christians had also been wrestling with the meaning and implications of radical evangelical apocalypticism as they watched events unfolding around the globe. While they did not always see eye to eye with their white counterparts and they did not participate in the white-led premillennial movement, their own engagement with apocalypticism reveals the ways race was functioning through both white and black expressions of Christianity, as well as how race helped eventually define fundamentalism. The African-American apocalypticism that emerged around the turn of the century blended the long tradition of black jeremiads against racial injustice with prophetic interpretations of current events. Black leaders longed for an end to inequality and anticipated the day when they would rule with Christ during the new millennium.

During the Gilded Age and Progressive Era, minister T. G. Steward used Daniel and Revelation to discuss the coming apocalypse. But rather than affirming the white premillennialist view that the Antichrist would soon take power over a restored Roman Empire in western Europe, he saw the devilish tyrant assuming control of the United States. "We may quite safely identify," he wrote in *The End of the World,* "the successors of this Roman kingdom with all those European nations which have developed the current civilization, whose people blended together in a common citizenship make up the population of America." For Steward, the restoration of the Roman Empire predicted in Daniel was the restoration of the people of the old Roman Empire into a new empire—the United States. Americans, he warned, had provoked the wrath of God because they substituted for the true gospel an Anglocentric message that applied "great ideas of liberty, fraternity and equality" only to people of their own race. Meanwhile "Christian America . . . robbed Africa of millions of her population and committed unheard of horrors," and "representatives of all Christendom in America have Christianized the Red man off the face of the earth." Under white rule, the tribulation predicted in Revelation had already begun for Native and African Americans. But destruction would soon come to Anglo Americans as Jesus set all things right.[33]

Steward emphasized the prophetic significance of Psalms 68:31, a passage widely heralded by African Americans (and African Christians) but mostly ignored by whites: "Princes shall come out of Egypt; Ethiopia shall soon stretch out her hands unto God." According to some African-American theologians, this passage indicated that at the end of the age, a holy remnant of Africans will rule with Jesus. "The bloody wave will soon have spent its force," Steward wrote, "and then shall the end come—the end of war and oppression; the end of the insolence of white pride and black contempt, and the ushering in of a new era in which righteousness shall prevail, and the peaceful, loving spirit of the Lord

Jesus Christ shall reign over all the earth." With the United States and other Western nations rendered powerless, Christians like Steward expected "the church of Abyssinia" to inaugurate the new millennium.[34]

The significance of the princes of Egypt passage was not lost on African-American minister James T. Holly either. He preached that Christians of African ancestry would play a special role in the coming kingdom. "The African race has been the servant of servants to their brethren" during "the Hebrew and Christian dispensations. And it is this service that they have so patiently rendered through blood and tears that shall finally obtain for them the noblest places of service in the Coming Kingdom. . . . The crowning work of the will of God," he explained, "is reserved for the millennial phase of Christianity, when Ethiopia shall stretch out her hands directly unto God."[35]

Just before the assassination of Ferdinand and the start of the war, the African-American newspaper *Chicago Defender* ran a long sermon about the impending fall of the Ottoman Empire and its meaning and relationship to the second coming of Christ. Writer D. W. Forde explained that evolving power relations in Europe had meaning in the context of the predictions outlined in the books of Daniel and Revelation. "The student of prophecy who has studied, and witnessed the fulfillment of every line of prophecy connected with" the Near East "thus far, without one failure, awaits the coming issue." He saw a great war on the horizon with horrible and bloody destruction in Europe and Asia. Meanwhile, premillennialism continued to spread more broadly in the African-American community. The *Chicago Defender* noted that numerous black churches in 1914 had announced sermons on prophecy and the second coming.[36]

The outbreak of war gave African Americans the opportunity to reassess their expectations. Seattle minister James Morris Webb expected the kaiser's plans for world rule to come to naught. Yet the German leader still inspired Webb to look beyond the battle of Armageddon to Jesus and his millennium. "As the Kaiser failed through his efforts to establish himself as a Universal King," Webb preached, "his career caused my mind to be lifted to a summit and view some Biblical prophecy, that there shall come a Universal King." But this was not the king so prevalent in the white imagination. "According to Biblical History," Webb continued, "he will be a black man with wooly hair." Then, taking a jab at Wilson, he concluded, "his ruling will be safer than Democracy. For there will be no discrimination and segregation under his dominion." Webb used biblical history to argue that Jesus, through Mary, had "black" blood, which would be apparent at the time of the second coming.[37]

At times African-American Baptists predicted an imminent apocalypse; at other times they warned their constituency to guard against millennial fanaticism. "Union-Review readers," the editors of the *National Baptist Union-Review* cautioned during the war, "should not be carried off their feet by modern prophets who are predicting things of which in the very nature of the case they can have no certain knowledge. Beware of the dealer in Bible prophecies." The paper offered a different kind of analysis of the war that looked at the role non-Western nations played in the ongoing crisis. "Who is prophet wise enough to deny that Africa is to be again the seat of world civilization? China, too, is awakening from a long sleep, which may presage a transference of Caucasian advance from Europe and America to the yellow people of Asia." The message of a black-led millennium appeared again and again among African-American Christians as the world descended into chaos.[38]

As the influence of premillennialism continued to spread, African Americans and whites routinely read prophecy, the coming judgment, and the millennium in racialized ways. White Americans rarely saw calls for social equality in the Bible. They displayed little sensitivity to the kinds of injustices experienced by their African-American brothers and sisters in Christ or to what those injustices might indicate about tribulation and prophecy. The idea that people of color would or could ever emerge as God's chosen did not cross white radical evangelicals' minds. Instead, they constantly—and naively—praised the United States as exceptional and perhaps more righteous than other nations. African Americans in contrast demonstrated much more awareness of the meanings and varieties of tribulation in this world as well as the next, and they had a more comprehensive view of the social changes God had promised to inaugurate during the millennium. They produced a counternarrative that sometimes offered a different image of the divine and often provided a very different analysis of the United States' supposed benevolence. The juxtaposition of white and black readings of prophecy and current events demonstrates how powerfully race functioned and what it obscured—especially among the white premillennialists who would soon shape the fundamentalist movement. While African Americans wrestled with Americans' growing fascination with apocalyptic theology, they had almost no role in shaping the broader premillennial movement.

Although radical evangelicals did not always agree on issues of patriotism and pacifism, their apocalyptic theology inspired a mostly consistent critique of Wilson's justification for entering the conflict. They saw democratizing the world as neither a worthwhile nor a sustainable goal. "We are reminded by the inspired prophets," *Christian Workers* cautioned readers, "that the ascendancy of democracy, though certain, is not lasting." In fact, the editors believed that Daniel's metaphor of clay mixing with iron foretold a period of democracy over the earth just before totalitarian governments arose against their subjects, opening the door for the Antichrist. *King's Business* had an even more cynical take. American leaders, the editors explained, had encouraged citizens' full participation in the conflict, promising "that the result of this awful war will be that all tyrannical government will end and that there will never be another war." But they were not buying what Wilson was selling. "This is a pleasant hope, but it is absolutely without warrant either in what we know of man or what we know of the teachings of the Bible." Furthermore, these Los Angeles–based editors believed that the government was misleading the American people. Saving democracy "may sound well for a Fourth of July celebration and as an appeal to thoughtless people, but it simply is not true and it is well that it is not true." Instead, the editors explained, the United States had entered the war in response to German aggression and specific violations of Americans' rights. "We have no more right to force Democracy upon Germany by bomb and bayonet than Germany has a right to force Autocracy upon us in the same way."[39]

Pentecostal Frank Bartleman was even more skeptical, suspicious that major Wall Street corporations were driving the United States' war efforts. "The common people are used up in the interests of the rulers, capitalists, etc.," he preached, echoing the criticisms of left-leaning dissenters like Eugene Debs. "Their lives and interests are wholly at their disposal. And the mandate of the government declare[s] them so. They must fight for 'capital,' while death is their reward and glory." But such criticisms were uncommon. While some premillennialists identified as economic outsiders, many others came from the middle and upper middle classes and more often identified with capitalist leaders rather than leftist dissenters.[40]

Not surprisingly, Mark Matthews differed from his coreligionists in that he supported the president and his justification for war. Matthews believed that the war represented "a death struggle between force and faith; between militarism and democracy; between brutality and humanity; between rationalism and Christianity." Germany, he harangued, "is fighting to make the world safe for Demon-ocracy—America is fighting to make the world safe for Democracy." The United States' Christian commitments, he vowed, would guarantee the nation's victory. He also pledged to help Wilson make the case for the war. He wrote the president suggesting that he "let those of us who are your friends and who would die for you and yours, go throughout the country and expose the infamy of the criticisms and of the critics. Now is the time to fight both in America and in Europe." Wilson responded by telling Matthews that his letter "warms the cockles of my heart." While the president seemed unwilling to ask his supporters directly to go after critics, he admitted that Matthews "may be sure that I would forgive any friend of mine for anything they might do in that way."[41]

Mobilization for the conflict required drastic action on the part of the Wilson administration and Congress. Shortly after the president called for war, legislators passed the Selective Service Act, which required all men ages twenty-one to thirty to register for the draft (which legislators later expanded to include men between eighteen and forty-five). Twenty-four million men registered by the war's end. The war also provided Wilson with the opportunity to expand dramatically the power of the federal government, taking control of industry, labor, and the economy in order to secure victory. Congress supported his agenda, establishing the War Industries Board, a mammoth bureaucratic agency that oversaw the wartime economy, as well as the Food Administration, led by Herbert Hoover, the Fuel Administration, and the Railroad Administration, among many other new federal entities. To finance the war, Wilson raised taxes on corporations and on personal income. The ratification of the Sixteenth Amendment just a few years earlier had made the latter possible.

Recalling predictions outlined years earlier by Blackstone and others, many premillennialists saw ominous signs in Wilson's consolidation of federal power and interventions in the economy. "The way is being paved," Bartleman wrote, for the Antichrist. "Men must obey. They must take the 'mark of the Beast.' They are to be simply the separate parts of a great State machine to be used up as ordered for the wild Beast's glory." Just a few years after Mauro's encounter with the *Titanic* tragedy, he had a similar response to changes on the home front. "The principles of Socialism," he wrote, "which were utterly opposed to monopoly, have led to the greatest monopoly that has yet appeared in the world. . . . We have seen the establishment of Government control of public-service corporations, Government control of incomes (both of corporations and individuals), Government control of food and fuel, and Government control of the *persons of individuals themselves,* for life or death—so far as their lives are supposed to be required in order 'to make the world safe for democracy.'" For Mauro, this was not necessarily a criticism but something he interpreted as inevitable. There was little reason to object to what had been laid out thousands of years earlier in the scriptures. In fact, Mauro was thankful that the "adoption of socialistic principles" in the United States had occurred without the kind of bloodshed paralyzing Russia at the time.[42]

To win the support of the public, Wilson established an effective propaganda board, the Committee on Public Information. The board enlisted the help of writers, filmmakers, and scholars to shape public opinion on the war. It also encouraged vigilant patriotism, even suggesting that neighbors spy on neighbors suspected of disloyalty. Evangelical W. W. Fereday saw this as yet another ominous sign of the end times. "The demand of the State will leave no room for freedom of thought, or independence of action in any direction whatsoever," he wrote. "The circumstances of the War have already furnished the machinery for this. . . . The authorities have felt constrained to take practically everything and everybody under their control." Fearful that the federal government could take away their religious freedom at any minute, radical evangelicals kept a wary eye on the state.[43]

As premillennialists surveyed the changing global landscape, they continued to align current events with biblical prophecy. Along with

German religion and philosophy, the kaiser became an object of evangelical scrutiny. Some believers even wondered if the prophet Daniel had foreseen Wilhelm II. Billy Sunday proclaimed that the German leader, "his nibs," fit biblical predictions of the end-times tyrant more closely "than any prince in the world today," while G. R. Eads linked him to the "little horn" of Daniel and suggested that he could be the Antichrist. "The end of the age is approaching with lightening speed," he asserted in the *Baptist and Commoner,* "and in the midst of the crash of the falling kingdoms of this world may we not look for the coming of our Lord." African-American religious leader Charles Mason used questions about the kaiser as Antichrist to emphasize the shortness of time in a sermon on "The Kaiser in the Light of the Scriptures." The fulfillment of prophecy, he explained, combined with "present events proved that we are living in the last days and the end was near."[44]

The majority of premillennial leaders, however, did not believe that the kaiser fit the mold of the Antichrist. Nevertheless, they had to address the issue in response to the many questions they received on the topic. James Gray laid out reasons why he believed that Wilhelm did not match the biblical description of the evil one and he asked his premillennial colleagues to speak to the issue. I. M. Haldeman, C. I. Scofield, Arno Gaebelein, and W. J. Erdman all agreed with the dean of MBI. The kaiser might foreshadow the Antichrist, they explained, but he was not the long-awaited man of prophecy.[45]

The role played by the Vatican during the war also troubled premillennialists. While most did not believe that the pope could be the Antichrist, they remained suspicious of Catholic intrigue. "Rome has her eye upon the triumph of the Kaiser and upon an alliance with him for the domination of the world," *King's Business* informed readers. "The greatest danger to our Republic is not from the Kaiser, but from Rome. We do well to be alert and to watch and pray." Wilson's efforts to prevent a German-Catholic alliance by bringing Rome into the Allies' camp troubled them as well. They criticized the president's plan to send an official government representative to the Vatican and insisted that recognizing the Roman Catholic Church as a political entity violated the separation of church and state, an argument they repeated for decades to come.[46]

The faithful watched Russia very closely as well, sure that it represented the northern empire that would compete with and do battle against the Antichrist in the last days. As early as 1868 Darby had written to his brother explaining that "Russia is Gog, unquestionably," in reference to the Ezekiel 38:2 phrase "Gog, the land of Magog." The *Scofield Reference Bible* solidified this view in 1909, interpreting the phrase as a reference "to the northern (European) powers, headed up by Russia." As a result, premillennialists saw great significance in events happening in eastern Europe. Following the 1917 February Revolution, Tsar Nicolas II abdicated the throne, opening the way for a new democracy to take shape. But premillennialists knew better. Gray rejoiced "with Russia in her newfound freedom" but added that "as a faithful interpreter of the Word of God" he would not be "surprised if the democracy of Russia were short-lived."[47]

He was right. In October 1917 Bolshevik rebels led by V. I. Lenin overthrew the new democratic government of Russia, vowing to lead a socialist world revolution. For premillennialists this proved extremely significant. Writing in the *Weekly Evangel,* Ernest A. Paul noted that Bible students should have expected Russia to break with the Allies one way or another before the end of the war. "The withdrawal of Russia comes not at all as a surprise, but as a thunderous reminder that not a word God has spoken shall fail to come to pass." Matthews, meanwhile, beseeched the president not to recognize the new "infamous hell born Soviet government." Premillennialists believed that the Bolshevik revolution represented a clear sign that the great power of the North, Magog, was preparing for the battle of Armageddon. "The spirit manifested by the Bolsheviki," Gaebelein groused, "is rising among the nations and is preparing the way for the time of lawlessness predicted in the word of God."[48]

The prophetic significance of Wilson's overtures to the pope, the rising power of communism through the Bolshevik revolution, and premillennial visions of the kaiser as a forerunner of the Antichrist had all titillated prophecy watchers. But nothing equaled their ebullience over the fate of Jerusalem. Right from the outbreak of hostilities, radical evangelicals hoped that the war would transform the Middle East and pave the way for more substantial immigration of Jews to Palestine. "The present war," Torrey forecast, "will very likely result in a restoration of Palestine to the Jews." With the Ottoman Empire in shambles, this was not hard to imagine. "It is glorious to think," Dixon wrote his wife from London, "that the inscrutable Turk is going to lose his power to persecute and will be driven out of Palestine." The Kentucky-based *Western Recorder* seemed equally sure. "Soon the Turk will make his last stand at Jerusalem, the day of salvation will end, the great day of the Lord will begin, the time of trouble such as never was will suddenly break upon the world, the King of glory will appear, and the great conflict so long waged with sin will forever end."[49]

As premillennialists longed for the restoration of Jews to Israel, they recognized that the presence of Muslims in Palestine presented a major obstacle. Before the war began Bartleman warned, "Mohammed is rising up against the Christ. He is the great religious opposer of these last centuries." Then, during the war, radical evangelicals linked alleged Muslim oppression with German aggression, hoping that to discredit one was to discredit the other. Billy Sunday called the kaiser a "defender of Mohammed, a deserter from Jesus Christ"; *King's Business* claimed that Wilhelm represented "Mohammedanism pure and simple." Others believed that the Germans had intentionally excited religious prejudices to foster chaos. "The Kaiser," H. C. Morrison preached, "has done all in his power to inaugurate a religious war, turning the hordes of Mohammedans loose in merciless rapine to deluge the whole Christian world with fire and blood."[50]

While the expansion of the war into the Middle East fueled premillennialists' anti-Muslim rhetoric, Blackstone continued to lead the evangelical Zionist charge. Having failed to secure a Jewish homeland in Palestine in 1891, he resurrected his memorial with the hopes of persuading Wilson to support the creation of a new Jewish state. Time was running out and he believed that Wilson's public acceptance of the petition would have "some influence upon those who are left behind" after the rapture—especially Jews.[51]

As Blackstone worked to this end, he developed relationships with important American Jewish leaders including progressive reformer, philanthropist, and Macy's department store magnate Nathan Straus, prominent liberal rabbi Stephen Wise, and future Supreme Court justice Felix Frankfurter, who at the time was working in the Wilson administration. Blackstone's most significant partnership, however, was with Louis Brandeis, the first Jew to serve on the US Supreme Court. In one of the strangest premillennialist partnerships of the twentieth century, the author of *Jesus Is Coming* and the celebrated jurist forged a unique relationship around the cause of a Jewish homeland in Palestine. Brandeis even purportedly remarked at one point that Blackstone was the true "father of Zionism" since his work "antedates" that of Theodor Herzl.[52]

Remarkably, Blackstone never hid from any of these prominent leaders his belief that in the end times Jews would face horrific persecution at the hands of the Antichrist and that the only way individual Jews could avoid this anguish was to accept Jesus as the Messiah. "Oh," he wrote to Straus, "would to God that you and every other Jew could believe and realize this glorious truth. But not many do accept this." He sent similar messages to Brandeis and Wise. Constantly peppering his letters with interpretations of prophecy and predictions of Jesus's imminent second coming, Blackstone hoped in vain to convert his most powerful Jewish allies. At one point he even warned Straus that the rapture was "to occur within the next few days" and pleaded with him to keep *Jesus Is Coming* close at hand in order to make sense of the event.[53]

The Blackstone–Brandeis relationship became even more bizarre in 1917. Blackstone oversaw a trust for world evangelism established by evangelical millionaire oilman Milton Stewart. Blackstone wanted to ensure that the money was used effectively. He asked Brandeis to help him draw up legal documents to transfer the trust to Brandeis to use for the Zionist cause in the event of the rapture. Apparently Brandeis agreed to help. The justice maintained a safe deposit box with Blackstone's legal papers, copies of his premillennial tracts, and sealed documents that Blackstone instructed Brandeis to open only in the event of rapture. These documents would further instruct Brandeis on how to find salvation in a world ruled by the Antichrist.[54]

In the late fall of 1917, a new Jewish homeland looked like a real possibility. British troops under the command of General Edmund Allenby engaged in a series of battles against Ottoman regiments in the Middle East. As the Allies neared Jerusalem, British foreign secretary Arthur Balfour wrote Lord Walter Rothschild, the most prominent Jew in Great Britain, to inform him that "His Majesty's Government view with favour the establishment in Palestine of a national home for the Jewish people, and will use their best endeavors to facilitate the achievement of this object." Just a few weeks later, Allenby marched into Jerusalem, making Balfour's promise a reality.[55]

This British success undermined Blackstone's efforts to use his memorial as an end-times tool for evangelicalism. Rabbi Wise wrote Blackstone that "when recently the British pronouncement was made . . . I thought of you, of your own faith and of your own effort of twenty years ago and more. We always think of you as one of our warm friends." However, the Zionist movement had grown beyond Blackstone's vision. Brandeis and Wise had promised the premillennialist that they would present his petition to Wilson when the time was right. They stalled for a couple of years, and then shortly after the Balfour declaration, Wise showed the president the memorial but did not leave it with him. Wise and Wilson apparently agreed that the White House would make no formal acknowledgment of it. Nevertheless, Blackstone continued to lobby his allies with the expectation that the rapture was imminent and that Wilson's reception of the memorial would both spare the United States from God's judgment during the tribulation and serve as a sign to the Jews of God's grace. But events on the ground had rendered Blackstone's proposal irrelevant to Jewish Zionists. While Brandeis initially supported the memorial's call for international rule over Palestine, he saw more limited, British-led supervision of the territory as a better option. Once that became a real possibility, he quashed the memorial while Blackstone waited in vain. Meanwhile, Brandeis wrote a friend that he still hoped to use the "Blackstone crowd" to support his agenda. The Blackstone-Brandeis friendship marked the beginning of a premillennialist-Zionist partnership of mutual opportunism, a relationship that has continued to this day.[56]

Premillennialists around the nation rejoiced at the news of Britain's victory, which seemed to fulfill literally Jesus's words: "Jerusalem shall be trodden down of the Gentiles, until the times of the Gentiles be fulfilled" (Luke 21:24). The times of the Gentiles, the great parentheses in the dispensational scheme, seemed near completion. The premillennialist response was uniform and widespread. "The capture of Jerusalem is more that a prophetic event," preached A. E. Thompson. "This," he gushed, "'is the climax of the ages.' We have entered a prophetic era." C. I. Scofield wrote to his friend and *Sunday School Times* editor Charles Trumbull, "now for the first time we have a real prophetic sign." Canadian minister P. W. Philpott explained that many of the "signs of the times" had been apparent in the past, with one major exception. "The

Jewish sign," he wrote, "has only recently been hung out, and that is why we feel the others are so deeply significant." Evangelist Henry Stough later remarked that this event should have been "a trumpet blast of warning to all nations" that prophecy was rapidly being fulfilled.[57]

In addition to bolstering premillennialists' faith, the capture of Jerusalem further fueled their anti-Muslim sentiments. "When General Allenby entered the city . . . the doom of Mohammedanism was sealed," Thompson preached at a major premillennial prophecy conference. "The day is soon coming when men will no longer honor the prophet of Mecca, but the Prophet of the Highest will be acknowledged. . . . Not Mahomet, but Christ; not the crescent, but the cross; not Mohammedanism, but Christianity; were triumphant when the British flag was planted upon the tower of David." Gaebelein was equally enthusiastic. "It has come to pass as we hoped and expressed," he exclaimed. "Jerusalem has been for about 1200 years under Moslem rule, or rather, misrule. . . . Jerusalem has been delivered and is freed from the domineering of the Turk." The *Western Recorder* jumped into the fray as well. "All too long the star and crescent, the royal insignia of Death and Hell, have been permitted to wave in insulting defiance to Christendom. . . . The Turk at his best is but a barbarian, without credible performance in the past or plausible promise for the future." The premillennial critique of Islam, which blended racial and religious stereotypes, grew in significance over the course of the century alongside the rising power of the Middle East and Arab-Jewish turmoil. Radical evangelicals had taken a clear position from which they would not waver.[58]

Despite their relatively small numbers, radical evangelicals trusted that their actions could steer the fate of empires. Near the end of the war they called on the president to declare a day of prayer and insisted that if he did, "the war would be brought to a very sudden and a very satisfactory close." In other words, if Americans made like Old Testament Israel, God would hear their prayers and intervene on their behalf. Wilson eventually proclaimed a day of prayer, humiliation, and fasting, leading *King's Business* to predict, "if it is observed as it should be, and if the people who pray meet the conditions of prevailing prayer, this day will prove the turning point in the war."[59]

Apparently it was. As the war wound down, radical evangelicals recalled that the day of fasting and prayer "was very widely observed" and "God heard the prayers that went up on that day, heard them in a way that has made the whole world wonder." As a result, "The tide of battle completely turned." They credited "the Lord God Almighty" with the result. Overwhelming military force may have helped as well, but premillennialists had no reservations about taking credit. They believed that God actively intervened in history in response to the prayers of his people.[60]

The conclusion of hostilities raised new issues for the premillennial movement. Since a cease-fire rather than the apocalypse marked the end of the war, believers had to return to the biblical text once again in search of insights into the future. Though their predictions that the war would lead to Armageddon proved wrong, they did not feel any sense of defeat, continuing instead to see in many global trends evidence of prophecy's ongoing fulfillment. In a short booklet summarizing the meaning of the war for Christians, Torrey emphasized that more than ever they could feel confident that "the Coming of our Lord Draweth Nigh." While most Americans celebrated peace, radical evangelicals predicted that an even greater war loomed on the horizon. Blackstone starkly telegrammed Wilson at the Paris Peace conference, "do not forget the prophetic word of God . . . 'For when they shall say, Peace and safety; then sudden destruction cometh upon them.'"[61]

Premillennialists believed that destruction might well come through the proposed League of Nations—a central topic at the Paris conference. During the war Woodrow Wilson had identified "fourteen points" that he hoped would define the peace and prevent another conflict from happening. They included freedom of the seas, open commerce, national self-determination, reduced armaments, and a handful of stipulations about postwar Europe. But for Wilson, the most important point was the last one. Repudiating generations of American isolationism, Wilson foresaw the creation of a League of Nations, in which the United States would be a member. He hoped that the league would transform and stabilize international relations, bringing true peace to the globe. As the Senate debated the merits of such a league, so did the American public. Did the proposed league infringe on American sovereignty? Would it hamper American aspirations for empire? Would it obligate the United States to military action in its defense? In treating nations equitably, would it undermine racial hierarchies and white dominance?

For radical evangelicals, however, another issue moved to the fore. They believed that the League of Nations would facilitate the rise of the Antichrist by bringing together the major nations of the world under the command of a single leader. They took an uncompromising stand against the league, revealing how directly premillennialism was shaping their politics. Premillennialists had long expected the Antichrist to take power through a ten-nation confederacy centered in Rome. While the geography of the proposed league did not precisely fit their reading of prophecy, the league's purposes matched their expectations closely enough to raise substantial concerns. After all, this was an international coalition that promised world peace potentially at the expense of individual nations' sovereignty. Mauro identified the league as the vehicle that would likely "wield the political authority of the world at the time of the second coming of Christ." French Oliver predicted that the coming league leader "will be the Politico-Beast described in Daniel, and in the Book of Revelation . . . the Anti-Christ!" Speaking for tens of thousands of radical evangelicals around the nation, Gray pledged his support for the Senate's "irreconcilables," the senators who made it their mission to defeat the peace treaty and US entry into multinational organizations. He characterized these men's position "as the safer and more consistent. . . . History leads us to believe this, without speaking of the Bible." Then, speaking of the Bible, he instructed Christians to be wary. "That the present League is the predicted one" for the last days "would be too much to say, but it is significant."[62]

Not all premillennialists adamantly opposed the league, however. In London, A. C. Dixon explained that his earthly citizenship presented different demands than his heavenly one. While he fretted that if "a League of Nations is to be organized which ignores the Bible and Christ, it . . . may become the nucleus of the Kingdom of Anti-Christ," he also worried that the Senate's failure to ratify the treaty "would be a world calamity." "Personally," he explained in an interview, "I believe that, if such a calamity should come, the United States would become a stench in the nostrils of the world." He further lamented that if the United States remained aloof, the rest of the world would likely line up against it, which would "mean another war even more terrible than the one through which we have passed." Wilson ally Mark Matthews also supported the league. When the legislature voted down the peace agreement, the preacher sent an irate telegram to the White House: "The rejection of treaty by United States Senate has made me ill." Then Matthews penned a scathing letter published in the *New York Times.* "The United States Senate," he declared, "has committed the crime of crimes against the liberty, peace, prosperity and future happiness of the world. . . . Away with men who could put America in such a disgraceful position by rejecting the treaty!" Although the League of Nations debate was not settled until the 1920 presidential election, the opposition of most radical evangelicals to US participation in global peacekeeping organizations illustrated their commitment to prophecy and how it shaped their politics.[63]

Just days after the armistice was signed, premillennialists convened in New York City for yet another major prophecy conference. Organizers rented Carnegie Hall for the keynote addresses, and both President Wilson and Vice President Marshall sent notes of welcome and encouragement. Many of the nation's leading premillennialists, including R. A. Torrey, Lewis Sperry Chafer, William Bell Riley, J. Wilbur Chapman, Ford C. Ottman, William Pettingill, and W. H. Griffith Thomas, spoke on the war, the capture of Jerusalem, current events, and prophecy. Audiences numbering over seven thousand people filled many of the services to capacity. Conference sponsors and "chairmen" included a number of wealthy Americans and captains of industry. That premillennialists had the support of politicians and business leaders revealed how substantially the movement had grown over the course of the war—it was fast becoming a major force in American Christianity. This was no movement of disinherited outsiders but one that attracted a broad array of advocates and sponsors from all social and economic classes.[64]

Arno Gaebelein wrote the introduction to the book that included the conference proceedings. "No one knew," he observed, "that when the appointed time for the Conference came the world-wide war would be over. The Lord knew that it would be so and that another prophetic testimony was needed to call attention to the real character of the age and the divine forecast of the future." The conference sermons included in the book reinforced the messages that premillennialists had preached throughout the conflict. They critiqued evolution, higher criticism, and German theology and worried that Americans had abandoned the scriptures. Many speakers also reminded the audience of events to come. Torrey warned that postwar optimism was futile. "Such hopes are delusive; they will end in disappointment and dismay. . . . When men's hearts are quaking for fear . . . look up, for your redemption draweth nigh."[65]

Although the war was over, the United States never ratified the Treaty of Paris. Europe remained fragmented, something the entire world realized just two decades later. While in retrospect it seemed that so much bloodshed had settled so little, the war had been extremely significant for at least one group of Americans. Premillennialists emerged from the fight better organized and with more momentum than ever. They carried with them a sense of urgency and vindication that they brought to their politics. They had been right—humankind was not ready for peace. But success drew opposition. As more and more Americans began taking premillennialists' apocalyptic ideas seriously, liberal Protestants increasingly spoke out against the newest incarnation of Christian millennialism. A major religious controversy began to brew; out of it American fundamentalism was born.

3

THE BIRTH OF FUNDAMENTALISM

ON A BRISK SPRING MORNING in 1922, popular liberal minister Harry Emerson Fosdick stepped up to the pulpit of Manhattan's First Presbyterian Church to deliver what became one of the most famous sermons in American history. The homily titled "Shall the Fundamentalists Win?" exposed the revolution under way in American religious life. The articulate, audacious cleric answered the question posed by his sermon title with a resounding and emphatic no. But Fosdick was mistaken; over the course of the twentieth century fundamentalists did triumph in important ways. They have played a decisive role in shaping modern Christianity, they have impacted nearly every facet of American life from politics to child-rearing practices to popular culture, and they have spread their faith to the ends of the earth.[1]

The "fundamentalists" Fosdick condemned that morning were the same radical evangelicals who had worked for almost a half century breathing new life into apocalyptic millennialism. By the early 1920s they had broadened their agenda. They began calling themselves fundamentalists to highlight their focus on resurrecting not just the early church's millennialism but also what they saw as numerous other historic foundations, or fundamentals, of the faith. In so doing they sought

alliances with other antimodernist evangelicals and churchly conservatives. But as the movement grew, expanded, and evolved, premillennialism continued to give fundamentalism its distinctive character and shape.

Fosdick, like many liberal Protestants, felt troubled by the emerging
fundamentalist movement. He disagreed with radical evangelicals'
faith in the historicity of biblical miracles, the virgin birth, the iner-
rancy of the Bible, and the sacrifice of Christ as a total payment for
human sin. Their obsession with the second coming of Jesus particularly baffled him. Fosdick believed that only the widespread disillu-
sionment of the "chaotic" and "catastrophic" war years could explain
the rise of such an obscure doctrine, one that he had never encountered
in his youth "at all." He attributed radical evangelicals' success to Americans' distress over "new knowledge" about the origins of the universe,
human history, and comparative religions, each of which seemed to pose
a threat to Christian belief.[2]

As Fosdick assessed the fundamentalist movement, he determined
that more than simple debates over theology were at stake. He fretted
that fundamentalists' "illiberal and intolerant" tone was hurting the
faith and he accused them of campaigning to "shut" the "doors of the
Christian fellowship" to those who did not agree with them. "Just now,"
Fosdick preached, in reference to an ongoing debate within his own
Baptist denomination, "the Fundamentalists are giving us one of the
worst exhibitions of bitter intolerance that the churches of this country
have ever seen." His own tolerance having long ago reached its limit,
he concluded, "you cannot fit the Lord Christ into that Fundamentalist
mold." Over the course of the sermon Fosdick made clear that his differences with fundamentalists were twofold. First, he disagreed with
them on numerous points of theology regarding the nature of Christ,
the Bible, and salvation. Second, he differed with fundamentalists on
the practical implications of the Christian faith. While the liberal minister embraced the progressive politics of his generation, fundamentalists had crafted a different kind of politics. They maintained an absolute
sense of good and evil and viewed compromise as sinful. They had no
faith in liberal reform.[3]

"Shall the Fundamentalists Win?" received widespread attention and
was quickly reprinted in multiple religious journals and also as a tract.
Through this sermon Fosdick helped define the parameters of the bur-

geoning fundamentalist movement. While the liberal-leaning Protestants who called themselves modernists tried to paint fundamentalism as a short-term, wartime aberration, they also knew that it was growing by leaps and bounds. Fundamentalists did not fit the stereotype of disinterested stargazers but represented an active and engaged army of militant believers who threatened progressives' power and influence. Radical evangelicals aggressively combated liberal trends in Protestant theology that denied the scriptures' historicity and miracles and that turned the Bible into a book of social ethics rather than a divine, sacred text. They identified the work of liberals like Fosdick as evidence that the last-days religious apostasy predicted in Revelation was upon them.

As the differences between radical evangelicals and theological liberals began to harden, each came to believe that the soul of Christianity was at stake. Hoping to discredit the power of Protestant liberalism, premillennialists strategically downplayed some of the more controversial aspects of their faith in order to find common ground with other white evangelicals and conservative Protestants. At times a few even tried to shift the focus away from premillennialism. Their belief that the time was nigh always influenced their actions, but they interpreted this belief as the product of rather than the foundation for right theology. If they could convince other Protestant antimodernists to stay focused on reading and interpreting the Bible accurately, then questions of eschatology would work themselves out in the end (literally and metaphorically). While modernists became obsessed with disparaging apocalypticism, fundamentalists repeatedly tried to return to what they viewed as more foundational issues of faith, prophecy, and biblical interpretation. They did not see themselves as defending a particular eschatological system but instead were engaged in all-out war over the very nature of the Christian faith.

Radical evangelicals had been wrestling with theological modernism for decades, but they had not intended to build a new Christian movement. Then the Great War began, accentuating the real-world ramifications of what had begun as a somewhat esoteric theological controversy. It pushed the premillennialist–Social Gospel schism beyond questions of beliefs and tactics to debates over patriotism and citizenship, which proved disruptive to the nation and the nation's Protestant churches. Radical evangelicals and liberals disagreed about their obligations as Christian citizens to the state, about the role the United States should play in World War I, and about the reconstruction of the postwar world. Their differences had ramifications for the American people as a whole, bringing substantial outside attention to the controversy. Modernists questioned the loyalty of fundamentalists and portrayed them as rabble-rousers whose pessimistic faith and lack of patriotism undermined the nation. As radical evangelicals fought back, they learned important lessons that in the postwar years helped them wed fundamentalism to Americanism. During the 1910s and early 1920s, fundamentalism came to represent the public expression of apocalyptic evangelical Christianity.

Few men were as instrumental in building the fundamentalist movement as Lyman Stewart. In his youth Stewart dreamed of becoming a missionary. Then his life changed dramatically. After oil was discovered near his hometown in northwestern Pennsylvania, he invested the money he had saved for his missionary venture into the oil business. Unfortunately for him, the investment and his career plans disappeared down the hole of a dry well. After Civil War service in the Union army, Stewart tried his hand at wildcatting, a high-risk, high-reward practice in which he had some success. He eventually sold his growing business to Standard Oil in response to John D. Rockefeller's tightening grip on the eastern US oil trade. In 1883 he moved west, where he plunged right back into the search for black gold. In California he hit pay dirt, or rather what was below it. Along with his brother Milton he helped establish Union Oil. He eventually served as Union's president. The company became one of the nation's most successful oil businesses, making Lyman and Milton Stewart millionaires. Like Rockefeller, and especially John D. Rockefeller, Jr., the Stewarts decided to use their wealth to support religious work. But while the Rockefellers subsidized the growth of liberal Christianity through such institutions as the University of Chicago and Manhattan's Riverside Church (built for Harry Emerson Fosdick), the Stewart brothers financed the growing premillennial movement.[4]

In 1891 Lyman Stewart helped establish the Pacific Gospel Union (now Union Rescue Mission—one of the largest private social relief agencies in the nation) in downtown Los Angeles. A few years later he attended a Bible conference at Niagara-on-the-Lake where he encountered the teachings of premillennialist pioneer James Brookes. The experience changed his perspective on Christian activism. "Only the gospel of Christ," he came to realize, "has power to save men. Humanitarian work may make their condition here more comfortable, and their surroundings more pleasant, but only the gospel can be of permanent value to them." In a letter to a friend, he revealed how directly premillennialism had reshaped his understanding of his role in the world. "I have been interested," he wrote, in "the Anti-Saloon League and also Good Government work, but it has begun to dawn upon me that if the saloon is closed and good government established, there will still remain the same work to be done, that of giving the people the gospel." He now understood that he had put the cart before the horse. "By giving them the gospel first, the closing of saloons and establishing of good government will logically follow." Yet this did not mean that he had abandoned his fellow citizens. Having found a more efficient means of helping his neighbors, he assured a Los Angeles reformer that he was "promoting good government along another line."[5]

Stewart's reasoning reflected that of many radical evangelicals across the twentieth century. Rather than reject outright the desperate pleas of the poor and oppressed for relief, or ethnic and racial minorities for civil rights, white premillennialists argued that they offered true liberation through faith. If they provided people with the gospel and changed hearts, social conditions would inevitably improve. Such ideas undermined generations of activism by nineteenth-century evangelicals who had often been leaders in social reform.

Stewart called Brookes's premillennial work "exceedingly instructive, and particularly helpful because of its sounding continually a note of warning in reference to the great apostasy." He felt "deeply impressed" about the need to spread Brookes's apocalyptic message to ministers all over the nation. "A great many good, honest men," he concluded, "were teaching error because they had never been properly instructed." Creeping liberalism troubled him as well, although he claimed not to be "a heresy hunter." He decided that if he ever had the means to educate those responsible for preaching the gospel he would do it. He felt called, he later explained, "to work along pre-millennial lines so far as Bible teaching is concerned."[6]

Stewart was an avid reader and he devoured books on premillennialism. Whenever he found one he especially liked, he bought copies for his friends and for college libraries around the country. He supported Scofield's work on the *Scofield Reference Bible* and distributed it widely. But one book in particular really thrilled him. Persuaded that William Blackstone's *Jesus Is Coming* clearly and succinctly summarized the most important message of the day, Stewart decided to send it to ministers around the nation. He reached out to Blackstone and together they assembled a new, updated version of the influential book that included endorsements from radical evangelicals from all over the nation, among them James Gray, R. A. Torrey, J. Wilbur Chapman, A. T. Pierson, L. W. Munhall, Ford C. Ottman, W. J. Erdman, William Moorehead, A. B. Simpson, and Robert Speer. The revised text once again emphasized how current events indicated that the rapture was imminent, imparting a sense of urgency to readers. As one elderly woman wrote to Blackstone, her discovery of *Jesus Is Coming* "was like a new conversion."[7]

The success of the expanded *Jesus Is Coming* pushed Stewart to dream even bigger. A faithful believer in the power of the written word to educate the mind and then transform ministry, the oilman decided to finance a far more ambitious project that could potentially have an even greater impact. As liberal ideas continued to make inroads in American Protestantism, Stewart wanted to do what he could to combat it. Like Blackstone and many other radical evangelicals, he believed that liberals' lack of commitment to premillennialism did not simply reflect different approaches to eschatology but that at the root of the pre/post-millennial divide lay a fundamental difference in approaches to the Bible. On the one side were those who believed that the Bible was scientifically and historically accurate and that it provided an unchanging, immutable, and infallible guide to all of life. On the other side were those who saw the ancient book as a valuable tool that offered important moral truths that could be extracted from the text itself and developed over time and applied in different ways to various issues and contexts. How each group viewed human history, the second coming of Christ, and the future of humanity simply represented the most obvious public manifestation of competing methodological approaches to and presuppositions about the Bible. Stewart believed that if he could convince ministers to adopt a more faithful, more literal reading of the Bible, they would then see that premillennialism worked in conjunction with other more historic fundamentals of the faith (such as Jesus's virgin birth, miracles, and literal death and resurrection). Stewart's goal was to reach those moderate religious leaders who had not yet succumbed to the heresies of liberalism. To this end, he began thinking about financing a new series of publications.

Stewart first shared his plan with A. C. Dixon. He approached the minister on a Sunday afternoon in Los Angeles after hearing Dixon deliver a powerful sermon critiquing theological liberalism as a dangerous heresy. As he later recalled in a letter to the minister, "you were replying to something that one of those infidel professors in Chicago University had published." After the service, Stewart asked Dixon if they could talk. "It seems as though the Lord must have given me courage to ask for the interview," he explained to the cleric, "as I naturally have a great shrinking from meeting strangers, and this matter which I had to present to you I had never mentioned to a single soul, not even to my own wife. So you were the first that heard it, and when you remarked, 'It is of the Lord; let us pray,' I was very deeply impressed."[8]

Stewart eventually decided to publish a series of books on the "fundamentals" of the Christian faith. He wanted to send them free of charge to every (presumably white) English-speaking Protestant minister, evangelist, professor, theology student, YMCA and YWCA leader, Sunday school superintendent, and religious periodical editor in the world. Dixon helped by serving as the first editor. When the minister later accepted a call to the Metropolitan Tabernacle in London, Louis Meyer took over the job. When Meyer's health failed, R. A. Torrey saw the project to completion. Between 1910 and 1915, Stewart distributed three million copies of individual volumes of *The Fundamentals: A Testimony to the Truth* at a cost of about two hundred thousand dollars, which he initially paid for by converting some of his oil stock. Eventually, his brother Milton helped subsidize the project as well. The brothers chose to remain anonymous, identified only as "two Christian laymen."[9]

The Stewart brothers represented just two of a few dozen exceedingly wealthy patrons who over the course of the twentieth century helped support and finance the spread of radical evangelicalism. But they were not using religion as an opiate for the masses; they were true believers. They laid their fortunes on the altar of the gospel, sure that God had blessed them with wealth to use for his purposes.

Lyman Stewart hoped in organizing this project to bring together antimodernist evangelicals of many different denominations, trusting that "more can be accomplished through interdenominational" collaboration. The editors solicited essays from many respected scholars, influential ministers, and evangelists from around the English-speaking world. They were all white men. The editors never considered how women or racial or ethnic minorities might enrich the movement or broaden its appeal. Contributors included an all-star roster of premillennial teachers such as Dixon, Torrey, A. T. Pierson, G. Campbell Morgan, Philip Mauro, James Gray, Robert Speer, L. W. Munhall, William Moorehead, W. H. Griffith Thomas, Charles Trumbull, Charles Erdman, C. I. Scofield, and Arno Gaebelein.[10]

The *Fundamentals* included personal testimonies and covered such topics as the virgin birth, the deity of Christ, the inspiration of the Bible, higher criticism, Catholicism, and new religious movements such as Mormonism and Christian Science. Numerous articles analyzed science and Darwinism, a topic on which the radical evangelical jury was still out. Scotland's James Orr, for example, indicated in his essay that Christians could accept some forms of theistic evolution. The series generally avoided political topics, with the exception of socialism, which Erdman attacked directly. However, he acknowledged that socialists had in some cases shown more compassion for the poor and the oppressed than many of the faithful. "Christian doctrines and Christian duties cannot be divorced," he wrote. The "social teachings of the Gospel need a new emphasis today." But, he stressed, "this does not mean the adoption of a so-called 'social gospel.'" Criticizing postmillennial promises of an earthly utopia, he called for renewed attention to the ramifications of biblical prophecy for addressing social problems. "The real blessedness of the Church and of the world," he concluded, "awaits the personal return of Christ."[11]

The editors wove premillennialism through the series, yet they were reluctant to make it a definitive test of orthodoxy. They understood that a range of opinions on eschatology existed and they did not want to close off any potential alliances with churchly conservatives or other antimodernists who might have somewhat different views. Their overriding goal was to defend what they interpreted as the true faith; they did not want to get sidetracked by issues of eschatology. They viewed premillennialism as the product of right theology not as an a priori presupposition. Furthermore, the battle among premillennialists decades earlier over whether Christ would return before or after the tribulation—a relatively minor point on which premillennialists have continued to disagree—had essentially destroyed the late-nineteenth-century Niagara Bible Conferences, where early premillennialists had met to study the Bible and prophecy. Radical evangelical leaders tried to prevent secondary issues of interpretation from overshadowing their common goal of calling Christians back to what they interpreted as the classic, historic faith now under siege by theological liberals.[12]

Nevertheless, analyzing and explaining premillennialism had in part motivated Stewart to publish the *Fundamentals*. As *King's Business* explained, "he had the vision of a prophet. Believing in the warnings and admonitions of the Bible and its prophecies concerning the last days, he earnestly desired to help other believers to be on their guard." The editors initially planned to print numerous articles on prophecy, the signs of the times, the various dispensations, the meaning of Daniel and Revelation, and many other related topics. But this proved more challenging than they anticipated. At the start of the project Dixon commissioned an article from Gaebelein on the second coming, but the piece he submitted, according to Dixon, was "not at all satisfactory." Scofield had promised to write on prophecy as well, but he was "very slow in fulfilling his promise." Well into the project Dixon complained to Stewart that though "there is much yet to be written along the lines of prophecy" and "the Second Coming of Christ," he had been unable to get quality, timely contributions on the specific topics he hoped to cover. "It has been difficult," he grumbled, "to induce the men who are most proficient in this line, like Schofield [sic], Louis Myer [sic], and others to write what we want but we shall keep after them until we succeed." Stewart followed up on Dixon's update with another letter to Scofield asking for an article on prophecy, apparently to no avail. The controversies that still surrounded the details of the premillennial scheme, along with its failure to take hold among many of the lettered academics the editors sought to include in the series, likely hampered Stewart's efforts.[13]

A few years into the project, its leaders had apparently still not secured the articles they wanted on prophecy. "I would be greatly disappointed," Stewart admonished Torrey, "if The Fundamentals should close without having strong articles" on "fulfilled prophecy" and "unfulfilled prophecy" and also one "on God's plan of the ages." At one point the editors planned to dedicate the entire last volume to premillennialism, a fitting choice since they saw the second coming as the ultimate fulfillment of the fundamentals. But as the project neared completion, Torrey worried that he still had too much ground to cover to dedicate an entire volume to eschatology. He also knew that premillennialists often disagreed on details and that a lengthy discussion of the second coming might create unnecessary divisions that could undermine the very interdenominational work they had hoped to foster. He commissioned Charles Erdman to tackle premillennialism directly, knowing that Erdman would be sensitive to varying interpretations. Erdman did not disappoint. Although he called "the return of Christ . . . *a fundamental doctrine* of the Christian faith," the premillennialism he described was very general. He sought to unify various antimodernist Protestants who differed over the many nuances of eschatology by following his defense of premillennialism with a call for those who disagreed with him to join in the greater task of evangelism—the "*one great precedent condition* of that coming age or that promised return of the Lord."[14]

Others tackled premillennialism as well. John McNicol's article "The Hope of the Church" called the second coming the Christian's ultimate hope. "There are many indications of a revival of interest in the study of eschatology," he enthusiastically noted. He believed that the infallibility of the Bible and premillennialism reinforced each other. Premillennialism derived from believers' faith in the accuracy of the text and witnessing the fulfillment of the premillennial signs of the times affirmed the text's accuracy. Premillennialism also appeared in a piece on the inspiration of the Bible. A. T. Pierson explained that properly interpreting the holy book required attention to the Bible's various dispensations. This dispensation would end, he predicted, when the "Beast, Prophet, and Dragon" challenged the restored Israel followed by the second coming. Despite Pierson's allusion to Israel, the *Fundamentals* did not include an article on Jews and prophecy, which was a great disappointment to Stewart. Louis Meyer had planned to write an article on the topic, but he did not finish it before his death in 1913.[15]

The reception of the *Fundamentals* illuminated the growing Protestant schism. On the one hand the books gave those radical evangelicals who were most concerned about the present state of American Protestantism a clear foundation on which to build. On the other hand they further antagonized liberals. In 1913 *King's Business* ran a letter from a liberal minister who asserted that the *Fundamentals* would "retard the progress of the kingdom" by slowing down the church's embrace of modern methods of interpretation. He accused the contributors of employing "reactionary methods" to strengthen a "reactionary movement." Yet the writer assumed that the *Fundamentals* "will become theological curiosities in the not distant future." "The encouraging fact," he concluded, "is that these ancient arguments in these books will have little weight with the modern mind, and will soon pass away." Had he had as much faith in the prophetic abilities of his antagonists as they had in themselves, he might have realized how wrong he was.[16]

The controversy over the *Fundamentals* made public what premillennialists had known for decades—that American Protestantism was facing a crisis. Creedal conservatives and radical evangelicals found it increasingly difficult to join together with liberals in fellowship. Differences over theology and the practical application of the faith proved harder and harder to surmount. Furthermore, in the decades around the turn of the century many areas of intellectual inquiry had undergone professionalization. The rise of the modern university system, the development of the social sciences, and the efforts of academics to distinguish themselves from laypeople by forming guild societies had all transformed the nature and distribution of knowledge. Bible study was no longer just the domain of ministers; a new generation of scholars, working in universities, seminaries, and divinity schools, brought new approaches to the classic text. For the most part, the men and women who took an academic approach to the Bible rejected the methodologies and interpretations embraced by premillennialists. As a result, radical evangelicals had to develop their apocalyptic theology outside the traditional bastions of religious and intellectual power. But having assembled an impressive roster of highly credentialed men to author the *Fundamentals,* radical evangelicals did not yet realize how wide the divide was becoming between their work and that of those in academia.

At the same time that Stewart, Dixon, Meyer, and Torrey oversaw the *Fundamentals* project, theological modernists started to identify their differences with traditional Christianity in even more explicit terms. Shailer Mathews, a leading liberal and dean of the University of Chicago Divinity School, believed that Christianity was undergoing a revolution. In his 1913 article "The Awakening of American Protestantism" he explained that prominent theologians were reinterpreting faith "in the terms and under the influence of evolution and democracy." He foresaw the emergence of a new "evangelicalism" that embodied "not a theory about the Bible but the actual religious experience and ideals which are recorded in the Bible." American believers, he hoped, would abandon "the formal legalistic principle of Protestantism" dating back to the Reformation and instead focus on the "normative worth of the Christian experience that gave birth to Protestantism and the Bible itself." This new faith, he believed, would "in the long run" present a "gospel of a saved society as well as of saved individuals." In making his views so explicit, Mathews gave radical evangelicals a gift. Rather than claiming to represent the historic evangelical faith, he explicitly taught that faith had evolved over time and that Christians needed to catch up. He admitted exactly what his opponents had been claiming all along—that liberal Protestants were not practicing the traditional, historic Christian faith.[17]

Mathews knew that not everyone would agree with this "awakening." On the other side of the revolution, he wrote, stood premillennialists (among others), who had "little sympathy with the evangelization of social evolution." He called them "earnest Christians who, in the spirit of Tertullian, repudiate all efforts at re-thinking Christian faith and prefer a bald literalism in the treatment of the Scriptures." By framing the debate in such stark contrasts, Mathews was laying out a clear divide— liberals versus conservatives, progressives versus reactionaries, evolutionists versus traditionalists, and premillennialists versus postmillennialists. A religious war was in the making.[18]

Mathews's article provoked numerous responses. His crosstown rival James Gray wrote a rejoinder that interpreted the modernist's ideas through a premillennial lens, arguing that liberal theology heralded the destruction of the true faith. Gaebelein called the Mathews article "a demonstration of the climax of apostasy of which the New Testament speaks." Others complained that Mathews and his allies had not fairly represented them. In an article titled "Millenarianism Misrepresented," *King's Business* lamented that "eminent, learned" men "seldom miss a chance to give a fling" at premillennialism. "The marvel is not so much their misrepresentations, as that they venture at all to criticize what they are so egregiously ignorant of." To hammer home the point, the writer noted, "we cannot think they would maliciously misrepresent." In other words, in mischaracterizing premillennialism, liberals were not mean; they were just stupid. According to this editor they failed to understand the complexity and nuances of the premillennial interpretive scheme.[19]

Premillennialists' reactions to Mathews made clear not just that there was an awakening under way on the liberal end of the Protestant spectrum. It revealed the coalescing of an alternative new movement that centered on premillennialism and the *Fundamentals*. Although millions of American Christians did not fit neatly within either of the developing camps, the white, male leaders of the two groups would set the terms and much of the agenda for American Protestant faith in the twentieth century.

The growing liberal-radical evangelical divide over theology and eschatology had important and direct ramifications for adherents' beliefs about citizenship and war. World War I looked very different from the vantage point of a premillennialist than from that of a postmillennialist. While liberals hoped that the war would ultimately result in a permanent, enduring peace, premillennialists used it to justify their predictions of imminent destruction, as well as their long-standing criticism of reform movements. The seeming fulfillment of prophecy bolstered radical evangelicals' confidence, gave them extra incentive to spread their ideas, inspired their increasingly aggressive attack on the faith of modernism, and made their message all the more compelling. If the war was setting up the battle of Armageddon then the great religious apostasy of the last days was certainly under way in the guise of liberal Christianity.

Premillennialists linked the war raging in Europe with the intellectual battles occurring in the United States. They believed that German theological liberalism was not only responsible for the conflagration abroad but that its influence, through American higher education, was also undermining values at home. Popular New York minister John Roach Straton called on Christians to go on the offensive against theological liberals and their "rationalistic and skeptical tendencies in religious thought," which had "come overwhelmingly out of modern Germany." He insisted that Americans "not only defeat Germany with our armies on the field of battle" but "also defeat Germany in the realm of mind and spirit."[20]

The attack on rationalism and skepticism was a drum that radical evangelicals kept beating. Torrey lamented that the poison German gas deployed on the battlefront "is not one tithe so dangerous and damnable as the poison gas that German university professors have been belching into the universities and theological seminaries of America." Cortland Myers opened a prophecy conference by declaring, "the Abomination of abominations in the modern religious world is that ripe, rank, rampant, rotten new theology made in Germany." Mixing racist jokes and nativist fears of immigrants, he admonished Americans to make war on theological liberalism. "I hate this traitorous stuff," he preached. "I hate it! I hate it! I hate the new theology as I hate hell, from which it came!" L. W. Munhall called the Bible the "'gas mask' with which the Christian can turn back the damnable 'made in Germany' infidelity that is undermining our churches and schools."[21]

Although only a few radical evangelicals were actually reading the works of German theologians, they rightly understood that liberal theology had its intellectual roots in Germany, and they wanted to make sure that everyone else knew it as well. Their criticism was especially potent because Americans were expunging all things German from their culture, going so far as to rename German shepherds "shepherd dogs" or "Alsatian shepherds" and sauerkraut "liberty cabbage." No one wanted to be identified with the kaiser's empire. Premillennialists had long-established, close ties with British and Irish theologians and scholars who had contributed to the development of modern premillennialism. They saw in the trenches of Europe a metaphor for the theological conflagration in the United States.

Even more than the battle over theological origins, the real-world ramifications of premillennialism exacerbated the growing wartime theological schism. Premillennialists' conflicted views on military service and democracy, as well as their lack of faith in ultimate victory, raised questions among many Americans about their loyalty. Leading theological liberals carped on these issues in a series of publications and public addresses. The University of Chicago's Shirley Jackson Case was the most vocal. While the United States needed "every ounce of the nation's energy," Case wrote, premillennialists "were advocating a type of teaching which is fundamentally antagonistic to our present national ideal." He accused premillennialists of "primitive thinking" and "mythological interpretation," claiming that they represented a tremendous danger to the nation. "Under ordinary circumstances one might excusably pass over premillenarianism as a wild and relatively harmless fancy." But not during the war. "In the present time of testing it would be almost traitorous negligence to ignore the detrimental character of the premillennial propaganda." Painting premillennialists as cold and heartless, he continued, "the retention of a vain hope of catastrophic world-renewal begets indifference, if not actual hostility, toward all remedial agencies designed to improve the present order of existence." Because premillennialists viewed Woodrow Wilson's efforts to make the world safe for democracy as doomed to failure, Case believed that they were in fact indirectly, and maybe even directly, aiding the enemy. The *Christian Century* agreed, warning that the "most serious menace of millenarianism is its inevitable effect upon the loyalty, courage and devotion of our citizenship in the present world war." What the liberals did not realize was that rather than withdraw from political engagement, premillennialists were developing a new kind of local and global politics derived from their very particular faith. They did not expect to improve conditions around them but rather to battle the forces of evil as they prepared the world for the coming judgment.[22]

Liberals' accusations of fundamentalist disloyalty were a serious matter in a period of hyperpatriotism. From the start of the war, the Wilson administration worried that the public did not fully support US participation. The president therefore encouraged the Committee on Public Information to quash dissent and to pressure ordinary citizens to support the effort. Congress backed the president's agenda, passing the Espionage and Sedition Acts, which severely restricted Americans' constitutional rights. Meanwhile a host of voluntary and vigilante organizations sprang up, coercing and enforcing patriotism in local communities. Overall the war provided the context for multiple egregious violations of Americans' civil liberties.

Shailer Mathews, who had in many ways fired the first shot in what became the fundamentalist-modernist controversy with his 1913 article, condemned premillennialism during the war for its social and political implications. On the opening page of his book *Will Christ Come Again?* he justified his assault on fellow Christians. "Partly because of the war, partly because of the extensive circulation of its literature, partly because of its literalistic appeal to the Bible, partly because of the lack of theological education on the part of active Christian workers, premillenarianism is a danger." The movement, he explained, "forces men to choose between the universally accepted results of modern culture, and diagrams from the book of Daniel, elevations of church members into the sky, and interpretations of the prophets which reach the heights of absurdity in aeroplanes, tanks, and the Kaiser." He accused adherents of subscribing to faulty Jewish apocalyptic expectations about the coming of the Messiah that undermined the war effort.[23]

Once again, premillennialists took the bait. Haldeman called Mathews's book "nothing less than a burlesque, a grotesque and dishonoring caricature of one of the most sacred, immense and initial subjects of Holy Writ." John MacInnis slammed it as "the rankest kind of propagandist literature," noting that it was rooted in German ideas. "What a pity," Torrey sarcastically responded, "that the Apostle Paul and the Lord Jesus Christ could not have attended Chicago University before they said or wrote anything." Though premillennialists rarely claimed explicitly that modernists were tools of the Antichrist, they often implied it. "The author little realized," Mauro explained, "when penning his scoffing remarks, and raising his puny weapon of ridicule against 'the promise of His (Christ's) coming,' that he was fulfilling the very prophecies he was endeavoring to discredit." The most incisive response to Mathews's book appeared in *Christian Workers,* where minister Daniel Bryant attacked the Chicago theologian's disregard for the "Jewish" nature of early Christian theology. "Dr. Mathews," he explained, "holds that we cannot know what the Bible teaches until we have rescued it from its orientalism and have translated it into the terms of occidental life. . . . I hold precisely the reverse to be the case." He criticized modern Western philosophy, asking whether Christians living in the midst of a major European war really believed their culture ranked above that of the New Testament.[24]

As the controversy grew, additional modernists jumped into the fray, supporting and reaffirming the positions of Mathews and Case while premillennialists responded in kind. The Methodist *Sunday School Journal* ran a series of articles denouncing premillennialism. The author, James Allen Geissinger, complained that it "paralyzes every impulse to Christianize the world" and that its adherents ignored "unjust wages, bad housing conditions, child labor, and every other social and moral problem." The *Christian Century* and *Biblical World* each published lengthy series disparaging premillennialism as well. George Preston Mains, in an unimaginatively titled book, *Premillennialism: Non-scriptural, Non-historic, Non-scientific, Non-philosophical,* attributed the success of the movement to the "unprecedented world war," which incited "a new expectation of the imminent coming of Christ for the ending of the world" and a period of "systematic, persistent, and even audacious propaganda of this faith." He added that the modernist attack on premillennialism revealed the "growing conviction that the movement no longer should be allowed to pass unchallenged." Mains was certainly right. The war had transformed what might otherwise have remained a somewhat obscure theological conviction on the fringes of Protestant life into a major force. It verified in a way that nothing else could that premillennialist doomsday scenarios and their implications for current affairs had to be taken seriously.[25]

T. C. Horton relished the attention premillennialists were getting. "Our Postmillennial brethren are on the warpath," he wrote. "For forty years or more they have held their peace. They had but one text book on the subject. . . . Now they are everywhere on the alert, writing books, declaiming from the rostrum, sounding the alarm from pulpit and press. 'Beware of the Premillennialists!'" Then he cut to the heart of the controversy. "What's the matter, brethren? Why the sudden arousement?" His answer: "now these good brethren are finding fault because the dear saints are flocking to hear the preachers and teachers who are premillennialists."[26]

Modernists searching for radical evangelicals' weaknesses questioned the funding at the root of the premillennialist crusade. Case hinted that the phenomenal spread of premillennial ideas from coast to coast and border to border in every major denomination in the previous few years might be a German-financed ploy to weaken American resolve. "With a thoroughness suspiciously Teutonic," he wrote, "the premillennial movement in its present activities is everywhere making its influence felt, and felt in so subtle a way as to threaten our national enthusiasm at one of its more vulnerable points." Case may have also called for a government investigation into the financial sources undergirding premillennialism, further raising radical evangelicals' ire. "While the charge that the money for premillennial propaganda 'emanates from German sources' is ridiculous," Torrey responded, "the charge that the destructive criticism that rules in Chicago University 'emanates from German sources' is undeniable." One thing was certain—radical evangelical apocalyptic thought, in the context of a world war, had become an issue of national consequence.[27]

As controversies about premillennialist funding continued even past the cessation of hostilities, Keith L. Brooks somewhat disingenuously responded that there was not "one iota of evidence that there is or has been an organized movement devoted to the teaching of the Second Coming, 'backed by millions upon millions of dollars.'" If the critics, he suggested, could put their "finger on the leaders of such a movement let him do so, and would he kindly put us in touch with just a few of the more generous of the contributors? . . . Any millionaire who believes the Lord is coming would, no doubt, be glad to assist us." What Brooks did not acknowledge—although he was very well aware of it— was that the Stewart brothers had paid for in whole or part the distribution of *Jesus Is Coming,* the creation and distribution of the *Fundamentals,* the publication of *King's Business,* and the construction of the Bible Institute of Los Angeles. There were in fact millionaires subsidizing the premillennial movement. But despite Case's allegations they had no ties to Germany.[28]

At the same time that premillennialists objected to modernists' efforts to portray them as bad citizens, they scrambled to reframe the debate. Postmillennialism, James Gray asserted, was the true threat to the nation. "The whole theory of postmillennialism is pregnant with the idea that the world is morally growing better all the time, the corollary of which is that military armaments are a menace and to be discouraged at every point." He pointedly blamed postmillennialists for naively playing into Germany's hands by supporting superficial peace movements and discouraging American armament. The premillennialist, in contrast, sets his mind "on the surest methods of winning the war." Turning back to the larger religious issues at stake, he argued that his theological opponents had "little real familiarity with what God is doing in the world and the place which this war occupies in His plan."[29]

Despite Gray's protests, most wartime suspicion centered on radical evangelicals rather than liberals. Government censors, who aggressively sought to ferret out subversive materials from the mail and from libraries in military camps, banned Blackstone's *Jesus Is Coming,* which by that point had sold over a half million copies and been translated into twenty-six languages. Infuriated, Mark Matthews wrote Vice President Thomas Marshall asking him to get to the bottom of the situation. The Seattle minister believed that either Catholics close to the administration or Shailer Mathews were behind the ban. Matthews promised that if the issue was not rectified he would "cross the continent and say a few things about the infernal crooks who are clothed in the livery of Heaven and who are parading in the garb of patriots that will stir a few people out of their conceit and self-confidence." In response to an evangelical lobbying effort, the director of military intelligence apologized, claiming that he had meant to prohibit a different publication with the same title.[30]

Nor did premillennialists' problems end with the armistice. Lingering wartime suspicions about radical evangelicals' apocalyptic politics and suspect patriotism, combined with their postwar political fervency, continued to provoke government attention. In 1919 agents from the newly formed Bureau of Investigation launched an inquiry into the work of R. A. Torrey. They believed that the Los Angeles minister and Bible institute dean might have violated the Espionage Act during a sermon denouncing Wilson for his advocacy of the League of Nations. Torrey apparently had called the president a "traitor" who had "dragged the honor of his nation in the dust." Eventually the bureau backed down, but the investigation demonstrated the seriousness of premillennialism for the body politic. It could be a subversive faith. As radical evangelicals saw their loyalty questioned over and over again during the war and in its immediate aftermath, they resolved to find new ways to integrate their faith with patriotism and their politics with the larger interests of the nation.[31]

To fend off liberal attacks and appeal to as many Americans as possible, end-times-oriented evangelicals felt compelled to prove that they were good citizens. While Darby and Scofield had emphasized the inherent contradictions between premillennialism and nationalism, the stakes were evolving as the premillennial movement grew and expanded. Adherents wanted the general public (and the government) to see them as loyal citizens, even as the hypernationalism and violence of the era challenged their ability to remain faithful to their religious ideals.

Most premillennialists reacted to questions about their loyalty with explicit demonstrations of their support for the US government and the war effort. Moody Bible Institute, for example, sold Liberty Bonds, canvassed for the Red Cross, and encouraged students to support the war. But the relationship between premillennialism and patriotism was not a simple one. During the conflict many Americans began to venerate the flag as the symbol of the nation. *Christian Workers* waved the Stars and Stripes proudly, essentially making it an object of worship. But for many other premillennialists, veneration of the flag was problematic. They believed that it had become for too many Americans a false idol. In an Independence Day issue, *King's Business* editors criticized flag manufacturers for commercializing patriotism to hawk their wares. "Many of those who display the U.S. flag most ostentatiously are those who will be the last to make any real sacrifice for the defense of country. And on the other hand, many of those who have made the greatest sacrifices for the country in times past, do not see the need now of flaunting their patriotism by wearing a flag in their buttonhole, or carrying it on their automobile, or draping it over their doors or windows." They encouraged readers to buy Liberty Bonds rather than flags if they wanted to support the war.[32]

Since the Assemblies of God had renounced combat duty, church leaders felt particularly obligated to demonstrate their national allegiance in other ways. During a wartime annual convention, they affirmed their "unswerving loyalty" to Wilson and vowed to help bring "the present 'World War' to a successful conclusion." This pledge followed on the heels of a powerful sermon on the second coming in which "again and again the preacher was stopped by the unbounded enthusiasm of his audience, and again and again the whole company of saints arose." Apparently convention delegates saw no contradiction in mixing the second coming with patriotism. Nevertheless, the loyalty pledge troubled at least one local congregation. The Spokane, Washington Assembly of God felt "*so strong* against war" that it believed that the denomination's promise to "support" the president was "unacceptable." Such protests, however, were rare.[33]

African-American leader and head of the Church of God in Christ Charles H. Mason, like other pentecostals, also struggled to prove his patriotism. His explicit pacifism, as well as the fact that some of his white followers were of German descent, captured the attention of the Bureau of Investigation. Mason was arrested during the war and temporarily jailed for denouncing military service. As a result, he felt even more obligated to pledge his loyalty to the US government. "I cannot understand," he explained in a sermon on the war, "after preaching the gospel for twenty years and exhorting men to peace and righteousness, how I could be accused of fellowshipping the anti-Christ of the Kaiser." He too counseled followers to buy bonds to support the war effort.[34]

Over the course of the war, premillennialists and postmillennialists waged a battle of pens, typewriters, tracts, and books, taking no prisoners. The war highlighted and exaggerated their differences, propelling the controversy forward. By the time Woodrow Wilson returned from treaty negotiations in France, Protestant leaders knew that a major schism was in the works. How it would end nobody knew. Recognizing that the future of American Protestantism was at stake, neither side sought an armistice.

The publication of the *Fundamentals* and the ensuing wartime controversy with modernists helped radical evangelicals sharpen their faith. But they understood that more work had to be done to establish a lasting movement. R. A. Torrey and James Gray agreed that it was time for "a blow" to be "struck," "a good strong one and not . . . a puny one," against modernism. But they disagreed on how best to do it. When Gray proposed a conference to bring together radical evangelicals, Torrey warned him that the debate over premillennialism could be divisive. "I doubt very much," Torrey wrote, "whether we ought to make the acceptance of premillenarianism a condition of attending this conference. There are other questions that are more fundamental." Meanwhile, evangelist Henry Stough was thinking along similar lines. He wrote John Roach Straton suggesting that "while the Lord tarrieth" they organize a movement that combined "the Fundamentalist's position" with social reform in order to "keep the way open to preach the gospel."[35]

Ultimately the more controversial William Bell Riley spearheaded the most successful effort to organize premillennialists. He called for a "confederacy of conservatives" to challenge theological modernism. To that end he helped launch the World's Christian Fundamentals Association in 1919, which provided a new venue through which many of the nation's leading radical evangelical ministers and teachers from many different denominations could work. The association's organizers— once again an all-male, all-white group—hoped to identify as clearly as possible their differences with theological modernists and to chart a course for the future. Riley described the first meeting of the World's Conference (a little too enthusiastically, it turns out) as "an event of more historical moment than the nailing up, at Wittenberg, of Martin Luther's ninety-five theses. The hour has struck," he declared, "for the rise of a new Protestantism." Pentecostals, however, were excluded from the group. Many non-pentecostal premillennialists continued to dispute the perpetuity of spiritual gifts and practices and they felt uncomfortable fellowshipping with those who spoke in tongues.[36]

Gray and Torrey were disappointed that Riley had become the public face of the movement, and for good reason. Riley could at times represent the darkest elements of radical evangelicalism—including anti-intellectualism, racism, and anti-Semitism. Torrey eventually joined the World's Christian Fundamentals Association, but Gray kept his distance. He was careful not to align MBI with Riley. Critics were already accusing MBI of seeking to "disrupt the churches," and he feared that the association would further solidify that image. Gray and the businessmen who oversaw MBI sought to balance radical evangelical faith with mainstream credibility. Despite their commitment to fundamentalism, they went to great lengths to distance their organiza-

tion from anything that seemed "sectarian" or out of step with traditional Christianity. Yet without Gray the association could not claim
the Moody network, which undermined its ability to represent premillennialism in total. In many ways the differences between the approaches of Riley and Gray foreshadowed the differences that would
later divide the leaders of the National Association of Evangelicals from
those of the American Council of Christian Churches.[37]

While Riley was building a new interdenominational network, his
fellow Baptists were waging a fight over doctrine within the Northern
Baptist Convention. In 1920, minister and editor Curtis Lee Laws
helped organize a "fundamentals" Baptist conference immediately preceding the denomination's annual meeting. He recorded the proceedings in the *Watchman-Examiner*. These conventioneers tackled the issue
of premillennialism and its relationship to the "fundamentals" right at
the start. Laws argued that while all premillennialists were theologically conservative (this was a bit of a misnomer—there was little "conservative" or traditional about premillennialism), not all theological
conservatives were premillennialists, and therefore "premillennialism"
did not adequately describe the Baptist antimodernist movement. The
group then decided to settle on a term to describe itself. They rejected
"conservatives" as "too closely allied with reactionary forces in all walks
of life," and they discarded "premillennialists" as "too closely allied with
a single doctrine and not sufficiently inclusive." In challenging liberalism within their churches and seminaries, they hoped to cast as wide a
net as possible in order to draw as many allies as possible. "We suggest,"
Laws summarized, "that those who still cling to the great fundamentals
and who mean to do battle royal for the fundamentals shall be called
'Fundamentalists.'"[38]

Laws made explicit what had been implicit for some time. "Fundamentalism" signified the rise of a new, aggressive, militant, interdenominational movement. Although the Baptist leader tried to distinguish
the more inclusive "fundamentalism" from the specific doctrine of premillennialism, this proved nearly impossible. It was premillennialism that
had separated radical evangelicals from traditional, creedal, churchly
conservatives and inspired the most fervent activism. Premillennialists'
sense of an imminent apocalypse, along with premillennialism's many
ramifications, gave the fundamentalist movement its most definitive

shape and character. This was especially true during the war years, which proved pivotal to the movement's origins and development.

Nevertheless, the role of premillennialism in shaping fundamentalism was always contested. At its root, the divide between fundamentalists and modernists reflected a difference in presuppositions about the Bible's design and function, leading to varying and often conflicting interpretations. Premillennialism served as the proxy for underlying methodological and hermeneutical differences. Fundamentalists' belief in the imminent second coming grew out of their more foundational faith in the centrality and historicity of Jesus's work as well as in the literal accuracy of the biblical text. But over the first decades of the twentieth century premillennialism became the most significant point of debate in the fundamentalist-modernist controversy because premillennialism, more than anything else, expressed, represented, defined, and shaped the very different approaches of fundamentalists and modernists to the Bible as well as to the world around them. Premillennialism, more than any other theological issue, fashioned the ways that radical evangelicals lived and structured their lives, which is why it took center stage in the debate with modernists.

As the fundamentalist movement grew, expanded, and provoked increased scrutiny, its leaders felt compelled to define its relationship to premillennialism. They tried mostly in vain to focus on the interpretative issues that undergirded the question of Christ's return rather than obsess over debates on the return itself. "The uninstructed," the *King's Business* editors explained in a special "fundamentals" issue, would gather from the ways the controversy had unfolded "that the battle of the age was between liberals and premillennialists. Why try to camouflage the matter in this way? The real battle," the editors argued, "is between skepticism (downright infidelity in many cases) and evangelical conservatism. The question of 'pre' and 'post' appearance of Christ is not to the front." *Moody Monthly* took the same position.[39]

Yet radical evangelicals, including those writing for *Moody Monthly* and *King's Business,* often treated fundamentalism and premillennialism as synonymous, especially because the latter could serve as an almost fail-proof litmus test to identify the former. While a person might claim to accept many of the tenets of orthodoxy, what he or she actually believed could still be elusive. But if a person affirmed premillennialism, his or her orthodoxy was almost guaranteed. J. Frank Norris

As this cartoon illustrates, fundamentalists insisted that the belief in the premillennial second coming of Christ was instrumental for properly interpreting the scriptures.

   E. J. Pace, *Christian Cartoons* (Philadelphia: Sunday School Times Co., 1922).

explained it this way: if a person was a premillennialist, "I know what he believes on the inspiration of the Scriptures. I know he believes the Bible literally. . . . I know what he believes concerning the Godhead. I know what he believes concerning the Virgin Birth. I know what he believes concerning the atonement. I know what he believes concerning the resurrection." For this reason he called premillennialism "THE MOST VITAL DOCTRINE OF ALL." Indeed, for most fundamentalists, premillennialism guaranteed theological orthodoxy.[40]

Premillennialism, however, was more than just a proxy. Apocalyptic faith provoked substantial debate because it moved fundamentalism beyond ideas and beliefs to questions of social and political action and citizenship. More than any other "fundamental," premillennialism affected the ways its adherents lived. Believing that Armageddon was imminent transformed how the faithful understood every part of their lives. Their eschatological convictions made them unwilling to champion the war effort and encouraged them to question Christians' roles in the military, refuse to support Wilson's vision for world democracy, and abandon hope in a lasting peace. In an era when the United States was beginning to emerge as a global power, mainstream Christians worked to plant the American flag around the world, while premillennialists were more interested in diagnosing current events in search of signs of the Antichrist. Premillennialists took unpopular positions on the basis of their convictions at a time when supporting the American empire was of the utmost importance.

Nevertheless, a small number of conservatives connected to the fundamentalist network rejected premillennialism. J. Gresham Machen, dubbed "Dr. Fundamentalis" by acerbic journalist H. L. Mencken, was arguably the most gifted of the group. He lamented the ways the premillennial debate had come to define the battle with modernists and called it "highly misleading when modern liberals represent the present issue in the Church, both in the mission field and at home, as being an issue between premillennialism and the opposite view. It is really an issue between Christianity, whether premillennial or not, on the one side, and a naturalistic negation of all Christianity on the other." But he could not change the fact that premillennialists had waged the most consistent and strongest fight against theological liberalism. They gave fundamentalism its militancy and urgency. In fighting the equation of premillennialism with fundamentalism, Machen was acknowledging the substantial hold of premillennialism on the movement. He was the exception that proved the rule.[41]

As the use of the term "fundamentalist" spread, some members of the movement wished that they had better defended their claim to the more historic term "evangelical." "Dear brethren," Moody Monthly advised, "do not let the old name slip away from us and become the property of those who would apply it in an unholy propaganda." James

Gray did not like the term either. "I do not call myself a fundamental-ist, not because I lack sympathy with the Bible truths for which that name now stands, but because I think the name itself is unnecessary and perhaps undesirable." Presbyterian minister Donald Grey Barnhouse agreed. "I never have been willing to call myself a fundamentalist . . . even though I know I am absolutely fundamentalist in my doctrinal po-sition." Dixon, despite editing the *Fundamentals,* consistently defined himself as an "evangelical" against modernism in the 1920s rather than as a fundamentalist.[42]

And yet the name stuck. In the interwar period, "fundamentalism" came to define the interdenominational network of radical evangelical apocalypticists who joined together to publicly and aggressively herald the imminent second coming while challenging trends in liberal theol-ogy and in the broader American culture. Their reading of the Bible alongside current events assured them that time was running out, which gave them a shared sense of militancy and determination. Modernists' aggressive attacks, which focused primarily on the doctrine of premil-lennialism, as well as fundamentalists' equally combative responses to those attacks created the fundamentalist-modernist controversy. The controversy, in turn, wreaked havoc in many denominations.

During the 1920s, pentecostals joined the controversy. Like other radical evangelicals, they worked to stake out an identity vis-à-vis the new fundamentalist nomenclature. Aimee Semple McPherson, one of the few female premillennialists to assume a public role, preached a Sunday night illustrated sermon—the kind of theatrical fare that made her famous—titled "Trial of the Modern Liberalist College Professor versus the Lord Jesus Christ." In this sermon the evangelist played the role of prosecutor in a mock trial that focused on the infiltration of liberalism into American churches. The faux jury, which consisted of a broad representation of the American public, was charged with deter-mining how leading institutions of revivalism in previous centuries, such as Yale University and Princeton University, currently stacked up next to the word of God. As exhibits, McPherson quoted modernist professors and preachers, including Social Gospel pioneer Walter Rauschenbusch and modernists Harry Emerson Fosdick and Shailer Mathews, among others, revealing how thoroughly aware McPherson was of the leaders and issues fundamentalists were battling. The

While women often played only secondary roles in the premillennial movement, a few pioneers, such as Aimee Semple McPherson, distinguished themselves as leaders and innovators. Here McPherson uses her "Gospel Car," painted with the message of Christ's imminent coming, to draw crowds as she tours the nation in 1918.
   Courtesy of the International Church of the Foursquare Gospel.

evangelist's case rested simply on the Bible, the words of respected fundamentalists, and the views of George Washington and Abraham Lincoln. By citing American presidents along with theologians, McPherson intentionally associated fundamentalism with patriotism and theological liberalism with un-Americanism. Her actions anticipated the marriage of faith and patriotism that would soon become a hallmark of the fundamentalist movement.[43]

Members of the Assemblies of God identified as fundamentalists as well, and occasionally as "Pentecostal Fundamentalists." In response to a question from a layperson, E. N. Bell explained that the Assemblies opposed "all modernism or infidelity in the church. . . . They believe in all the real Bible truths held by all real Evangelical churches." Another Assemblies minister called the "new theology" a "menace to society and to the nation," likening it to Bolshevism. The denomination's Central Bible Institute even offered a course titled "Fundamentals of the Faith 'Plus.'" The "plus" referred to "the Baptism of the Holy Spirit with signs following." But this difference could at times raise tensions with other fundamentalists. On one occasion the *Evangel* ran an ad for a book by popular prophecy writer Louis Bauman. Influential Assemblies missionary Alice Wood complained to denomination leader Stanley Frodsham that the Assemblies was promoting a book by a person who had been critical of pentecostals. Frodsham acknowledged first that fundamentalists had good reasons for some of their criticism, as some pentecostals had gone to unhealthy extremes. Furthermore, he explained, "we should greatly rob ourselves if we refused to have anything to do with the Fundamentalist preachers and writers who do not see eye-to-eye with us. . . . There is no doubt that God has many precious children among the Fundamentalists who are doing all they can to preach the gospel. I believe the Lord wants us to take a very charitable attitude towards them." Indeed, these small steps taken by Frodsham and others like him would lead to big things in the coming decades.[44]

As the fundamentalist-modernist controversy played out in numerous venues in the interwar era, denomination after denomination faced civil war. Annual church conventions, parochial schools, theological seminaries, and missions boards became arenas for testing or challenging orthodoxy. The *Christian Century* summed up the controversy in 1924. "The differences between fundamentalism and modernism are not mere surface differences, which can be amiably waved aside or disregarded, but they are foundation differences, structural differences, amounting in their radical dissimilarity almost to the differences between two distinct religions." Sounding more like a radical evangelical than a liberal, the writer acknowledged, "the God of the fundamentalist is one God; the God of the modernist is another. The Christ of the fundamentalist is one Christ; the Christ of the modernist is another. The Bible of fundamentalism is one Bible; the Bible of modernism is another." The differences were clear. There would be no rapprochement.[45]

But much more than religious ideas were at stake. The controversy was also about power and control of churches, property, and resources. "Nine out of ten . . . dollars, if not ninety-nine out of every one-hundred of them," William Bell Riley lamented, "spent to construct the great denominational universities, colleges, schools . . . theological seminaries, great denominational mission stations, the multiplied hospitals that bear denominational names, the immense publication societies, and the expensive magazines, were given by Fundamentalists and filched by modernists. It took hundreds of years to collect this money and construct these institutions," he continued. "It has taken only a quarter of a century for the liberal bandits to capture them." Fundamentalists wanted to win the battle of theology but they also wanted to maintain control of the major resources managed by the nation's historic Protestant churches and schools. As a result, many refused to separate from traditional denominations.[46]

The American public, daily newspapers, and the nation's major magazines all covered the ebbs and flows of the controversy. The *Washington Post* ran an editorial that accused fundamentalists of reviving discarded theological practices and advocated instead liberty of conscience. "Medieval history is crowded with records of such clashes and incident bitterness, but the history of these times should be free from them." International papers also took up the story. The *Manchester Guardian* ran an article on "the religious crisis in America" linking fundamentalism to medieval religious violence. The fundamentalist movement, the paper asserted, "quickly took on the character of a crusade and made astonishing strides." The *New York Times* summarized the growing controversy. "Protestant religion has been overtaken by what seems to be a far-reaching crisis," P. W. Wilson explained in the Old Gray Lady. "The issues now raised are as deep as any decided by the Reformation. The battleground of the struggle is limited to the United States . . . but the echoes of the conflict resound throughout the world. It is safe to predict that this religious affair, in all its bearings, will occupy as much of public attention as many a political problem."[47]

Premillennialism often served as the focus of articles on the fundamentalist controversy. The *Boston Globe* ran a story on the debate wreaking havoc in the Northern Baptist Convention under the headline "Is Christ Coming Soon to Rule the World by Force?" "An exciting religious storm is swirling around Boston," the article began. "Religious weeklies are filled with red hot letters for and against the doctrine of the 'pre-millennialism' and 'the second coming of Christ.'" The *Atlanta Journal-Constitution* printed a series of articles that described the "Errors of Adventism" and lamented the rise and popularity of premillennialism. The author criticized James Gray, R. A. Torrey, I. M. Haldeman, and William Blackstone for misleading thousands of earnest believers. But at other times journalists praised these same premillennialists for bringing new life and vitality to the Christian faith.[48]

As the religious chasm grew over the next few years, it occupied an important place in American culture and in the headlines. The controversy revealed that fundamentalism was never simply about doctrine or subscribing to a series of essential beliefs. Countless Christians in the United States could affirm the "fundamentals." The fundamentalist movement represented something else. It marked the rise of a network of apocalyptically oriented radical evangelical ministers, teachers, and radio personalities who insisted that the end was nigh and the apostasy predicted in Revelation had begun. As skepticism, secularism, and scholarly criticism grew, they believed that evil was enveloping the earth. This conviction, in turn, demanded an urgent and militant public response by the faithful and a new way of living until Christ's return.

The fundamentalist-modernist controversy, like the prophecy conference movement that preceded it, originated among white evangelicals. While many African-American Protestants embraced the "fundamentals" of the faith, they mostly remained on the sidelines as public debate raged in the leading white religious denominations and periodicals. At no point did white evangelicals consider reaching out to the nation's black churches. Despite fundamentalists' talk of doctrinal purity as the foundation for Christian fellowship, the color line always trumped theology. White fundamentalists were not interested in cultivating African-American allies or bringing them into the fundamentalist network, even if those African Americans were in perfect harmony with fundamentalist beliefs. Meanwhile, for black evangelicals racism often represented a hallmark of the white fundamentalist faith.

Although African Americans did not participate directly in the fundamentalist movement, the nation's black churches felt the effects of the religious controversy. The National Baptist Convention made its commitment to fundamentalist doctrine clear. "All colored Baptists are fundamentalists," explained an editorial in the *National Baptist Union-Review,* "except a half-dozen imitators of Ingersoll, Darrow, Fosdick, and Dieffenback, the so-called 'Intellectuals' of our race." The paper called modernism a "cancer on the body ecclesiastic" and then proudly noted that "the infection of false teachings afflicting white Baptist churches, schools, and homes balks at the color line because

Colored Baptists will have none of it." Church leaders counseled young ministers not to spend time studying "Evolution" or "Liberal Religion"; instead they "should be devoted to prayerful, strongly mental meditation of the Word of God as held and taught by Baptists throughout the ages."[49]

And yet substantial differences distinguished black evangelicals from white fundamentalists. The president of the National Baptist Convention, E. C. Morris, delivered a major speech that emphasized the importance of clinging to the historic doctrines of the Christian faith. In the same address, however, he denounced lynching and justified African Americans' pursuit of their civil and social rights. His ability to move seamlessly from criticizing modernist theology to expressing concerns about social justice revealed a substantial divide. Whites simply did not—and did not have to—think about how their faith related to issues of injustice and discrimination.[50]

Other African-American religious leaders made their differences with white fundamentalism even more explicit. Minister A. B. Adams, who had a regular column in the *Pittsburgh Courier,* rejected modernism and emphasized the importance of what he saw as the classic faith. Nevertheless, he understood the racialized nature of fundamentalism. If "the worn out theological conceptions of the white man have not sufficiently benefitted the Negro youth," then ministers should "impart to them the teachings of God. . . . Proclaim the Word of God. We have too many man-made faiths in the world." He flayed modernists, including ministers like Fosdick, whom he accused of abandoning the scriptures. But lest anyone mistake him for a fundamentalist, he concluded by asserting his independence. "Please do not misunderstand me being a fundamentalist. I am not, although the fundamentalists are a little better than the modernists."[51]

Others did not think that fundamentalists were better at all. Some African Americans feared that fundamentalism could set decades of hard work and rights activism backward. In a pointed editorial, Ernest Rice McKinney explained in the *Amsterdam News,* "a Fundamentalist is nothing more than the same old reactionary strutting forth in a brand new robe. . . . The Negro race is filled to overflowing with these 'Fundamentalist' gentlemen. They are everywhere and in everything. They keep us poor, ignorant and weak. But, some day, we will revolt." Then in a *Pittsburgh Courier* column McKinney lamented the stereotype that

African Americans had by nature "childlike religious faith." He feared that as blacks embraced fundamentalism the stereotype would gain traction. Only ignorance, he wrote, could explain white or black predispositions to such simple versions of Christianity. Some African Americans expressed concerns that clinging to the fundamentals in the face of modern advances risked making religion irrelevant to young people. An article in the *Pittsburgh Courier* blamed the decline in church attendance among younger African Americans in part on church leaders' "fundamentalism" and lack of engagement with the Social Gospel and current thought.[52]

While many African-American religious leaders took sides in the controversy, others opted to stay out of the increasingly vitriolic war raging among white Protestants. In a series of news summaries, Roscoe Simmons—who at one point identified himself as a fundamentalist—warned African Americans to keep their distance. "American white people are still fighting over religion," he explained in the *Chicago Defender,* "maybe the Modernists and Fundamentalists arguing about creeds will stumble up on true religion." A few weeks later, he quipped, "no doubt as to our white people having religion. Getting them to use it every day is something else." Then, in another column, he advised, "don't follow our smart white people off in this religious war. . . . Our white people are tangled up. Pray for them; don't follow them." Nevertheless, Simmons and other black leaders saw a potential opportunity for African Americans in the fundamentalist-modernist war, one that echoed the sentiments of generations of black millennialists. "Keep up the controversy," he wrote, "fifty years hence the priesthood of the New World will be children of the New World's slaves."[53]

The idea that African Americans could emerge from the white church controversy as the nation's spiritual leaders also appeared in a *Pittsburgh Courier* editorial. "The layman stands aghast while he listens to this bitterness as it belches forth from the mouths of professing Christians—and more, men called of God." The paper then called for a return to a simple faith in Jesus and his teachings and an acknowledgment of the mysteries of God. "We must look to another than the Caucasian Church," it concluded, "for a true and reliable exemplification of the life of our common brother." Once again, African Americans prayed that Ethiopia would soon stretch forth her hand.[54]

Despite many African-American religious leaders' interest in the fundamentalist-modernist theological controversy, it proved insignificant in the face of the social and political issues black Christians faced. The *Chicago Defender* published a letter on fundamentalism that observed, "the trouble with fundamentalists is that they fail to deal in fundamentals. Social, economic, and spiritual relations were the only subjects that Jesus preached about." Atlanta minister J. Raymond Henderson agreed; he preached that supposed orthodoxy was not a good thing. "Most Negro Baptists have second-handed conception of religion" he lamented, "our ideas are not ours but rather a passed-on product of the white man." In a sermon to white Emory University students, he targeted white hypocrisy. "This is the Bible belt where people profess to believe in the Bible from cover to cover," he preached, "and where a fundamentalist conservative religion is matched by an equal degree of bigotry, and injustice, which makes peons out of the poor of your group and of mine, and even eventuates into the most awful evil of society, namely lynching. Here in the south we have a religion that is so good that a colored youth would contaminate it. . . . The curse of the south is its religion, it is too fundamentalistic, theoretical, doctrinarian, and priestly." He longed for the day that the South would "shake off outmoded religious conceptions." This was a cry that would echo all the way into the 1960s civil rights movements and beyond. African Americans' experience with white fundamentalists shaped their evaluation of the merits of fundamentalism. Meanwhile, white fundamentalists' racial orientation fashioned the way they read and taught the Bible and where they put their emphases and energy. The racial divide proved impossible to surmount.[55]

During the 1910s, radical evangelical apocalypticists—galvanized by the war—constructed a distinct movement led by an interdenominational network of white preachers, evangelists, writers, and Bible institute teachers. They had a theology codified in the *Fundamentals* and a name thanks to Curtis Lee Laws. As fundamentalism's power and influence increased, movement leaders continued to wrestle with their responsibilities to the larger American society. In one of the most insightful articles to run during the war, BIOLA faculty member John

MacInnis laid out a strong justification for more explicit fundamentalist cultural and political engagement. "What," he asked, "must be the
attitude of the Church while she waits for the return of her Lord?" To
answer this question, he turned to Jesus's parable of the minas, also
called the parable of the talents (Luke 19). In this story, a king leaves
minas—money—with his servants and instructs them to "occupy till I
come." Those who invested the money and thereby earned more won
the praise of the king. He rewarded them for "occupying" while he was
away. This, MacInnis wrote, "is the Lord's own picture of this age. . . .
We make a tremendous mistake when we take the attitude that the
world is a hopeless wreck from which we are simply to redeem a few
chosen ones." So what was the alternative? "The devil has no right to
rule the commercial, political and social life of this world," he wrote.
"Every legitimate impulse of life in the universe belongs to the Son of
God and ought to be harnessed to His glorious chariot." The vast majority of premillennialists came to embrace MacInnis's logic. They believed that God had called them to bring all things under his dominion
as time wound down.[56]

Fundamentalism was never simply about theology or spirituality. It
was always a perspective and an attitude toward this world, the next
one, and the road between the two. The faithful believed that Jesus's
imminent coming had ramifications that touched every part of life,
giving them a determined confidence. They knew that God had called
them to occupy the world until he returned. However, they had not
yet fully established what that meant in terms of politics, social issues,
and relationships to the broader society. But fundamentalists, having
long since abandoned the separatist ideas of Darby and Scofield, were
ready to find out as new technologies, social movements, and powerful
forms of mass media promised once again in the 1920s and 1930s to
revolutionize their world.

4

THE CULTURE WARS BEGIN

IN 1918 JOHN ROACH STRATON ACCEPTED a call to Manhattan's Calvary Baptist Church. Shortly after assuming his new post he launched
a campaign against Broadway, the most iconic institution in his new
hometown. Straton promised the people of New York that he would
"put up a man-sized fight" against the theatre's "forces of sin and godlessness." He described the theatre as "a covetous, Mammon-worshipping,
money-seeking institution" that appealed only "to the lower instincts of
the race." He called female actors "brazen licentiates" and alleged that
they routinely bore "illegitimate children." Sunday curtains troubled
him as well. Broadway, the tall, gaunt minister harangued, "deliberately
and persistently" violated "God's holy law concerning the Sabbath,"
putting it "into direct and deadly competition with the church and
Sunday School." Finally, he drew on anti-Semitic stereotypes to undermine the legitimacy of theatre, asserting that godless Jews used the
stage to undermine Christian values. For fundamentalists like Straton,
Broadway represented how far the culture had slid toward Gomorrah.[1]

This charismatic, spotlight-loving fundamentalist guru of Gotham
pummeled the Great White Way like no one before him. His incendiary messages on the theatre and especially its flaunting of sexuality

garnered substantial attention. While many New Yorkers praised the minister, his unbridled actions occasionally troubled members of his own congregation. "You are cheapening yourself and your church," one member wrote, "we are laughing stocks. Your much sought publicity is not only poor taste and tawdry, but is disgusting to people of refinement. Your attack on sex relationship shows thoroughly that you are the victim of a filthy mind." A young man worried that Straton's sensationalizing produced the opposite of its intended effect. "I feel quite certain," he wrote, "that scores of people attend services at Calvary . . . for amusement, and if something sensational or shocking is introduced, so much the better." Yet another disgruntled church member insisted, "the pastor's invective against stage and dance hall spectacles belong to erotic literature rather than to the pulpit." But such criticisms did not faze the minister. When critics knocked his "Puritanism," he claimed the epithet as "a badge of honor." Far better to be a Puritan, Straton retorted, than "the silly charlatan, the mocker, the cigarette dude, the profane person, the roué of a rollicking Bohemia, the swaggering, swearing, painted woman and the cynical, sensuous, self-indulgent man." The minister trusted that in sensationalizing evil he was doing the Lord's work.[2]

While Straton's explicit discussion of sexual sins offended some churchgoers, other New Yorkers supported him and offered suggestions for expanding his crusade. One anonymous "member of a secret society" wrote Straton with the names and addresses of four houses of ill repute. "Cannot we exterminate pimpism and prostitution?" the writer asked. A "mother" who worried about the influence of a "disorderly house" on her children told the minister about a tenant in her apartment building who ran a brothel where over thirty men visited each night. Another "wife of a lodge member" complained of the sexually suggestive entertainment that characterized male-only clubs. "People talk about the Turks and their harems but our own husbands are not missing much of the sights that the Turk enjoys." Illicit sex was a concern of a member of Straton's own congregation as well. Responding to the minister's claim that young women had to trade their bodies for roles on Broadway, this "Christian actor" told Straton that the minister had not gone far enough. Women, he explained, were not the only vulnerable ones. "Have you ever heard," he asked Straton, "of the state of sodomy prevalent in the N.Y. theatrical offices? Do you know that clean young men who come from small stock houses to N.Y. have their manhood assailed even more than do young girls?" According to this actor, "when a man fights these beasts he is immediately boycotted. . . . The profession has many many men in it who are notorious for this degeneracy." Such accounts enflamed fundamentalists' polemics against Broadway.[3]

Straton routinely preached on premillennialism and rejected what he perceived as liberals' misguided reform work. Echoing Dwight Moody, he explained, "the supreme duty of the church today is not to patch up and paint a wrecked world but to get out the life-boats and take as many souls as possible off of the wreck." And yet he was a culture warrior who remained deeply involved in reform efforts of many kinds. Near the end of his life, he tried to make sense of these seemingly conflicting impulses. "I wish . . . to make one matter very clear," he wrote in the late 1920s. "I am really not a reformer. I do not believe in 'social service.' . . . I believe in regeneration rather than 'reform.' I believe in salvation as the only source of true social service." Yet he reasoned that some social reform could facilitate the spread of the gospel. "To improve environment," he explained, "gives a better chance for the transforming truths of God to reach the hearts and change the lives of men—and that is the Christian philosophy of social service."[4]

In the 1920s and 1930s fundamentalists like Straton preached apocalypse while working to increase Christian influence within sinful society. They believed that since World War I had ended short of Armageddon, they had one last chance to prepare their churches, their communities, and their country for the second coming. As humankind approached the last days, the faithful believed that a series of cultural and moral signs would herald the coming apocalypse. Jesus had told his disciples that at the time of his return conditions would parallel those that forced God to destroy the entire world during Noah's generation and the cities of Sodom and Gomorrah in the days of Lot (Luke 17:26–28). Social, cultural, and sexual debauchery, fundamentalists believed, had provoked God's judgment on ancient cultures, and humans' unrighteous behavior would call down God's wrath again.

While fundamentalists' moral views often mirrored those of many other Christians and social conservatives at the time, their ability to frame their convictions in the language of premillennialism distinguished them. Their assurance that Jesus was coming and was coming soon instilled in them an elevated sense of determination and passion, an uninhibited willingness to share what they loved and loathed, a sense of impatience with incremental reform, and a total intolerance for those who differed with them. They embraced the most radical of tactics and the harshest of words to save all whom they could. Fundamentalists saw echoes of the world of Noah in popular amusements like the theatre, movies, and dancing, and they believed that widespread challenges to traditional gender and racial hierarchies matched the chaotic social order that had doomed Sodom and Gomorrah. Embodying the parable of the talents, they aggressively worked to "occupy" this world until the rapture by judging all manner of morals and fighting last-days depravity. Completing the revolution radical evangelicals had begun at the turn of the century in which they used premillennialism as the inspiration for aggressive action, fundamentalists transformed premillennial apocalypticism into a moral crusade on contemporary culture.

In the aftermath of World War I, *King's Business* ran one of the bleakest issues in the magazine's history. The cover set the tone. It showed an American flag and a Christian flag hanging over signs that read "sensualism," "despising of government," "wars," "Bolshevism," "man deified," "infidelity," "apostasy," "isms of all kinds," and "spiritism." The caption simply read "Signs of the Times." Indeed, the times did not look very promising. In a series of related editorials inside the magazine, fundamentalists explained the various "signs" they observed in all parts of American life. Nations waged "war" for "commercial supremacy." The "elimination" of the Bible from the public schools and "paganism" in the universities signified impending Armageddon. The Christian church had "sought to compete with the world and provide literary entertainments and semi-worldly amusements," but "the world has resented its efforts and laughed at its silly pretensions." The editorials condemned the state of society as a whole. "The devil is rampant. Divorces multiply, homes are broken; children neglected; crime increases; churches are closed; jails are filled; taxes increase, and the little dilettante lecturers go on singing their lullaby of 'Keep sweet, all is well.'" Indeed,

In the wake of World War I, fundamentalists had to acknowledge that their predictions of Armageddon had not been fulfilled. Nevertheless they remained confident that the signs of the coming Antichrist were appearing all around them.

King's Business (July 1919), cover.

seemingly declining moral conditions in the United States signified how rapidly the world was approaching the apocalypse.[5]

Fundamentalists did not have to look hard to see evidence of a return to the days of Noah all around them. At precisely the same time that they began to assess the dangers of popular culture, record numbers of Americans dedicated unprecedented amounts of time and money to all kinds of secular amusements. In the interwar years, dancing emerged as a popular entertainment for working and middle-class youth. Large halls hosted enormous parties where young people could mingle beyond the supervision of their parents, listen to live music, and practice the latest steps. Fundamentalists, however, saw in social dancing little more than a shortcut to perdition. Rather than humbly thank God for victory over Germany, the cocksure Bob Jones lamented, "we got off our knees and we began to dance. We danced on the coffins of our dead soldiers. We danced to the tune of their dying groans and America has danced the vilest dances since the World War the world has even seen since Rome went to hell." A Georgia minister linked dancing with nativist fears, convinced that popular styles had their origins in "foreign" cultures. "The modern dances," he summarized, "are beastly and heathenish." As usual, however, Straton said it best. He suggested that only "a fossilized octogenarian, or a self-complacent mollycoddle with ice-water in his veins, or a dandified dude, or a society sissy, or a pleasure-cloyed Don Juan, or a vitiated fop, who doesn't know whether he is a man or a woman" could dance with "a throbbing, beautiful young woman, with about half of her body exposed—and the other half clothed largely with good intentions . . . and have nothing stronger than Sunday School maxims running through his mind."[6]

Prizefights represented another form of popular and controversial entertainment. Many Americans in the late nineteenth and early twentieth century viewed boxing as a healthy form of exercise. But as the sport professionalized, it grew more closely associated with gambling. By the 1920s, many social conservatives believed that it represented a reversion to savagery. Nevertheless, championship matches drew enormous crowds and tremendous media attention. The opportunity to see a major fight firsthand proved too tempting for Straton to pass up. In 1921 he accepted an invitation to attend the highly anticipated Jack Dempsey–Georges Carpentier heavyweight championship bout in

Jersey City in order to share what he witnessed with the American public. The histrionic minister promised to "reach the American ear with a Christian protest against the horror and infamy of the whole thing," and that is exactly what he did.[7]

While fundamentalists consistently denounced the theatre, dances, and prizefights, nothing matched their anxiety over the most popular form of entertainment in the United States—the movie. In the 1920s, tens of millions of Americans enchanted by the silver screen attended movies every week. They also followed the personal lives of their favorite actors. Hollywood studios created fan magazines and fed stories to gossip columnists to ensure that their stars garnered the latest and greatest headlines. Such efforts often blurred the lines between what happened on screen and off. For fundamentalists tawdry film represented much more than cheap amusement. It too was a sign of the moral depravity that Jesus prophesied for the last days.

Evangelist Gerald Winrod blamed films for the decline of American culture. If "millions" of people, he preached, see films every week that reek "of filth" and "all manner of crime, deception, immorality and infidelity; do not be surprised if they go out of those places of amusement and pattern their lives according to what they have seen." The major fundamentalist magazines reiterated this message. "There is probably no institution that is doing more in our day to corrupt the morals, both of old and young," the *King's Business* editors wrote, "than the Movies." When a subscriber asked *Christian Workers* whether a Christian could attend movies, the editors answered with a straightforward "no." The magazine's unqualified response provoked strong reactions from readers, demonstrating that not all fundamentalist laypeople saw the evils of Tinsel Town so clearly.[8]

The morals of individual actors, salaciously reported in gossip sheets, provided fundamentalists (and other morally conservative Americans) with further ammunition. The most popular star of the era, Charlie Chaplin, had long antagonized some Americans with his womanizing, partying, and refusal to seek American citizenship (he was born in England). Douglas Fairbanks and Mary Pickford's decision to divorce their spouses and marry each other garnered even greater outrage. Straton attacked them from his pulpit, provoking a public response from popular actor Lillian Gish, who defended her colleagues' work on the stage and in Hollywood. One actor, however, outflanked the rest in the race toward total moral degradation. "Capping the climax" of Hollywood sin, Straton proclaimed, was Fatty Arbuckle, "standing before the nation with his idiotic, leering grin on his face."[9]

Few events galvanized more public concern over the morals of the nation's celebrities than the Arbuckle trial. In 1921 Arbuckle rented a bloc of hotel rooms in San Francisco for a series of parties. An aspiring actress became ill at one of the parties and eventually died. Investigators accused the actor of raping and then accidentally killing her when he allegedly caused her bladder to rupture under the weight of his fat body. The newspapers sensationalized the event and also began looking more closely into the morals of Hollywood. A jury acquitted Arbuckle, who then went on tour to tell his side of the story. When Mark Matthews learned that the actor planned to be in Seattle, he wrote a public letter of protest. Arbuckle responded with a letter of his own informing Matthews that he was "just as good a Christian" as the popular minister. He also reminded the preacher that Christ taught the virtues of "faith, hope, charity and forgiveness." Fed up with the values emanating from Hollywood, fundamentalists suggested that a constitutional amendment against film would be "a righteous judgment against a wicked industry."[10]

In the aftermath of the Arbuckle scandal, studio bosses recognized that their success depended on an approving public. They walked a fine line, keeping enough titillation on the screen to entertain their audiences while also working to keep critics mollified. Hoping to head off government intervention and censorship in the 1920s, the studios required actors to sign morals clauses and issued guidelines to regulate film content. They hired Presbyterian Will Hays to coordinate their efforts. Fundamentalists, however, did not believe that the Hays Office would make any difference. "Given the moron audience and the moron picture, the moron actor and the moron director are inevitable," *King's Business* editorialized. Straton was equally dubious. He called Hays "a respectable false front," conjecturing that "when any real issue came up, especially if it touched the box office, he would be like a little child in the hands of these shrewd and powerful manipulators." Tapping into anti-Semitic stereotypes, fundamentalist preacher Harold John Ockenga alleged that Jews ran Hollywood and that they injected anti-Christian messages into movies. "Will Hays," he fretted, "may say that the movies are not giving propaganda for any agency but they are filled with propaganda against religion, and very often that is instigated by some atheistic Jewish producer."[11]

Nevertheless, a few fundamentalists believed that despite all of the problems with Hollywood, film still offered tremendous possibilities. Evangelists Paul Rader and Bob Jones produced silent pictures in the late 1920s chronicling their revivals. Bible colleges and some churches also used movies to attract audiences. Aimee McPherson even incorporated her own film company. She did not expect to produce dramatic films, she explained, but to record and distribute her sermons around the globe. But these efforts stoked controversy. For the most part fundamentalists and their evangelical successors remained suspicious of the silver screen and its potent mass appeal until after World War II.

Radio, however, was another matter. While radical evangelicals worked to spread the message of an imminent apocalypse, they made the most of this new technology. Despite some Christians' fears that when the apostle Paul dubbed Satan "the prince of the power of the air" he had foreseen the new medium, most radical evangelicals saw radio as a powerful tool. Moody Bible Institute and BIOLA built radio stations in the 1920s, following the lead of evangelists like Paul Rader and Aimee Semple McPherson, both of whom had taken to the airwaves with great success. McPherson called radio "a beautiful priceless gift from the loving Hand of our Father God." It presented a "most unheard of opportunity for converting the world, and of reaching the largest possible number of people in the shortest possible time." For McPherson, the conviction that the end was near justified taking bold and unprecedented action. Harold Ockenga, Donald Grey Barnhouse, John Roach Straton, Louis Talbot, J. Frank Norris, and African-American preacher Lightfoot Solomon Michaux, among many others, all effectively preached premillennialism over the air, delivering apocalyptic diatribes into countless living rooms throughout every part of the country.[12]

Los Angeles evangelist Charles Fuller took Christian broadcasting to entirely new levels. He began broadcasting from BIOLA's studio in 1924 and then gradually expanded his ministry. In 1936 Fuller formed a partnership with a new national network, Mutual Broadcasting, and soon thereafter he preached his first coast-to-coast sermon on the newly dubbed the *Old Fashioned Revival Hour*. The show was a hit. By the mid-1940s, it had an audience estimated at twenty million. A typical broadcast included upbeat hymns, a selection of inspirational letters from listeners read by Charles's wife, Grace, and then a short sermon delivered in simple, plain language on the fundamentals of the Christian faith. Fuller's program succeeded by blending the best of the nineteenth-century evangelical revival tradition, a premillennial sense of urgency, and the latest twentieth-century technology. In fact, fundamentalists were much better at integrating mass media into their ministries than their liberal counterparts, an advantage that played an important role in building the movement and spreading doomsday convictions.[13]

Fundamentalists' concerns about the messages and values emanating from popular culture reflected in part their larger anxieties about perceived threats to American society. In the wake of the war, many Americans grew deeply suspicious of various groups—religious and ethnic—who seemed less than 100 percent American and who challenged Protestant dominance. Immigrants, Jews, Catholics, and alleged communists suffered at the hands of various nativist movements. Fundamentalists invested substantial energy in defending what they understood as traditional, God-given gender and racial roles. They believed that challenges to those roles symbolized the last-days decline of Western culture and the social chaos that had provoked God's Old Testament wrath. They feared that perceived "others" were contaminating American society and promoting socialism, communism, and anarchy, making it harder for them to orchestrate revival as the world approached the last days. While they often claimed to oppose the morals and values that pervaded American culture, in reality fundamentalists conformed to the white mainstream on questions of race and gender. In defending exclusionist racial and gender hierarchies, they did not look like religious radicals at all but more like prototypical white Americans.

The war and then the Red Scare fostered widespread anti-immigrant sentiments nationwide. Fundamentalists, joining a majority of Americans, called for an overhaul of the nation's immigration laws with the goal of reducing the number of "undesirables." They feared that immigrants were weakening the nation and in so doing were engaging in the work of the Antichrist. The increasing number of Catholics and

Fundamentalists not only crafted a creative theology that spoke to the terrors of the modern age; they also made excellent use of the latest technology to spread that theology. Nobody mastered the medium of radio better than Los Angeles evangelist Charles Fuller.

Courtesy of Fuller Theological Seminary.

Jews in the United States, they suspected, would align against them in the last days as they sought to combat the schemes of the devil. Anti-immigrant sentiments were so widespread at this time, however, that fundamentalists rarely had to appeal to their religious beliefs to justify their prejudices. Anglo-Americans just "knew" that these suspicious

looking immigrants could not be good for the country. "We must create a national spirit," Matthews explained in an interview. "There is no
room in America for any hyphen. . . . We will not submit to any quali-
fying word before the word 'American.'" He believed that the purpose
of the American "melting pot" was to "destroy the un-American dress
of the world"—it was not to let immigrants "dilute the strong waters of
Americanism." Billy Sunday agreed with Straton's assessment. "They
call us the 'melting pot,'" he preached. "Then it's up to us to skim off
the slag that won't melt into Americanism and throw it into hell or
somewhere else."[14]

For many fundamentalists, Jews sometimes represented that slag.
Straton's and Ockenga's comments on Jewish producers running Broadway and Hollywood were typical; many fundamentalists, like Americans more generally, harbored strong anti-Jewish prejudices. Popular
radio minister Charles Fuller called "the history of the Jews" little more
than "a wicked and willful rebellion against God, until such time as
His long-suffering and mercy had ceased to have any good effect upon
them." At the same time radical evangelicals preached that Jews were
God's chosen people and promised that the Almighty would reward
those who defended them, they fostered prejudice through repeated
references to ugly stereotypes. Their views matched those of many
other Protestants across the theological spectrum. But what distinguished fundamentalist anti-Semitism from other forms of bigotry was
the ways it aligned with premillennial hopes and fears. Apocalypticism
gave fundamentalists a powerful framework for justifying their prejudices and incentive for seeing dangerous, global conspiracies all around
them.[15]

The responses of fundamentalists to a series of anti-Semitic publications in the 1920s illustrated their schizophrenic views and demonstrated how their prejudices related to their apocalyptic convictions.
The fraudulent *Protocols of the Elders of Zion* claimed to reveal the plans
of a secret group of influential Jews who were scheming to take over
the world. "The International Jew," a series of articles published in
Henry Ford's virulent anti-Semitic *Dearborn Independent,* supported the
Protocols' message of a Jewish cabal determined to rule the globe. Fundamentalists' willingness to see Jewish conspiracies as integral to last-
days scenarios reinforced the negative stereotypes in which many in

the movement traded. Their anti-Semitism makes their relentless Zionism, and Jewish leaders' willingness to work with them, all the more ironic.

Some radical evangelicals linked the *Protocols* directly to their reading of prophecy. "The protocols' profound if unconscious knowledge of prophecy makes any likelihood of their being a fake extremely remote," concluded British minister D. M. Panton in an article on the coming Antichrist. Evangelist Luke Rader quoted extensively from the *Protocols* to demonstrate that a great global conspiracy was under way that would soon produce the Antichrist. Arno Gaebelein believed that the *Protocols* was not only an authentic document but one published by "a believer in the Word of God, in prophecy . . . a true Christian." In 1919 Mark Matthews sent a copy of the infamous document to President Wilson. He asked Wilson to use it to purge the government of Jewish influence and accused Jews of orchestrating the Bolshevik revolution. "They are today antagonistic to our principles of government," he wrote. They are "willing to produce a collapse in government and in finances in order that they might bring out of the collapse a Jewish Government over all."[16]

When Henry Ford came under attack for his publication of "The International Jew," fundamentalists rallied to his defense. The *Dearborn Independent,* the editors at *Moody Monthly* concluded, "simply gave to its readers what had been well known for some time to the thoughtful people of Great Britain." Even the usually levelheaded James Gray supported Ford in the controversy. He believed that the assertions printed in the *Dearborn Independent,* like the *Protocols,* lined up with prophecy. When former president William Howard Taft denounced the series as anti-Semitic propaganda, A. C. Dixon called it "fitting" that an "avowed and aggressive Unitarian" should be associated with "his co-religionists, the Jews, whose Sanhedrin nineteen hundred years ago condemned the Lord Jesus Christ to death." When Ford finally apologized for the harm his paper had done in perpetuating fraudulent ideas, *Moody Monthly* editors viewed the confession as additional evidence of the Jewish conspiracy. "Indeed," the editors concluded, "the pressure brought to bear upon Mr. Ford to make his confession was in itself such corroborative evidence. This pressure came from the Jews all over the world, and in the face of it Mr. Ford was panic-stricken."[17]

Gaebelein's writing on Jews (and African Americans) caught the attention of the American left. The League of American Writers accused him of attacking "Jews as 'Red anti-Christs'" and called his ministry "a pseudo-religious organization whose main purpose is to promulgate 'Aryan,' 'Gentile' and 'white supremacy.'" The churlish Gaebelein was not pleased. He called their characterization "a slanderous misrepresentation," which he interpreted in apocalyptic terms. "Such attacks and slanders," he harangued, "show how the enemies of the truth of God and the enemies of the Cross of Christ are getting ready for the final Struggle." He even asserted that his premillennial screed *The Conflict of the Ages,* which was loaded with anti-Semitism, had "the Lord's most gracious approval."[18]

While many fundamentalists traded in anti-Semitism, two individuals took their prejudices further than most. William Bell Riley constantly peppered his sermons with bigotry. He blamed Jews for America's economic crises, World War I, and the decline of the Democratic Party (which had fallen "into the contorting hands of the mugwump Jew, Raskob, and his communistically inclined confederates"). He also praised Hitler in 1934 for clamping down on supposed Jewish communism, which excited "the wrath of all Jews and of deceived Gentiles throughout the world." Gerald B. Winrod, whose independence and extreme views on many issues generally kept him outside the fundamentalist network, went even further. He complained of Bible teachers who engaged in "meaningless sentimental gush . . . excusing every sin against God and man of which the Jewish race is guilty." "The Jew is essentially an egotist," he wrote. "He is capable of sinking to depths untouched by those of lesser capacity."[19]

A few fundamentalists, however, challenged the virulent streak of anti-Semitism that ran through post–World War I fundamentalism. William Blackstone immediately recognized the *Protocols* for what they were and wrote Ford calling for the *Dearborn Independent* to cease publication of "The International Jew." Surprisingly, J. Frank Norris, who harbored many prejudices, rejected the *Protocols* as well and disputed the notion that a relationship existed between Jews and communism. Assemblies of God leader Stanley Frodsham lamented that "so many of our good fundamentalist friends are taking such a stand against the Jewish people." H. A. Ironside, pastor of the Moody Church, "regretted" that "the Protocols are being used not only by Godless Gentiles but even by some fundamentalist Christians to stir up suspicions and hatred against the Jewish people as a whole." A few even repented of anti-Semitism. Keith Brooks of BIOLA evolved from an anti-Semite to a crusader against prejudice, taking on fellow fundamentalists, including Winrod, Riley, and Oswald Smith, for their bigotry.[20]

The dominant tenor of fundamentalists' views on Jews and immigrants, along with their deep-seated anti-Catholicism, brought them into direct contact with the Ku Klux Klan. Unlike the Reconstruction-era Klan, which used violence and intimidation to maintain white supremacy over newly freed African Americans, the 1920s Klan had a more comprehensive agenda. Klansmen feared that immigrants, Catholics, African Americans, urbanites, and intellectual elites were threatening the power of small-town, white, rural Protestantism. They promoted patriarchal families, held Klan picnics and parades, defended Prohibition, worked with local government to enforce community moral standards, and advocated a generic Protestant Christianity as the authentic American religion. Although the Klan shared many of the same values as fundamentalists, the relationship between the two groups was awkward and conflicted.[21]

Some radical evangelicals interpreted the Klan within their premillennial scheme. J. W. Welch, an early leader of the Assemblies of God, viewed the Klan within the context of what he called last-days developments. "We believe that the coming of the Lord is imminent, and that antichrist will appear in the midst of conditions such as may grow out of the conflict between Catholicism, K. K. K., and other such organizations." As a result, denominational executives discouraged ministers from joining the hyperpatriotic organization.[22]

Other fundamentalists focused on less esoteric elements of the Klan. The editors of *Moody Monthly* struggled to articulate a consistent position on the organization. They acknowledged that while much of the Klan's agenda matched their own, they had some reservations. "Why cannot such a mission," the editors asked, "be carried out without secrecy, without increasing race and religious animosity, and without going about the country in disguise?" The next month the journal ran an article by Texan A. R. Funderburk who asked the question: is the Ku Klux Klan of God? His answer was a clear no. He criticized the

Klan for its treatment of immigrants and Catholics (even though "we recognize in Roman Catholicism an enemy of true Christianity. Their teaching is the teaching of Antichrist") and noted that the Klan's use of mob violence belied their claim to stand for law and order. The Klan's treatment of Jews also troubled Funderburk. "We see that the religion of Ku Kluxism is not the religion of Jesus Christ. How could the Klan embrace Christianity," he asked, "when its very constitution would bar the Founder of Christianity from membership? Our Lord Jesus Christ was a Jew." He ended by reminding readers that Satan can appear as an "angel of light."[23]

A few months later *Moody* editors printed a reply to Funderburk from Pennsylvania minister John Bradbury. He called the initial piece a "transgression of the laws of righteous publicity" and insisted, "the article is wrong so far as the K. K. K. is concerned." "This country has arrived at the watershed of destiny," he continued. "For years a silent penetration of our national institutions has been going on. Subtle mischief is at work. Nefarious combinations have grown so powerful as to present a national menace." The Klan was helping to expose this menace. As Bradbury went one by one through Funderburk's accusations, he demonstrated that the Klan and fundamentalists saw eye to eye on many issues. "So far," Bradbury concluded, "I have found that the churches never had a more active ally, the state a more determined champion, our homes a more resolute defender, and lawlessness and vice a more powerful foe than the Ku Klux Klan."[24]

In response to a flood of letters denouncing the Bradbury piece, the editors explained that they only endorsed articles "over our own names, or which are found on our editorial pages." However, they believed "in giving our readers an opportunity to hear both sides" of controversial subjects and clearly the Klan and radical evangelicals shared some of the same fears. A few months later, *Moody* editors denounced the Klan in vague and ambiguous terms, while printing in the same issue a letter in support of the organization from influential Los Angeles fundamentalist "Fighting Bob" Shuler. He called the Klan a "hopeful" secret society and a "positive and active friend of Protestant Christianity."[25]

While fundamentalists expressed some qualms about working with the Klan, Klansmen and women had no problems seeking alliances with fundamentalists. The organization ran an ad in Norris's magazine that praised the minister's work and the Texas Tornado later received a warm letter from the "Women of the Klan" thanking him for a sermon he preached over the radio. "While you did not say that it was a Klan Sermon," they wrote, "those of us who were fortunate enough to have heard it, both over the Radio and in the Church feel like it was." When Straton criticized the hooded group, he received a long, articulate letter in response from an "imperial klokard" who assured him, "your place is with us, and not with our enemies." Billy Sunday's sermons also earned him commendations from at least one local branch of the Klan. The most famous Klan-fundamentalist encounter, however, involved Aimee Semple McPherson. After a Colorado revival, the infamous men in peaked white hoods "kidnapped" the evangelist and a *Denver Post* reporter. Masters at using the media to garner attention, they presented McPherson with a bouquet of white flowers, which the Klan explained was symbolic of the "purity" of her character and ideals. She accepted the gift, warned them that God could see behind their hoods, and challenged them to live up to their motto of protecting the powerless.[26]

As fundamentalists prepared for the end times, they occasionally had trouble discerning friend from foe. Their failure to take a clear position on the Klan reflected the ambiguity of their primary mission. If they intended simply to promote the fundamentalist theological agenda, they would have had little use for the Klan. But their agenda was always about more than correct theology; it was also about reclaiming and then occupying American culture. Fundamentalists' lack of tolerance for contrary opinions and their commitment to relentless action, fostered by their apocalyptic sensibilities, made them attractive allies for the nation's leading nativist groups. That fundamentalists and Klansmen and women recognized in each other cobelligerents in the culture wars reveals the exclusivist nature of interwar fundamentalism, as well as the ways fundamentalists reflected the prejudices characteristic of their times.

The racial views of fundamentalists mirrored those of many other white Americans regardless of creed. Most radical evangelicals were suspicious of Jews, worked to clamp down on immigrants, and supported hyperpatriotic Americanism campaigns. They also treated African Americans as second-class citizens. For decades Jim Crow segregation had characterized the nation and the nation's churches. White fundamentalists and black evangelicals drew on similar theologies, but they applied their faith to the world around them in very different ways. As some African-American evangelicals joined black liberation movements and others supported groups like the National Association for the Advancement of Colored People, white fundamentalists grew progressively more defensive. They policed the color line with great tenacity and viewed racial tensions as a sign of the times, when they acknowledged race at all, rather than an evil to attack. Even the most racially progressive members of the radical evangelical movement—pentecostals—regressed in the 1920s as the lines of segregation hardened.

Segregation was so prevalent in churches around the country that it rarely provoked comment. Short-term revivals featuring celebrity evangelists, however, often forced the issue. People of all races and colors flocked to see famous preachers. In most cases in the South the nation's leading revivalists offered segregated meetings. During a revival in wartime Atlanta, for example, Billy Sunday had held a special service for "Negroes" since they could not attend the regular services. At that meeting he acknowledged "his lack of familiarity with the colored race," but that did not keep him from offering what the *Atlanta Constitution* praised as "some of the finest advice that was ever given to a crowd of colored people by any man from the north or from the south." What was Sunday's advice? He told his black audience that "southern whites are Negroes' best friends" and that they should not migrate north, and he admonished the North to keep its "hands off" the South. The white southern press saw his self-serving counsel as a breakthrough and called the evangelist a "promoter of interracial harmony." When he followed up the meeting by inviting a thousand African-American singers to serve as the choir for the next white service, *Current Opinion* concluded that nothing like it had ever been attempted before. "Both races felt that an important step had been made in the right direction." That journalists interpreted the appearance of a black choir at a Sunday meeting as a novelty illustrates the customary nature of strictly segregated revivals.[27]

While Sunday's efforts may have delighted some white southerners, they did not impress African Americans. After a long Washington, D.C., campaign a local minister noted that Sunday "was brought here by the whites for the benefit of the whites." Over the course of a multiweek revival, Sunday denounced dozens of different kinds of sins, yet he ignored "the devil of race prejudice, rotten, stinking, hell-born race prejudice," which would "be just as strongly entrenched in the white churches and in the community as it was before he came." Sunday, the minister concluded, "at times, seems to be a little courageous judged by his vigorous denunciation of many sins; but when it comes to the big devil of race prejudice, the craven in him comes out; he cowers before it; he is afraid to speak out; at heart he is seen to be a moral coward in spite of his bluster and pretense of being brave. What are you afraid of Mr. Sunday . . . ?" The *National Baptist Union Review* leveled a similar charge. "It will not suffice for Mr. Sunday to invade the Southland," the paper editorialized, "and denounce adultery, fornication, liars, hypocrites, bums, hobos, rascals, scoundrels, crap shooters, tramps and loafers, and leave untouched the lynchers, the ballot box thief, the segregator, the discriminator, the Negro hater, the promoter of racial strife and the mob leader, who burns human beings at the stake because they are black." White fundamentalists simply proved unable to recognize race prejudice as a real problem. For them, inequality most often reflected God's order rather than the sins of humanity. For African Americans the equality of all people represented an essential component of the fundamental gospel.[28]

In contrast to most other radical evangelicals, some early pentecostals interpreted the severing of racial barriers as a positive indication of an imminent rapture. "One token of the Lord's coming," exclaimed a participant at the Azusa Street revivals, "is that he is melting all races and nations together and they are filled with the power and glory of God." During Aimee Semple McPherson's itinerant days she regularly included African-American preachers in her campaigns and fought for integrated worship services in the South. While preaching in Key West in 1918 she tried to convince African Americans that they could safely enter her tent alongside whites; when they refused, she left the white community. "My soul was so burdened for the dear colored people," she wrote, "that I announced from the public platform that I had done my duty in the Lord toward the white population of the Island, and must risk their displeasure and disapproval now by going to the poor colored folk." Cognizant of the racial tensions within the community, she continued, "at first the throngs of white people attending our camp meeting . . . felt we should not go to the colored section," but this did not matter because "God so definitely called us that we could not hesitate." However, segregation did not last for long. At the "Colored Camp Meeting," McPherson explained, "it was impossible to keep the white people away. So for the first time on the Island the white and colored attended the same place of worship and glorified the same Lord side by side." "Glory!" she enthusiastically concluded, "all walls of prejudice seem to be breaking down." But they did not always break down. In other locations, she like Sunday offered separate "colored" services. These, however, proved to be controversial because of her gender. For a white woman to preside over a meeting that included African-American men threatened southern hierarchies in a way that Sunday's "colored" meetings did not. When she opened her mammoth Angelus Temple church in Los Angeles in 1923, she encouraged African Americans to seek membership in local black churches rather than in hers. Despite the work of early pentecostals, by the 1920s the movement had split along racial lines into separate predominately white and predominately black denominations. As white pentecostals angled for position within the fundamentalist movement and more mainstream Christianity, they left their black brothers and sisters behind.[29]

Most fundamentalists not only practiced segregation on Sunday mornings; many also defended racial hierarchies in the broader society. Presbyterian minister and popular radio preacher Donald Grey Barnhouse appealed to nineteenth-century biblically inspired arguments to justify the inferior social position of African Americans. In a sermon on "the black man" preached over the Columbia Broadcasting System, he moved from emphasizing the unity of all people in Christ to the allegedly inferior nature of African Americans. He claimed that they still bore the "curse of Ham" and that God had destined "the colored peoples" to serve the "Semites" (Jews) and "Japhethites" (white Gentiles). "The streams of history," he explained, "have run in the channels that God marked out for them with His prophetic finger so long ago." By grounding racial differences in a supposedly inerrant Bible text, fundamentalists made it very difficult for opponents of segregation to mount an attack.[30]

Fundamentalists applied their racialized reading of the Bible in varying ways. "I can find no Biblical demand that racial differences be obliterated," Riley asserted. "Nature's ways, which must be God-ordained, are opposite!" He claimed to prefer "pure-bred" humans like "pure-bred dogs." Invoking the ideas of Booker T. Washington, he called for "the five races, like the fingers of the hand" to "be separate and yet co-operative!"[31]

Other fundamentalists blended their racial views with their class prejudices. *Moody Monthly* editors defended the tradition of prohibiting African Americans from traveling in first-class passenger cars, a practice they claimed was not based on "color . . . but on questions of manners, cleanliness and intelligence." Nor did fundamentalists feel compelled to support black voting rights. A. C. Dixon believed that the federal government had erred in giving male former slaves the franchise shortly after emancipation. "It was the blunder of the age," he wrote, "and it will take time to counteract its effects. Ignorance, whether black or white, has no right to the ballot." *Moody* editors agreed that most African Americans—along with uneducated whites—were unworthy of suffrage. "Some day," the editors warned, "universal suffrage will turn and rend the governments which bestowed it."[32]

Fundamentalists' mixed responses to the lynching crisis further illustrated their inability to understand the challenges African Americans faced. Many fundamentalists disavowed lynching because of their commitment to law and order. "It is awful," missionary L. Nelson Bell wrote, "when mob rule prevails; an awful indictment of our laws which have become so lax in so many places." But not all fundamentalists saw lynching in this light. Riley denounced his fellow Baptists' support of antilynching legislation and he apparently defended a naval officer who lynched a man who had supposedly raped the officer's wife. A letter to the editor in the *Pittsburgh Courier* criticized fundamentalists like Riley who seemed unable to recognize how antithetical lynching was to Christian ideas of justice.[33]

Concerns over the ballot and lynching, however, remained secondary for most white fundamentalists. As many sermons and publications made clear, at the root of their racial anxieties was a deep-seated fear of intermarriage, a fear they shared with the vast majority of white Americans in the interwar era. In a series of sermons denouncing race riots and lynching in both the North and South, Straton repeatedly perpetuated negative stereotypes of African-American men as rapists and murderers who longed for the bodies of white women. Yet he encouraged the "better" members of the race to lead the way to a more promising future and called for the application of the "principles and practices of true Christianity" to the "race problem." But egalitarianism was apparently not a principle of Straton's true Christianity. "This does not mean," he qualified, "that there should be any breaking down of those barriers between the two races which were erected by God Almighty for the protection of both. Any blending of the two races by marriage is a monstrous thing." The purity of the white race remained a key component of fundamentalists' ideology.[34]

Over and over again fundamentalists criticized African Americans' quest for rights, which they saw as code for gaining access to the bodies of white women. For an African American "to assert and practice the right to intermarry with the whites," Dixon preached, "is to doom his race to extinction." Texas evangelist John Rice viewed marriages between white women and African-American men as unnatural. "Those two have not become one flesh. Any such marriage is wrong and doomed to misery and unhappiness." He told readers of his magazine, "it is always wrong for whites to marry Negroes." Extending his logic, he suggested that since whites and blacks should not intermarry, they had no cause for social interaction. W. O. H. Garman lamented the "race suicide" caused by birth control, the "intermarriage of inferior and superior races," and "foreign contamination." Bible Institute of Los Angeles president Louis Talbot also opposed intermarriage. "Personally, I think the Negroes are far happier with their own race. Furthermore, I am convinced that God intended that it should be so, and that the two races should not intermarry."[35]

A transcript of one of Billy Sunday's famous sermons captured his sentiments on intermarriage and the ways fundamentalists routinely used class to reinforce their racial ideals, as well as a revival crowd's enthusiastic response to his race-baiting. "Talk about social equality!" Sunday preached in Philadelphia in 1922. "There never will be social equality between the white and the black. (Applause). . . . The black man is entitled to civic equality. . . . When you are out on the highway with your Pierce-Arrow limousine you have got to give half of the road to that darkey with his tin lizzie. (Laughter.) Civil equality is all right. Social equality is another proposition." Then he turned to the bugaboo of sex. "No decent negro man would want to marry a white woman. No decent white man would want to marry a negress." The former baseball player's messages reified white Americans' racial prejudices. Not only did he fail to see racial equality as a component of the Christian faith, he saw segregation as a characteristic of godly living.[36]

A handful of leading fundamentalists, however, occasionally recognized racism as a problem. Barnhouse, a civil libertarian, had reservations about the way his fellow believers stomped on minority rights (despite his belief in the curse of Ham). He was one of the few fundamentalists who praised the work of the new American Civil Liberties Union (ACLU). In a message to his followers he quoted a *New York Herald-Tribune* columnist who he believed best expressed American hypocrisy.

> No Jews allowed in this hotel;
> They're noisy, clannish and they smell.
> Don't play with Michael Murphy, child;
> Those Catholics are bad and wild.
> If Negroes vote in Alabama
> They'll violate your wife and mama.
> This country, proud Americans,
> We wrested from the Indians.
> For liberty's sake we fought and spoke
> To free us from the British yoke.
> Remember that this glorious nation
> Is built on the rock of toleration.
> Unjust, tyrannical, unfair
> Is Hitlerism over there.
> We're met tonight in freedom's cause,
> America for all. (Applause).

Barnhouse followed the piece by noting, "we are quite well aware that the irony in some of these lines may cut even some of our readers deeply" yet he believed that the only way to protect Christian liberties was to protect minority liberties. "Any Christian," he concluded, who failed to defend the rights of minorities, even though they may be *"enemies of our truth,* is an enemy of the liberty of the Gospel of Jesus Christ."[37]

Ockenga also recognized that racism was a sin. In a sermon in the mid-1930s he called the "rise and the expansion of the white race" one of the "most sordid chapters in human history. Brutality, frauds, pillage, plunder, cruelty, knavery, and human terror, have followed in its trail." Citing the nation's lynching epidemic, he determined "that a judgment upon the white supremacy of the earth is not far in the future." Then he turned to the miscarriage of justice in the Scottsboro trial, a case in which a group of young black men riding a freight train with two white women were accused of rape. "Why should nine boys," Ockenga asked, "have to face death or imprisonment on an unproved charge simply because white men are on the jury?" In the same sermon he also took on the Immigration Act of 1924. "We are also guilty of discriminatory immigration laws whereby we have offended certain races of people." Finally, he lamented, "Christians have never repudiated the crusades which still are a source of grave antagonism between us and the Mohammedans." Yet he too was leery of race mixing. While he insisted that all people were equal before God, he later preached, "to attempt to abolish racial distinction is folly and impossible."[38]

The statements, sermons, and practices of white fundamentalists in the 1920s and 1930s guaranteed that African-American evangelicals would keep their distance from the fundamentalist movement. They understood that white fundamentalists were far more likely to oppose black efforts to gain equality than to practice the social and racial egalitarianism that most African Americans saw in the work of Jesus. But they did occasionally challenge white leaders. "You said that this is a white man's country," one "Negro Mother" wrote J. Frank Norris, "but the Bible tells me the earth is the Lord's and the fullness there of. . . . The negro has been buffeted, he has been lynched, he has been cursed and no earthly help was nigh, but there was an all-seeing eye who hath said vengeance is mine I will repay." But such letters had little impact on the views of Norris or his wide network of allies. As much as white fundamentalists liked to claim that they practiced the true, universal faith, it was a faith most often defined by race. Preparing individuals for the coming judgment meant maintaining rather than undermining white "purity" and racial hierarchies.[39]

Although the United States' racial problems provoked significant fundamentalist commentary, changing notions of gender, sex, and family sparked even greater concerns. Radical evangelicals often returned to Jesus's warning that at the time of his return moral conditions would approximate those of Noah's and Lot's days. Defiance of the Almighty's supposed gender hierarchy and moral order had triggered his rage in the Old Testament and fundamentalists felt confident that the changes happening around them would soon incite God's last-days wrath. Their passionate reactions to evolving gender ideals represented in part the unintended consequences of the fundamentalist-modernist controversy, in that these reactions solidified fundamentalists' commitment to the home as sacred space. While American churches had fallen to heresy, the faithful were not going to give up their families to the forces of the Antichrist. As women gained more and more equality, fundamentalists dedicated more and more time to restricting their roles at home and in the church. Furthermore, many fundamentalist leaders like Riley, Norris, and Straton were obsessed with issues of masculinity. They reacted against anything that threatened their sense of self.

Same-sex relationships, fundamentalists believed, represented one important symbol of the nation's growing sexual depravity. In the interwar era the term "homosexual" made its way into popular parlance. Meanwhile gay subcultures took root in some of the nation's major cities. As gay and lesbian men and women assumed an increasingly public presence, fundamentalists joined a majority of Americans in denouncing what they interpreted as deviant forms of sexuality. But for fundamentalists more was at stake than simply who was shagging whom. They interpreted the rise of "sodomy" and its evocation of the sins of Sodom as explicit proof of Jesus's apocalyptic prophecies and evidence that the last days had commenced.

A handful of fundamentalists spoke out against same-sex relationships. Barnhouse criticized what he interpreted as the celebration of same-sex relations in popular culture and lamented the rise and spread of "unnatural vice." He interpreted both as signs of the imminence of Armageddon. Journalist and evangelist Dan Gilbert called homosexuality "one of the ugliest blotches upon American civilization" and identified it as "one of the surest signs that the days of Noah are closing in upon us." Fretting that "well-financed and highly-organized cults of homosexuals sponsor all sorts of propaganda to woo and win new addicts to their horrible vice," he called on the public to "stamp out this plague in our midst." Moody professor Wilbur Smith called same-sex relations "another dreadful tendency of our time." "It is the curse," he preached, "of all large penal institutions, of all concentration camps, internment areas, and great bodies of soldiers kept within military areas for long periods of time. . . . Our Lord Himself said that Sodomic conditions would again be manifest before the coming of the Son of Man." Some fundamentalists even believed that the Antichrist would be gay, on the basis of Daniel 11:37, "neither shall he regard . . . the desire of women." Although in the interwar era most fundamentalists did not acknowledge the existence of same-sex relations, the few who did viewed them as a menacing sign that confirmed the imminence of Armageddon.[40]

While homosexuality troubled the few fundamentalists bold enough to address the topic, the evolution of women's "traditional" roles represented a far more common and alarming trend for most believers. In many ways the faithful sought to defend an imagined past in which Christianity provided the foundation for every home, the Bible served as the center of social life, godly leaders ruled the nation, and men and women knew their places. When fundamentalists perceived challenges to these ideals, they went on the offensive. They routinely peppered their critiques of changing gender roles with premillennial references to the last days and the rise of the Antichrist.

In the first decades of the twentieth century, unprecedented numbers of women defied traditional stereotypes. They sought increased access to birth control, education, and professional jobs. Some crusaded for the right to vote; others worked to have a greater voice in shaping their communities. Still others donned new fashion styles, and younger women in particular began talking about and experimenting more openly with sex. Although nineteenth-century evangelicals had often supported women's rights, with the rise of fundamentalism came a rigorous call for limiting women's power and opportunities. Billy Sunday summed up the fundamentalist position. "The average little frizzle-headed, fudge-eating, ragtime flapper who can't turn a battercake without splattering up the kitchen," he preached, "knows more about devilment than her grandmother did when she was 75 years old. . . . Yes sir, woman is the battleground of the universe." The ball player was right—fundamentalists had identified women and their bodies as a significant battleground.[41]

Fundamentalists saw interwar fashion trends and especially shorter skirts as a manifestation of greater problems. "The man that can look at some of these Janes today," Sunday opined, "the way they get themselves up with dresses above their knees and their stockings rolled down and the flesh of their legs showing and their stockings looking like lattice work. . . . well if a man can look at a girl like that and not have a moral blow-out, he ought to have a pension." Shrinking hemlines also caught Straton's attention, if not his gaze. His criticism of female fashion provoked varying responses. One woman asked why she should "be ashamed of the well formed body her creator has bestowed upon her." A young man supported the minister's diatribes against short skirts. Although "by nature I want to be good," this thirty-one-year-old salesman fretted, "the beguiling, I might say seductive, manner" of young women, "to-gether with the manner in which they dress, as well as the 'approaches' which they deliberately invite," proved too much for him. He ended by asking Straton to "understand a young man's problems." Straton did, and so did Bob Jones. "I have ceased to hope for men to live pure until women dress modestly," Jones preached. "God will hold you women accountable for the downfall of thousands of men." Jones's views were typical; fundamentalist leaders almost always blamed women rather than men for the nation's supposed sexual decline.[42]

Hair, like skirts, represented another issue for the faithful. Fundamentalist leaders despised the short "bob" cut that had become one of the symbols of the "new woman" of the interwar era. *Moody Monthly* provided the most extensive discussion of the trend. The journal repeatedly criticized bobbing and reiterated the Pauline claim that a woman's "long hair" was a glory to her. This did not convince all the journal's readers, however. Women flooded the *Moody Monthly* offices with a record number of critical letters. The editors replied with another statement staking out an even clearer position against the bob, which they positioned within both the scriptures and the broader social context. They claimed that since the Great War they had witnessed "a great slump" that "has been even more marked in women than in men." Some women, they explained, "wish to ape men, their dress, their amusements, their manners. The cigarette, the cane, the knickerbockers, the crossed knees illustrate it. . . . The bobbed hair seems to belong to the penciled eyebrows, the painted cheeks, the low necks, the naked arms, the short skirts, the movies, the beauty parade, and the fox-trot." Most other male fundamentalist leaders shared *Moody*'s perspective. Pentecostal Frank Bartleman's tract *Flapper Evangelism, Fashion's Fools, Headed for Hell* warned that "every bobbed head is a token of rebellion against God's decree," while Texan John R. Rice denounced the bob in his infamous *Bobbed Hair, Bossy Wives, and Women Preachers.*[43]

Fundamentalists saw the women's movement as another sign of last-days degeneracy. Calling "the woman question" the "burning question of the day," Peter Z. Easton outlined a very specific sex hierarchy. "Man," he explained, "represents the Creator, and woman the creature." To challenge this hierarchy was to challenge God. "All the evidence, there-fore, goes to show that emancipated woman, trampling under foot the laws of God in nature and revelation . . . is herself an incarnate demon, with nothing womanly in her but the name." That the women's movement had moved from the domain of "short-haired women and long-haired men" to that of the "noblest men and women in the church" made it all the more necessary, he believed, for fundamentalists to "sound the alarm."[44]

At the heart of the women's movement was the battle for the ballot, which many fundamentalists interpreted within their end-times apoc-alypticism. Most (although not all) opposed giving women the vote. In 1913 *Christian Workers* slammed female intelligence before linking the suffrage fight to last-days prophecy. "Without any implied slight," the editors explained, it is "evident that woman has not the same intellec-tual position in life that man has. With greater leisure at her command, the educated woman would have asserted her intellectual equality long ago if she had possessed the power to do so." The evils of suffrage and the need to maintain traditional gender roles was a message the journal repeated again and again. *Our Hope* also came out strongly against woman suffrage. "Woman leaving her sphere," Gaebelein editorialized, "becomes by it an instrument of Satan and the result can hardly be pictured. Corruption of the vilest kind must follow." He called British suffragists "wicked women . . . possessed by demons," and he was one of many fundamentalists who connected the civil disobedience of ac-tivists to the "lawlessness" predicted for the end times. Although women won the right to vote in 1920, antisuffragists believed they would have the final word. "There is a full-fledged rebellion under way," Keith Brooks explained, "not only against the headship of man in government and church but in the home. . . . These conditions are marks of the apostasy. . . . Toward what the movement is tending, is plainly evident." It was moving toward Armageddon.[45]

During the 1920s, women began to take jobs outside of the home in increasing numbers. They most often found employment in sex-segregated professions, serving as teachers, nurses, retail clerks, and office secretaries. The choice to move beyond the "traditional" role of mother and homemaker—for many different reasons—provoked strong criticism. Paul Rader contextualized changing gender roles within prophecy and concluded that women "are taking a place that God has already shown in the scripture they will take in the Antichrist age." His apocalyptic sensibilities gave him a determined confidence to speak what he saw as the truth. Fundamentalists had nothing to lose in denouncing popular trends; the world itself would soon end.[46]

Moody Bible Institute administrator Harold Lundquist best summarized fundamentalists' views on the changes under way. "The American home is not what it was a generation ago," he warned. "There can be no doubt that the Scriptures teach that a woman's place is with her family in her home. Only on exceptional occasions does God definitely call her into another place of service." This was the standard fundamentalist position. "Women as a rule should be trained for motherhood," King's Business sermonized, "motherhood in its highest and best sense, rather than for the various forms of public life." Horton lamented the decline of "real" mothers in the United States. "God designed woman as the home-maker, but somehow she seems to have been side-tracked." Dixon agreed. "As president, governor, judge," he wrote, "she would be out of place. Think of a woman policeman!" Matthews, never afraid to speak bluntly, instructed wives to "go home." But unlike many ministers he did not lay the blame for American decline at the feet of women alone. "The average husband," he preached, "is a coward. The average wife is a bully. . . . Women ought to be forced to go home. But their husbands are too cowardly to force them."[47]

Nevertheless, as women worked to understand their place in this world, some believed that God had called them not only to step out of the domestic sphere but to preach, a phenomenon that dated back to colonial times. The most famous woman preacher in the interwar era was Aimee Semple McPherson—a divorcee whose success rivaled the most influential male evangelists of the period. Her work provoked mixed responses from other fundamentalists. Some supported her. "Cowboy Evangelist" Jay C. Kellogg, for example, took seriously the prophet Joel's prediction that "in the last days" women would "prophesy." He believed that this was in fact happening. "God is using women in the ministry today as never before. The devil," he explained, "does not like the women preachers." Straton agreed. But others believed that McPherson and female evangelists like her were modern-day Jezebels engaged in the work of Satan.[48]

For many fundamentalists, woman's relationship to man was based both in the biblical account of creation and in biology. But Henry Stough took this conviction further than most. The evangelist developed a novel theology of gender that he preached in revivals around the country. He believed that the "first man was hermaphrodite; that is both male and female." Then "God created woman, not as a separate entity, but out of the man." "What is the particular difference then between men and women?" he asked. "Sexuality. Every peculiarity of sexual organism woman now possesses was at her creation taken out of the man." He even provided a new translation of Genesis. "God said, 'It is not good for this hermaphrodite Adam to live alone.'" So God created Eve and established marriage for the reconstruction of the holy hermaphrodite. "No wonder," Stough explained, "marriage becomes an increasingly solemn thing when thus considered." No wonder indeed. As fundamentalists sermonized and editorialized on proper gender roles, most drew on traditional nineteenth-century ideas of male-female differences. But Stough's radical theory demonstrates how deeply fundamentalists invested in defending and maintaining gender difference.[49]

As fundamentalists fought contemporary gender trends, they also emphasized the importance of having children and properly raising them. In part they feared that white, middle-class Americans' declining birthrate coupled with massive immigration from eastern and southern Europe threatened the nation's traditional white Protestant foundations. Once again the purity of the white race was at stake. Straton complained of young couples in Manhattan adopting dogs instead of having babies. "Not big, noble dogs—there might be some consolation in that!" he preached, "but miserable little scraps of hair and hide, with bleary eyes, wobbly legs, pink ribbons, and . . . little coats and pants upon them." Matthews fretted that "childless homes, made so by the premeditated plans of society-loving women, are to blame for the social corruption, degradation and infamy now confronting the world." Stough saw marriage without children as "a failure." "The marriage that refuses motherhood in the sight of God is nothing but legalized adultery," he preached. "The woman that refuses to become a mother has thwarted the plan of God."[50]

For those men and women who did have children, fundamentalists offered plenty of advice. They challenged Americans who denounced corporal punishment and reminded the faithful that the Bible instructed believers that to "spare the rod" was to "spoil the child." "The greatest disservice that a parent can ever do to a child," Barnhouse warned in a radio address, "is to fail to spank the child." Rice was also a strong believer in physical reprimands. He called on parents to demand "strict obedience," which should be "enforced by whipping." Corporal punishment, he promised, will keep children out of the penitentiary and out of hell. He even shared a personal example. Apparently one of his toddlers "was so stubborn and rebellious" that the minister had little choice. "I applied the palm of my hand so vigorously to the place God provides for spanking babies that later the blue prints of my fingers could be seen on the precious little body." He blamed "columnists, educators, feminists, and psychologists" for trying to undermine "godly discipline in the home" and for turning "American children" into "a race of undisciplined, pleasure-seeking, willful despisers of authority and breakers of law." With the tribulation looming, fundamentalists believed that it was essential to raise disciplined children who could stand boldly against the schemes of the Antichrist.[51]

Fundamentalists often linked their anxieties over new philosophies of child rearing, women's changing roles, and the more open sexuality of the era with the growing birth control movement. In the 1910s and 1920s, more and more Americans spoke openly about contraception. The most famous example, Margaret Sanger, provoked the ire of social conservatives across the country with her willingness to distribute information about sex and to publicly defend contraception.

Although a few fundamentalists believed that artificial birth control might be appropriate for married couples, most did not. Opponents often couched their arguments in nativist terms, lamenting the alleged decline of the white race. *King's Business* editorialized against "race suicide," hoping that the war had "awakened many people to the folly of the recent vigorous agitation in this country to promote the limitation of families." Gaebelein in turn quoted a race-baiting speech given by Italy's Benito Mussolini about the decline of the white race in the United States. Il Duce predicted the imminent rise of an "Africanized America" that could put a "negro in the White House" within a century. "Who is responsible for these conditions?" Gaebelein asked. "The agitators of the companionate marriage, this legalized prostitution, and the agitators of birth control." The *Sunday School Times* identified "birth control, divorce, and Hollywood" as "the chief enemy of the Protestant home."[52]

Closely linked to the question of birth control was that of abortion. Since most fundamentalists opposed contraception, they also opposed abortion. Not many discussed publicly the topic in the first half of the twentieth century, but those who did equated the practice with murder. Billy Sunday alluded to the issue in a women-only revival meeting. According to the *Atlanta Constitution,* Sunday "painstakingly" went into "detail" regarding the many pitfalls that could ensnare women and declared "the murder of unborn babies the curse and damnation of America." Straton also dealt directly with abortion; his Manhattan vice crusades pretty much guaranteed that he would have to acknowledge the topic. He received numerous letters encouraging him to take on the practice. One distraught mother begged him to expose a clinic where "criminal operations" had been performed on her daughters, while another described abortion as "the shedding of innocent blood, the sin of blood-guiltiness, the unpardonable sin, the MURDER OF THE UNBORN." John Rice also called abortion "murder" and made the case for life at conception. "After a male sperm cell has united with a female ovum," he preached, "and the body of the child thus conceived begins to develop in the womb of the wife, to destroy that little life and so prevent a normal birth of a child is called abortion. . . . And abortion is murder." *Moody Monthly* supported the pope's 1930 encyclical on the sanctity of marriage and against artificial birth control and abortion, although the editors hoped that in so doing they would "not be accused of going over to Roman Catholicism."[53]

Henry Stough preached on abortion more often than most fundamentalists of the era. He called abortion a "crime" and refuted the commonly held notion that abortions were morally justified prior to quickening, calling it a "devilish tradition." "For every child permitted to see the light of day," he warned, "it is said one is cruelly aborted; half the race is murdered." He too believed that life began at conception. When the "spermatozoa" enters the egg and the egg closes over it, he preached, "imbedded now in the heart of the ovum is the life of the male—and at that moment an immortal soul is born. Touch it if you dare. To do so is to have committed murder. It is just as much of a crime before God to murder a child that is two minutes old as it is to murder a man seventy years old."[54]

Like Sunday, Stough often tackled this issue during women's meetings, where he would occasionally read letters from "distressed" females. His purpose was to encourage the members of his audience to guard their bodies. In one such letter a young woman shared the story of her seduction by a man who promised that if she became pregnant "he would take care of it, so no one would ever be the wiser." She had heard that "such things could be done," and so she "yielded to him" and eventually needed an abortion. The anonymous letter writer ended with a plea for Stough: "tell parents and young girls to keep out of such things. Talk about the White Slave Traffic—I am a slave and worse than a slave." During another meeting, Stough read a letter from a woman who was repeatedly raped by her brothers before she had turned twelve. Once she left the house, she was sexually active and became pregnant. A friend took her to an abortion provider, "and in three months from that time," she wrote, "I gave birth to a three month old baby that I had killed." Stough indicated that women alone bore the responsibility for these problems. He did not assign blame to men or encourage them to treat women with more respect. It apparently never occurred to him that men could be sexually responsible.[55]

For a few fundamentalists, however, the issues of birth control and abortion seemed more complicated—especially as they approached Armageddon. Brooks vacillated on birth control and he occasionally mentioned abortion without any clear sense of affirmation or condemnation. He was not sure whether Christians should bring babies into an increasingly dangerous world that would soon be under the rule of the Antichrist. "As the Tribulation time draws near," he wrote, "this will be more and more a baffling problem as indicated by our Lord's own warning concerning the end days." Over time, however, he became more decisive, adopting the fundamentalist party line. "The birth control movement," he preached, "has given birth to a thousand evils far worse than those it was intended to remedy. . . . The stench of Sodom is coming upon the land."[56]

Indeed, the stench of Sodom and its evocation of the end of days smelled real to fundamentalists in the interwar era. The signs of the times were manifesting everywhere. The faithful set themselves apart from many mainstream Christians and from the broader culture by critiquing popular trends around them ranging from dancing to stage plays to movies. Meanwhile they conformed to popular middle-class white American understandings of race, gender, and sexuality. Confident in the wake of World War I that current events were rapidly fulfilling prophecy, they found ways to make faith relevant. Sure that they would be rewarded when Jesus returned for the final judgment, they developed a bold, relentless, uncompromising approach to addressing controversial social and moral issues. Through their efforts, fundamentalism evolved beyond a simple expression of radical Christian apocalyptic theology. It became a new and unique form of faith that touched every part of life. Fundamentalists understood occupying until Jesus came as a call to culture war. Although they enjoyed few permanent victories, their lack of success did little to dampen their enthusiasm. Rather, it confirmed their belief that the last days were settling on them. But while Jesus tarried, they determined to make the most of their time. The destiny of the nation, fundamentalists believed, was in their hands.

5

AMERICAN EDUCATION ON TRIAL

IN THE LAST YEARS of William Jennings Bryan's life, he took on a foe far greater than the Republican candidates who had three times derailed his quest for the presidency. He pledged to defeat the new science that he believed threatened the souls of the nation's schoolchildren. In 1922, the *New York Times* asked the former presidential nominee, past secretary of state, and staunch Presbyterian to explain his crusade to eradicate evolution from public school curricula. In a long article, the Great Commoner offered many criticisms of evolution, but his religious arguments resonated most widely. "Not one syllable in the Bible" supported evolutionary theory, he asserted. It "destroys man's family tree . . . and makes him a descendant of the lower forms of life." He warned that schoolroom peddlers of Darwinism were "undermining the faith of Christians," "raising questions about the Bible as an authoritative source of truth," and "teaching materialistic views that rob the life of the young of spiritual values."[1]

Bryan's well-publicized attack on evolution provoked the ire of many religious liberals. Harry Emerson Fosdick responded with his own rejoinder in the *Times,* claiming to "voice the sentiments of a large number of Christian people" who were "quite as shocked as any scientist . . .

at Mr. Bryan's sincere but appalling obscurantism." He called Bryan the true enemy of the Christian faith and alleged that the Commoner represented those who insisted "on setting up artificial adhesions between Christianity and outgrown scientific opinions." "Mr. Bryan," Fosdick worried, proposed "that we shall run ourselves to his mold of medievalism. He proposes, too, that his special form of medievalism be made authoritative by the State." If Bryan succeeded in his crusade, Fosdick promised, "multitudes" of Christians would "fight against him in the name of their religion and their God." Two months later Bryan was clearly on Fosdick's mind when the Manhattan minister preached, "Shall the Fundamentalists Win?" In that historic sermon the liberal cleric urged his followers to stop the fundamentalist crusade against science in its tracks.[2]

To the great chagrin of fundamentalists, by the mid-1920s battles over the truth of Darwinian evolution had come for many Americans to symbolize the heart of the fundamentalist-modernist controversy. It brought the fundamentalist movement back into the headlines, and positioned it as an adversary of progressive politics and education. For most fundamentalists, however, evolution was a mere symptom of larger issues. Just as debates over premillennialism had never been solely about theology but had also always been about Christians' relationship to the present and future, so too was the evolution controversy about much more. Were humans moral creatures made in the image of God or were they the descendants of soulless animals seeking no more than self-survival? Was the Bible a reliable and eternal source of truth or a flawed product of its times? Was the purpose of education to raise godly children or to expose them to the latest scientific ideas?

At the heart of these questions lay fundamentalists' concerns over the relationship between faith and secular schooling. Fearful that the deck was stacked against them, fundamentalists redoubled their efforts to reclaim the nation's primary and secondary schools. At the college level, however, they knew they were fighting a losing battle, so they accelerated their exodus from the nation's great centers of learning and established their own insular institutions. At the same time that fundamentalists were embracing isolationism in foreign policy, they adopted a position of academic isolationism. Their work revealed how much they feared the major intellectual trends emanating from Europe, which ranged from Darwinism to Marxism to modernism. Their self-imposed exile and their skepticism toward conventional secular research and scholarly science ensured that they would have a difficult time competing for a hearing in the marketplace of ideas. It also reinforced their self-perception as besieged outsiders who were increasingly at odds with a culture rapidly ceding ground to the forces of the Antichrist. Nevertheless, like guerilla warriors who attack an enemy and then retreat to safety, fundamentalists thrived in their alternative evangelical universe one step removed from the mainstream of American intellectual life, where they continued to refine their apocalyptic theology and to apply it to every part of life.[3]

Contrary to popular stereotypes, fundamentalists were never anti-intellectual. Many of the men who shaped the early premillennial movement held advanced degrees from prestigious schools, including Yale, Princeton, Johns Hopkins, and the University of Chicago. But as they looked to train successors, they recognized that American higher education was undergoing substantial changes. In the late nineteenth and early twentieth centuries, many schools instituted a series of modernizing reforms. Rather than continuing to educate students primarily in the classics and moral philosophy, they elevated science and scientific reasoning. They began incorporating the new social sciences such as psychology, sociology, and anthropology into the curriculum. Religion, and Christianity in particular, represented simply another lens through which to view the world rather than the foundation on which to build a holistic education. Mandatory chapel services disappeared at many private schools and fewer and fewer clergy served as college presidents. The leaders of the nation's elite private universities, many of which had been founded by devout Christians, increasingly moved to secularize their schools.

Fundamentalists correctly understood that the philosophy at the root of modern university education differed in substantial ways from their own. Furthermore, if the time was nigh, why waste it providing students with a general education? Many opted instead to set up new institutions to train workers as efficiently as possible to disseminate the fundamentalist message of instant and eternal redemption. The goal of these schools was simple—they hoped to empower students with the practical tools necessary to bring people into the kingdom before Armageddon. Fundamentalists did not necessarily intend to compete with more established colleges, but to offer something entirely unique and different that fit the times in which they were living. The schools they built provided effective breeding grounds for succeeding generations of premillennialists to develop skills essential for spreading the movement's apocalyptic message and accelerating its growth.

Moody Bible Institute and the Bible Institute of Los Angeles became the nation's two leading fundamentalist schools. Moody Bible Institute grew out of the work of Emma Dryer, a Chicago laywoman who had started a Bible study to train female urban missionaries. Impressed with Dryer's work, Dwight Moody helped her and William Blackstone raise the necessary funds in the 1880s to establish a more comprehensive training institute for men and women. Under the leadership of R. A. Torrey, who led the school from 1889 to 1908, and then James Gray (dean and then president, 1904–1934) MBI thrived. Blackstone contributed money to the school and occasionally taught classes. In 1901 MBI launched a highly successful correspondence course, which spread the premillennial gospel throughout the nation. A handful of prominent businessmen, led by Quaker Oats mogul Henry Parsons Crowell, served on the school's board of trustees. They helped ensure that the mission of the school aligned with their market interests, promoting a gospel of salvation that celebrated individual attainment and the free market. Like Quaker Oats, the fundamentalism disseminated at MBI was guaranteed pure.[4]

Moody Bible Institute leaders hoped to project an image of respectability by matching the standards set by the nation's top schools in every area, from academic rigor to facilities to dress. In the midst of a humid 1908 summer, a disgruntled Dean Gray sent a strongly worded letter to the faculty. "I have observed members of the faculty during this warm weather sitting in their offices without coats or vests. . . . I beg that the practice may not grow upon us because of its effect on the students who need our example of conventionality." Department meetings, and the grumblings of faculty who had to attend them, were also a conventional part of life at Moody. Wilbur Smith worried that the meetings were inhibiting his ability to discern the signs of the times.

"Would it be possible," he asked Dean Harold Lundquist, "for you to excuse me from Faculty meetings for the rest of this term." They "are an awful trial to my soul. . . . I really believe my own efficiency in the Institute would be increased did I not have to endure these long, tedious sessions." While many a professor—then and now—has felt Smith's pain over faculty meetings, he was not excused.[5]

Minister Louis Talbot and oilman Lyman Stewart founded BIOLA in 1908 to build the premillennial movement on the West Coast. Once again, Blackstone had a hand. He and his wife had moved to Pasadena, California, in the early twentieth century, and they shared Talbot's vision for the school. Blackstone served on the founding board of directors and was the school's first dean; R. A. Torrey, who had left Moody, took over in 1912. Stewart was so committed to ensuring that the school remained true to the fundamentals that he inserted into the deed to the school's property a clause stating that if false teachings entered the curriculum, "the property will revert to the heirs of the donors, any of whom may bring suit for the purpose of obtaining title to the property." Well aware of the drift of universities like Harvard, Yale, and Andover away from their explicitly Christian foundations, he wanted to protect his investment in the radical evangelical faith.[6]

Stewart viewed the four hundred thousand dollars he put into BIOLA as a means of furthering both the cause of Christ and the betterment of California. As the fundamentalist controversy grew, he regarded BIOLA as an alternative to the University of Chicago's liberal-leaning divinity school, which had been heavily subsidized by his arch–business rival and "old enemy" John D. Rockefeller. Although Stewart believed that BIOLA's primary purpose was to get people saved, he also believed that the school would strengthen the local community. In a letter to streetcar magnate Henry Huntington he boasted that the school had transformed eight hundred men "who were a part of what is regarded as the lawless and dangerous element" into members of "the law-abiding and progressive forces of the community."[7]

In organizing Bible schools, premillennialists had to reconcile their faith in an impending rapture with the need to hire a permanent staff and house students. Initially, Stewart believed that BIOLA should make use of existing property "in view of the imminence of the Lord's coming." "I do not think," he wrote, "it wise to use any portion of this

While fundamentalists have long been stereotyped as rural, southern, and ignorant, in reality they often thrived in the hearts of the United States' great cities. The Bible Institute of Los Angeles, with its illuminated "Jesus Saves" signs flashing over downtown, provided an excellent training ground for many prominent fundamentalists.
Courtesy of Biola University.

fund in purchase of real estate or putting up buildings." Over time he changed his mind. "Until very recently," he confided to his brother, "I felt that it was a serious mistake to put the Lord's money into brick and mortar"; but he came to see such things as necessary to prepare missionaries for the field. Someone had to train the next generation of workers in case the Lord tarried. Torrey justified such projects as well, explaining, "there is no reason why those who believe that the Lord may come at any time should not build the very best buildings they can for the most effective carrying on of His work until He comes." He conveniently made this claim after school planners had already erected a large new church to house his ministry. That both men felt compelled to address the issue underscores the seriousness of their expectations of an imminent apocalypse.[8]

Although fundamentalists came to appreciate the significant role that the Stewart money played in supporting the movement, not all had initially greeted their entry into Bible institute–building warmly. When James Gray learned that plans were under way to establish BIOLA, he sarcastically wrote an MBI ally, "Bible Institutes don't start themselves. . . . There is a new one at Los Angeles (in contemplation), some rich oil king being back of it. . . . Why not make a trust of all these Institutes and set ourselves up as Bible Barons?" When word reached the Stewarts that Moody leaders had been grousing about BIOLA's "extravagance" in building comfortable dormitories, Lyman complained, "this does not come with a very good grace from them, in view of the fact that I have been a contributor to their work."[9]

Moody Bible Institute and BIOLA represented two schools among many. In the early twentieth century, fundamentalists opened Bible institutes all over the nation. William Bell Riley established the Northwestern Bible and Missionary Training School in Minneapolis in 1902; Colorado fundamentalists opened the Denver Bible Institute in 1914; C. I. Scofield started the Philadelphia School of the Bible in 1914; the Assemblies of God launched Central Bible Institute in Missouri in 1922; Aimee Semple McPherson opened LIFE Bible College in Los Angeles in 1923; Robert C. McQuilkin founded the Columbia School of the Bible in South Carolina in 1923; Lewis Sperry Chafer opened Evangelical Bible College in Texas in 1924 (later Dallas Theological Seminary); Bob Jones began the school that bears his name in Florida in 1927; and Edmund Ironside, fundamentalist leader H. I. Ironside's son, opened the Dallas Colored Bible Institute in 1928, where he and his white colleagues trained dozens of African Americans in the fundamentalist faith. Riley interpreted the success of the many Bible schools as proof that God was preparing a faithful remnant for the final days.[10]

Fundamentalist schools generally drew from a common core curriculum. They placed heavy emphasis on English Bible study, evangelism, and practical ministry. Students learned how to properly interpret the

Fundamentalists made very little effort to draw African Americans into their
movement. One exception was the Dallas Colored Bible Institute, where
fundamentalists trained dozens of African Americans in the faith. Each of these
graduates proudly carries a *Scofield Reference Bible* along with his diploma.
    Courtesy of the Southern Bible Institute.

scriptures, sing hymns on key, direct choirs, minister to children, and
make effective use of simple tools like chalkboards to teach lessons. But
clear differences set BIOLA and MBI apart from most of the other schools.
When Gray suggested to Torrey that they should establish a "league" of
Bible institutes, Torrey dismissed the idea immediately. "The educational
standard that we demand [at BIOLA] is way, way above anything that I
think is possible for the other Bible Institutes excepting your own
[MBI]." He went on to criticize the shoddy work being done at most
fundamentalist schools, which often had low admissions standards and
did not demand much intellectually of their students.[11]

    Bible institutes attracted mostly white men and women, reflecting
the demographics of the fundamentalist movement as a whole. Although
movement leaders did not usually view female students as candidates

for the priesthood, many fundamentalist school administrators welcomed women into their classrooms. They believed that women could
play important supportive roles in the movement. Western and northern schools like BIOLA and MBI also enrolled a token number of African Americans, Asians, and other minority students. Among Moody's
most famous alumni (of any race) was Mary McCloud Bethune, who
became an influential member of Franklin Roosevelt's New Deal administration. But despite Moody's self-proclaimed egalitarianism,
around 1910 MBI leaders began requiring African-American students
to live off campus rather than integrating housing with white students
(this policy was not rescinded until 1938). Moody's correspondence
courses proved to be a popular alternative for African Americans. Southern fundamentalist schools almost always admitted whites only. That
fundamentalist institutes and colleges in the first few decades of the
twentieth century trained tens of thousands of white ministers, teachers, evangelists, radio preachers, and missionaries, compared to only a
handful of African Americans, helps further explain why premillennialism did not have the same impact on black Christianity as it did on
white. African Americans remained separate from the fundamentalist
movement in almost every way.[12]

Two other schools played important roles in fundamentalism. Wheaton College, founded just outside of Chicago in 1860 by evangelical
reformers and abolitionists, was always a breed apart from other fundamentalist institutions in that it offered a full liberal arts curriculum and
emphasized classical studies rather than just training for ministry. Nevertheless, under the leadership of Charles Blanchard (president 1882–1925)
and then J. Oliver Buswell (president 1926–1940), Wheaton became a
mainstay of premillennialism and one of the fundamentalist movement's
most intellectually respectable colleges. But despite the school founders'
progressive views on race, in the first half of the twentieth century
Wheaton admitted very few African-American students.

The other major initial training ground for fundamentalists was
Princeton Theological Seminary. Princeton had long been a bastion of
old-school Presbyterianism and conservative Protestantism where at the
turn of the twentieth century eminent theologians, including Charles
Hodge and B. B. Warfield, challenged liberal approaches to the scriptures. In the 1920s, J. Gresham Machen served at Princeton as professor

of New Testament. Despite his discomfort with the term "fundamentalist" and his criticism of premillennialism, he taught some of the most important fundamentalist ministers of the interwar era, including Harold Ockenga, Donald Grey Barnhouse, and Carl McIntire. But as Princeton began to liberalize, Machen led an exodus of conservatives out of the school and formed Westminster Theological Seminary as an alternative Presbyterian school. He was angry at having been passed over for a promotion and he disagreed with school leaders' efforts to reorganize the seminary, a move intended to take power away from conservative members of the faculty. In making the decision to separate from Princeton, conservative Protestants ceded to moderate and liberal Christian leaders one of the most intellectually respectable seminaries in the nation and one of the few places where fundamentalists could receive a top-tier graduate education that did not directly undermine their faith.

Bible institutes and evangelical colleges provided training for those fundamentalists who planned to go into full-time ministry, but they served only a small part of the movement. Church leaders knew that the vast majority of their college-bound congregants planned to attend state colleges and universities. They did everything they could to combat what they perceived as threatening trends in American higher education. They believed that religious and political liberals, as well communists inspired by the Bolshevik revolution, were proselytizing through American schools. "Godless faculties," evangelist John Ham contended, "are producing moral and spiritual Bolsheviks a thousand times faster than the agents of communism about which our State Department is alarmed." Brooks alleged that "Soviet agents and sympathizers now occupy chairs of learning in many of our colleges." Riley warned that a conspiracy to destroy the nation's Christian foundations was taking root. Modern universities' "God-denying, Christ-reputing, Bible-scorning theories," he preached, would lead to the Soviet "triumph in America" and "the overthrow of the Christian state." For many fundamentalists, the communist threat and the modernist threat had merged into one.[13]

In the interwar period, journalist and evangelist Dan Gilbert became fundamentalism's most prolific critic of secular education. He believed that modern educators were inadvertently brainwashing students in order to prepare them for the coming Antichrist, but rather than abandoning the fight he hoped to motivate Christians to do something about the many pitfalls he saw in the nation's universities. "Unscrupulous professors," he lamented in both the *Pilot* and *King's Business,* "are using tax-supported schools as agencies through which young students are recruited to Satan's army of godlessness and infidelity. Students are poisoned with free-love propaganda and directed into ways of immorality which end in prostitution, crime, disease, and even suicide." He was one of a few fundamentalists to add to the communist threat fears of abortion. He hoped to shock readers by informing them that each year in American colleges "36,000 girls lose their virginity" and "more than 2,000" get abortions. He claimed that professors encouraged legalization of abortion "as part of their program to make free-love a 'safe and practical proposition.'" The schools had gotten so bad that many fundamentalists bemoaned the dramatic increase in the number of students enrolling. "Once our hearts would have rejoiced greatly over this," minister T. C. Horton confessed. "Now a great fear possesses us. What does it portend when we consider the present attitude of so many of the professors toward the Word of God?"[14]

Fundamentalists highlighted the dangers of public education in order to arouse their fellow citizens from apathy. Decades before Governor Ronald Reagan promised to clean up the "mess" at the University of California, Berkeley, Gilbert called for an end to the state's financing of the university system in response to the work of faculty he deemed anti-Christian. He also lobbied Christians around the nation to write and support ballot initiatives that banned the teaching of atheism, free love, and communism from public schools; and he hoped to make it a punishable crime for a teacher to "poison the minds of students with atheist and communist propaganda." Gilbert claimed to have "one purpose only: that is to stir the Christian citizenry to action, to an appreciation of the conditions, and to a correction of them."[15]

Fundamentalists coupled their concerns over communism and abortion with their frustration over the inclusion of evolutionary biology in university curricula. In a commencement address at Moody, John Roach Straton warned, "the wave of immorality which is menacing the integrity" of youth "dates from that time when the dark and sinister shadow of Darwinism first fell across the fair fields of human life. . . .

Monkey men," he concluded, "make monkey morals." Fundamentalists loved to cite the Bobby Franks murder case to illustrate this point. In 1924 two wealthy and intelligent young men, Nathan Leopold and Richard Loeb, kidnapped and killed the thirteen-year-old Franks, hoping to pull off a "perfect" crime. Their lawyer, the famed criminal defense attorney Clarence Darrow, blamed the students' embrace of a survival-of-the-fittest ethos and their reading of moral relativist philosophers, such as Friedrich Nietzsche, for having influenced their actions. That they matriculated at the University of Chicago made the story all the more rich for fundamentalists. "If anything of so horrible a nature were needed to show the debasing danger of some of the radical teachings now being permitted in some of our colleges," *King's Business* editorialized, "it is afforded by this crime." *Moody Monthly* advocated the death penalty for Leopold and Loeb, arguing that this was the punishment God laid out in the Bible.[16]

Fundamentalists' conviction that godlessness was pervasive and that the second coming was imminent, combined with their sense that public schools were hostile to the Christian faith, shaped their relationship to education in the interwar period. Women seemed to be defying their God-given roles, new forms of mass media were glorifying all sorts of sin, and now even the youngest and most vulnerable citizens were being trained to question the Christian faith by their teachers and curricula. Changes in education reinforced fundamentalists' anxieties about the direction of the culture. They relentlessly criticized American colleges and universities while erecting dozens of interdenominational Bible schools. Many fundamentalists abandoned established universities, seminaries, and divinity schools in exchange for independent Bible institutes, practically guaranteeing that the faithful would become intellectually isolated. The generation of believers who came of age between the world wars, indoctrinated by monolithic faculties and freed from having to engage with those who disagreed with them, had a difficult time making an intellectually persuasive case to outsiders for the radical evangelical faith. Had Jesus returned as they expected, this would not have been a problem. But he didn't. Fundamentalists' decision to downplay the importance of education in the context of last-days priorities left them susceptible to charges of anti-intellectualism, sometimes valid, sometimes not, that dog their descendants to this day.

The concerns of fundamentalists and other social conservatives over American higher education paralleled their apprehension about changes occurring in primary and secondary schools. In the nineteenth century, public schools, many of which had their origins in evangelical reform efforts, often featured Bible reading and Christian training as part of their core mission. But as curriculum began to evolve in conjunction with changes inspired by the work of reformers like John Dewey, the evolution of higher education, and the increased diversity of student populations as a result of immigration, many American schools began to secularize their curricula. These new trends in education riled fundamentalists, who interpreted such changes as another sign of the immoral days in which they were living and of the coming tribulation. They expressed their greatest concerns over evolution and reductions in Bible reading, but they also fretted about sex education and what they perceived as the growing influence of communism in the classroom. Instead of abandoning public schools to secular trends as they had colleges and universities, fundamentalists went to war, convinced that at the state and local levels they could still turn the tide against liberalism.

Beginning in the mid-nineteenth century, some school boards, and occasionally the courts, began to take seriously the growing religious diversity of public school students. In response to the pleas of freethinkers and some Catholic, Jewish, and liberal Protestant parents, administrators slowly began to reduce explicitly Protestant schoolroom practices, including daily reading from traditionally Protestant versions of the scriptures. The debate over Bible reading continued for decades, ebbing and flowing. In the early twentieth century, fundamentalists inspired by new court decisions jumped into the fray. In 1910, foreshadowing the 1963 US Supreme Court decision *Abington v. Schempp,* the Illinois Supreme Court declared that reading scripture verses each morning in public schools violated the Constitution's First Amendment. Many states followed Illinois's lead. Norton Brand insisted that this trend indicated "the total secularization of government and society," while William Bell Riley called it "the greatest calamity that has befallen the modern state." In California, some fundamentalists fought back by working to pass legislation to get the Bible back in the classroom. McPherson helped place a proposition on the California ballot requiring that the Bible be placed in all public school classrooms with the hope that it would be read. But her embroilment in a sex scandal at the same time undermined her efforts. "Aimee was going to put the bible into every classroom in our public schools," novelist and California resident Upton Sinclair sarcastically explained to journalist H. L. Mencken, "but now it is too easy to prove that bible reading produces immorality." In the 1930s a minister from the Pacific Northwest put the Bible-reading controversy in the context of prophecy and called on Franklin Roosevelt to undo the damage that had been done. "I believe the greatest mistake this country ever made," he wrote the president, "was when the Bible was taken out of our public schools. The result has been the Faith of our children in the fundamentalist principles of the gospel of Jesus Christ is undermined. Materialism and the spirit of the anti-Christ is sweeping the foundations from under all the governments of earth."[17]

Fundamentalists and other conservative Protestants blamed many different groups for declining Bible reading, but Catholics often served as their favorite targets. The faithful believed that Rome was working to undermine the historic ties between Protestantism and public education in the United States while simultaneously training a new generation of dedicated foot soldiers to take control of the nation. "Our Romanist friends," *King's Business* alleged, "have outwitted us by retaining their own children, of early age, in their own schools, while the Protestant children have been denied the benefit of Bible reading in the public schools." The editors responded to Roman Catholic cardinal James Gibbons's lament that Americans were losing interest in religion by blaming the cardinal's church. "Were it not for the opposition of the Roman hierarchy the public schools would not be the godless schools that they are," they complained. "Besides, to the influx of European Catholics we owe the worst elements of our restless and lawless populations." Henry Stough alleged that Catholics had systematically taken control of local school boards in order to ban Bible reading from the curriculum. He called them "destroyers of Protestant Education, Faith and Morals & Propagandists of Catholicism." *Christian Workers* insisted that the effects of parochial education demanded "the attention of every patriot." Fundamentalists believed that if they did not mount a stronger defense, they would soon be the slaves of the Vatican.[18]

A few fundamentalists expressed concerns as early as the 1910s about the introduction of sex education into school curricula. Teachers and school leaders were hoping to educate children about the basics of sex and to instruct them in "sex hygiene." *King's Business* believed that sex should be a topic for parents to discuss with their children, not something taught at school. *Christian Workers* took a clear stand against sex education as well, since "attention of innocent persons is thus called to things they should not know, and their curiosity being aroused, they seek information in improper ways." Gilbert warned that "in many states courses in so-called 'sex instruction' have been established in the schools" and admonished fellow fundamentalists to reclaim sex education. Schools in the eyes of fundamentalists seemed to be abdicating their responsibility to raise virtuous, godly students. Instead they were planting immoral and subversive ideas in impressionable young minds.[19]

Although many school-related issues troubled fundamentalists, they saved their most impassioned language and concerted efforts for fighting biological evolution in public school curricula. Their skepticism about evolution reflected the views of the majority of Americans at the time. Fundamentalists insisted that Darwinian theories undermined the belief that humans represented a distinct creation made uniquely in the image of God. Notions of random chance, natural selection, and the survival of the fittest threatened their beliefs in godly creation. Billy Sunday, with his typical gusto, preached, "If you believe that your great-great-great-great-granddaddy came from a monkey, and wrapped his tail around the branches of a tree, take your ancestor and go to the devil with him." On the basis of various Old Testament genealogies and the calculations of seventeenth-century bishop James Ussher (which were reproduced in the Scofield Bible), many fundamentalists believed that humans had only been around for about six thousand years, regardless of the age of the earth. If humankind was millions of years old, then fundamentalists' reading of the Bible was flawed. They insisted on a literal interpretation of Genesis and believed that any skepticism about human origins opened the door for a denial of Biblical miracles, including Jesus's resurrection, which cut to the heart of the evangelical faith.[20]

Nevertheless the issue of evolution was not as black-and-white among premillennialists and early fundamentalists as it would eventually be-

come. The *Fundamentals* included multiple viewpoints on the topic im-
plicitly acknowledging a range of "orthodox" views. A *Christian Workers* study on the first chapter of Genesis left room for interpretation as
well. Although the authors insisted that God had created the universe
and everything in it, they did not define the process precisely and they
included evolution as a possible divine mechanism. "There is a remarkable agreement," they wrote, "between modern science and the account
in Genesis. The Biblical accounts by their wording provide for both
creation and the evolutionary development of created things." The
"days" of Genesis, they added, were not necessarily literal twenty-four-
hour days. In subsequent editorials, *Christian Workers* affirmed the possibilities of both an old earth and microevolution. Editors essentially
maintained that Genesis required a belief in a first cause (God) and that
animals and humans represented distinct creations. Beyond those two
issues Chicago fundamentalists seemed open to competing theories of
change over time.[21]

Other fundamentalists found a possible gap in Genesis that allowed
for an old earth. Although Barnhouse believed that humans had only
been around for six thousand years, he cited the Bible's silence on the
time between the creation of the universe and the creation of humankind to postulate that the old earth revealed through contemporary
geology did not contradict Genesis. Talbot and other fundamentalists
even suggested that a pre-Adamic race of beings might have roamed the
earth. "The many fossils that are discovered today," he wrote, "which
would indicate life upon this earth millions of years ago, may be the
relics of the pre-Adamic days."[22]

However, World War I proved for many fundamentalists to be a
turning point in the evolution debate. They believed that the integration of liberal theology with Darwinian philosophies had inspired the
German war machine. "Right at the bottom of this war," Dixon
preached from his London pulpit, "is this evolutionary theory; the belief in what is called 'the struggle for existence', the survival of the fittest
in that struggle." Torrey called the German war effort "evolutionism
carried to its logical issue. . . . For the safety of the whole human race,"
he continued, we must "get this soulless, cruel, remorseless philosophy
of evolutionism . . . out of our universities, colleges, and high schools."
Christian Workers summarized the fundamentalist view. "The harm
that Charles Darwin did to human thinking," the editors explained,

"can never be estimated on earth. That he made valuable contributions to science will not be denied, but the conclusions that he and his followers have drawn from them have darkened men's souls and made them the beasts that Prussianism demonstrates today."[23]

Once the German threat abated, many fundamentalists began to associate communism with Darwinian ideas. "Evolution," T. C. Horton wrote on behalf of the World's Christian Fundamentals Association, "is the devil's device to undermine the very foundations upon which our nation is founded. . . . Now this Godless, Christless, senseless, Satanic imposition—bred in hell, boosted by the devil and his demons, broadcasted by puny specimens of scholastic attainment—is creating a Bolshevistic spirit which will—if unchecked—Russianize America."[24]

During the 1920s, the strident opponents of evolution overshadowed the voices of moderation and reconciliation. Enough fundamentalists had linked Darwinism with military might, atheism, communism, and Protestant liberalism that the voices of those who in the past had not viewed Darwin as a major threat went mute. James Gray represented fundamentalists' growing opposition. In a pamphlet titled "Why a Christian Cannot Be an Evolutionist" he argued that faith and evolution were mutually exclusive. Christians who tried to blend the two were both bad Christians and bad evolutionists. This position was slowly becoming the party line. "The Bible is in full conformity with all that we see," F. C. Jennings declared, "evolution is opposed to it." A Kentucky minister agreed that it was "impossible" for an evolutionist to be a Christian. "It goes without saying," he concluded, "that we should be merciful to this species, as we are commanded to be merciful to beasts, and this, of course, should include the progeny of beasts." Dixon concluded, "there is only one thing worse than atheistic evolution and that is the theistic evolution, which makes God responsible for this infernal method of doing things." The African-American *National Baptist Union-Review* counseled young ministers to avoid spending time studying "philosophy, if it is a philosophy that ascribes man's origins to protoplasm, to mollusks, to tadpoles, to mud. No time to explain how man sprang from the monkey or the ape, the orangutan, or from any other inferior creature. His mission is to preach man as a direct creation of the Almighty."[25]

Skepticism about evolutionary theory drove many white fundamentalists and some black evangelicals to doubt the value of science as a

Fundamentalists often linked their opposition to Darwinian evolution with their opposition to communism. They saw both as part of a larger satanic conspiracy to undermine Christian beliefs and convictions.
  "Away with God," *King's Business* (May 1925), 197.

whole. "The devil," *King's Business* asserted, was using scientists and Bolsheviks "in his deadly desire to destroy the faith of men in the Christ of the Bible." Rather than seek to penetrate the academy and engage with the ideas of the day, the faithful instead chose to abandon it. Their oversimplification of evolutionary theory and wholesale rejection of modern science further encouraged critics' depiction of fundamentalists as anti-intellectual.[26]

As radical evangelicals ramped up their efforts to expose the "falla-cies" of evolution, their language—that evolution was an unproven and unprovable theory rather than a fact—stuck. John Roach Straton took on New York's American Museum of Natural History over the issue. The museum had opened a new exhibit, the "Age of Man," built on the assumption that humans had evolved from lower forms of life over time. Straton claimed that the exhibit was "a misspending" of "tax-payer's money" and was "poisoning the minds of New York school children by false and bestial theories of evolution." The minister called on the museum to offer an alternative exhibit displaying the Genesis creation account. He received a thoughtful reply from one of the cura-tors explaining in great detail why the minister's proposal did not align with the museum's mission and methods. Museum president Henry Fairfield Osborn was less gracious. "This is a very serious matter," he told Straton. "I would remind you of the scriptural quotation, 'If any of ye offend the little ones, which believe in me, it were better for him to hang a millstone around his neck and plunge into the depths of the sea." Turning the tables on the minister, he accused fundamentalists of deceiving children. As the evolution debate grew, a *Los Angeles Times* journalist suggested that one way to "start a war" was to "whisper 'evo-lution' in the ear of a fundamentalist." As fundamentalists and the press well understood, the battle for the hearts and minds of the nation's schoolchildren was just beginning.[27]

The fundamentalists who took up the cudgel against evolution found an ally in the person of William Jennings Bryan. After drop-ping out of Wilson's cabinet during the war, the Great Commoner dedicated his twilight years to hawking Florida real estate and ad-vocating traditional Protestantism. He challenged theologically liberal approaches to the Bible, believing that modernist interpreta-tions had wreaked havoc among both his fellow Presbyterians and Christians more generally. He had little interest in premillennial-ism but simply defended what he saw as the classic faith. As he honed his message, he began to view Darwinian evolution as a primary symbol of the dangers of modern thought. His bout against evolu-tion brought unprecedented attention to the fundamentalist movement and positioned it as an adversary of progressive thought and politics.[28]

Bryan's message resonated with many people, including—but certainly not exclusively—fundamentalists. He toured the country, preaching against Darwin in churches east and west, north and south. His rousing addresses condemned evolutionary theory, its social implications, and the educators who brought it into their classrooms. He believed that Darwinism undermined the faith of students and that a secular bias had overtaken American education. "The special reason," Bryan preached in 1921, "for bringing to the attention of Christians at this time the evil that Darwinism is doing is to show that atheists and agnostics are not only *claiming* but *enjoying* higher rights and greater privileges in this land than Christians; that is, they are able to propagate their views at *public expense* while Christianity must be taught at the *expense of Christians*." Bryan shared with fundamentalists a strong desire to hold schools accountable for the curricula they put into their classrooms. He encouraged taxpayers to demand that their teachers stop instructing students in scientific ideas that undermined faith. Always the populist, Bryan believed that local communities, not school boards or professional educators, should be dictating the curriculum utilized in tax-supported classrooms. In response to those who questioned why he had plunged into a religious controversy, the Democratic leader explained that his antievolution campaign did not represent a career change. "I have not turned aside from politics," he forthrightly declared. Instead he viewed the battle against evolution as part of his long battle for good government and a healthy nation.[29]

Bryan began his antievolution crusade as no more than a tangential part of the fundamentalist movement. He cared little for the quintessential fundamental, individual salvation. He was a postmillennialist, a reformer, and a political progressive who preached toleration and practiced it by working regularly with Catholics and Jews. He also lacked interest in many of the social issues that animated fundamentalism. Although he rejected the liberal biblical criticism emanating from seminaries in the United States and Europe, he had no interest in turning the Bible into a set of propositions that when aligned revealed a hidden plan of the ages. Rather, the Great Commoner represented the American Protestant majority, neither fundamentalist nor modernist but something in the middle. Nevertheless, as the evolution debate intensified, Bryan came to represent for many Americans the face of fundamentalism.

Like Bryan, fundamentalists had been working to eradicate evolution theory from public school curriculum. J. Frank Norris led the charge in Texas, where he lobbied the state legislature. He also rallied both BIOLA and MBI to the cause. Faculty at BIOLA called for citizens "to demand" that the government not use their taxes to support the "enemies of the Bible who are used of Satan to spoil the lives of the students." In Arkansas, Ben Bogard published a document identifying how candidates for state office voted on evolution bills. "Our motto," he counseled, "should be PUT NO EVOLUTIONIST IN OFFICE THIS YEAR." Then he told parishioners and readers of his magazine exactly how to vote. Straton's effort to eradicate the teaching of evolution in the New York public schools provoked numerous impassioned and insulting responses. "When Darwin said man originated from a monkey," one disgruntled correspondent wrote him, "he must have seen your face." Fundamentalists encouraged their fellow believers to elect school board members who would prioritize Bible instruction in public school curriculum.[30]

As fundamentalists' efforts to get evolution banned from public schools continued, they sensed the most potential in Tennessee. As a result, many prominent leaders, including Riley, Norris, Straton, Sunday, Bryan, and Baptist T. T. Martin, visited the state to urge citizens and representatives to act against evolution. In 1925 they achieved their greatest victory. The Tennessee state legislature passed the "Butler Bill," named after its sponsor, John Butler, which prohibited schools from teaching "any theory that denies the story of Divine Creation of man as taught in the Bible, and teach instead thereof that man descended from a lower order of animals." Violating the law resulted in a misdemeanor fine ranging from one hundred to five hundred dollars.[31]

The Butler Bill caught the attention of the young American Civil Liberties Union (ACLU). Founded in response to government repression of citizens' rights during World War I, the ACLU defended the First Amendment liberties of Americans from all walks of life. Because ACLU leaders interpreted the Butler Bill as a violation of free speech as well as academic freedom, they offered to defend any teacher accused

of violating the new law. They ultimately hoped to challenge the con-
stitutionality of all antievolution bills. Learning of the ACLU's offer,
local city boosters in Dayton, Tennessee, sensed an opportunity to
bring attention to their city. They recruited twenty-four-year-old John
Thomas Scopes, a science teacher and football coach, to confess to
teaching evolution and to serve as the ACLU's defendant in a test case.

As Scopes and local prosecutors prepared for trial, events quickly
spiraled out of their control. Although Bryan had not practiced law in
many years, he volunteered his services to the prosecution. Then famed
criminal defense attorney Clarence Darrow volunteered for the defense. He later explained that his goal was not just to defeat the Butler
Bill but to challenge the growing fundamentalist movement as a whole.
"My object, and my only object, was to focus the attention of the
country on the programme of Mr. Bryan and the other fundamentalists
in America." The nation, he believed, was "in danger" of succumbing to
"religious fanaticism." Darrow saw himself as a crusader for truth and
righteousness, just a different truth and a different righteousness than
Bryan professed. "To me it was perfectly clear that the proceedings bore
little semblance to a court case," Darrow recalled, "but I realized that
there was no limit to the mischief that might be accomplished unless
the country was roused to the evil at hand." He publicly offered his
services to Scopes and the ACLU, leaving the organization little choice
but to accept. This was the only time Darrow ever worked for free.
The ACLU's goal of overseeing a narrow test case was soon overshadowed by the actions of those with much larger agendas. Scopes would
no longer really be on trial. Instead, Bryan and Darrow planned to
debate the facts of evolution, the nature of true religion, and the proper
balance between individual liberty and majority rule.[32]

Journalists from around the nation and world descended on Tennessee
for the trial, where they joined Darrow in framing it as a contest over
fundamentalism, despite the fact that millions of Americans who had
nothing to do with fundamentalism rejected evolution. No writer had a
greater impact on the unfolding controversy than the famous and acerbic
critic H. L. Mencken. Like Darrow, the sage of Baltimore labeled just
about everyone who disagreed with evolution theory a "fundamentalist"
regardless of his or her actual religious affiliations. His reporting—
imprecise as it was—helped decouple the term "fundamentalism" from

the movement that had made it. The rest of the nation's leading journalists followed suit, linking opposition to evolution with fundamentalist Christianity even though evolution had not been a significant
factor in the rise of the fundamentalist movement, nor had fundamentalism been at the base of Bryan's crusade, nor were fundamentalists
the only Americans uncomfortable with Darwin's theories. By 1931
Frederick Lewis Allen could easily—although incorrectly—assert that
the fundamentalist-modernist controversy "reached its climax in the
Scopes case." As much as fundamentalists tried to emphasize their
broader agenda, the connection between their work and that of the antievolution movement stuck. They hoped to prepare humanity for the
second coming of Christ; instead, they were locked in a no-win debate
against the nation's most respected scientists, sharpest skeptics, and
leading journalists. Fundamentalism, in the eyes of much of the nation,
represented a retrograde religion that evoked histories of medieval crusades and inquisitions.[33]

The trial began on Friday, July 10, with jury selection. Darrow
opened the defense's case the following Monday with a dramatic speech
that linked the antievolution movement with fundamentalism, ignorance, and bigotry. "Hard as it is for me to bring my mind to conceive
it, almost impossible as it is to put my mind back into the sixteenth
century," he told the packed courtroom, "I am going to argue" the case
"as if it was serious, and as if it was a death struggle between two civili-
zations." He claimed that evolution was not an issue until "the fundamentalists got into Tennessee" and warned that "fires . . . have been
lighted in America to kindle religious bigotry and hate."[34]

When Bryan finally got a chance to address the court a few days
later, he reiterated the arguments he had been making for years. As the
Great Commoner spoke, the large crowd frequently interrupted him
with cheers and amens. "The question," he explained, "is can a minority in this state come in and compel a teacher to teach that the Bible is
not true and make the parents of these children pay the expenses of the
teacher to tell their children what these people believe is false and dangerous?" Bryan repeated his usual warning that undermining Genesis
undermined the rest of the Bible, which in turn transformed students
into moral relativists. Then he turned the tables on the defense team.
Scopes's attorneys had earlier tried to humiliate Bryan by reading from

his old statements on the benefits of religious liberty; he responded by reading from Darrow's defense of Leopold and Loeb. Darrow had argued that his clients' exposure to Nietzsche and Darwin through scholars, libraries, and the University of Chicago helped explain their crime. Bryan seized on this point to argue that even Darrow knew that evolution corrupted vulnerable students.[35]

Mencken was not impressed with Bryan's courtroom performance. "He can never be the peasants' President," Mencken wrote, "but there is still a chance to be the peasant's Pope. . . . It is a tragedy, indeed, to begin life as a hero and end it as a buffoon." Sensing that his job was done, the journalist left town before the trial had ended. He assumed that all that remained "of the great cause of the State of Tennessee against the infidel Scopes is the formal business of bumping off the defendant." But on the seventh day of the trial God did not rest. Judge John T. Raulston had been worried all along that his second-floor courtroom could not bear the weight of the unprecedented crowds squeezed into it, so he decided to move the monkey trial outside. Darrow immediately objected to a large sign on the courthouse wall that counseled, "Read Your Bible." The prosecution pounced, noting that Darrow's team had just finished trying to prove that the Bible and evolution were compatible; hence they should have no objection to an admonition to read the Bible.[36]

Then the defense made a stunning move. Bryan had attacked Darrow's expert scientific witnesses, asserting that although they might be able to testify regarding science, they could not speak on biblical interpretation or what Genesis did or did not mean. This gave Darrow an opening he eagerly exploited. He called opposing counsel William Jennings Bryan to serve as an expert witness on the Bible. Bryan took the bait, asking that in return for taking the stand he get a turn to question the questioner. Darrow began by asking Bryan if he interpreted the Bible literally. The former presidential contender answered carefully, explaining that he interpreted passages as their authors intended them. Metaphors, he explained, were metaphors, and he understood them as such. While Bryan believed that Bishop Ussher's chronology placing the creation of humans at about 4004 B.C. was accurate, he acknowledged that he thought that God did not create the planet itself in six twenty-four-hour days and that it was much older. Darrow relentlessly kept at Bryan for hours, quizzing him on the story of Jonah and

Although generations of Americans have viewed the Scopes "Monkey" Trial of
1925, especially the dramatic interrogation of William Jennings Bryan (seated with
fan) by Clarence Darrow (standing), as the climax of the fundamentalist-modernist
controversy, the trial's true legacy was its facilitation of a redefinition of the term
"fundamentalism."
  Courtesy of Library of Congress, LC-USZ62–114986.

the whale, the origins of Cain's wife, and the account of Joshua making
the sun stand still. Skeptics had long asked Darrow's questions and
Bryan delivered the traditional orthodox responses.

The verbal chess match often turned testy. Bryan, whose answers
Darrow repeatedly cut off, insisted that defense counsel allow him to
give full replies. Darrow objected, asking that the judge ensure that
Bryan not make speeches "every time I ask him a question." At other
times, however, the duel was more lighthearted. Darrow interrupted
one of the witness's responses by imploring him not to talk about "free
silver"—one of the pillars of Bryan's famous 1896 presidential campaign
(a campaign Darrow had supported). For the most part Bryan answered
the self-proclaimed agnostic's challenges fairly well, but there was not a
witness alive who could completely fend off this master interrogator.[37]

The other members of Bryan's prosecution team repeatedly asked the judge to end the examination, but Bryan refused to budge from the stand, insisting that he was willing to undergo questions for as long as Darrow wanted to keep asking them. "These gentlemen have not had much chance," he explained. "They did not come here to try this case. They came here to try revealed religion. I am here to defend it and they can ask me any question they please." Then things got nasty— Bryan accused Darrow of referring to the locals as "yokels," and Darrow told Bryan that the Commoner insulted "every man of science and learning in the world" with his "fool religion." His animosity aroused, Darrow explained that his purpose in continuing the testimony was to prevent "bigots and ignoramuses from controlling the education of the United States." Bryan responded that he was "simply trying to protect the word of God against the greatest atheist or agnostic in the United States."[38]

Bryan never had a chance to cross-examine Darrow. The next morning the judge expunged Bryan's testimony from the official record and turned the case over to the jury. Bryan had prepared a lengthy closing argument, but since the defense chose not to deliver a summation, by rule the prosecution could not do so either. After nine minutes of deliberation, the jury found Scopes guilty. Even Darrow had asked for a guilty verdict so that he could appeal the case to the state supreme court. Bryan responded with a short but very prescient speech about the significance of the trial, noting that eventually the "people"—the ultimate jury—would rule on the issues fueling the controversy. Darrow, never one to cede the last word, interpreted the case differently. He believed that it represented the rebirth of religious bigotry. "I think this case will be remembered because it is the first case of this sort since we stopped trying people in America for witchcraft."[39]

Bryan immediately made plans to publish his undelivered closing argument, which summarized and contextualized his antievolution campaign. The speech revealed how substantially his work differed from that of fundamentalists. He had no expectation of a coming apocalypse but was still the same reformer who had advocated woman suffrage, direct election of senators, and a graduated income tax. "By paralyzing the hope of reform," he warned, the evolutionary hypothesis "discourages those who labor for the improvement of man's condition." Bryan, in contrast, believed that "every upward-looking man or woman seeks to lift the level upon which mankind stands, and they trust that they will see beneficent changes during the brief span of their own lives." Bryan represented the classic evangelical reform tradition, not the fundamentalists with whom he had made common cause on the issue of evolution.[40]

On Sunday, July 26, 1925, less than one week after the trial had ended, the Great Commoner died in his sleep in Dayton during an afternoon nap. Responses to the news varied. "Bryan was a vulgar and common man," Mencken wrote, "a cad undiluted. He was ignorant, bigoted, self-seeking, blatant and dishonest. His career brought him into contact with the first men of his time; he preferred the company of rustic ignoramuses." More than happy to spit on Bryan's grave, he continued, "he seemed only a poor clod like those around him, deluded by a childish theology, full of an almost pathological hatred of all learning, all human dignity, all beauty, all fine and noble things. He was a peasant come home to the dung-pile." Mencken advised his readers, "The job before democracy is to get rid of such canaille." If Americans did not, he predicted, the populist rabble of society would "devour" democracy.[41]

Fundamentalists had a different take. "Unlike Clarence Darrow," Moody Monthly editors wrote, "we never voted for him [Bryan] for President. His politics were not ours." Nevertheless, Bryan's moral and religious views had earned him their friendship and loyalty. King's Business eulogized him as well, comparing him to biblical heroes Joshua, David, Daniel, Paul, and the early-church martyrs in his forthright stand for the faith.[42]

While fundamentalists mourned Bryan, some recognized that the Scopes trial had damaged the credibility of their movement. Bryan "was the only man in the country," Moody editors acknowledged, who could have brought evolution "before the world as it is today." But "had our counsel been sought and taken in advance, the fight would not have occurred in the place and under the circumstances in which it did." Barnhouse, a libertarian who tended to be more temperate than many of his fundamentalist colleagues, was even more critical of the monkey trial. "We say that the bill never should have been passed. . . . We do not believe that any majority should force its opinion upon a minority in a religious matter and—more important yet . . . you cannot legislate men into believing or being anything." Barnhouse's opinion, however, was not common among the faithful.[43]

At the time of the trial much of the African-American religious press supported Bryan's crusade. The *National Baptist Voice* ran the Great Commoner's entire ten-thousand-word address unedited over multiple issues of its denominational magazine. Black intellectuals, however, had a different appraisal. W. E. B. DuBois complained that the fundamentalist's "answer to Science is Dogma; and his reason for bringing it forward is again, not perverse hatred of the Truth, but the Shape of Fear." National Association for the Advancement of Colored People leader Walter White praised Darrow for his lifetime of work on behalf of African Americans. "He has shown that the agnostics and free thinkers are friends of the Negro rather than the fundamentalists whose religion, which should make them the best friends of the people of other races, actually stops at the color line." The *Chicago Defender* also criticized Bryan. An unsigned editorial warned that the Great Commoner had "died fighting for FUNDAMENTALISM in Christianity" while "also fighting against your fundamental rights in the Constitution."[44]

By the late 1920s, fundamentalists were still waging a relentless battle against evolution. But rather than keep beating their heads against a scientific brick wall, a few began to assess the strengths and weaknesses of the fundamentalist position. *King's Business* ran a series of articles, "Errors of Fundamentalist Science," by Dudley Joseph Whitney. He cataloged the sloppy scientific work done by fundamentalists and demonstrated how their errors encouraged evolutionists to ignore them. "There are in fact many very convincing reasons for believing in at least a large amount of evolution," he wrote, "and if in addition it happens that much of the conviction in favor of evolution comes from mistakes in fundamentalist science, an urgent need exists for the fundamentalists to correct their errors."[45]

Moody Monthly cautioned the antievolution zealots, fearing that numerous state bills, especially in the South, were poorly crafted. Editors believed that schools should provide space for discussions of some less controversial forms of evolution. "We believe the law should be carefully drawn, and that in drawing it legislators should seek the aid of conservative scholars. . . . Not a few of our lawmakers are in need of

instruction on the subject of evolution lest their laws recoil against the
position they are enacted to promote or maintain." The editors later clarified their position: "no intelligent person opposes the teaching of evolution as a 'theory,' a hypothesis, a guess, whether it be in state-supported
schools or in any other schools, if only it is kept in its proper place as a
theory, or hypothesis, or guess." Foreshadowing the intelligent design
controversy of the late twentieth and twenty-first century, the faithful
wanted their view of creation taught alongside Darwinian evolution as
equal, competing theories.[46]

Fundamentalists worked hard to try to dispel Darrow's and Menck-
en's claims that they proved unable to engage intellectually with major
issues or that they were a regressive movement. When the World's
Christian Fundamentals Association scheduled a debate between William B. Riley and Harry Rimmer on the "days" of creation (Riley
believed they were eons while Rimmer thought they were solar days),
Charles Trumbull told readers of the *Sunday School Times* that the purpose of the debate was "to show the public that Fundamentalists were
not so narrow as to insist on agreement in every detail of Bible interpretation and that they could have honest and legitimate differences of
conviction." Most of the time, however, those differences resulted in
new schisms rather than respectful debate.[47]

Perhaps the most important legacy of the Scopes trial was not its
impact on American education but its central role in facilitating the
redefinition of fundamentalism. Before Scopes, "fundamentalism" referred to a well-defined, close-knit radical evangelical apocalyptic
movement. After the trial and its coverage in the national media, fundamentalism still referred to a specific network of radical evangelicals,
but the meaning of fundamentalism in the popular imagination had
changed. Thanks to the work of Bryan, Darrow, Mencken, and many
others during the antievolution crusade and Scopes trial, "fundamentalism" was transformed for many into a pejorative term. The press,
liberal intellectuals, and theological modernists began using it generi-
cally to refer to all socially conservative, antimodernist, antiscience,
antieducation Christians, whether they had any relationship to the
fundamentalist movement or not. Because many southerners seemed to
fit the new, broader definition of the term, "fundamentalism" evolved
from an apt characterization of a relatively small network of Christians

based primarily in the North and West, with some key players in the South, into a more stereotypical term applied to expressions of Christianity that appeared anti-intellectual, antiprogressive, rural, and intolerant (and often southern-based). The faithful spent the next decade and a half trying to reclaim the term before realizing that their efforts were futile.[48]

As the Scopes trial receded from the headlines, many Americans—especially journalists and religious liberals—expected fundamentalists to grow complacent and to fade into obscurity. But they did not. Their mobilization against the teaching of evolution at the local and state levels signaled their growing political sensibilities and activism. As they sought to integrate faith with broader cultural currents and to use their talents to occupy their nation more fully so as to be prepared for the rapture, new allies and new enemies emerged. Over the decade of the 1920s, fundamentalists' political convictions crystallized, and their willingness to work with others expanded as they labored to challenge the schemes of the Antichrist and to bring revival to the land.

6

SEEKING SALVATION WITH THE GOP

IN 1928 AL SMITH SET his sights on the Democratic nomination for president of the United States. That the New York governor could possibly win the election troubled fundamentalists. Smith seemed to represent everything they had been combating since the end of World War I. He was a product of big-city machine politics, he owed his success to New York's infamous Tammany Hall, and he was the Roman Catholic grandson of immigrants. He opposed Prohibition and he drank and smoked. Fundamentalists feared that to let their country fall into the hands of a wet Irish Romanist was to bring down the wrath of God on their nation. They saw the Smith campaign as a call to action and an opportunity to embody Jesus's call to occupy this world until his return.

"Texas Tornado" J. Frank Norris led the fundamentalist crusade against Smith. This Baptist firebrand presided over a five-thousand-member church in Fort Worth. He had long used his pulpit and radio station not just to instill faith but also to combat perceived evils from evolution to modernism to communism. "Instead of deploring controversy," Norris preached, as "some spineless, weak-kneed, pussyfooting folks say, we should rejoice in the opportunity that it presents to advance the truth."[1]

For Norris, advancing the truth often meant battling the political influence—real and feared—of Roman Catholics. His efforts turned tragic, however, in the summer of 1926, when Catholic businessman D. E. Chipps barged into Norris's church office. He had allegedly come to warn Norris to stop disparaging the local Catholic mayor. Never one to cower in the face of a threat, the minister calmly opened his desk drawer, pulled out a loaded revolver, and emptied the chamber. Three bullets slammed into the chest of the unarmed Chipps. In a spectacular murder trial a few months later, the jury affirmed the minister's claim that he had acted in self-defense. The verdict confirmed the power of white Protestant religion in the South, as well as a broader indifference to Catholic rights and liberties. Norris returned to his religious work immediately after the trial.

For the first time in American history, Norris warned during the Smith campaign, the pope might succeed in putting one of his lieutenants into the Oval Office. He determined to do everything he could to foil the Vatican's plans. Despite his long-standing membership in the party of Andrew Jackson, he was not going to vote Democrat if Smith won the nomination. In a typical sermon against the governor, Norris opened with the classic premillennial text 2 Timothy 3:1: "This know also, that in the last days perilous times shall come." Linking the Smith campaign with the growing power of Italy's fascist leader Benito Mussolini, Norris believed that an end-times, worldwide apocalyptic Catholic conspiracy was afoot to subvert legitimate government and the Christian faith. As the election neared, he preached all over the South, encouraging fundamentalists and other white Protestants to vote for Republican candidate Herbert Hoover. He hoped to mobilize radical evangelicals from around the nation whose political loyalties had traditionally been shaped more by region than religion.[2]

Norris's work exposed the subtle changes under way among radical evangelicals. Over the first decades of the twentieth century the political differences between northern and southern fundamentalists slowly eroded. Together they watched and routinely commented on national politics while developing a political philosophy that paradoxically blended calls for an activist, interventionist government on social and moral issues like Prohibition with a growing commitment to states' rights in education and social welfare. Northern fundamentalists, in alignment

with business leaders, advocated limited government and an unregu-
lated economy in all areas, except where the state could serve their particular interests. Southerners were less enthused about defending the
rights of corporations, but they worried about the direction in which
the Democratic Party was moving as the power and influence of urban
ethnics grew. Arch-antifundamentalist Shailer Mathews called it "no
accident that the Fundamentalist in his effort to rehabilitate the theology of a pre-democratic, pre-industrial, pre-scientific society should be
as much of a Tory in social affairs as he is in theology." While Mathews's
vitriol often overshadowed his analysis, he was right—in the wake of
the world war, fundamentalists were lining up with economic and political conservatives more closely than ever. Whatever inhibitions some
early premillennialists may have felt about political engagement had almost vanished as northern and increasing numbers of southern fundamentalists made a home in the right wing of the GOP. By the end of the
1930s, fundamentalists North and South were emerging as the leading
voices of Christian political conservatism.[3]

Fundamentalists and their predecessors had long believed that the state
could serve as a tool of moral suasion. Although they worried that the
federal government would eventually succumb to the Antichrist, they
had little trouble in the meantime asking political leaders to use their
authority to regulate the entertainment industries or to craft strict laws
governing questions of morality. No issue, however, was as important
to early fundamentalists as securing and then enforcing Prohibition.

Jesus may have turned water into wine, but his fundamentalist followers did not. Nor did they approve of drinking Satan's brew. In the
nineteenth century evangelicals worked alongside other reformers to
curb the influence of alcohol in American life, especially among the
immigrant and working classes who seemed to suffer most from its
abuse. They had some success, especially at the local and state levels,
and in the twentieth century their fundamentalist successors followed
suit. The battle against booze reinforced fundamentalists' faith in concerted political action and the power of the federal government to dic-
tate morality. As increasing numbers of states and counties went dry,
James Gray rejoiced. "These wonders," he preached in the early twen-

tieth century, "are enough to awaken the expectation that the Millennium is at hand." But before he got too carried away, he reminded his audience that it was "not to be expected in this way, good as this way is." Still, fundamentalists had a responsibility to improve the world around them. Too many Americans, Gray lamented, thought that fundamentalists were "so absorbed in . . . heavenly citizenship, as to have no interest in the citizenship of earth. But this is not so." Instead he reiterated to the faithful the importance of engaging with the world. "I appeal to you, my brethren! Do not despise your earthly citizenship. Do not commit political suicide. Do not disenfranchise yourselves."[4]

During World War I, fundamentalists denounced liquor in no uncertain terms. They saw the conflict as an opportunity to press the government to enact national Prohibition. "What a monster," *King's Business* editorialized, "remorseless, cruel, conscienceless, the liquor traffic is! It would seem as if every owner of brewing or distilling stocks must feel as if his fingers were dripping blood, and he must shudder when any one even hints the word, patriotism." That President Wilson did not use his executive authority and wartime powers to curb the manufacture of alcohol infuriated the faithful. "Why," the fundamentalist magazine asked, "is our President who is not afraid of Kaiser Wilhelm so afraid of Kaiser Beer?" The editors further suggested that American businesses stop wasting money and resources on the production of candy, ice-cream sodas, soft drinks, and chewing gum. While fundamentalists did not often fit the stereotypes of dour killjoys, attacks on ice cream could not have helped their public image.[5]

Billy Sunday led the fundamentalist assault on booze. "I am the sworn, eternal, uncompromising enemy of the Liquor Traffic," he preached in his most famous temperance sermon. "I ask no quarter and I give none. I have drawn the sword in defense of God, home, wife, children and native land." He routinely offered dramatic testimonies to illustrate the impact of alcohol on families and claimed that drink manufacturers had repeatedly threatened to silence him. In a typical New York City revival meeting he shouted what journalists described as "invectives" at the liquor traffic and declared, "no man can pray 'Thy kingdom come' and then walk up and vote for the dirty, stinking saloon. You can't pray 'Thy kingdom come' and keep booze on your sideboard." Impressed with Sunday's work, William Jennings Bryan predicted that when Prohibition finally happened, the baseball player–evangelist would deserve the credit.[6]

Fundamentalists rejoiced in early 1920 when the Eighteenth Amendment to the US Constitution took effect. It prohibited "the manufacture, sale, or transportation of intoxicating liquors within, the importation thereof into, or the exportation thereof from the United States and all territory subject to the jurisdiction thereof." The battle over booze proved that the work of godly people could change the law and that the government could legislate morality. Although fundamentalists had played only a minor role in the amendment's passage, they soon became its staunchest defenders. They had a knack for picking losing battles.

Fundamentalists' economic views proved less consistent than their ideas about alcohol. Some, like Billy Sunday and the leaders of Moody Bible Institute, worked closely with corporate barons, and they praised the benefits that big business brought to the nation. Others, however, questioned the merits of free market capitalism. During the early twentieth century those radical evangelicals who were not taking substantial offerings from captains of industry routinely viewed the rise of huge, powerful corporations and the exploitation of labor as indications of the nation's growing degeneracy. They interpreted economic consolidation and corporatization as signs of the imminent rapture. Blackstone called the "accumulation of riches, in the hands of a few men . . . characteristic of the present times" and proof that the tribulation was near. "The spirit of combine represented by Rockefeller, Morgan, and the great trust idea," pentecostal W. H. Cossum wrote, "is finding an enlarged sphere in the call for [an] international federation with a world president," who "will evolve in a few successive stages into the Antichrist." Like their Social Gospel counterparts, these premillennialists emphasized the responsibilities of the rich to the poor and often supported the rights of workers to organize and use strikes in their quest for justice. Few premillennialists, however, marched with workers. They interpreted growing economic inequality as an inevitable sign of the last days, but they did not see it as something they should work against.[7]

Many early premillennialists criticized not just large corporations but wealthy individuals. "He is coming!" one pentecostal warned, "but the millionaire continues to grind down the hire of the laborer, whilst he goes on piling up his heaps of gold and silver, or spending lavishly on fabulous feasts and orgies, all unconscious that he is a proof that we are in the last days." Scofield believed that economic inequality would inevitably provoke God's wrath. "Is it not among the possibilities that almighty God may have something to say of this civilization, by way of judgment, by way of catastrophe," he wrote, because Americans had created "a social order which is founded upon greed and avarice?" Government, he argued, had two functions—the protection of life and property. It had failed on both accounts. "Governments have never learned yet how to so legislate as to fairly distribute the fruits of the industry of their people." Echoing Jesus's condemnation of the rich young ruler, *King's Business* explained, "the rich with their idleness and display and mad waste of wealth and stuffing of their overfed and diseased bodies, are the real authors of the most desperate and dangerous forms of anarchy." However, these denunciations never translated into action. The premillennialists who had access to corporate leaders were far more likely to solicit donations than to confront their patrons about workplace injustice.[8]

Around the turn of the century premillennialists carefully watched as working-class men and women organized. Workers hoped that unionization would help them deal more effectively with the tremendous power of corporations. Philip Mauro saw the growth of organized labor and working-class dissent as precursors to the rise of the Antichrist. His tone, however, displayed the populist sympathies common among many early premillennialists. He noted in 1912 that rapidly increasing consumption had so transformed American society that "the toilers" dedicated too much of their lives and energies to producing unnecessary goods for the wealthy. "Is it then to be wondered at," he asked, "that the working people are ready to demolish a social system which operates in such manner that while they are providing expensive contrivances for the amusement of the rich, the cost of the actual necessities of life to themselves is steadily advancing?" Mauro was less troubled, however, by how his own highly lucrative work helping corporations protect their intellectual property rights had affected the toilers.[9]

Into the 1910s radical evangelicals sometimes sided with workers in labor-management conflicts. Arno Gaebelein, for example, supported strikers during the Ludlow Massacre, a catastrophe in which the Colorado state militia attacked and killed protesting miners in 1914. He strongly condemned the Rockefellers, who owned the mines, and interpreted the tragedy in the context of prophecy. Alluding to James 5:1 he warned, "the weeping and howling of the rich men will surely come." Cognizant of the Rockefellers' financial support of liberal Protestantism, he was probably hoping to be around to see them howl. He later noted that "rioting and different acts of violence and lawlessness" among strikers "have to be expected and will increase as this age comes to its prophetic end."[10]

In 1919, labor leaders launched the largest wave of strikes ever to hit the United States. During the war wages had risen and workers in many industries had gained union recognition. Corporations had essentially been forced to the bargaining table by the Wilson administration in order to keep the economy running. When the war ended, workers moved to secure and expand their power while corporations acted to reverse the concessions they had made. The result was substantial and sustained conflict.

Early in Norris's career he sided more with labor than capital. In a sermon in response to violence associated with the 1919 strikes, the Texas Tornado called "the individual bomb thrower who destroys law" not "one whit worse than the powerful profiteer who defies law. When it comes to pass," he preached, "that a few men can sit around a mahogany table and fix the prices of all that we eat and wear, overriding and defying the law of humanity and the law of God, I care not how reputable, how influential, how respectable that coterie of gentlemen may be, they are no more nor less than anarchists and should be dealt with as such." Something, he continued, "is wrong in the system of economics in which we live." He concluded by citing James 5:1, the same verse that had animated Gaebelein.[11]

But the rich were not weeping or howling. In the wake of World War I, political conservatives and corporate leaders discovered that they could exploit the upheaval caused by the Bolshevik revolution to stir fears of workers' organizations and of the subversives supposedly embedded within them. They insisted that communist agitators and "foreign" troublemakers had hijacked the labor movement and that these "aliens," rather than workers' employers, were responsible for unrest. Their claims melded easily with fundamentalists' persistent fears of outsiders and their eschatological expectations of end-times chaos and violence, which helped widen the gulf between fundamentalism and organized labor.

Many Americans fretted that at the root of postwar worker agitation lay the Soviets' 1919 move to foster world revolution through the creation of the Communist International. Seeing communism as the cause of labor strikes reinforced Christians' long-held conviction that Russia was the prophesied great northern kingdom of the last days. The faithful believed that the USSR was seeking global dominance as the world approached Armageddon and that Americans should do everything they could to impede the Soviets' plans. "We are living in the day of the rising tide of color, and that color is RED," Charles Waehlte observed. "In the Book of Revelation we find that everything connected with the Antichrist is Red. . . . Lenine [sic] is simply the awful shadow of the great Red king that is surely coming to reign over a great Red world." L. Nelson Bell, who as a missionary encountered communism firsthand in China, believed that it came "from the bottom of Hell alone." He predicted that "the spirit of the Bolshevists" would "animate the armies which fight against Christ at Armageddon." Fundamentalists' convictions about the coming end times and the rise of "Magog" kept them keenly aware of the expansion of communism around the globe and its potential role in mobilizing working-class discontent.[12]

While American fundamentalists' eschatological expectations substantially influenced their views of communism, there were other reasons for despising all things Red. American anticommunists claimed that Soviets' critiques of traditional marriage fostered exploitative free love and amorality. In Russia, Billy Sunday exclaimed, there isn't "a girl 14 years of age or over that is a virgin." Why? Because once a girl turned fourteen, any "bewhiskered, God-forsaken old scoundrel" could have her. At the same time that African-American evangelicals worried that communists were preaching false religion to southern blacks, white fundamentalists interpreted communists' commitment to racial equality, which they read as code for intermarriage, as further proof of the dangers of the movement. Torrey called Bolshevism one of the "great perils of this country" while *Christian Workers* concluded, "Bol-shevism and the Christian religion can not both survive."[13]

At times fundamentalists' anticommunist fears bordered on the ab-surd (a trait they shared with nonfundamentalist Red-hunters). The faithful identified Albert Einstein as a significant threat to the nation as an intellectual, a scientist, a German, and a Jew. Los Angeles minister Louis Bauman called Einstein an "anti-God crusader" who had devel-oped "that non-understandable something known as 'relativity'" sim-ply to fool people into thinking he was smart. Gaebelein associated Einstein with the "apostate Jews" supposedly responsible for master-minding communism and called him a "much over-rated" scientist. "Doctor Jekyll of mathematics," he lamented, "became the crouching Mr. Hyde of radicalism." William Bell Riley even took a swipe at Ein-stein's masculinity. "For Einstein, a Communist renegade from his own land, welcomed to this country with open arms by the Intelligentsia, the flag of the stars and stripes should be torn from its staff, lest its silken folds entangle the long hair of this German Communist." Ein-stein became a convenient canvas on which many fundamentalists pro-jected their fears about gender, communism, Jews, and science.[14]

Convinced that the United States needed to do more to protect itself from the communist threat, the faithful cheered the work of those government agencies that made it their mission to root out subversives. Fundamentalists particularly praised Attorney General A. Mitchell Palmer and Bureau of Investigation director J. Edgar Hoover, who had orchestrated a campaign against alleged Reds residing in the United States. Showing little regard for civil liberties or constitutional rights, Palmer and Hoover oversaw a series of raids that led to thousands of incarcerations and hundreds of deportations. Supporting the Depart-ment of Justice's aggressive tactics, the *Western Recorder* insisted that the Bolshevik "anarchist as justly deserves death for spreading this poison as does the convicted murderer." A few fundamentalists, however, re-sponded to the communist threat by doing more than just preaching against radicalism. Mark Matthews repeatedly offered his services to J. Edgar Hoover. "We are in critical times," he wrote Hoover. "I no-tice from present reports that you yourself and your Department are being double-crossed and spied upon. I might be of great service in detecting and helping in such things, as I move in the several spheres in which information might be secured." He asked only for a bureau badge in return. Hoover politely informed the minister that "only regularly appointed Special Agents" could claim the credentials of the FBI. Matthews's G-man badge was going to have to come from God. Despite the rebuff, for the next half century fundamentalists and their evangelical successors saw J. Edgar Hoover as an important ally.[15]

Fundamentalists' anticommunist efforts, like their support of immigration restrictions and their hostility to various civil rights movements, illustrated their profound sense of besiegement. Apocalyptic theology encouraged action but it also encouraged suspicion. If, as fundamentalists believed, they were really on the verge of the greatest cataclysm in history, then they could trust no one. Outsiders—political, religious, and ethnic—represented threats to their religion and to their nation. Their job was to expose those threats until Jesus returned.

As the American anticommunist movement grew, fundamentalists realized that they could turn Red fears to their advantage in the battle against theological liberalism. Communism seemed to be working in conjunction with modernism to fulfill many of the end-times signs that they had predicted decades earlier and embodied all of the attributes of Antichrist rule. James Gray warned in his aptly titled sermon, "Modernism a Foe to Good Government," that the inroads of liberal faith threatened the nation's foundations and ultimately made the United States vulnerable to foreign, communist powers. The modernists' "will for peace, the social gospel, the league of nations, resolutions of conventions, laws of congress, the abolition of our army and navy," Gray explained, represented a "sinister pacifism" crafted in Moscow. He warned that the continued growth of modernism would "result in only one thing, and that is the overthrow of our government." While fundamentalists' politics had been under suspicion during the war, their loyalty would never be questioned again. In the postwar period they turned the tables on modernists, linking liberalism of thought and deed with communism and atheism. The move ensured a vigorous concern with politics both domestic and global.[16]

Fundamentalists' anxieties over communism influenced their views of organized labor in the postwar period. As concerns about socialists, atheists, and immigrants intensified in the 1920s, fundamentalists' empathies shifted. They began to see worker unrest rather than corporate exploitation as a sign of the times. In a representative revival sermon, Billy Sunday claimed that "weasel-eyed, hog-jowled, good-for-nothing, God-forsaken, iniquitous, rapacious buffoons and charlatans, and mountebanks and poltroons and marplots and moral perverts" had deceived the working class. A sense of mistrust and suspicion clouded the faithful's views. Rather than trusting workers to know what was in their best interests, radical evangelicals began to see laborers as misguided dupes of subversives.[17]

With the Red Scare gaining momentum, fundamentalists began to accuse unions of doing the work of the devil. They no longer interpreted the rise of behemoth corporations as a bitter sign of last-days injustice. While James had predicted that as the end of the world approached the rich would be weeping and howling, fundamentalists instead honed in on workers' groups as the most likely source of devilish trouble that would help set the economic stage for the Antichrist. Communists' explicit atheism combined with their call for the workers of the world to unite spoke directly to fundamentalists' fears that efforts to organize American workers concealed a darker agenda. "Trade Unionism is a menace to the country," fundamentalist Walter Scott wrote, "and numbers of Christian men are groaning under a tyranny which they are powerless to resist." He further believed that unionism—not corporate monopolies—was paving the way for the Antichrist to take control of the economy. W. O. H. Garman agreed, calling the "hordes of unbelieving reds . . . members of labor unions and the hundreds of thousands of members of other devil created organizations" the "skirmishers of the onrushing forces of the Anti Christ." Mark Matthews's position in Seattle gave him a front-row seat for observing labor agitation and the tactics of the radical Industrial Workers of the World. Focusing on the large numbers of immigrants who were unionizing, he pleaded with President Wilson to force the Department of Labor to take a more aggressive stance. "Issue warrants at once for these enemy aliens and let us deport them," he admonished the president. "Clean the shores of America of the infamous vipers." Billy Sunday, whose bark was always greater than his bite, offered his own unique solution to the problem of labor unrest. He pledged to "smash the radicals," the "Bolshevists and the I.W.W.'s and the Communists . . . who wriggle their damnable carcasses out of the slums of Europe and cross the Atlantic."[18]

The fundamentalists associated with MBI rarely sympathized with labor. In reference to a United Mine Workers' strike that had turned violent, *Moody Monthly* asked, "How long is this going to last in this free country? Has the public any rights which such groups are bound to respect?" The editors praised the historic importance of labor unions but then conveniently complained that they had exceeded their purpose. They singled out progressive labor leader Eugene Debs for blame, alleging that he was "sowing the seed of unrest and hate among the industrial workers of this country." Showing their antistatist colors, the editors called for the federal government to stay out of strikes and complained that government intervention in the economy "checks initiative and thwarts enterprise." "Employers and employees," they clarified in another editorial, "should be left to work out their own problems with as little interference as possible on the part of the Government."[19]

In the postwar era, fundamentalists came to view both the power of organized labor and federal intervention in the economy as dangers to the nation. They believed that labor leaders' and progressive reformers' proposals intended to meet the nation's problems would open it to communism. The rise of massive numbers of workers, many of them immigrants, moving in unison alongside a stronger state met fundamentalists' expectations about last-days conditions. They believed they had no choice but to act against organized labor with the same dedication and urgency that characterized their evangelistic efforts.

As fundamentalists reacted to labor unrest and the communist menace, they evolved from occasional critics of monopolistic corporations into apologists for free market capitalism. For Billy Sunday, securing the nation's Christian foundations meant a return to small government and laissez-faire economics. "There are two schools of thought in our land," he preached. "One is that each individual man and woman shall have his or her right to determine what shall be your happiness. . . . There is the other school where the individual effort, my friends, and initiative is controlled by the State or by force." He made clear that Jesus was no parlor pink. "No man," he preached, "who thinks as Jesus thought can ever be a socialist. No man who thinks as Karl Marx thought can ever be a Christian."[20]

Sunday's perspective mirrored that of the majority of fundamentalists in the 1920s. While earlier generations of premillennialists had little interest in defending the rich and powerful, the Red Scare put the fear of a communist revolution into the souls of fundamentalists. They no longer stood apart from labor-capital conflicts as neutral voices calling for workplace justice but instead became mouthpieces for the wealthy. Amid the shifting social mores that left few traditional customs untouched, fundamentalists sought less conflict, more stability, fewer questions, and more certainty. Nor were they the only Americans to move to the right in the post–World War I years. Their political evolution represented widespread changes under way in the United States as Progressivism died a slow death, changes the Republican Party began to masterfully exploit.

For fundamentalists, as for many other Americans, presidential politics had become an important venue where engaged citizens debated a variety of issues, including those related to drink, labor, the economy, and foreign policy. The 1920 campaign provided fundamentalists with the opportunity to respond to wartime doubts about their loyalty and their commitment to serving their nation by demonstrating how their beliefs intersected with national policy. The faithful felt particularly concerned about the ongoing controversy over the League of Nations, sure that the league had significant implications for Bible prophecy. They hoped to help steer the nation away from foreign entanglements and onto a godly course.

In 1920 Democrats nominated Ohio governor James Cox and former assistant secretary of the navy Franklin Delano Roosevelt for president and vice president; Republicans nominated Ohio senator Warren G. Harding and Massachusetts governor Calvin Coolidge. Like Wilson, the Democratic nominees supported ratification of the Treaty of Versailles and with it American entry into the League of Nations. The Republicans, in contrast, refused to take a clear position. The debate over the treaty fanned many fundamentalists' misgivings about the Democratic Party. Most northern fundamentalists were not likely to vote Democrat anyway, but the League of Nations controversy drove southern fundamentalists to reexamine their loyalty to the Democratic Party. On the Sunday before Election Day, Norris preached against the league, alleging that it might empower the coming Antichrist. Arkansas minister Ben Bogard, who also believed that the League of Nations was foretold in the Bible, laid out for his southern audience the key issues in the presidential campaign. "Liquor and Big Business Will Win No Matter Which Party Wins at the Polls," he lamented. However, one difference separated the Republican from the Democrat candidates—their contrasting positions on the League of Nations. "If you favor the league of nations . . . you should vote for Cox. . . . If you oppose the league," he preached, "you should vote for Harding." He instructed followers not to vote blindly Democrat. Expressing a sentiment that would become increasingly common among southern fundamentalists over the next few decades, he assured his audience that "each one of us can vote as we please with no party collar about our necks." With this campaign, the solid Democratic South began to show some signs of cracking.[21]

Mark Matthews was one of the few fundamentalists who publicly supported Cox. He accused the Republican presidential candidate of being either the puppet of reactionary forces or a liar. "Mr. Harding," he preached, "is either foolish or insincere." He then assured his congregation, "If we were in the League at the present time we could bring about world peace, tranquility, progress, and prosperity." Strange words for a premillennialist, yet they illustrated the continuing tension believers faced as they anticipated the second coming while simultaneously working to occupy the nation and prepare the way for the return of Jesus.[22]

The election proved to be a significant victory for the Republican Party. Harding polled sixteen million votes to Cox's nine million. During the campaign, Harding had famously avowed, "America's present need is not heroics, but healing; not nostrums, but normalcy; not revolution, but restoration; not agitation, but adjustment; not surgery, but serenity; not the dramatic, but the dispassionate; not experiment, but equipoise; not submergence in internationality but sustainment in triumphant nationality." In many ways his call for a return to normalcy represented a repudiation of the reform efforts of progressives. That such sentiments proved so popular reflected the changing political temperature of much of the nation at the time. Harding was leading the Republican Party and the American people to the right and radical evangelicals were happy to go along for the ride.[23]

Fundamentalists responded to the Republican victory in numerous ways. Blackstone sent the president-elect a copy of *Jesus Is Coming* and telegrammed him some advice. "The restoration of Israel to their homeland in Palestine," he warned, "betokens the approaching end of

the times of the Gentiles." He hoped that the president would help facilitate this restoration. The popular writer also counseled the Ohio
Republican to "beware of International entanglements. God has reserved our nation for special service in the impending crux of human
history." *Moody Monthly* reacted to the election results with a short but
insightful editorial noting that "in the North at least, evangelical men
of the conservative type, and especially those known as Bible teachers
and students of prophecy," voted Republican. In part their vote was a
response to the League of Nations debate, but it also reflected the
growing antistatist, antitax sensibilities of northern fundamentalists.[24]

As president, Harding proved to be popular among fundamentalists
who appreciated his repeated invocations of God and the "old time
religion." T. C. Horton called him an "example" to "stir the hearts of
the laymen of the country." *Moody Monthly* editors praised Harding for
keeping the nation out of the league and "free from entangling alliances." "We are thankful just now for a Federal administration," they
further editorialized, "which seems honestly disposed to do its best for
the nation, for it is generally admitted that the President has gathered
around him an efficient cabinet with a genius for team work." But un-
beknownst to fundamentalists, Harding's administration was one of
the most corrupt in American history. Its most famous debacle—one of
many—was the Teapot Dome scandal; secretary of the interior Albert
Fall leased oil-rich federal lands in Wyoming to private companies in
exchange for large bribes. He was the first cabinet officer ever to go to
jail. Nor did Harding's private life measure up to fundamentalist standards. He had many affairs, including one with a much younger woman
who regularly visited him for trysts in the White House.[25]

When Harding died in 1923, fundamentalists seemed truly saddened.
Despite Mark Matthews's opposition to Harding during the campaign, he
preached a moving sermon about the "Christian statesman, the Christian
gentleman, the Christian husband, and the Christian brother." He called
Harding "as gentle as a virgin" (an ironic choice of words given Harding's
penchant for taking rather than preserving virginity). Aimee McPherson, unaware of the president's wild antics and corrupt politics, preached
a funeral oration on "Harding, the Christian President." Lyman Stewart
praised him as "an earnest Christian man," who "in all his speeches . . .
advocated a return to the Bible and to Bible righteousness."[26]

Vice president Calvin Coolidge succeeded Harding. The former Massachusetts governor had impressed fundamentalists in 1919 when he took an uncompromising stand for "law and order" against striking Boston policemen. Once Silent Cal assumed the presidency, fundamentalists praised his "quiet courage and determination." Coolidge had only been in office for about a year when the 1924 presidential campaign got under way. Supporting the incumbent was an easy decision for Republican Party leaders; Democrats had a more difficult choice. Convention delegates split between William McAdoo, the favorite of prohibitionists and southerners, and New York governor Alfred E. Smith, the choice of wets, immigrants, and easterners. Bob Jones attended the Democratic Convention and cautioned the party about the consequences of choosing a candidate who rejected Prohibition. "Party lines are not so strong as they used to be," he warned. Alluding to Coolidge, he continued, "the sentiment for law and order is greater than ever." Should the delegates opt for Smith, the southern evangelist threatened, "it will split the solid South."[27]

The convention proved to be a disaster for the Democratic Party. Americans spent sixteen days listening to delegates mock and criticize each other's religions and home regions over a live radio broadcast. Meanwhile, in the midst of the convention, Democrats debated whether to condemn the revived Ku Klux Klan (they did not). *Moody* editors blamed Catholics for the chaos at the convention, alleging that Rome was conspiring to take over the United States. The party eventually settled on compromise candidate and Wall Street lawyer John W. Davis.[28]

As the election neared, a few fundamentalists jumped into the fray. Southerner Ben Bogard criticized Davis for serving the interests of liquor and the Catholic Church. "Coolidge," he preached, "is not much better but he has at least had the decency to keep his mouth shut. . . . Some of us are either going a fishing this next election day or we shall vote for Coolidge." *Moody* editors simultaneously pledged to keep partisan rancor out of their magazine while defending Coolidge's probusiness economic policies. Progressive taxation, they insisted, "heads us backward not forward, though commonly its advocates are radicals who are supposed to be very progressive. They are ignorant of history, that is all." The periodical had warned readers that increasing government regulation was bringing the United States into line with the devil's plans for world domination. The editors predicted that "government control" will not "halt" until "the government itself may need governing." This, they believed, could open the door for the Antichrist.[29]

On Election Day, most northern fundamentalists sided with the incumbent, while southern fundamentalists likely continued to vote Democratic. Coolidge won easily. Praising the president's states' rights philosophy, *Moody* editors asserted with the president that centralization "results in bureaucracy, tyranny and decline." They called Coolidge "a man among men to whom the people of the United States should give heed without respect to party. He is wiser than Roosevelt," they gushed, "and more transparent than Wilson. To our mind he comes nearer Abraham Lincoln than either of them and somehow or other our thought often goes back to George Washington." While Silent Cal has not usually been remembered as a president on par with Lincoln or Washington, his political and economic conservatism made him a hero to many leaders of the fundamentalist movement.[30]

The 1928 election proved for fundamentalists to be the most pivotal presidential contest since their organization as a distinct Christian movement. Over the previous decade, fundamentalism had grown substantially. Fundamentalist Bible colleges were churning out effective evangelists, movement leaders continued to exploit their close relationships with powerful businessmen (and businessmen's deep pockets), and radio preachers all over the country were winning converts. The growth of radical evangelicalism played out in many arenas, but few were as obvious as politics, where premillennialists' apocalyptic presuppositions set much of the tone and shaped many of the goals of believers.

Well before most Americans were beginning to think about the campaign, rumors began circulating that influential members of the Democratic Party planned to renominate Al Smith. The *Atlantic Monthly* responded to the rumors in the spring of 1927 by publishing an open letter to Smith from attorney Charles Marshall. Despite Americans' admiration of the governor, the letter began, "there is a note of doubt, a sinister accent of interrogation . . . as to certain conceptions which your fellow citizens attribute to you as a loyal and conscientious Roman Catholic." The Episcopalian explained that many Americans wor-

ried that conflicts existed between the Catholic Church and the Constitution, which, he reminded Smith, "as President you must support
and defend." Marshall then listed a handful of official church teachings
to argue that Catholic doctrine conflicted with the American commitment to the separation of church and state. He concluded by asking
Smith to declare where his ultimate loyalty as president would lie—to
the US Constitution or the Roman Catholic Church.[31]

Smith published an immediate reply. He pledged himself to American ideals and claimed that they did not conflict with the tenets of his
church. "I believe," he wrote, "in the worship of God according to
the faith and practice of the Roman Catholic Church. I recognize no
power in the institutions of my Church to interfere with the operations
of the Constitution of the United States. . . . I believe in absolute freedom of conscience for all men. . . . I believe in the absolute separation
of Church and State." He could not have expressed his convictions any
more clearly. But it didn't matter.[32]

Fundamentalists, along with substantial numbers of other Americans,
had long feared that Catholics were conspiring to take over the United
States. "A Roman Catholic president will be the next issue tried for,"
Frank Bartleman predicted in 1911. "The pope to dominate us." A few
years later *King's Business* claimed that Catholics were "doing everything
in their power to Romanize the Government of the United States."
Woodrow Wilson's efforts to build an alliance with Rome added fuel to
their fears. When word leaked that the president was contemplating a
meeting with the pope at the Vatican during his postwar tour of Europe,
Matthews wrote Vice President Thomas Marshall asking him to plead
with Wilson not to do something so foolish. "In cool, calm, prayerful
deliberation I say to hell with the Pope. . . . For God's sake wire him
[Wilson] and tell him to stay away from the infernal pro-German 'Dago.'"
When Wilson did in fact see Benedict XV, the fundamentalist response
was predictable. "The nation as a whole," Torrey warned, "will not tol-
erate the bowing of our Chief Magistrate to that strange and pernicious
mixture of politics and religion that is headed up at Rome." He presciently hinted that if Democrats continued to court the Catholic vote,
their days of southern dominance would come to a quick end.[33]

In the summer of 1928, both political parties held nominating
conventions. The GOP met in Missouri, where delegates selected

Secretary of Commerce Herbert Hoover to serve as their candidate for president. The Democrats held their convention in Texas. Lewis Sperry Chafer wrote missionary Ralph Norton from the Lone Star State with his analysis. "The Democratic Convention is on at the present time and we are promised a very strenuous presidential campaign this year," he predicted, "with very unsavoury exposures of the working of the Catholics. All this might easily lead to riot and bloodshed. How very near our Lord's return must be, and how greatly we desire His coming!"[34]

There were other signs of the Lord's imminent return as well. Smith, the Democratic front-runner, did not attend the convention in Houston but remained at the governor's mansion in New York awaiting the party's decision. A summer storm began to rage in Albany shortly after delegates in Texas cast their final votes, officially making Smith the party nominee. The foul weather forced the Democrats to cancel their notification of nomination ceremonies. Straton claimed that this was "no mere coincidence, but an omen of what the future would bring." In response, the minister received a letter from the mayor of Stamford, Connecticut. "Some of the boys up here," the mayor wrote, "are very anxious to go on their vacations and would like to know whether or not you have arranged to have the rain turned off long enough for them to enjoy pleasant weather, or whether or not once you get the rain turned on you can get it turned off, or whether or not you should be blamed if it continues to rain." "P.S.," he sardonically added in reference to Prohibition, "rain or shine, the people of Connecticut can be counted upon to stay wet."[35]

Fundamentalists did not waste any time mobilizing against Smith. They felt sure that the governor was little more than the pope's shill. "We are not advising Christians to jump into politics," *King's Business* admonished, "but we do feel that we are called upon by the New Testament to do our duty toward the government whose protection we enjoy, and which we can in a measure protect from designing office-seekers." Minister Walter Lingle assured fellow believers that "it is perfectly proper to vote against a man because of the political platform of his church." Despite many pentecostals' longtime reputation as apolitical, they too worried about Smith. Assemblies leader J. Narver Gortner told congregants that there was no comparison between the candidates. "Hoover is a gentleman as well as a statesman. He stands for honesty, for decency, for good government." Smith, in contrast, was a "creature of Tammany" and represents "an element in American society that stands on a much lower moral plane than does the element represented by Herbert Hoover."[36]

Others did more than just editorialize. John Roach Straton wrote J. Frank Norris proposing the creation of an explicitly political fundamentalist organization. "The time is ripe in this country," he wrote, "for a drawing together of all truly patriotic Americans for the defense of the faith of the fathers, religious, domestic, political and educational." He noted that despite the "idealism" of the Klan, "we have long needed in this country a truly adequate Fundamentalist organization that will have teeth." The proposed organization did not materialize; nevertheless Straton and Norris soon emerged as the most politically active fundamentalists in the nation.[37]

As the election neared, Straton decided to use his influence to encourage southerners to vote Republican despite their deep animosity toward the GOP. He left his pulpit in Manhattan to return to Dixie, where he had spent much of his life. He preached across the South on the evils of Smith, Tammany Hall, alcohol, and Catholicism, on the basis of his firsthand experience in New York City. His purpose was to convince fellow Christians that voting for Hoover was not a sign of disloyalty to the old Confederacy.

In making his case, Straton was not above race-baiting. According to an Alabama paper, he told a southern audience that African-American boxing champion Jack Johnson "was a Democrat and his wife was a white woman and a Democrat." For southerners to blindly support the Democrats, he continued, was akin to aligning "with this negro pugilist and his white wife." Indeed, race played a major role in the southern campaign. A Floridian wrote Straton imploring him to further emphasize Smith's work with African Americans in New York. "Make as much capital" as possible, she advised, "out of Smith's negro affiliations." The candidate's supposed push "to 'force' social equality between whites and blacks on the South" would prove much more important "to the southern mind," she added, than debates over Prohibition.[38]

While many southerners felt leery of Smith, they were not necessarily prepared to vote Republican. A Texan knocked Straton for using "the pulpit of a church" to fuel disloyalty to the Democratic Party. He

A national network of socially engaged, apocalyptically oriented religious activists
gave the fundamentalist movement its distinctive character. Few were as popular or
effective as Texas's J. Frank Norris (left) and Manhattan's southern-born John Roach
Straton (right). Together they helped begin to unify northern and southern
fundamentalists around a common set of religious and political principles.
  Courtesy of Library of Congress, LC-DIG-ggbain-34064.

claimed that the Republican's "cardinal principle" was to "subjugate" the South "to the will of the black man; to blend the races, as far as the south is concerned, into a race of mulattoes." A Georgian who supported Straton's anti-Smith campaign called on the minister to fight the Republican Party's alleged practice of putting "negro politicians in our Southern States." "We need the United States Government," he wrote, "run by such men as Roger Williams, George Whitefield, Wesley, the Puritans of Georgia and the French Huguenots. We see this ideal carried out in the K. K. K." While the Klan-Williams comparison might have caused the Puritan advocate of liberty of conscience to roll over in his grave, the correspondent's point was clear. Fundamentalists' racial views could help defeat Smith in the South.[39]

Straton's controversial campaign provoked many critical responses. One person accused the Manhattan minister of opposing Smith and the Democrats' wet platform because he was on the take from bootleggers. Another told him, "the place for you is down south with the niggers. Smith will make a bum out of you." Pro-Hoover voters worried that Straton was doing more harm than good. "If any one thing would sway my vote" for Smith, a Baptist Republican wrote, "it would be your intolerant, radical, prejudiced and unjust attitude." Another explained, "Herbert Hoover gets my vote for President, but as between you and Al Smith as Christian Gentlemen, Al gets my vote with a cheer." An anonymous correspondent called the minister an "old dog" and warned "we will get you." The writer also told Straton he was "not clean enough to wipe Smith's ass." Another barely literate correspondent denounced Straton in the strongest language he could muster. He called him a "Cocksoaker" and "hipogrit" and then offered "for Chists seek, let me give you a tip . . . why don't you and all other cocksoackers ceep your moth shot when you are in your Church." He concluded, "I hope the Devil get you S. of a b. befor long." The letter was signed, "A 200% AMERICAN."[40]

But not everyone criticized Straton. Over the course of the campaign, he received a lot of positive correspondence encouraging him to keep up the fight. One supporter told him that a primary reason for opposing Smith was that "the constitution says a catholic must not be president. The founders of constitution should be respected. They knew what they were doing." Another wrote, "Protestants founded America and only they should run it." A southern Democrat called the minister a "Moses" to "bring the deluded multitudes of the South . . . out of the wilderness of darkness into light and show them how they can remain 100-percent Democrat without voting for Al Smith." A manufacturer of toilet brushes counseled Straton to keep up the fight against "Al (co-hol) Smith." The Klan also praised Straton. The "Exalted Cyclops" of the Jamaica, New York branch of the Ku Klux Klan told Straton, "it is indeed gratifying to know a man of your high calibre and standing in the religious world is so nobly championing the cause of American Protestantism." The cyclops invited Straton to address twenty-five hundred Klansmen along with Imperial Wizard Hiram Wesley Evans shortly after the election and suggested that the visit could "be a purely secret one if necessary." The Long Island branch of the Klan assured the minister, "this fight is not only a battle against Rome but against all the evil forces in America, cutthroats, thugs, the scum from the cesspools of Europe, etc." The Klansman concluded by assuring Straton, "you have hosts of friends."[41]

While the Manhattan minister earned the praise of the Klan, Cath-olics were not as enthused about his actions. One pro-Hoover layper-son warned Straton that his bigotry was driving Republican Catho-lics to Smith. He asked Straton to "be good" and to let anti-Smith Catholics lead the charge against the candidate. Meanwhile a priest claimed that "a more stinking skunk" than the minister "does not ex-ist in America." Another Catholic questioned Straton's masculinity and sexual orientation, demanding that he recant. "Be a man and not a molly-coddle or an old woman as you look like in the papers. You only have to look at your picture to tell what you are." The many let-ters Straton received illustrated the costs of politicizing fundamental-ism. This minister's overarching message—that individuals needed salvation—disappeared far below controversies over his involvement in politics.[42]

Contending with Straton for the title of most vigorous fundamen-talist opponent of Smith was the Texas Tornado. Norris routinely claimed that he came from a long line of staunch Democrats. However, he criticized the Democrats in 1920 over the League of Nations, and he privately admitted his loyalties to the GOP in 1927, writing to Re-publican Party leader R. B. Creager, "for many years I have been of the conclusion that it was in the best interest of this country that the Republican Party administer its government." Nor did he think that he was the only one. "Multitudes of Democrats have been just wanting an occasion where they could, with respectability and show a good face, have a justifiable excuse to vote the Republican ticket." The Smith nomination gave them that occasion.[43]

Norris preached repeatedly on Smith's opposition to Prohibition as well as his supposed drinking habits. Although he denounced Smith in his magazine, his message did not always reach its intended audience. An "old" subscriber to the *Fundamentalist* complained to Norris that his issues were being stolen from the mail. He called it "a grave and diabolical trick on the part of some member of his Satanic majesty the Pope whose mission on earth seems to be to destroy the light and cover up the truth." Whether or not this correspondent was being satirical, there is no doubt that fundamentalists believed that the pope would go to great lengths to undermine their movement.[44]

Despite Smith's stand on Prohibition and his Catholic faith, Norris, like Straton, understood that many southern Democrats would have a very difficult time voting for the party of Lincoln. But he too knew that there was one far more explosive issue that could best be turned to the advantage of the GOP in the South—race. As governor, Smith worked with African Americans and generally supported racial equality. Norris urged Republicans to take full advantage of this issue. He offered to help Republican Party operatives by securing "the addresses of fifty thousand Klansmen," for "mailing list propaganda" although it "would cost a little expense." He also warned the Republicans that they needed to replace African-American convention delegates with white men to secure the votes of southern states. "Otherwise," he warned, "Mississippi will go for Al Smith regardless of rum and Romanism." One "very old lady" even suggested that the Baptist minister remind African Americans that a Republican, not a Democrat, freed them from slavery. She suggested that any "Negro" who votes for Smith "should be thrown back into slavery." Along with a handful of other prominent fundamentalists, Norris understood that the Republicans could not simply let Smith dig his own grave; they had to play on southern racial fears if the party wanted to expand its base in Dixie.[45]

In 1928 many fundamentalists feared that Democratic presidential candidate Al
Smith's Catholic faith, relationship with New York's infamous Tammany Hall, and
opposition to Prohibition would lead the nation to ruin. Texas minister J. Frank
Norris put this cartoon on the cover of his 1928 collection of sermons against Smith.
   J. Frank Norris, *Is America at the Crossroads? Or Roman Catholicism vs. Protestant Christianity*
   (Fort Worth: J. L. Rhodes, 1928), cover.

   While Straton and Norris led the fundamentalist charge against
Smith, they had a legion of allies working alongside them. William
Ward Ayer, who at the time was leading a Baptist church in Indiana (he
would later take Straton's Manhattan pulpit), asked Norris for some
"ammunition for the bombardment I am endeavoring to carry on in

Indiana . . . am doing the best I can to tie a few knots in the tail of the Tammany Tiger and keep good Protestant Hoosiers from kissing the Pope's toe at election time." Southern Baptist leader D. N. Jackson called the nomination of Smith "the boldest attempt that the pope of Rome has ever made to get hold of the United States, and he has come by way of the saloons to make his bid." Blissfully ignorant of the way his own actions undermined church-state separatism, Jackson wrote, "to elect Smith President would be a step toward Romish intolerance and a union of church and State." Billy Sunday jumped into the fray as well, filleting Smith repeatedly over Prohibition.[46]

Many fundamentalists interpreted the election in the context of premillennial expectations. Oklahoma minister and evangelist Morde-cai Ham—just a few years before he would preside over the conversion of a young student named Billy Graham—wondered what the Smith campaign meant for prophecy. In a letter to Norris, he explained, "the time has come when the fundamentalists better be getting together some sort of a very aggressive campaign. Unless I am badly deceived, we are right in the closing days of this age." Norris agreed, writing Ham that if Smith was elected, "it will be the beginning of the final plunge into the day of apostasy." North Carolinian Rev. S. J. Betts eagerly anticipated hearing Norris "shell the woods on Rum Roam and For-eign Emergration." Turning to prophecy, he explained, "the coming of our Lord is the only hope. . . . The ten kingdoms are being formed. We are in the last 'Times.' "[47]

Ben Bogard was yet another influential southern fundamentalist preacher who saw no irony in using the argument of church-state sepa-ratism to campaign against Smith. "We are tolerant," he assured his followers. "We believe that no man should be discriminated against because of his religion. . . . We believe in the separation of church and State and we believe in free speech and free press. That is exactly why we are opposed to any Roman Catholic being in office." In a nation where Protestants had long dominated public life, fundamentalists simply did not conceive of their own efforts as bigoted or as a violation of the separation of church and state.[48]

Bogard, more than any other prominent fundamentalist, most overtly and unapologetically injected race into the anti-Smith campaign. He challenged those southern Democrats who believed that abandoning

the Democratic Party would lead to dire racial consequences. He called
Smith a "friend of negro rapists" and added, "if you believe in negro
equality you can vote for Smith." He fretted that southern journalists
had been ignoring the "'nigger' question." Smith, he warned, "would
take his 'nigger' equality views with him to Washington." Listing a
series of "facts" regarding Smith's commitment to racial equality, he
encouraged his readers to "Stick that under the nose of the next man
who says 'NIGGER.'" He also used photographs to make his case. He
ran a "disgusting" photograph in the *Baptist and Commoner* of an African-
American man dressed in a suit sitting behind an office desk next to a
secretary who was taking notes in order to illustrate what happened in
Smith's administration. The caption under the picture read, "Here Is the
Buck Negro with His White Stenographer." Although most fundamentalists did not go as far as Bogart, their racial views became unapologetically explicit during the 1928 campaign.[49]

As the election neared, fundamentalists continued to fret. A congregant wrote P. W. Philpott, the pastor of the Moody Church, just weeks
before Election Day, asking that the congregation and its leader take a
clear stand against Smith. "There's a lot of difference between a pulpit
devoted to politics to the neglect of the spiritual—and the refusal on
the part of a church to refute that devil's lie that a man can vote for 'Al'
Smith and still be a good Christian and a patriot." In another letter, the
same layman warned, "It's time to get out into the open with EVERY
man and EVERY gun we've got. . . . Onward Christian soldiers! The
fight is ON!" On Reformation Sunday, which fell just before the election, James Gray preached a sermon on "intolerance" in which he essentially justified voting against a Catholic on the basis of religion. He
claimed that taking such a position was not "intolerant" because Rome
had designs on the US government. "American opposition to a Roman
Catholic president is based on something more than his religion . . .
something more than intolerance and bigotry."[50]

The 1928 election was a tremendous victory for Hoover and the
Republican Party. The secretary of commerce garnered twenty-one
million votes to Smith's fifteen million. He swept most of the North
and also won a handful of southern states, including Florida, Texas,
North Carolina, Tennessee, and Virginia. The new president invited
Norris to the White House as a reward for his hard work. The preacher

described Hoover after the meeting as "a strong believer" in the "fundamentals of the Christian faith." But for the minister, the election was simply the start not the end of a long struggle. He wrote to a friend, "I believe that we are just in the beginning of the most terrific fight with the same evil powers. The war is on and while we won the recent great battle, yet we would make a colossal blunder to go to sleep on the job." Norris would ensure that they did not go to sleep. He and his many fundamentalist allies kept a close eye on the Catholic threat. Ironically, however, during the early Cold War the Texas Tornado shifted gears and became one of the first major fundamentalists to join forces with Catholics against the threat of communism.[51]

While the election of Hoover cheered most fundamentalists, *King's Business* perceptively saw potential trouble in the returns. The editors noted that Smith's support came from "the large cities" while Hoover's support was based in "rural districts and smaller towns." With a major migration of rural Americans into cities under way, "how long will it take to wipe out the Hoover margin?" they asked. "There is still need for prayer, even if the president-elect does all that is expected of him." Soon their fears about shifting demographics would be realized as cities came to dominate American electoral politics and new threats emerged.[52]

Over the course of the 1920s, premillennialism helped frame the way many fundamentalists understood politics. Prophecy directly inspired their organizing against the League of Nations and those politicians who supported it. They expected the league to facilitate the Antichrist's assumption of global leadership, the international transmission of foreign leaders' diabolical religious ideas, and the efforts of atheistic communists to take over the world. They insisted that the league would curtail religious freedoms and demand loyalty to an all-powerful state. The league also reinforced their conviction that Roman Catholics were engaged in a conspiracy to undermine American sovereignty in order to help shape a false religion that the Antichrist would soon exploit. But apocalypticism also had many indirect consequences. The faithful brought their prophetic expectations with them into the voting booth as they sought to answer questions about the state, the economy, and social policy. The countdown to Armageddon had begun, and although the twenties provided a bit of a lull between the chaotic years of World War

I and the Great Depression, fundamentalists still felt motivated to do their part to protect the nation from the oncoming tribulation.

As the new year began in 1929, fundamentalists, like all Americans, had no idea what was in store for them. When Hoover accepted the Republican nomination, he audaciously declared, "we in America today are nearer to the final triumph over poverty than ever before in the history of any land. The poorhouse is vanishing from among us. We have not yet reached the goal, but given a chance to go forward with the policies of the last eight years, and we shall soon, with the help of God, be in sight of the day when poverty will be banished from this nation." Gaebelein saw the economy in similar terms, although he worried about its spiritual state. "Never before have the optimistic dreams of mankind been so bold and soaring as during the closing weeks of 1928. The world sees nothing but progress and prosperity ahead. All appears as a bright and rosy future." Little did the president elect or the preacher realize that their world was about to turn upside down.[53]

In the fall of 1929 the stock market crashed, revealing that underneath the glamour and glitz of the Roaring Twenties the economy had sputtered to a halt. As the nation's financial state worsened, Chicago evangelist and popular radio preacher Paul Rader issued a dire warning. "Satan stirs man up about community morals, great governmental reformations and educations, mass social movements that teach good environment as the basis of human salvation." But these were false hopes, he asserted. He compared the proposals of modern political progressives to those offered by Satan to tempt Jesus during his forty-day sojourn in the wilderness (Matthew 4:1–11). When the devil told Jesus to turn stones into bread, he was suggesting that Jesus solve the world's hunger crisis. When the devil showed Jesus the kingdoms of the world, he was suggesting that Jesus join the devil in "the big national and international reformation, cultural and uplift programs." When the devil told Jesus to throw himself off of the pinnacle of the temple to show that he would not be hurt, he was encouraging Jesus to "become a great spectacular leader of a vast mass movement." But Jesus wisely rejected Satan's liberal politics. As the world plunged into a depression, fundamentalists would try to do the same.[54]

7

THE RISE OF THE TYRANTS

IN LATE 1933, missionary and medical doctor L. Nelson Bell sat down at his desk in Qingjiangpu, China, to write his weekly letter home to his mother. As usual, he dedicated most of the missive to discussing the activities of his children. Thirteen-year-old daughter Ruth, he explained, had written him a "lively" report of events at her boarding school in Pyongyang, Korea. While ironing some clothes, Ruth spontaneously blurted out to a classmate, "Oh just think, the end of the world may come soon and then we will be so happy." Apparently, her friend was not at all surprised by the outburst. She merely responded, "Oh you Bell girls . . . surely are stuck on the end of the world."[1]

Both Ruth, who would grow up to marry evangelist Billy Graham, and Nelson, who would become one of the primary architects of modern American evangelicalism, were indeed "stuck" on the end of the world. And they were not alone. In the 1920s and 1930s, American fundamentalists—at home and abroad—felt a new sense of urgency. For generations they had been carefully combing both their Bibles and their daily newspapers for evidence that Jesus's return to earth was nearing. With Benito Mussolini planning to restore the Roman Empire, Adolf Hitler driving Jews out of Europe, Joseph Stalin institutionalizing state atheism, and nations around the globe drowning in an economic tsunami, fundamentalists trusted that the countdown to Armageddon had begun. Global events in the 1930s so closely paralleled their long-held predictions that they spent little time fretting about past prophetic mistakes. Their concerns about the imminent return of Christ animated everything from their most private conversations to their loudest political expressions. Although the Antichrist had not yet revealed himself, the faithful felt sure that Satan was orchestrating global events in preparation for the coming of a new world leader. But whether the United States would succumb to the Antichrist remained an open question, one fundamentalists vowed to help answer.

In the wake of World War I, fundamentalists amplified their apocalyptic preaching. They saw signs of the times appearing at home in the seeming celebration of immorality, the decline of public schools, the decay of their culture, a Catholic candidate running for president, and growing religious apostasy. As they looked abroad, the signs seemed even clearer. Fixating on Jesus's prophecy regarding wars and rumors of wars, fundamentalists felt sure that conflict was on the horizon.

Christabel Pankhurst, the former British suffrage leader and convert to fundamentalism, believed that the time was nigh. Although she never renounced her strong feminist inclinations and steadfastly defended woman suffrage, she matched her commitment to gender equality with her passion for preaching the end times. While most fundamentalists still insisted that women should not preach, they had a hard time arguing with Pankhurst's success. Like Aimee McPherson and teenage preaching sensation Uldine Utley, Pankhurst routinely captured the attention of the press and helped reach new audiences with the fundamentalist gospel by connecting it to geopolitical developments. She told all who would listen that the Antichrist was "living in the world at this present time." However, she promised that if humankind repented, "its doom might be averted as was the doom of Nineveh when they repented at the preaching of Jonah." She made it her mission to convert the masses while warning them of the destruction to come.[2]

Critics saw Pankhurst as a symbol of premillennialism's continuing danger to the nation. New York Unitarian minister Charles Francis

Potter invoked typical modernist denunciations of premillennialism to criticize the woman evangelist. "Millennialism at its worst," he insisted, "produces insanity and suicide and at its best is an enemy of social reform." He called on fellow Americans "to treat such preachers as we treat the other enemies of society: examine them as to their sanity, put them on probation, give them a guardian or lock them up." African-American minister A. B. Adams was no fan of Pankhurst either. Writing in the *Pittsburgh Courier* under the heading "false predictions" he warned, "untrue vaticinations of the coming of Jesus Christ have wrought havoc to the faith of many."[3]

But the faithful remained undaunted. Buoyed by what seemed to be incontrovertible evidence of prophecy's fulfillment, a few fundamentalists began privately setting dates for Christ's return. They did not, however, make public predictions, knowing that they might be mistaken. William Blackstone determined in 1927 that the rapture would most likely happen on the Jewish Day of Atonement (Yom Kippur), which also happened to be his birthday. Later that year he wrote to a friend that 1935 marked 2,520 years since Jerusalem had been destroyed by Nebuchadnezzar, a date that would herald the battle of Armageddon and the end of the seven-year tribulation. If he had calculated correctly, the rapture and the "the manifestation of the antichrist" all had to happen "before the fall of 1928." Intrigued by this interpretation, his friend joked that if the rapture occurred as Blackstone predicated they would meet again in the sky "and you will surely be able to say to me 'I told you so.'" But then, invoking the typical premillennialist sense of occupying until the second coming, he reminded Blackstone (who didn't need reminding) that their convictions required them to labor as if Jesus was not coming back for another millennium. "No matter what happens," he wrote, "we are under marching orders." Fundamentalists like Blackstone had spent a half century anticipating the rapture while simultaneously spreading apocalyptic fundamentalism as aggressively as possible. Their sense of determination and commitment fueled their relentless passion for expanding their movement. They never forgot that they were under marching orders.[4]

With the tribulation seemingly imminent, Blackstone concocted a new plan. Believing that during the reign of the Antichrist a remnant of faithful Jews would refuse to take the mark of the beast but would instead flee into the wilderness, he determined to assist them from on the other side of the rapture. He surmised that they would most likely escape to the ancient rock city of Petra (in today's southwest Jordan), so he hid boxes of Bibles and premillennial literature printed in Hebrew, Yiddish, and Aramaic throughout the region. He hoped that Jews would discover the materials he left behind and then realize through them "that Jesus Christ is truly their Messiah, and that He will come to deliver them." Blackstone's actions demonstrate that in predicting an impending rapture, he was deadly serious. He put his money and his energy into saving as many people as possible from the coming catastrophe.[5]

Some groups of African-American evangelicals also took note of unfolding prophecy in the late 1920s. "We see the predicted signs being fulfilled before our eyes that 'the coming of the Lord draweth nigh,'" the National Baptist Union-Review exulted. The National Baptist Voice also indicated that the time was at hand. "According to the plain prophetic teaching of God's Word, and the rapid fulfillment of prophecy," the paper editorialized, "it seems that the most awful time of consternation, mourning and trouble that this world has ever witnessed is due to take place very soon." The writer ended with a word of warning to those left behind after the rapture: "do not take the mark of the Beast, for that will mean certain damnation." He recommended martyrdom at the hands of the Antichrist as the better option.[6]

Various African-American ministers emphasized racial turmoil as last-days signs. Pentecostal pioneer Charles H. Mason preached a 1926 sermon on the total destruction of a town known for "much race hatred" by a supposed act of God. He ended his sermon by admonishing his listeners that such signs indicated that Jesus's return was imminent and they should be ready for the rapture. African Americans' sense of anticipation grew as they recognized that they had far more to gain from the destruction of this world and the coming of a new millennium than many of their white counterparts.[7]

For other African Americans, millennialism continued to have black liberationist implications. Seattle minister James Webb, an active member of Marcus Garvey's Universal Negro Improvement Association (UNIA), blended prophecies of the second coming with visions of a black Jesus and African nationalism. In 1924 the New York Times quoted his speech at a UNIA meeting. "The whites," he explained, "feel they have the black men frightened and they have frightened all who haven't studied biblical history." But those who studied the scriptures knew differently. The prophets taught "that the universal black king is coming," and his arrival will reinforce and justify UNIA efforts. "A great victory is coming," Webb boasted, "not by human but by divine power, as foretold by Daniel." African-American pentecostal R. C. Lawson promised that a black deliverer was soon to appear. Since "the white brethren don't preach the fatherhood of God, and the brotherhood of man irrespective of color or nationality, and exemplify the true spirit of brotherhood and equality to all, their civilization is doomed. However," he continued, "God will bring deliverance from another quarter, and will raise up a people who will preach it, and exemplify it in their lives and relationship to their fellowmen." As African Americans waged a steady battle against Jim Crow, many found hope in the evidence that the millennium was imminent.[8]

The onset of the Great Depression and changing global conditions provided prophecy prognosticators with substantial new ammunition. William Bell Riley summed up their feelings. The daily newspaper, he explained, was "an index finger pointing down the path of fulfilling prophecy. The age to which we have come is one of which Isaiah and Jeremiah wrote; of which Daniel dreamed; of which the apostles prophesied, and of which Christ Himself uttered alike words of warning and wisdom. Indeed, the signs were lining up as never before. *"Can man know the future?"* Arno Gaebelein provocatively asked. "We answer without hesitation, *Yes.* We can know the future through the Bible, the Word of God." Premillennialism consistently provided its adherents with confidence. In a darkening age, they alone understood the significance of cascading world events. While the rest of humanity naively marched toward the coming tribulation, fundamentalists looked forward to the rapture and then millennial bliss.[9]

As the global economic crisis spread, Christian publishers eagerly capitalized on substantial reader demand for more material on prophecy. *King's Business* began a new monthly column in 1931, "There Shall Be Signs," written by Los Angeles pastor and fundamentalist leader Louis Bauman. He opened the column by declaring that the coming of Christ was close at hand. "By 'close,'" he clarified, "we do not mean a thousand years, or a century, or possibly so much as a score of years.

His coming is imminent." Bauman's articles on prophecy were among the most popular items printed in fundamentalist magazines in the 1930s and he wrote for just about all of them. When at one point he tried to quit the *King's Business* column, the editors told him that his articles "received more favorable comment . . . than anything else in the magazine." A member of the circulation department even quipped, "Why, as far as subscriptions are concerned, Dr. Bauman *is THE KING'S BUSINESS.*"[10]

Indeed, Christian editors had long understood that nothing attracted more readers to their religious rags than speculation about the destruction of everyone outside the faith. While fundamentalists tried to embody the virtues of love and charity, premillennialism could feed the darker elements of human nature. The faithful found something satisfying in anticipating the ultimate destruction of those who had long ignored them or mocked and derided their faith. They were offering the world a clear choice—join them or face annihilation. For a person to reject the message fundamentalists were offering was to seal his or her fate.

The letters provoked by Bauman's columns revealed how some laypeople understood premillennialism. One Sunday school teacher complained that in his church, "I dont think there was ever a sermon here on the second coming . . . they don't no nothing about it, at all." He asked Bauman to send him some books on what had "taken place since the war, I mean prophesy." A woman who knew the blazing heat of hell first hand as a resident of California's Mojave Desert hoped to start a bible class on prophecy. However, she wondered if her gender precluded her. "I feel that the time is so short," she wrote, "I want to reach all I can in as little time as possible." Bauman responded enthusiastically, explaining, "the Bible gives the woman a perfect right to teach and to preach." For some fundamentalists the urgency of the times demanded that as many people as possible get the message out regardless of gender; however most leaders still insisted that preaching remained men's work.[11]

Laypeople badgered the editors at the *Pentecostal Evangel* for additional information on prophecy. One man requested more pieces on "world conditions from a prophetic viewpoint." He was curious about "who these present Dictators are and what part they are playing in God's great plan." But he also raised some concerns. The *Evangel* occasionally printed ads for prophecy books that included teasers—compelling, intriguing tidbits of information intended to encourage magazine readers to purchase the books. This writer complained that poor readers like himself "who are really hungry for more of God and an interpretation of world conditions in the light of prophecy" were cut off from important prophetic analysis "because they lack the $.75 or the $1.50 to buy the book or paper advertised." As global events affirmed premillennial expectations, laypeople tried to get their hands on as much material as possible in as many different formats as they could afford.[12]

The leading fundamentalist periodicals *Sunday School Times, Revelation, Our Hope,* and *Moody Monthly* responded to reader interest with their own regular columns on prophecy and the news. *King's Business* editor and Bible Institute of Los Angeles faculty member Keith Brooks even began a new publication in the late twenties, *Prophecy Monthly,* to focus specifically on these issues. Donald Grey Barnhouse praised the "solid front" of evangelical prophecy interpretation disseminated by these magazines; he believed that God was using them to prepare the world for what was soon to come. As the editors rediscovered readers' insatiable appetite for end-times speculation they even used special "prophecy" issues to recruit new subscribers. While Bauman occasionally fretted that "religious editors need to avoid all appearance of commercializing prophetic truth," that ship had sailed long ago.[13]

Numerous international events in the late 1920s and 1930s reinforced fundamentalist convictions that Armageddon was just around the corner. As tensions around the globe increased, radical evangelical leaders had plenty of new information from which to draw. They studied global news, certain that they could discern emerging patterns in changes occurring in Europe and Asia.

Fundamentalists put substantial energy into analyzing the rise of Benito Mussolini. Since the time of Darby, the faithful had expected the Antichrist to take power through a ten-nation confederacy led by a resurrected Roman Empire. That Il Duce seemed to fit the prophetic bill almost perfectly captivated fundamentalists around the nation. Speculation about Mussolini's significance began shortly after he formed a new government in Italy. Bauman boasted that he had first identified Mussolini in 1922 as the probable Antichrist. A few years later he warned, "if Mussolini does not prove to be Antichrist he is certainly a

Men and women from all social classes and geographic regions regularly turned to
biblical prophecy in search of solutions to the world's ills. Sometimes they
worshipped in lavish urban churches; other times they congregated in small shacks
like the one in Modesto, California photographed here by Dorothea Lange in 1940.
  Photo by Dorothea Lange, Courtesy of the National Archives and Records Administration,
  521623.

magnificent fore-shadow of Antichrist!" In 1927 Charles Fuller—before
he acquired national fame on the radio—invited Bauman to speak at his
church in Placentia, California, on what was soon to be one of the hottest
topics among fundamentalists. "We would be glad to hear something
about Mussolini or some phase of the Lord's return," he entreated.[14]

   As global conditions deteriorated, premillennial speculation snowballed. Luke Rader called Il Duce a "curse to the human race" and the
possible Antichrist. "Since Mussolini is resurrecting Rome," his brother
Paul warned, "the eyes of all students of prophecy are upon him."
Norris warned a friend to keep his eyes on Mussolini. "I firmly believe," he explained, "we are coming to the climax of the ages." Bell
summarized fundamentalist thought in a letter to his mother. The
"way is being paved for the final restoration of the old Roman Em-

pire. . . . What a joy," he wrote, about events that seem less than joyful, "to have the hope of His Coming before us, rather than the mirage of a world getting better and better."[15]

Such bold prophecies occasionally caught the attention of the nation's major media outlets, which capitalized on premillennial prognostication. Like fundamentalists editors, secular journalists sensed in apocalypticism a surefire formula for engaging with audiences. The speculation of radical evangelicals provided a plausible framework for interpreting deteriorating global conditions, striking a chord with countless Americans who were struggling to make sense of their place in this world.[16]

In one of the great ironies in fundamentalist history, Mussolini had no idea how closely he was being watched by fundamentalists. Then he met Ralph and Edith Norton. The Nortons were probably the most influential and well-known fundamentalist missionaries of the interwar era. They ran the Belgium Gospel Mission and corresponded with most of the significant fundamentalist leaders of the era. In the early 1930s, they embarked on a tour of Europe with plans to publish a series of articles based on their impressions in the *Sunday School Times*. A meeting with Mussolini marked the climax of the trip. "Do you intend to reconstitute the Roman Empire?" they asked the prime minister. At first Mussolini had no idea what they were getting at. Then the Nortons walked the Italian fascist through biblical prophecy. As they proceeded, Mussolini apparently "leaned back in his chair and listened fascinated." "Is that really described in the Bible?" he asked the missionaries. "Where is it to be found?" By the time the Nortons were through with him, Mussolini apparently believed—and maybe even hoped—that he was the long-awaited world dictator prophesied in the book of Daniel. True to form, Il Duce had no reservations about taking on the role of the prophesied Antichrist.[17]

Fundamentalists also kept a close eye on Mussolini's relationship with the Vatican. They believed that in the last days the Antichrist would establish a universal false religion led by a person described in Revelation 17 as the "whore of Babylon." While fundamentalists never reached a consensus on this issue many believed that the Antichrist's spiritual ally would be the pope. Bauman claimed that Mussolini was already laying the foundations for just such an alliance. He told followers that it was impossible to read Revelation "without seeing papal Rome in every delineation of the scarlet-clothed woman astride this beast." H. A. Ironside came to the same conclusion, calling Catholicism "the bride of the Antichrist, the false harlot system that masquerades as the wife of the Lamb."[18]

In 1935, Italy's invasion of Ethiopia raised fundamentalist interest in Mussolini to new heights. Harold John Ockenga, who would soon emerge as the leading spokesman of evangelicalism in the post–World War II era second only to Billy Graham, preached an enthusiastic sermon on the relationship between the prophecies of Daniel and the Italian campaign in Africa. He promised that humankind was standing "on the brink of the greatest international upheaval and tribulation of history which will mark the end of the present era." Many fundamentalists agreed that Italy's actions in Africa matched biblical predictions. Prophecy, or at least their interpretation of prophecy, seemed to be coming true. Bauman also saw the invasion as an important step on the road to Armageddon. "It is time for Caesar again to ride. His legions are marching. Where? Is it to Armageddon? Armageddon—*via Ethiopia?* To the student of the sure word of prophecy, the present movements of kings on the international chessboard could hardly be more significant." Inspired by events abroad, John R. Rice preached sermons in his Texas church titled "Is Mussolini the Anti-Christ?" and "Mussolini Restores the Roman Empire." Both were printed in his fledgling newspaper *Sword of Lord*. The articles produced a flood of positive correspondence and helped Rice eventually make *Sword* one of the most influential Christian papers in the nation.[19]

A few fundamentalists were so sure about Mussolini's role in endtimes prophecy that they felt compelled to share God's cosmic plans with national policy-makers. One Atlanta man suggested that fundamentalists open "a Sunday School in Washington to study Prophecy and History and invite the House and Senate and the President and his Cabinet to become students." Others wrote President Roosevelt directly. A Texan, who promised to keep FDR up-to-date on the "signs of the times" named Mussolini as the Antichrist and predicted that out of the Ethiopian crisis "a ten League of nations will come, which shall be governed by Mussolini, which shall stand for seven years" preceding the return of Christ. A Pennsylvania Presbyterian wrote Roosevelt as well, encouraging him to study prophecy "with its amazing secrets for the Statesman." Roosevelt, he believed, should be making policy on the basis of premillennialism. "In international relationships," he counseled, "it would be of priceless worth to know that the map of Europe will be reshaped according to Biblical Prophecy, of which the strength of Rome to-day is an interesting indication." These letters indicated how seriously the faithful took their analysis. They believed that they could and should help American leaders make wise decisions on the basis of their premillennial interpretations of the Bible.[20]

Some African-American evangelicals agreed with white fundamentalists that the Italian campaign represented another sign of the approaching last days. African Methodist Episcopal leader Noah Williams wrote from Europe that the imminent global world war was certain to conclude at Armageddon with "the Second Advent of Jesus Christ." The editors at the *Union Review* offered similar interpretations. "No generation since our Lord's day has been given such tremendous proofs of the veracity of Biblical Prophecy as our generation. Prophecy after prophecy has been fulfilled before our eyes during the last twenty years in the most striking way."[21]

But for other African Americans, the war and specifically the end-times role of Ethiopia took on much greater significance. Many black religious leaders had long read Psalm 68:31, "Princes shall come out of Egypt; Ethiopia shall soon stretch out her hands unto God," as a prophecy of their redemption and a key verse about the last days. They expected Ethiopia ultimately to triumph over Rome and to play a substantial role in Christ's new kingdom. But the news out of Africa did not look good. A columnist for the *Atlanta Daily World* encouraged church leaders to discuss Ethiopia and biblical prophecy with their congregations. All African Americans, he observed, were "following with bated breath this piece of history in the making" as the "last independent unit" controlled by "the BLACK MAN anywhere" came under attack. Writing in the *Chicago Defender,* Dan Burley called Mussolini "a militant, merciless dictator, who after all, is symbolical of the white spirit of today." Linking the invasion, American racism, and traditional premillennial tropes, he warned that the predictions of Daniel were being fulfilled as "the white man's civilization" imploded. The world, he surmised, was "headed for Biblical Armageddon." Another columnist writing in the *Defender* cautioned that for African Americans a threat against Ethiopia represented "a direct affront to their belief in the fulfillment of the prophecy for their complete redemption." He encouraged "the blacks of America" and "the blacks of the world" to "continue to watch, pray, believe in the prophecies." A Harlem resident wrote the *Amsterdam News* expressing his hope that what was happening in Africa might undermine European colonial efforts. "Let us keep our eyes in the Bible and modern history and await developments." This writer could be certain that African-American evangelicals were doing exactly that.[22]

At the same time, some black leaders saw the Ethiopian tragedy as a call to repentance. Chicago resident W. M. Butler viewed Ethiopia's humiliation as a symbol of the destruction that was soon to befall humankind for failing to heed the signs of the times. "Today," he wrote to the *Defender,* "the Negro is in the midst of the most amazing fulfillments of Biblical prophecy. . . . This is the Negro's warning. It points out an impending crisis." He hoped that such events would spark a renewed interest in biblical prophecy. The *Union-Review* used the war as an opportunity to denounce theological liberalism, which the paper linked to Sunday movie showings, evolution, and communism. The Old Testament prophets, the editor asserted, "appear to have gotten 'a scoop' on the Italo-Ethiopian war." For many radical evangelicals regardless of race, war simultaneously represented the fulfillment of prophecy and God's judgment of sin. But for some black evangelicals, it also reminded them of both the oppression they faced in this world and the liberation that was soon to come.[23]

For white fundamentalist Robert Hockman, Mussolini's invasion of Africa represented more than just a spiritual threat. Hockman, who had a medical degree from Northwestern University, sailed with his wife to Ethiopia in late 1933. The couple planned to serve as missionaries and aid workers. They noted that on the ship they kept hearing "Mussolini," which was the only Italian word Robert knew besides "spaghetti and ravioli." By 1935, Hockman realized that he had a front-row seat at the coming war. "Italy all the time," he wrote home, "is mobilizing more and more forces and now there is quite an army in Africa. War seems inevitable here and it seems to be a matter of time."[24]

When the war began, Hockman sent his pregnant wife to Egypt for her safety while he went to work for the Red Cross. He had planned to join her there for Christmas and to meet his new baby. But the fighting intensified. "The Italians," he wrote his family, "bombed our town twice thus far and have circled over our camp every time but have not done anything." Still he remained unfazed. "Do not worry about me. I am as safe as I would be if I were in Wheaton for I believe He will keep me here as anywhere for I believe this is what the Lord wants me to do right now." As Christmas neared he learned that the Red Cross was "in an uproar" about his plans to leave the front. Although his missionary agency had granted him permission to go, local Red Cross leaders persuaded him to skip Christmas with his wife and to remain in Ethiopia. He hoped that "the Lord" would "make it up a hundred fold to both of us for the sacrifices we have been called upon to endure."[25]

Life on the front was dangerous, but Hockman made it more dangerous than necessary. He baited, chased, and taunted the local wildlife and toyed with explosives dropped by the Italians. He and his buddies "unloaded" deadly bombs and kept fuses for souvenirs. He also collected "specimens of incendiary bombs and explosive bombs which did not go off." But there were accidents too. "One of the big bombs," he wrote home, "which I have described exploded and did it make a noise!!" That was his last letter. He never reunited with his wife and he never met his baby daughter. Just over a week later, he died at age twenty-nine while handling another undetonated Italian bomb. Hockman was the first American casualty of World War II. For most fundamentalists, deciphering prophecy presented an exciting and interesting challenge. But for Hockman, reading the Bible while face-to-face with Il Duce's army was deadly.[26]

While Rome drew substantial fundamentalist attention, it was not the only region inspiring prophetic analysis. Fundamentalists expected Germany to play an important end-times role as well. The faithful had long believed that Ezekiel's reference to "Gomer" (Ezekiel 38 and 39) referred to Germany. Following the prophet's words, they anticipated that in the last days Gomer would align with Magog—Germany with

Russia. Together they would form the great "northern kingdom." The faithful also kept a close eye on Germany's relationship with Jews. Since fundamentalists believed that massive numbers of Jews would return to the Promised Land just before the battle of Armageddon, they interpreted growing European anti-Semitism as part of God's plan to drive Jews to Palestine to set the stage for Jesus's return.

The rise of Adolf Hitler stimulated fundamentalists' hopes and fears. In early 1932 Donald Barnhouse drew on biblical prophecy to predict that the National Socialist German Workers' Party would soon be in power. "Those of us who look at the world and its men and events through the magnifying glass of the Word of God," he declared, "are not in darkness." He described Hitler's anti-Semitism as "of great interest to the Bible student" since it had the potential to force Jews out of Central Europe and to Palestine. *Revelation,* he later claimed, "was the first religious magazine in the world" to discuss *Mein Kampf,* even "before it had appeared in English."[27]

In 1933, Hitler became chancellor of Germany. Fundamentalists were among the few groups in the United States to recognize almost immediately how central anti-Semitism was to the new regime. "The Hitler government," Brooks wrote shortly after Hitler came to power, "is doing its best to suppress the news until the work of exterminating the Jews is done." Bell expressed concern as well. "This persecution of the Jews in Germany is a strange thing," he wrote from China. It "shows colossal ignorance on the part of Hitler and his party." Fundamentalists believed that God would eventually punish Hitler for his actions. They insisted on the basis of Genesis 12:3 that to "bless" Jews was to guarantee God's blessing, while to persecute Jews was to anger the Almighty. Trumbull summed up their perspective by describing anti-Semitism as "a deadly boomerang" that would provoke God's wrath.[28]

While many fundamentalists lamented Jewish persecution, most saw it as part of God's end-times plan. In the Old Testament God had regularly used pagans to accomplish his geopolitical purposes and/or to punish his chosen people. This was no different. "Hitler does not know it," Ockenga concluded after a tour of Europe, "but he is an instrument in the hand of God for the driving of the Jews back to Palestine." Charles Fuller informed listeners of the *Old Fashioned Revival Hour* that the Jewish migration confirmed that the rapture was nearing. He explained that the "budding of the fig tree"—the repopulation of Palestine by Jews—was under way, which meant that the battle of Armageddon had to occur within the next fifteen years. Nevertheless, an editorial in the *Sunday School Times* reminded readers, "the fact that the Nazis are fulfilling prophecy does not excuse them." Fundamentalists believed that as they neared the return of Christ more and more evil would envelop the earth. Their responsibility was to wage war against it.[29]

Fundamentalists' interest in the Soviet Union, long an object of serious prophetic scrutiny, continued to grow in the 1930s. The Bolshevik revolution and then Stalin's consolidation of power reaffirmed their sense that Russia was moving into line with the plan of the ages. "No other nation on earth does so completely fit into the divine portraiture of a completely anti-God nation as does modern Russia," Bauman wrote. "If, as all signs clearly indicate, we are at the closing hour of Gentile domination on this earth, than what other nation could possibly be the 'Gog' of Ezekiel's prophecy if Russia is not?" A "European" writing in the *Pilot* informed readers that "Russia is rapidly preparing, if not already prepared, to take her part" in prophecy. For fundamentalists, there was no doubt that the USSR was the center of the great northern kingdom prophesied in the Old Testament.[30]

To the great chagrin of the faithful, Franklin Roosevelt did not understand God's end-times plans. Shortly after taking office in 1933, the president indicated that he might offer diplomatic recognition to the Soviet Union. Sensing what was coming, the World's Christian Fundamentals Association passed a resolution admonishing the government "to refuse to recognize Russia, because of the official and governmental atheism of that country and its sinister place in Bible prophecy." The protest was futile. In the fall of 1933, the Roosevelt administration officially recognized the Soviet Union. Fundamentalists responded with outrage. "We have recognized a bunch of atheists and murderers," Bell lamented. "I fear this move by our Government will have serious effects." The aging and increasingly irrelevant Billy Sunday wondered what "that blasphemous country" had "in common with us," while Gaebelein worried that FDR's "stupendous blunder" would facilitate "the rise and increase of communism in the United States."[31]

Church leaders and laypeople alike wrote the president to express their anger directly. A California minister warned that the United States "cannot expect to have God's blessing upon it as long as it recognizes the godless government of Soviet Russia." A Texan cautioned FDR that the USSR "is filling out the outlines of blasphemy, sacrilege and impiety" found in prophecy. He encouraged the president to live "in constant expectation of the Second Coming." "For a nation built upon Christian principles, such as ours is," wrote an Oregon minister "to join hands with a nation that is so flagrantly anti-God, anti-Christ, anti-Bible, and anti-religion, is to invite the certain judgment of Almighty God." It also invited the judgment of fundamentalists, who were no more forgiving.[32]

As fundamentalists mapped out the relationships between modern nation-states and those described in Ezekiel, Daniel, and Revelation, some wondered what role, if any, the United States played in the prophetic scheme. Biblical authors, writing thousands of years ago from locations around the Middle East, had no conception of North America. Nevertheless, some fundamentalists believed that God had secretly embedded references to the United States in the ancient scriptures. They eagerly searched the Bible seeking to demonstrate that their nation had a significant part to play in the last days.

Fundamentalists began their exegetical quest with Daniel's "king of the South" (Daniel 11), who they expected to battle the Antichrist and the great northern kingdom (Russia) at Armageddon. According to these fundamentalists, the "king of the South" probably referred to England. Then they juxtaposed this chapter with Ezekiel 38:13, which referred to "the merchants of Tarshish, with all the young lions thereof." They understood Tarshish as another reference to England while the "young lions" referred to current and former British colonies including the United States. Connecting these dots allowed fundamentalists to integrate premillennialism with American exceptionalism. On this basis Bauman predicted that Canada, the United States, Australia, New Zealand, and Great Britain "will be found protesting to the very end of the age against the ravages of the great Bolshevistic colossus of the north and its atheistic allies." Bauman even hoped that he would be able to keep his national citizenship in paradise. "Will the old Stars and Stripes," he wondered, "float aloft in

RUNNING ON
SCHEDULE TIME

THE THROTTLE
WIDE OPEN

E. J. Pace, the most popular fundamentalist cartoonist of the interwar era, often integrated apocalypticism into his illustrations. Here he depicts the efforts of fundamentalists to warn the world through their "advent testimony" that humankind was heading down the tracks of prophecy toward the battle of Armageddon and the coming judgment.

"Running on Schedule Time," *Sunday School Times,* May 13, 1933, 331.

glory in the Millennial Kingdom, not because she was without great national sins, but because she did refuse to join in any Satanic program to exterminate the 'earthly seed of Abraham'?" In one fell swoop Bauman perfectly blended premillennialism with American nationalism. Although such a move would have horrified Darby, Scofield, and other early premillennialists, it was one that fundamentalists increasingly made as war approached.[33]

Other fundamentalists thought that the prophet Isaiah, like Ezekiel, had foreseen the United States. "Looking down the vista of centuries," Gerald Winrod preached, Isaiah "saw a new nation born, the American ensign unfurled, and Old Glory blowing in the breeze." Canadian minister Canon F. E. Howitt promoted this view in *King's Business* and *Moody Monthly*. He offered a complicated argument in which Isaiah's allusion in chapter 18:1 to "the land shadowing with wings, which is beyond the rivers of Ethiopia" referred to the United States. William Blackstone had made the same argument to William Jennings Bryan a decade and a half earlier. Pentecostal Frederick Childe summarized the various theories offered by his fellow premillennialists. "This great nation that has taken such a prominent part in world politics in the past, and which is apparently destined to play a tremendously important part in world affairs in days to come. . . . Surely such a nation should find reference in the Word of God!" And indeed, Childe found those references in Isaiah 18:1, Revelation 12:14 (he believed that the reference to "two wings of a great eagle" referred to the United States) and Ezekiel 38 and 39. He further believed that the United States' support of a Jewish homeland in Palestine was evidence of Americans' prophetic role in the last days. "Perhaps," he wrote, "it is more than a coincidence that 'U.S.A.' is in the middle of Jerusalem! (Jer–USA–lem)."[34]

Other fundamentalists, however, believed that such speculation was misguided. "There is not a single clear and unmistakable reference specifically to the United States in the Bible," Rice insisted. Barnhouse warned that fundamentalists should "not try to seek exaggerated interpretations in prophecy where God has not intended to give them." This was a warning that most did not heed. As the world moved toward war, fundamentalists increasingly found prophetic significance in the actions of the United States, allowing them to connect themselves directly to the great chain of events described in Revelation. They wanted the nation of their birth to help make last-days history. Framing potential American military action as part of an inevitable and godly rebellion against the forces of the Antichrist laid the foundation for fundamentalists' wholehearted support of American action in World War II and then the Cold War. After all, to fight Mussolini,

Hitler, and later Stalin—Rome, Gomer, and Magog—was exactly what God had called the king of the South to do.[35]

While fundamentalists felt sure that Italy, Germany, the Soviet Union, and maybe England and the United States appeared in prophecy, they were less certain about what to make of the geopolitical changes occurring in Asia. Talbot believed that "the dark-skinned peoples—the nations of India, of China, of Japan, of the Mongolian hordes" would play an important role in the end times. He predicted that after the Antichrist had consolidated power in Europe and set up his capital in Jerusalem, the "kings of the East" (a reference from Revelation 16:12) would unite together under one leader and move to attack the Antichrist with an army of two hundred million people. Ironside predicted in the late 1930s that the leader of this "horde" would be Japan.[36]

The long history of US intervention in Asia shaped fundamentalist analysis of the region. American businesses had long benefited from the Open Door policy in China, which gave them access to the Orient's lucrative markets. Christians had invested heavily in China as well. Over the previous one hundred years, thousands of American missionaries had preached the gospel of Jesus and old-fashioned Americanism to countless Chinese. Missionaries believed that their efforts were rewarded in 1930 when Chinese leader Chiang Kai-shek, influenced by his Christian wife, converted. The 1931 publication of missionary Pearl S. Buck's best-selling book *The Good Earth* further enhanced American sympathies for the Chinese people. Fundamentalists believed that in China they would finally establish a foothold for Christian work around Asia.

Japan, however, had other plans for China. The Japanese government wanted better access to the natural resources on the continent and heralded Asia for the Asians. In 1931 Japan seized Manchuria. Then in 1937 Japan launched a full-scale war against China, to the dismay of most Americans, who felt particularly troubled that their nation was indirectly supplying Japan's war machine through trade. *Moody Monthly* defended China and encouraged readers to petition their national representatives to stop selling raw materials to Japan. Furthermore, the editors presciently added, "it is not at all impossible . . . that the very scrap iron which America is selling to Japan today will be the shells used on our own soldier boys not many months hence, as arrogant little Japan continues to dream of world conquest." Ockenga preached numerous sermons against the United States' indirect support of Japanese aggression as well. "Just as inevitable as there is a God," he harangued, "there will be a judgment of us for what we have done." Rice joined Ockenga in condemning American policy. "We deplored the sorrows of China," he sarcastically quipped, "but that was not nearly so important as the money we made out of the war!" Just months before Pearl Harbor he again warned that God was going to "bring America to judgment" for trading with Japan.[37]

But what did the war in Asia mean for prophecy? African-American minister Owen Troy predicted that Japan's militarism would lead to the establishment of an enormous Asian empire that would result in a race war, a "world war" between the "dark" and "white" races. Citing Revelation, he predicted that such a war would culminate in Armageddon. "Who knows but this war in China at the present time, and this state of unrest in India, are but the prelude of the awful battle of Armageddon, which will ring down the curtain of this world's history?" Assemblies of God missionary Elizabeth Galley, who was in China, admonished her family, "world conditions today are certainly threatening, and enough to make men's hearts to fail for fear if they are not centered and resting in the Lord and looking for His coming." The *King's Business* editors, trying to keep up with readers' endless cravings for articles on prophecy and world events, asked Lewis Sperry Chafer to write something on the "present Sino-Japanese conflict in prophecy." Chafer admitted to his friend Bauman that he knew nothing at all about the topic, and that "if anybody does know, I would go some distance to hear them give their definition." For a fundamentalist to acknowledge even privately that he could not put a major geopolitical event into a prophetic context was a rare thing. Nevertheless, fundamentalists all agreed that while the details might yet be vague, the conflict in Asia would soon lead to global war and eventually Armageddon.[38]

As events in Europe and Asia looked increasingly ominous, fundamentalists struggled to apply their theological convictions to real-world problems. The vast majority still harbored strong isolationist sentiments, but they also recognized that the increasingly volatile international situation abroad demanded a response. Jesus had called them to occupy their land. What did this mean in a world ruled by tyrants?

In 1938 the German army invaded Austria and Czechoslovakia. Hoping to convince Hitler to stop his aggression, French and English leaders met with Hitler in Munich. They agreed to cede the captured territory to Germany in exchange for Hitler's promise not to take any more land. British prime minister Neville Chamberlain heralded the pact as a guarantee of "peace in our time." H. A. Ironside, writing in his diary about the Munich conference, saw reasons for hope. "The war scare that kept us all exercised and in much perplexion for the past several weeks now seems to be over."[39]

But many fundamentalists feared that Munich had not really prevented war but instead made a major war all the more inevitable. Mark Matthews wrote a strongly worded letter to Chamberlain accusing him of kowtowing to Hitler, while Barnhouse criticized both the French and British for letting Hitler set the terms of the agreement. He worried that Chamberlain's Unitarian faith might have led in part to his poor decision-making. Bauman responded to the pact by reveling in the imminent cataclysm and coming slaughter. "The heavens are flashing signals that even fools should understand, to warn that the sun of man's day on this earth is about to set in vast seas of human blood." He privately told his editors, "events in Europe just now are taking place so fast that I am beginning to feel as though I would like to write a prophetic article every day!" Rice in turn reminded Christians that the "beast" of Revelation was coming. "The mystery is already working and the Bible is being fulfilled in Europe today." William Ward Ayer also predicted that the world might be rapidly approaching its denouement. The *New York Times* summarized his sermon, illustrating again that fundamentalists and their views were never as marginalized by the nation's major media as they sometimes claimed.[40]

In responding to the world's many crises, fundamentalists could not have positioned themselves any better. They promised Americans that only they could explain the causes of global turmoil, only they could anticipate where world events were heading, and most important, only they could guarantee adherents a means of escape from the impending global catastrophe. They, and they alone, could read beyond the headlines to help humanity navigate its way out of the coming earthly inferno and on to the millennial kingdom. If only the men and women they were trying to reach would listen.

By the late 1930s, fundamentalists' anticipation of the apocalypse reached all-time heights. And for good reason. The events they saw predicted in Jesus's sermons on the second coming and the prophecies of Daniel, Ezekiel, and Revelation all seemed to be converging almost exactly as fundamentalists had outlined decades earlier. The faithful had long believed that Jews would reclaim Palestine in the last days, a process that began during World War I and accelerated during the 1930s. They had also spent generations anticipating the rise of four competing empires around Palestine, which were taking shape before their eyes. The first and most important was the revived Roman Empire, led by Mussolini; the second was the northern kingdom, led by Stalin; the third was the southern kingdom, led by Great Britain and possibly the United States; and the fourth major empire, led by the "kings of the East," seemed to describe Japan. "For the first time in history," theologian Alva McClain wrote, "four great world powers are appearing contemporaneously in the precise quarters of the world as specified by prophecy *with the Jew back in his own land.*" Armageddon, fundamentalists reckoned, had to be imminent.[41]

On September 1, 1939, the German military invaded Poland. Tanks ripped over Polish terrain while planes provided air cover. The German strategy of blitzkrieg had begun. Within days of the invasion, Great Britain and France declared war on Germany. "It is terrible to think of," Ironside lamented in his diary. Mark Matthews, whose sense of himself knew no bounds, wrote Hitler directly. He called the führer a madman and recommended that he abdicate his office. "If you will so retire," he counseled, "send me a telegram of agreement. I think I can organize forces which will immediately begin working to present that promise and agreement to the world, thereby causing the cessation of fighting." Even more outrageously, the premillennialist promised to "begin efforts to organize the United States of Europe." A unified Europe was usually something that fundamentalists saw as a vehicle for bolstering the power of the Antichrist, not something they wanted to help create. But Matthews's premillennialism had never been terribly consistent. While outsiders and skeptics may not have seen fundamentalists as major players on a global stage, they always saw themselves as God's most powerful earthly ambassadors.[42]

Hitler encountered little resistance in Poland, in part because a month earlier he had signed a nonaggression pact with Stalin. The Nazi-Soviet pact stunned much of the world. Ideologically, the two nations could not have seemed further apart. Hitler was a right-wing fascist and Stalin a left-wing communist. Hitler had risen to power in Germany by playing on the German people's fears of communism, while communists around the world saw fascism as their mortal enemy. Fundamentalists, however, rejoiced over the news of the pact.

Radical evangelicals had long believed that the Germans and the Soviets—Magog and Gomer in Ezekiel's terms—would compose the end-times northern alliance. When this seemingly happened, they celebrated the fact that their reading of prophecy better anticipated coming events than did forecasts offered by the US State Department. "The unregenerate of this world's intelligentsia," Bauman boasted, "have long assured us that Germany and Russia could never march together to battle." But fundamentalists knew better. Dan Gilbert noted that if the world's great democracies had accepted the "Word of God" they could have prepared for this contingency. Ockenga preached a similar message to his congregation. "Bible students have long been foretelling that Germany and Russia would get together." Armageddon, he concluded, "may be closer than we expect."[43]

As fundamentalists witnessed what they interpreted as the ultimate fulfillment of the scriptures, their confidence grew. But a few of the faithful feared that their coreligionists were putting too much emphasis on premillennialism. Radical evangelicals' obsession with scouring the news for hints of the Antichrist took time and energy away from the work of helping to save humankind from the coming tribulation. "But is it not a fact," W. W. Shannon asked, "that many of the saints will cross the city and go many miles to hear about the Antichrist, but they would not cross the street to try to win a soul for Christ?" Roy Laurin, the new editor of King's Business, also felt troubled. "How much prophecy?" he asked. "One of the great temptations with which the alert preacher finds himself confronted in these stirring days is the temptation to deal disproportionately with the prophetic aspect of the Scriptures. . . . If Daniel is in the canon of Scripture—so is John. If Antichrist is a menace—Christ is the panacea. If totalitarianism threatens—regeneration is still our greatest hope." Nevertheless, Laurin expanded coverage of prophecy in *King's Business* the following year. "In line with readers' desires," he explained, "increased emphasis has been placed upon current events in the light of Bible prophecy." Fight it as he may, Laurin quickly learned that prophecy was essential for the success of his magazine.[44]

With war clouds looming, Moody Bible Institute professor Wilbur Smith dictated a long letter to Dean Will Houghton suggesting that the school renew its focus on prophecy. "Our Lord's return cannot be far away," he assured his colleague. "In the last five or six years we have seen prophecy fulfilled more rapidly, more universally than in any other similar period since the close of the Apostolic Age." Thinking boldly, he suggested that they dedicate the school's annual conference to reexamining prophecy books from the previous fifty years to demonstrate that events they predicted "are coming to pass." Charles Fuller saw the same signs. On New Year's Eve 1939, he took to the radio. "The Bible," he preached, "gives us a very *vivid, clear, comprehensive* word-picture of the days in which we are *now living,* and the remarkable thing about this word picture of the last days, of this age—the days in which we are now living—is that it was written some 1900 years ago." Finally, Rice spoke for fundamentalists around the country when he assured his congregation, "We cannot say that Jesus will come by December first, nor positively that He will come in 1940. But according to certain signs, we can definitely believe that His coming is near, very, very, near, is likely to come even today."[45]

With so much prophecy being fulfilled with such speed, many of the nation's major fundamentalist leaders decided to reconvene for the first time since the end of World War I to study the relationship between prophecy and world events. Gaebelein believed that in the same way that prophecy conferences had helped Christians make sense of World War I, a new series of conferences would prepare the faithful for the new war and coming rapture. But rather than follow the model of the World War I conferences, which were heavily publicized and sought to awaken all Americans to the hope of the rapture, in 1940 fundamentalists led by MBI's Will Houghton organized a series of low-key, closed-door meetings with the country's leading experts, where they could wrestle with the relationship between the scriptures and world events outside the curious gaze of the public. "Would you and could you meet," he asked, "with a group of Bible students of like mind, to spend a few days in prayer and Bible study, with particular thought as to prophecy and where we are today?" "Surely," he concluded, "in the light of the key position America holds in this dark day, God has something to say to American Christians, and perhaps if these leaders will get down in the dust of humiliation it may please God to say it to and through them." Attendees included prominent fundamentalists William Ward Ayer, J. Oliver Buswell, Charles Fuller, David Fuller, H. A. Ironside, Robert Ketcham, Robert McQuilkin, Harold John Ockenga, and L. Sale-Harrison.[46]

The white fundamentalist men who came together in Chicago discovered that apparently God did have something to say. Out of the conference came a series of resolutions. First the group attacked fascism, both at home and abroad. They blamed the world's "departure from revealed truth . . . for the collapse of civilization and for the isms, such as statism, classism, racism." Second, they asserted, "God is speaking very definitely to the nations through present world conditions," which meant that Christians should renew their focus on "the present plight of the world in light of Bible prophecy." Finally they defined their own obligations. "We increasingly feel it our solemn responsibility in this crisis hour to tell forth what God has clearly foretold in His Word, and thus enable the people properly to interpret the tragic events of our day." The men who cloistered at MBI emerged from their meetings with a renewed faith in their own significance. God, they believed, wanted them to speak truth to power in order to redirect the trajectory of their nation as war loomed in the distance.[47]

8

CHRIST'S DEAL VERSUS THE NEW DEAL

THE PRESIDENT HAD A PROBLEM. During the summer of 1935, a political operative working for Franklin Delano Roosevelt traveled the country hoping to gauge levels of support for the administration. The Democrats wanted to be prepared for the 1936 presidential campaign. The operative's August report contained such important conclusions that FDR's secretary insisted that the president read it personally. "In my opinion," the operative explained in the memorandum, "the strongest opposition to Mr. Roosevelt—in 1936—would come, not from the economic reactionaries, but from the religious reactionaries (if you can separate the two). . . . The opposition of what one can call the evangelical churches is growing steadily more bitter and open."[1]

The operative was exactly right. Fundamentalists interpreted Franklin Roosevelt's efforts to expand the power of the federal government and his internationalist inclinations in the context of their end-times expectations. Against the background of Hitler's persecution of Jews, Mussolini's restoration of the Roman Empire, Stalin's institutionalization of state atheism, and the global economic depression, the faithful believed that the Roosevelt presidency was marking the start of the countdown to Armageddon in the United States. The president's will

for power and global sensibilities seemed to augur the political philosophy of the coming Antichrist. Troubled by what they were witnessing
at home and abroad, white radical evangelicals began to view their
president and his administration not as God's emissaries on earth but as
tools of the devil. For the faithful living in the 1930s, to support Roosevelt was to support the Antichrist.

On the eve of the stock market crash, most Americans had little sense
that the economy was crumbling beneath them. The nation seemed
strong, the automobile industry was booming, new homes were pop-
ping up all over the country, and middle-class consumers had plenty of
money to spend on the latest goods, from vacuum cleaners to refrigera-
tors to radio sets. But within a couple of years, the economy had totally
imploded. Unemployment skyrocketed, prices for agricultural goods
plummeted, financial institutions collapsed, corporations laid off unprecedented numbers of workers, and banks foreclosed on record numbers
of home mortgages. The American people were suffering. Hoboes
took to the rails in search of work; others built makeshift residences
out of scrap materials in vacant lots derisively dubbed Hoovervilles in
honor of the president. Some Americans took to the streets as well,
demanding more action on the part of the federal government.

As the nation readied for the 1932 presidential campaign, fundamentalists prepared for action. The incumbent, Herbert Hoover, ran
for reelection on the Republican ticket. Democrats nominated Franklin Delano Roosevelt. The wealthy scion of an elite New York family,
Roosevelt had succeeded Al Smith as governor of New York. A charismatic speaker, he had the ability to energize the American public, but
he personified the liberal, urban progressivism that fundamentalists
and political conservatives abhorred. Fundamentalists saw an especially
ominous sign during the Democratic National Convention. On the
first set of convention ballots, Roosevelt received 666 votes. Six-six-six
was the number long associated with the Antichrist (Revelation 13:18).

Even more ominous was FDR's disdain for Prohibition. Fundamentalists fretted that the Democratic Party, seemingly beholden to urban
interests and immigrants, would lead the campaign for repeal. Although
most fundamentalists opposed federal expansion into the economy,

they seemed sure that Washington had an important role to play in restricting citizens' moral choices. Nelson Bell despaired that if the "wets" won the White House, "our country will be ruined." H. A. Ironside, along with Moody Bible Institute president James Gray, organized a mass meeting to address the question "What is the Christian's responsibility in reference to the question 'Shall We Repeal the 18th Amendment?'" Their answer was clear—don't let it happen.[2]

Fundamentalists used the Prohibition issue to instruct fellow believers to vote Republican. "The objective of the Democratic party is the return of liquor," the *Western Recorder* editorialized. "The objective of the Republican party is the conservation of our gains and the protection of our rights already secured." Individual preachers echoed the Kentucky-based magazine. "I took my stand in no uncertain terms in my pulpit," Bauman wrote a friend. "I came out as strongly as I could against Roosevelt and his whole sopping-wet program." Democratic-leaning fundamentalists were no more pleased with FDR than they had been with Smith. J. Frank Norris and transplanted southerner and old Wilson ally Mark Matthews—pastors of two of the largest churches in the nation—both despised the Democratic candidate. "What are you going to do about this infernal wet issue?" Matthews wrote Norris after the convention. "Roosevelt is worse than Smith." "I quite agree with you on Roosevelt's being worse than Smith," Norris responded, "and in addition to being wet, he is a Communist. I can not believe the country will elect him though it is in a mighty bad state of mind." Norris, however, sat out the 1932 campaign, which infuriated at least one supporter. A North Dakota farmer wrote the minister lamenting that the Texas Tornado was not "on the firing line, in front, in the thickest of the fight, dealing irresistible blows with the Sword of the Spirit, discomforting the enemy, making a valiant stand for God, pure and undefiled religion and Prohibition, as he did in 1928." That fundamentalists as far away as the Dakotas looked to Norris for political leadership revealed how far his influence had spread.[3]

While repeal aroused the strongest sentiments among fundamentalists, many also worried about taxes. *Moody Monthly* claimed that an unreasonable tax burden had "ruined the Roman Empire, and it will ruin the United States if a halt is not called." In a primitive form of trickle-down economic theory, the editors hoped that the government would ease the tax burden on the wealthy. "If some of our rich men, or rich corporations at least, were not as heavily taxed as they are, it would be much better for us poorer people." These Chicago fundamentalists, ignoring James's last-days predictions, defended the wealthy. Having long walked in lockstep with corporate leaders, they tried to insulate the rich from anything that might cause weeping and howling rather than see such weeping and howling as a sign of the evil days in which they were living.[4]

Like their white counterparts, many African-American evangelicals supported Hoover in 1932. But pentecostal minister Smallwood Williams, the leader of a growing church in Washington, D.C., saw things differently. He believed that Hoover "was insensitive to the economic needs of poor people. His Republican Party had become bedfellows with Big Business, making empty promises to poor people and fat provisions for the rich." Although Williams had never voted, he decided that something needed to change. "I became determined to do whatever I could to get rid of President Hoover and his policies." Prohibited by Jim Crow laws from registering his choice for president in the nation's capitol, he voted for Roosevelt by absentee ballot in his former home state of Ohio.[5]

The election was a tremendous victory for FDR, who decimated Hoover at the polls. For many fundamentalists, the results came as a disappointment. "Election went off quietly," Ironside confided in his diary, "but much to my regret Franklin Roosevelt was elected." The century-long effort of various Protestant groups to enshrine Christian morality in the Constitution through the Prohibition amendment seemed a failure. Reinforced by portentous changes abroad, Roosevelt's election represented not simply the triumph of a less-desirable candidate but the ascension of an interventionist government driven by secular philosophies. That so many Americans supported FDR boded ill for the preservation of fundamentalist values.[6]

Radical evangelical leaders throughout the nation knew beyond any doubt that their colleagues had lined up for Hoover and the GOP. "I am greatly concerned over the turn of the election yesterday," Lewis Sperry Chafer wrote to Ironside, "and feel we shall see much harder times before we see any relief." Fundamentalists did not simply frame their analysis around relevant political issues. Instead they believed that

Roosevelt's victory had moved the world one step closer to Armageddon. "The results of the past election in our beloved country," Hollywood minister Stewart MacLennan observed, "confirm the conviction that we are living in the end days of human government in the earth. . . . Surely the Lord must be at hand!" Bauman wrote a friend that the election "seems to have gone chiefly in a way that delights the devil's crowd, but these are the last days and what else are we to expect?" Fundamentalists rarely expected anything but the worst. But the worst often signaled good news in that it confirmed how quickly the rapture was approaching. Their longing to escape the tribulations of this world was reinforced by events both international and domestic that seemed to be aligning against them. They knew, however, that God had entrusted them with a mission to fulfill as they anticipated his return.[7]

As Roosevelt prepared to assume the presidency, Americans wondered how he would address the growing economic crisis. In accepting the Democratic nomination, he promised to provide "a new deal for the American people," but what he had in mind remained a mystery until the inauguration. From the East Portico of the US Capitol he guaranteed that the nation "will endure . . . will revive and will prosper." Then, delivering one of the most famous lines in American presidential history, he assured his audience, "the only thing we have to fear is fear itself—nameless, unreasoning, unjustified terror which paralyzes needed efforts to convert retreat into advance." He concluded the address by calling Congress into a special session to find solutions to the economic crisis and then warned that if legislators failed to act he would seek "broad Executive power to wage a war against the emergency." The president was prepared to use the bully pulpit to redefine the relationship between the federal government and the American people.[8]

In a short-lived moment of conciliation, some fundamentalists hoped that the president-elect's decision to take communion before his inauguration meant that he might actually be someone they could support. The *Sunday School Times* ran an unsigned editorial written by MBI professor Wilbur Smith praising Roosevelt's use of the Bible during his swearing-in ceremony, as president FDR consistently talked about his faith and invoked explicit Christian ideals. But fundamentalists soon determined that the commander-in-chief was simply posturing. After all, they believed that Satan was most effective when posing as an angel of light.[9]

In Roosevelt's first one hundred days, he engaged in a flurry of activity. With the support of a heavily Democratic Congress, he and his administration crafted and enacted substantial new legislation aimed at relieving poverty and reforming the economy. The president believed that the rise of behemoth corporations, huge bureaucracies, and the transformation of the market over the previous few decades required a new approach. The federal government was no longer the great leviathan that should be kept in check; instead it needed to play an important role in protecting individual liberties and freedoms from the many economic and political forces that threatened them. As the United States faced an unprecedented financial meltdown, he argued that the state needed to intervene aggressively into the economy to regulate big business and protect individual citizens. In crafting a new philosophy of government, FDR gave birth to modern political liberalism.

Roosevelt's actions did not surprise fundamentalists. With Mussolini in power in Italy, Stalin at the helm in Russia, and the Nazi Party on the ascent in Germany, they believed that the United States was ripe for its own totalitarian leader. During the campaign many fundamentalists predicted the inevitable rise of an American dictator, and that was exactly what they saw in FDR's aggressive policies. The editors of *Moody Monthly,* just a few months into Roosevelt's term, compared the president to Hitler and claimed that his actions were "preparing the people for what is coming later, and perhaps not much later—the big dictator, the superman, the lawless one at the head of the ten kingdoms of the prophetic earth." Wilbur Smith laid out typical fundamentalist logic in a letter to *Sunday School Times* editor Charles Trumbull. He called "the sudden, amazing rise of dictatorships throughout Europe" and the acquiescence to "dictatorship" in the United States "preparation for the coming of a great world dictator." As economic troubles increased, Smith explained, people would "look to one great super-man, and that is the perfect setting of the stage for the manifestation of Anti-Christ." Bauman believed that the president's programs were "presenting the world with a system of government, which carried to its limits, corresponds amazingly to the Biblical description of the government of the coming 'prince.'" Ockenga, Riley, Rice, and pentecostals Loren Staats and J. N. Hoover each claimed that Hitler, Mussolini, Stalin, and Roosevelt might be establishing confederacies that would lead to world domination by the Antichrist. An Illinois minister even confronted the president directly about these concerns. "I cannot quite see," he wrote, "why your administration should want to scrap the Constitution, concentrate power in your hands, put the Courts out of business, and turn this great Republic into a dictatorship after the pattern of Russia, Germany or Italy." For decades fundamentalists had expected end-times governments to represent what Daniel described as a mix of iron and clay—totalitarian control supported through popular democracy. Roosevelt seemed to be giving the nation exactly that.[10]

Fundamentalists not only worried about FDR's motives, they also fretted about the agendas of those who advised him. Dating back to his days as governor, Roosevelt had looked to academics rather than political cronies for solutions to social and economic problems. Although the press dubbed his key advisors the "Brain Trust," the faithful had little trust in their brains. "If the university professor's sole desire is to be right," *Moody Monthly* editors queried, "why is he found almost uniformly in opposition to the only righteous Man who ever lived, our Lord and Savior Jesus Christ?" A "poor country minister" called on FDR to "clean out a lot of them hot dog Harvard boys . . . that someway have squirmed into Washington and pretty nearly ruined your whole administration." An incensed Presbyterian minister from Fort Lauderdale advised FDR, "Mr. President, you have never had to work for a living. For that reason you are impractical, but being from Ha'va'd you don't know it. . . . Discard your crazy counselors; retrace your foolish courses." Bauman identified the majority of the New Deal architects, including Marriner Eccles, Harold Ickes, Mordecai Ezekiel, Felix Frankfurter, Benjamin Cohen, Henry Morgenthau, Charles Taussig, Rexford Tugwell, Harry Hopkins, and Frances Perkins as communists and socialists. That many members of the Brain Trust were Jewish likely worried him as well. He called them the "worst brains that ever directed our old Ship of State." Fundamentalists' animosity toward elite academics made them suspicious of these professors, who they assumed went from peddling Darwin and Marx in their classrooms to peddling the same diabolical theorists in Washington.[11]

Convinced that the personal was political, fundamentalists saw in FDR's family additional reasons to agonize over the state of the nation. Eleanor Roosevelt, a longtime progressive reformer, played an important role in shaping the New Deal, to the great frustration of the faithful who believed that she was either a socialist or a communist. That she became a symbol of women's mobility and freedom rather than solely a domestic partner troubled them as well. Some fundamentalists also picked on the family's personal morals, convinced that the Roosevelts set bad examples for the nation. "Yourself and Wife stand at the head of the list of the million cigarette smokers," wrote a Nazarene leader. "We certainly do hope and pray" that God will "deliver this nation before it is entirely too late." Stough disparaged the entire family in a revival sermon for their alleged divorces, drinking problems, traffic tickets, and bootlegging. The Roosevelt family, he scolded, "has helped undermine the ideals upon which the nation was founded." The president had become for radical evangelicals a stand-in for all the progressive attitudes that seemed to be turning Americans away from more traditional family-based values.[12]

Fundamentalists grounded their anti-Roosevelt sentiments in much more than personal differences, however. The policy innovations that defined the New Deal caused them substantial consternation. Within days of taking office, FDR signed the Beer-Wine Revenue Act, which set the stage for the repeal of Prohibition. Although the faithful had anticipated the move, they were furious. The president, Stough griped, had started "the nation downward into legalized drunkenness & debauchery" in an "agreement with Hell." Norris sarcastically quipped that turning the "rivers of liquor back on the homes of the American people" was the only campaign promise Roosevelt had kept. The president heard directly from many religious leaders about this issue. A Texas Baptist warned him, "God can not bless a Rum-soaked, dancing, nudist nation with total prosperity"; Los Angeles minister Gustav Briegleb feared repeal had produced "the finest crop of drunkards we have ever had." He sarcastically suggested that Roosevelt create a new agency to help deal with the growing crisis. Evangelist Mordecai Ham, not pulling any punches, quipped that the rise in employment among preachers was a consequence of the New Deal. Churches had found new relevance serving the victims of alcohol abuse.[13]

African-American evangelical minister and radio evangelist Lightfoot Solomon Michaux disagreed with those who condemned the president. He pointed out that if ministers spent less time harping on the president and more time leading their churches in righteousness, "they might be able to say as I can about my parish. . . . as far as we are concerned, America is still dry. Our slogan is, If the world wants liquor, let them have it, and the church stay dry that it may be a light and an example." A layperson and friend of Norris took a similar view. He called Prohibition "a post-millennial mistake." While this position may have been the most consistent with fundamentalist theology, most of the faithful believed that it was inimical to occupying until the second coming.[14]

Beer was far from the only problem fundamentalists had with the president's agenda in the first one hundred days. To help stabilize American industry, Roosevelt proposed the National Industrial Recovery Act. New Deal architects believed that part of the nation's economic problems resulted from too much marketplace competition. Working around antitrust regulations, they pressured major manufacturers in various industries to cooperate with the goal of stabilizing supply and setting uniform wages, hours, and prices. The act also threw a bone to workers, giving them the right to organize and collectively bargain. The program led in part to the creation of the National Recovery Administration (NRA). Participation in the NRA was voluntary; however, the government encouraged consumers to boycott those businesses that did not display its "Blue Eagle" symbol.

Many fundamentalist leaders criticized the NRA, confident that it undermined traditional American capitalist values. Billy Sunday believed that federal regulation of the economy meant that "the rugged individualism of Americanism must go," while Bauman carped that the NRA would likely "destroy individual action, and force cooperation with the group. Its promoters," he opined, "already have very much to say in depreciation of 'rugged individualism.'" On a more positive note, he hoped that the growing numbers of nudists—a popular trend in the interwar era—would don the Blue Eagle. The acronym could be reinterpreted, he wrote (missing his own double entendre), to mean "Nuts Running Abroad!"[15]

For many fundamentalists the NRA was problematic for reasons beyond its supposed impact on rugged individualism. The book of Revelation predicts that in the last days the Antichrist will require all people to display the "mark of the beast" (Revelation 13:17–18) in order to participate in the economy. The NRA seemed to foreshadow this prophecy. "Roosevelt's 'Blue Eagle' sign is certainly significant," Bell wrote. "If he succeeds in his present policy just watch European powers follow suit and then it will not be long until the 'mark of the beast' will be displayed." The majority of fundamentalists agreed with Bell that the eagle was a precursor but not the actual mark. In fact, editors Barnhouse *(Revelation)*, Trumbull *(Sunday School Times),* and Bogard *(Baptist and Commoner)* all participated in the NRA. Nevertheless, all of the fundamentalist periodicals took up the issue of the Blue Eagle in response to readers' questions about the relationships among current events, federal policies, and prophecy. Their concerns revealed that fears of Roosevelt as forerunner to the Antichrist were not just a top-down phenomenon generated by influential ministers but reflected the interests and anxieties of laypeople.[16]

While FDR and his Brain Trust worked to stabilize industry, they also sought relief for American agriculture. Since the end of the Great War, overproduction had driven prices down to the point that significant numbers of farmers had a difficult time staying financially afloat. To address the crisis in rural America, FDR pushed the Agricultural Adjustment Act (AAA) through Congress. Its purpose was to increase prices for agricultural goods by limiting production. To achieve this goal the act offered subsidies to farmers who agreed to reduce crop acreage and thereby reduce supplies, which policy-makers hoped would increase demand and make agricultural goods more profitable. Meanwhile, the cash farmers received from subsidies gave them the ability to buy industrial and consumer goods, which benefited the economy as a whole. However, by the time the bill made it through the legislature, many farmers had already planted their fields. The Roosevelt administration responded by paying agricultural workers to plow under new sprouts. It also subsidized the destruction of millions of squealing piglets and other livestock. While the economics of this policy might have been sound, the symbolism was awful. For the American people to see goods destroyed at a time of want sent a disquieting message.

Fundamentalists despised the AAA. "I cannot believe that God in heaven is pleased with such a program," a Missouri minister wrote to FDR, while an Alabama Baptist described it as "the biggest [*sic*] fool thing that any president has ever inaugurated." Gaebelein called the demolition of agricultural goods "the great sin of America." "Since 1933," he harangued, "when the godless in Washington advocated the wicked destruction of the Creator's kind gifts . . . disaster upon disaster has come." He warned Americans that ecological catastrophes such as drought represented God's answer "to the policy of men who think they can run nature . . . without the God of Nature." Meanwhile, Sunday linked the NRA with the AAA, calling them the "serpentine coils of this communistic, socialistic, atheistic, monster."[17]

Fundamentalists, who saw themselves as citizens of two worlds, moved seamlessly from prophetic utterances to political critiques of New Deal programs and back again. A Denver minister warned FDR that Jesus's return and the coming judgment were imminent but in the meantime still felt compelled to offer the president advice on the economy, a balanced budget, and the use of agricultural surpluses. A New York minister counseled FDR that the rebirth of the Roman Empire, the rise of the Soviet Union, and the return of Jews to Palestine all indicated that prophecy was "rapidly being fulfilled now." Then he scolded the president and called the destruction of foodstuffs and the slaughter of pigs a "crime." Premillennialism allowed the faithful to critique what they saw around them without forcing them to take responsibility for it. They believed that God had turned the world over to Satan until the battle of Armageddon. Until then, they could claim the moral high ground without having to get their hands dirty in the hard and imperfect work of social and economic reform.[18]

While Roosevelt and his staff worked with Congress on many new pieces of legislation, various Americans outside Washington proposed their own programs aimed at solving the nation's problems. One of the most popular was the Townsend plan. In the mid-1930s, Frances E. Townsend, a tall, thin, retired doctor living in Long Beach, California, put forward a proposal aimed at increasing the consumer spending of the elderly while also getting them out of the labor market in order to open up positions for younger people. His old-age pension plan called for the federal government to provide monthly payments of two hundred dollars to the elderly with the provision that they spend their checks in the month that they received them. Although the plan was economically unfeasible, it became quite popular. Millions of Americans all over the nation joined Townsend clubs and signed petitions calling on the president to make the plan a reality.

Fundamentalist leaders generally did not buy what Townsend was selling. John R. Rice called the plan "silly, wicked and dangerous." In part he detested the redistribution of wealth inherent in the proposal. "Higher taxes and increased Government spending do not mean prosperity. They never did, and they never will." Others rejected the utopian hopes nurtured by the plan. "Dr. T. affirms that poverty would vanish permanently in five years," Brooks wrote. "Our Lord knew of no such workable scheme when He said that the poor should always be with us." Not all fundamentalists felt that the plan was a bad idea, however. When *Moody Monthly* joined the anti-Townsend chorus, angry readers flooded the magazine with a wave of negative correspondence. Meanwhile, an "evangelist preacher" warned FDR that although the president was "facing some of the terrible conditions" predicted for the "last days" there was reason to hope. "But you can be elected president again," the preacher advised, "*if you are wise enough to quickly adopt the Dr. Townsend Old Age pension plan.*" According to this believer, the bespectacled Long Beach doctor could help thwart the last-days schemes of the devil.[19]

While keeping his distance from the Townsend movement, Roosevelt pushed the Social Security Act through Congress in 1935, creating the first comprehensive federal welfare program in American history. It had multiple components. Workers made payments into a Social Security fund that employers matched. The government, in turn, used these payments to distribute benefits to retired workers. The legislation also created a joint federal-state program that provided unemployment compensation to workers, relief to the poor, and payments to the indigent elderly and single mothers with dependent children.

Roosevelt hoped that the program would earn him massive popular support. In the fall of 1935, possibly in response to the summer memorandum he received on growing evangelical opposition, he reached out to the nation's religious leaders. "Because of the grave responsibilities of my office, I am turning to representative Clergymen for counsel and advice," he wrote. "I am particularly anxious that the new Social Security Legislation just enacted . . . shall be carried out in keeping with the high purposes with which this law was enacted. . . . Tell me where you feel our government can better serve our people. . . . We shall have to work together for the common end of better spiritual and material conditions for the American people."[20]

The response from fundamentalist ministers to Social Security was probably not what the president had hoped for. They believed that the more Americans turned to the federal government for help, the fewer rights they would retain. Eventually they would be powerless when the government ceded control to the Antichrist. "In my humble judgment," Wheaton College president J. Oliver Buswell explained to the president in less than humble terms, "you are seriously in error. In fact, the socialistic or communistic tendencies of your administration and of the legislation to which your letter refers, are entirely contrary to the spirit and the detailed teachings of the Word of God." Chafer warned FDR not to reproduce the "English dole system" and fretted that Americans were "anticipating too much from the federal government." J. Gresham Machen wrote the president as well. He opposed the Social Security Act as "inimical (1) to liberty and (2) to honesty." A number of other ministers moved effortlessly from discussions of prophecy to criticisms of the act. One man from rural Florida explained to FDR, "as I see prophecies fulfilling so rapidly," he began, "it fills me with fear and trembling." Then he lamented that the president had given the South "a dirty deal" and worried that Social Security would "never help the poor old farms."[21]

Other radical evangelicals integrated critiques of Social Security into their sermons and articles. Dan Gilbert believed that Americans had to choose between "personal security" and "social security." Do they want "the traditional American way" of "freedom," he asked, or "the alien way, whereby the government plans and provides what the citizen shall be, what he shall do, how he shall live?" Ockenga complained of "character disintegration" in "every one of these security movements, doles and unemployment protections," which made Americans "dependent more and more upon government." Gaebelein believed that among the consequences of FDR's unprecedented spending was "the creation of a new class of citizens, the class of 'dole-loafers.'" Foreshadowing modern racially coded allusions to supposed "welfare queens," he alleged that "colored maids" were impossible to find in Washington, D.C., since "they are all on the dole." Radical evangelicals

Religious activists found many innovative ways to spread their message. In 1939 a photographer captured this prophecy truck whose owner apparently hoped Congress would heed the message that Jesus was coming soon.

Photo by John Vachon, Courtesy of Library of Congress, LC–USF34–060110–D.

believed that the government had no business expanding its reach into the economy; policies that strengthened the state not only violated their political presuppositions but went against the eternal word of God. Fundamentalists' critique of Social Security spoke volumes about their politics and worldview. They simply did not believe that the government should be looking after the welfare of individuals. In so doing it was subverting God's order and assuming responsibilities that God had assigned to churches and local communities.[22]

A few fundamentalists, however, lobbied FDR for their own piece of the New Deal pie. An Illinois man wrote FDR that the depression could not end since the "Second-Coming-Of-Christ" was "Near at Hand." Nevertheless, he promised that in the meantime he could improve conditions around the country if Roosevelt would simply pay him $150 a week to hold evangelistic meetings. Joe Baird, an "evangelistic singer, Chautauqua entertainer, and war song leader," suggested that Roosevelt help Americans sing their way out of the depression. "There is nothing that will cause people to forget their troubles, pep them up for greater activity and give them that feeling of security, more than good wholesome singing." These requests, however, were not typical. Most fundamentalists believed that New Deal spending was antithetical to both Christian nurture and national blessings.[23]

Roosevelt, more than any president before him, provided fundamentalists with an opportunity to link their apocalyptic theology to their politics. Their relentless sense that they needed to make every minute count, their belief that they were engaged in an all-out battle against evil, and their reading of national and international events prepared radical evangelicals to discern evidence of the Antichrist almost everywhere. In FDR they saw a president who repudiated Prohibition, raised a family with questionable morals, surrounded himself with secular-minded intellectuals, and usurped the social welfare mission of the country's churches. His aggressive interventions into the economy reinforced their convictions. They could not believe that the president, like Mussolini and Hitler, was doing anything other than paving the way for the rise of a global tyrant.

Roosevelt's prolabor sympathies fired up the faithful as well. Dating back at least to the Red Scare, fundamentalists had believed that radicals and foreigners who threatened American freedoms had overtaken the labor movement. Fundamentalists agreed with political conservatives that the work of organized labor undermined individual rights and liberties and feared that a surging mass of discontented workers could foster social turmoil and chaos, inspiring political leaders to claim even greater power for the state. That the president seemed to side with workers more than businesses and that he offered them protections through the National Industrial Recovery Act and later the Wagner Act symbolized for fundamentalists yet another sign of his inability to separate the sheep from the goats. While FDR and his Brain Trust potentially set the stage from the top down for the Antichrist to assume power, godless labor leaders wittingly or unwittingly were doing the same thing from the bottom up.

Fundamentalists saw in labor organizations havens for the very people they most distrusted—political radicals, foreigners, and outcasts. Pentecostal Charles E. Robinson called unions "the most sinister thing in our government," while Rice groused, "you can hardly separate unionism and communism." Ockenga disparaged unions as well, convinced that they remained "a fertile field for communist propaganda." When workers chose to strike, fundamentalists blamed their actions on radicals and communists. They refused to see worker unrest as a reasonable response to deplorable workplace conditions. Instead, they steadfastly joined other political and economic conservatives in maintaining that the actions of subversives were driving the labor movement.[24]

As workers' frustration grew, some engaged in a new, more effective tactic—the sit-down strike. The most famous sit-down started in late 1936 in a Flint, Michigan, General Motors plant where assembly-line workers struck not by walking off the job or carrying signs but by occupying their workspace so that strikebreakers could not replace them. "Led by radicals and communists," Gilbert scowled, "strikers have . . . flouted Christian principles of morality and American principles of government." He accused them of resorting to "terrorism." An editorial in McPherson's *Crusader* saw important symbolism in the controversy. "Whether strikers sit down or rise up" they indicate "how tragically we have lost our good old American Rugged Individualism." Fundamentalists viewed private property as sacrosanct. For unions to occupy that property was therefore a challenge not just to their corporate bosses but also to the American way of life.[25]

While many fundamentalists groused that radicals had captured the working class, others blamed the president for labor problems. "This is the Roosevelt depression," Rice harangued, "not the Hoover depression." He reprimanded FDR for crafting policies that encouraged sit-down strikes and warned that the president had "angered and displeased God Almighty." Brooks wondered if FDR had given communists "a free hand to bring all commerce under control of a central dictatorship." Bell thought he knew the solution to labor unrest. "What we need," he proposed, "is a Government that stands for law and order and which will rule with an iron hand when necessary." That was not, he lamented, what the nation was getting. The popular American conviction that every man could and should pick himself up by his bootstraps remained central to the radical evangelical worldview.[26]

Driving most fundamentalist critiques of Roosevelt's handling of the economy was the larger presumption that the president was leading the nation down a slippery slope toward communism. "During the five months that have elapsed since Roosevelt became the President of the United States," Assemblies minister F. J. Lindquist complained, "our government has drifted far from the principles of Democracy, and very close to the Socialistic and Communistic ideals of Russia." Riley called FDR's supposed embrace of Soviet policies "stupid." A Texas premillennialist did not let his faith in the imminent second coming prevent him from expressing his displeasure directly to Roosevelt. He saw in "confiscatory taxes" the "hydra heads of Socialism and incipient Communism" whose "real object" was "the ultimate confiscation of all property and the utter destruction of private initiative in business." Norris also linked the New Deal to communism. "I hail from the South," he preached, "and since my ancestors set foot on the shores of South Carolina . . . they have always been Democrats." But he now believed "that the greatest menace that ever confronted America—is the 'New Deal'—no more or less than the American name for Russian Communism." Calling FDR's policies communistic provided fundamentalists with a rhetorically powerful device for undermining the president's plans for intervening in the economy and creating a more just tax system.[27]

Future fundamentalist movement leaders shared their elders' litany of concerns about the New Deal. O. E. Tiffany, a history professor at Wheaton College with a PhD from the University of Michigan, wrote

Roosevelt expressing the views of the school's faculty and students. He claimed that juniors and seniors were about two to one against the New Deal, sophomores about three to one, and freshman about four to one against it. He specifically criticized "the continuance of heavy expenditures on public or semi-public works"; "the increasing cost of the ever-enlarging number of seemingly unnecessary civil service workers"; and "higher taxes." "Many," he continued, "believe that your social program has been a hindrance to the return of prosperity."[28]

Apparently Tiffany's sense of the politics of the Christian school was on target. Roosevelt received another letter, this one from a local Wheaton man and former minister who lamented the Republican control of his Chicago suburb. He complained that the college had "well-nigh ruined the town" by bombarding its citizens with the "imaginary dangers of Socialism, Communism, Masonic and other secret orders, Theatres, Dance Halls, Liquor, Smoking, etc. . . . They speak quite openly," he continued, "that Washington is already Russianized." Veterans of the fundamentalist movement had little sympathy for the New Deal and modern political liberalism proved no more appealing to the younger generation.[29]

One white fundamentalist leader swam against the tide, however. McPherson, who was usually more irenic than most of her brethren, called FDR a "'godsend' . . . divinely placed at the head of this nation's government to guide it out of its most depressive, if not near-fatal period in history. There is no doubt about it," she told a reporter, because "he has accomplished so much in so short a time" and has responded so genuinely to "the people." While she shared the social and economic conservatism of other fundamentalists, she viewed FDR as an earnest public servant facing an unprecedented crisis rather than as a tool in the hands of the devil. Despite her strong premillennialist convictions, she did not see in the president echoes of the Antichrist. Her work demonstrates that within the fundamentalist movement, dissenting voices never went totally silent.[30]

Radical evangelicals' belief that the nation's economic problems could be traced to its spiritual problems found some support in unexpected quarters. "Business depressions," economist and popular writer Roger Babson argued, "are caused by dissipation, dishonesty, disobedience to God's will—a general collapse of moral character." He believed

in contrast that "moral awakening, spiritual revival and the rehabilita-
tion of righteousness" cured depressions. Most fundamentalists agreed
with Babson and accused the president of neglecting the spiritual life of
the nation. Percy Crawford, the leader of the Young People's Church of
the Air, warned the president that his failure "to honor Jesus Christ will
result not only in the downfall of your administration, but of the country as a whole." One Florida man complained to the president that he
had "added every letter of the alphabet to the New Deal except G-O-
D," while another shared a premillennial tract. He called on Roosevelt
to repent before the end-times tribulation began. Others recalled FDR's
invocation of the "forgotten man" whom the president had promised to
represent. "The 'forgotten man,' Mr. President," explained a Pennsylvania minister "is our Lord Jesus Christ." Conservative Presbyterian leader
H. McAllister Griffiths agreed. "In our collective national life God is
even more forgotten than your 'forgotten man.'"[31]

African-American R. C. Lawson believed that the depression was
an expression of God's divine justice. But the New York preacher's assessment of the causes differed substantially from that of white fundamentalists. He attributed it to God's judgment for "the terrible, atro-
cious things that happen down south, jim-crowism, lynching and
prejudice to the darker brothers." Yet his solution was the same as that
proposed by Babson and white fundamentalists. "Only by turning back
to God," Lawson surmised, "will He lift His hand off the neck of the
people." Rather than seek justice, however, most fundamentalists continued to turn a blind eye to racial oppression. They never saw racism
or segregation as national sins from which they needed to repent or
civil rights as worthy objects of federal legislation.[32]

As the 1936 elections neared, fundamentalists again preached action.
The same religious leaders who were most obsessed with end-times
prophecy remained most adamant about rallying Christians against the
New Deal. They made prophecy a means and inspiration for political
mobilization. Speculation about the future gave fundamentalist leaders
a profound sense of courage. While much of the nation supported the
president, Christians knew that Jesus was returning soon. Regardless
of the outcome of the campaign they would ultimately prevail. The
significance of their political efforts was not in the seeming contradic-

Fundamentalists often recognized the paradoxical nature of fighting to reform their world while simultaneously preaching an imminent, inevitable global cataclysm. This cartoon reminded the faithful that as more and more evidence of the Antichrist was starting to appear, urgent action was required.

"No Time for Sleep," *Sunday School Times,* December 2, 1939, 868.

tion between premillennialist determinism and political action. Instead the significance of their work was revealed through the ways in which premillennialism directly shaped the nature of fundamentalist political activity. While Roosevelt led the nation to the left, fundamentalists north and south, Republican and Democrat, informed by biblical prophecy, boldly pushed their followers to the right.

Fundamentalist leaders had no qualms about telling their followers how to vote. Directly challenging those Christians who believed that their citizenship in heaven negated their responsibilities on earth, Bible Institute of Los Angeles president and World's Christian Fundamentals Association leader Paul Rood warned followers that "subversive influences" were threatening the American government. A writer in the *Sword of the Lord* called on readers to "awake and repudiate" Roosevelt "at the polls" since the president had helped lead the nation away from God. Norris, in his typical hypermasculine rhetoric, called on "red-blooded, one-hundred percent Americans" from across the nation to make like the Old Testament warrior Sampson and put Washington's "uncircumcised Philistines out of business." The apocalyptic faith that these men had been honing for decades prepared them to see in FDR continuing evidence of Satan's earthly dominion. The urgency inherent in their beliefs fostered an aggressive, demanding, and uncompromising politics.[33]

As radical as fundamentalists' critiques of the president seem, their rhetoric intersected with and reaffirmed that of prominent, mainstream political conservatives. Herbert Hoover, for example, speaking at the 1936 Republican National Convention, compared the New Deal to the "march of socialism and dictatorships" in Europe and called on the American people to launch a "holy crusade for freedom." Senator Frederick Steiwer even suggested in his convention keynote address that Americans' religious liberty was in danger. The New Deal's "centralization of power," he warned, would likely grow to the point that "all human rights, including religious freedom, must yield to its tyranny." Some libertarian-leaning theological liberals also challenged the president. The most influential was possibly Los Angeles's James W. Fifield, Jr., who founded Spiritual Mobilization in 1935 to organize ministers and business leaders together to combat New Deal liberalism. He believed that government was undermining individual rights as well as the authority of churches.[34]

In battling the Democratic administration, fundamentalists most often reaffirmed the values and ideals of their corporate patrons and other political conservatives. Yet what distinguished their efforts from those of most of FDR's other adversaries was the apocalyptic nature of their overarching criticism. Alongside Mussolini's conquest of Ethiopia,

Hitler's brutal plans for the Jews, and the global spread of communism, the United States seemed to be falling into place in the premillennial plan of the ages. Radical evangelicals' religious convictions inspired dogmatic action and provided an overall framework for justifying choices. God, they believed, was calling the shots. In challenging FDR they were simply following the Almighty's lead.

Massive disenfranchisement kept the vast majority of African Americans from the ballot boxes. Of those who could vote, many black evangelicals shared their white counterparts' displeasure with the president. The *National Baptist Union-Review* printed article after article condemning the New Deal. "The American people," the editors admonished, "should hold tightly to their constitutional heritage—it has been tested by the years, and has been found good. If the people fail to do this, all that our forefathers gave to us will be destroyed." J. G. Robinson, editor of the influential *A.M.E. Church Review,* wrote the president directly. He called FDR a hypocrite for taking communion before his inauguration and then resurrecting the sale of liquor shortly thereafter. He criticized the Democratic Party's "attitude towards the Negro race" and advised FDR to "more thoroughly and earnestly consider the rights of the American Negro, and instead of pushing the 'New Deal,' give to them the principle of the 'Square Deal.' "[35]

Other African-American evangelicals supported the president. Michaux wrote Roosevelt an encouraging note. "If you are to be called a socialist and a wrecker of the Constitution because of your administration taking the bull of depression by the horn to throw him out of America in whatever way possible, you rejoice and be exceedingly glad, for great will be your reward in heaven." Pentecostal pioneer Charles H. Mason sent a reassuring telegram to Roosevelt praising him for jailing gangsters and building homes for the poor. Smallwood Williams commended FDR for changing "despair into hope and poverty into prosperity with New Deal policies" and applauded Eleanor for her contributions to civil rights. Future congressman Adam Clayton Powell, Jr., supported FDR and advised other African Americans to do the same. He adopted apocalyptic language to challenge those men and women who viewed the president as "the anti-Christ" and naively voted Republican "for Lincoln's and Jesus' sake." The Harlem minister pledged to put his money "on Roosevelt that he'd break the tape at the

Pearly Gates before the rest of the field." "Brothers," he concluded, "the Lord will not smite thee by day nor your forefathers turn over in their graves by night just because you have voted for Roosevelt." Many theologically conservative African Americans remained reluctant to support a wet Democrat for president, but some were beginning to see FDR's aggressive policies as part and parcel of the Christian gospel.[36]

On Election Day Roosevelt destroyed his Republican challenger, Alf Landon, at the polls, winning the popular vote by over twenty-four percentage points and taking every state but Maine and Vermont. How fundamentalists effected the election is difficult to gauge. Although hundreds of thousands, if not millions, of Americans adhered to the fundamentalist faith, many in the South likely remained loyal to FDR, and those who opposed the president—from all regions—probably had minimal direct impact. Nevertheless, by preaching cultural engagement and working for conservative political causes while simultaneously predicting an imminent Armageddon, fundamentalists made subsequent generations of believers aware of the dangers of modern liberalism. The faithful continued building a home—and a future—for themselves within the conservative wing of the Republican Party.

Despite radical evangelicals' steadfast faith in God's sovereignty, the president's overwhelming victory still stung. They had hoped that the 1932 election was a fluke. Roosevelt's victory four years later signaled to them nothing less than the last gasp of America's Protestant civilization and the solidification of the nation's move toward state-run communism. Rood explained that Roosevelt's plan to "repudiate our cherished national principles has met with the enthusiastic approval of the voters." *Moody Monthly* fretted that the United States was "headed toward liberalism and the passing of old-time American institutions. . . . We are headed, with the rest of the world, toward a dictatorship of communism or fascism." Norris called it a "Hitler revolution but with American ballots instead of Hitler bayonets. . . . The Constitution," he solemnly concluded, "has been repealed."[37]

Gaebelein, Brooks, and Bauman linked the election directly with prophecy. "The Election is over," Gaebelein groused. "All that is going on in the United States is in full swing with the predicted end of our age. . . . Political conditions revealed through Daniel 2,500 years ago are now universal." Brooks predicted that the president would use his sweeping victory to "ride roughshod over the Constitution into the seat of a dictator" as the scriptures predicted. Finally, in an unapologetic article, "The National Election Viewed beneath the Searchlight of the Prophetic Word," Bauman denounced "our benevolent American Dictator-President" and then stoked the nativist fires that many fundamentalist leaders had fanned throughout the decade. The majority of Protestants had voted for Landon, he claimed, but Jews and Catholics had overwhelmed them, turning the tide for the incumbent. "The Lord Jesus Christ," he argued, "receives no recognition at the ballot box." For fundamentalists the politics like the religions of Jews and Catholics worked in concert with the devil's schemes for world rule.[38]

As Roosevelt embarked on a second term, his actions did nothing to alleviate radical evangelicals' fear that he was slowly acquiring dictatorial powers. He controlled the executive branch and generally had the support of Congress. The Supreme Court, however, had been a thorn in his side. He proposed adding six new justices to the bench to counter the work of aging justices who had invalidated some important pieces of New Deal legislation. He claimed that enacting his plan would breathe new life into the Court and improve its efficiency, but he was really looking to secure a New Deal majority on the bench. The proposal became the greatest political miscalculation of his career.

Fundamentalists, like Congress and much of the public, responded with outrage. They had long worried that FDR would move against the Supreme Court. "All that stands between you, Mr. American Citizen," Bauman wrote in anticipation of the president's proposal, "and the tyranny of dictatorship—a Mussolini, or, perchance, a Hitler or a Stalin—is 'nine old men'!" America, he warned, "may begin with a benevolent dictator" (in reference to Roosevelt), "but dictators do not long remain benevolent! Benevolent dictator; then, tyrannical dictator; then, Antichrist." For the faithful, the United States was already well down the path to Armageddon. Bauman's rhetoric had become so fiery that he eventually felt compelled to temper his views somewhat. "Be it far from us," he wrote, "even to suggest that any President of the United States could ever become the Antichrist." That he had to state this explicitly so that his readers would not be misguided reveals how sensational and relentless his critique of Roosevelt had become.[39]

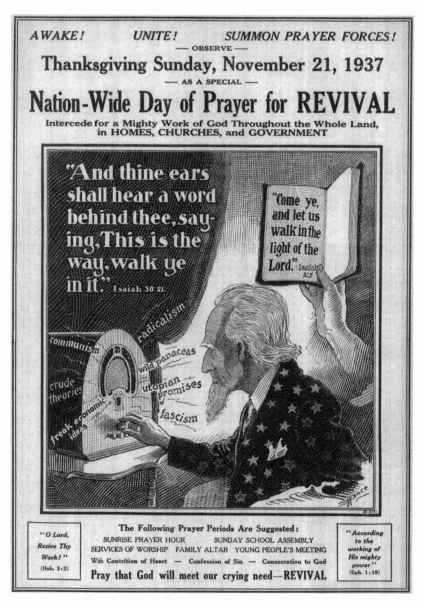

Fundamentalists regularly blended criticism of the New Deal with pleas for a return to the faith of the nation's founders. In this call for a national day of prayer in the midst of the ongoing depression, fundamentalists encourage Uncle Sam to turn away from the elusive promises of political liberals and to return to the Bible for guidance.

"Nation-Wide Day of Prayer," *Sunday School Times,* November 6, 1937, 784.

Once the president officially unveiled his Supreme Court reform plan, fundamentalists took to the airwaves, magazines, and pulpits. For evangelist J. E. Conant, the court-packing proposal was proof that the nation's "enemies" sought to nullify the Constitution. "If we fail to fight for our own rights," he preached, "we thus step aside and give Satan our permission to rob God of His rights in us." In other words, acceding to Roosevelt's plan to expand the bench was the equivalent of denying God his rights over humankind. Fundamentalists, in framing the debate over the Supreme Court, were making God subservient to the Constitution, rather than the other way around.[40]

Many of the nation's prominent fundamentalists weighed in on the controversy. Bell called the court-packing scheme "by far the most serious thing he has done for it is paving the way for a new form of government in America." Gaebelein clucked that if FDR had his way, "America will be no longer a free country, but be controlled by a dictator." Ockenga was outraged as well. He identified the Supreme Court proposal as an "attack upon American liberty" and the "outstanding" political event of 1937. Mark Matthews wrote an impassioned and lengthy letter to Senator Burton K. Wheeler begging him, "in the name of all that is sacred to this nation; in the name of all that involves the personal, religious, civil, and civic rights of the people of this country," to "defeat the bill!" Brooks characteristically saw Roosevelt's proposal through a premillennial lens, interpreting it as part of the United States' move away from its biblical and constitutional foundations. But such a move was never inevitable. He encouraged readers of *Prophecy Monthly* to write their congressional representatives to express their opposition to the president's plan.[41]

Congress voted down FDR's bill, handing the president a major defeat. A Nebraska minister summed up the fundamentalist perspective. "An attempt was made to subvert the independence of the Supreme Court, which is the last bulwark of Americanism against anti-christ, tyranny, and diabolical despotism. There was no power on earth which could stop this anti-God assault upon the rights and liberties of men." No power, that is, except one. "Only through the intervention of the Almighty God," he wrote, was the Supreme Court "saved." Such sentiments made explicit what had been implicit since early in FDR's first term. Fundamentalists believed that in waging war against the New Deal, they were leading a righteous crusade against the devil, the Antichrist, and his minions. Rather than surrender, they vowed to occupy their nation until Christ returned.[42]

Over the course of the 1930s, radical evangelicals' political sensibilities matured. As the world moved toward the precipice of war, fundamentalists began organizing more explicitly. To turn the tide in the nation and ultimately the world, they believed, they must defeat the forces of New Deal liberalism and restore the United States to its supposed Christian foundations. Writing for *Moody Monthly,* Gilbert summed up the fundamentalist position on the New Deal perfectly. "The most cursory observer of the present situation cannot escape the conclusion that the kind of government developing in America today approximates . . . the Antichrist setup." Yet Gilbert never preached apathy or fatalism. In 1940 he developed the most thorough and articulate fundamentalist political philosophy of the era, which he espoused in his own books as well as in columns in the leading fundamentalist magazines, including *King's Business, Sunday School Times, Sword of the Lord,* and *Pilot.* "There is a definite need," he explained, "for the clear enunciation of a *creed of and for conservatives*." Fundamentalists, he insisted, must "abolish the socialist bureaucratic encroachments" on constitutional government, fight to conserve "our Christian heritage," commit "to a crusade to reverse the whole prevailing trend," and "be militantly determined to alter drastically the course our nation is at present pursuing." The *Los Angeles Times* captured his sentiments in a sermon delivered before the World's Christian Fundamentals Association. The headline read: "New Deal's Reign Called Anti–Bible and Anti-Christian." Gilbert warned of "anti-Christ dictatorships" and called on Christians to "oppose New Deal trends" that threatened property rights.[43]

The message preached by Gilbert and his fellow fundamentalists not only resonated with apocalyptic church leaders and their parishioners but also reflected the ideals of a growing number of evangelical businessmen. The early relationships that radical evangelicals had developed with corporate leaders around the turn of the century had continued to grow over time. In the 1930s, they mobilized together against

FDR and the New Deal, attacking political liberalism from multiple angles. While the vast majority of Gilbert's writings explored the relationship of world events to biblical prophecy, his expansive call for a new conservative political movement was in no way a repudiation of his premillennial conviction that the rise of the Antichrist was inevitable. Instead, Gilbert represented the prototypical fundamentalist of the 1930s and 1940s—one part conservative political ideology mixed with one part apocalyptic fear mongering.[44]

As Roosevelt embarked on the fight for an unprecedented third term in 1940, fundamentalists believed that their fears of his dictatorial aspirations had again been justified. In their correspondence, in their magazines, and over the airwaves they pledged to stop him. The World's Christian Fundamentals Association adopted a resolution described by journalists as "flaying the New Deal and vigorously opposing a third term for President Roosevelt." Nebraska minister Theodore Epp took to the radio just before the election to condemn the president and warn the nation that it was at a "crossroads." "The battle to save our nation from encroaching dictatorship is not over," he preached. But if Americans did not stop "dictatorship" in its tracks, the consequences would be dire. Ockenga urged Americans to fight the president's devilish schemes. "If America is to be saved," he argued, "citizens must act. . . . To your tents, to the battle, O Americans, we will have no part in dictatorships." The editors of *Moody Monthly* concurred. "The battle lines are drawn. The war is on," they declared. "These evils must be corrected at the ballot box at once. . . . A conscripted army to save the property of America means nothing unless there can be self-conscription of patriots in an army set to save American ideals." Once again, fundamentalists believed that much was at stake. While they hoped to lead the American people in revival, they saw the Roosevelt administration working against them.[45]

Apparently there were still not enough patriots in the fundamentalist army, at least not yet. Bell had hoped in 1940 that the president would get "the licking he deserves," but it was not to be. Gaebelein admitted that word of FDR's victory "came as a disappointment. . . . The pace of age-end events," he determined, "is quickening." Although Brooks believed that the outcome matched the Bible's end-times predictions, he was equally confident that his fellow fundamentalists had

lined up with him. "While we made no poll of Fundamentalist leaders," he admitted, "so far as we were able to make contacts we found
practically all of them opposed to the third term, knowing the prophetic picture into which we are unquestionably headed." Yet this still
did not mean that Christians should succumb to the inevitable. The
Los Angeles evangelist used the campaign and its outcome to encourage fundamentalists to redouble their fight against the ruses of Satan.[46]

Fundamentalists' role in the campaign and views on politics attracted
substantial attention from laypeople. Many peppered their ministers
with questions about the spiritual significance of the election. Bauman,
whose prophecy articles in the major fundamentalist magazines made
him one of the best known premillennialists in the nation, received
numerous queries. "We should not be discouraged or pessimistic," he
replied to one correspondent. "These are dark days but the very shadows that are about us clearly indicate that the day break of the millennial age is at hand." Another wrote the California minister perplexed
about the results. "We are living in the last days," Bauman responded,
"and who could expect it to go otherwise than it did go?" But "if Jesus
tarries," he assured this writer, Americans would regret their choice
to reelect FDR. A third correspondent admitted, "We are pretty sick
about the election," but then she pointed to the silver lining. "Well, if
America is going down too, surely the time is very very near, so perhaps we should rejoice instead of grieve." Yet another celebrated the
outcome as a sign that the rapture was approaching. "From a human
viewpoint," she acknowledged, "I deeply regretted the result of the
Presidential election, but I have thought it might be part of the Lord's
plan for our country in the closing days of Gentile world power." Fundamentalists continued to find hope in the most dire circumstances,
sure that the world would soon be theirs.[47]

While most fundamentalists agreed with Bauman's outspoken opposition to Roosevelt, his integration of politics with ministry enliv-
ened at least one church member. Arthur Phelps's letters illustrate the
ways some premillennialists continued to question the political nature
of fundamentalism. "I presume I have things all wrong," Phelps wrote
Bauman. "I thought that we were in the world, but *not of* it; that we
had been '*called out* from among the nations . . .' that we are to '*come out
from among them* and touch not the unclean thing'; that Satan was the

prince and god of this political, religio-economic world-system; that *we* were 'not to be *unequally yoked with unbelievers,*' etc." He believed that both political parties were "made up of the riff raff and the rabble, rag tag and bob tail of society. How can Christians," he asked " 'yoke together' with such trash?" Peppering his missive with allusions to scripture, Phelps disputed Bauman's frequent references to FDR as a dictator, reminding the preacher that Roosevelt was democratically elected and that the other branches of government checked his power.

Phelps then unmasked the economic motives of some of FDR's enemies. "Who is it that is opposing Roosevelt? Who is it that is slandering him so viciously? *Men of wealth* primarily. Men who are the beneficiaries of privileges granted to them under republican administrations. Since when did you come into such wealth?" Phelps sarcastically asked Bauman. While most fundamentalist leaders joined business tycoons in their criticism of FDR, the issues at stake were more complicated for working-class Christians, many of whom had likely received aid during the depression from any number of New Deal programs. Phelps's pointed questions exposed some fundamentalists' discontent with the cozy relationship that church leaders had formed with economic conservatives. Although they had little power or influence, a handful of dissenting voices challenged the coupling of faith and the free market from within the movement.[48]

While 1930s-era fundamentalist critiques of New Deal liberalism may have seemed insignificant, irrational, or paranoid to many outsiders, politics and religion intersected in this decade to define the exploding fundamentalist movement and ultimately set the trajectory for evangelical activism across the rest of the century. Fundamentalists' continuing anxieties over foreign ideas and people, the continuing influence of women, the power of cities, and countless secular forces inspired them to redouble their political efforts. They honed a politics of dogged determination, aggressive action, and uncompromising self-righteousness. Fundamentalists' mobilization against the expanding state at the very moment of the New Deal's inception eventually paid tremendous dividends. The faithful helped lay the foundations for postwar religious mobilization; they perfected the antistate, promarket worldview that subsequent generations of evangelicals and other religious activists adopted and used to shape American politics; and their efforts to unify North and South under the banner of the GOP helped craft new national political alliances that eventually contributed to the rise of the Sunbelt. Fundamentalist political activism in the post-Scopes, interwar era is, therefore, essential to our understanding of the rise of modern Christian political engagement and ultimately the transformation of American politics and culture in the twentieth century.

As fundamentalists scanned the horizon in 1940, they saw little but dictatorships, destruction, and death ahead. The world was at war, the United States seemed to be abandoning its Christian foundations, and religious apostasy and immorality were on the ascent. Armageddon seemed more imminent than ever. John Rice asked his legion of followers living throughout the United States, "Will America get in World-Wide War?" His answer was unequivocal. The United States deserved to be punished, and punished badly. "If America has sown to the wind of sin like European nations," he asked, "why should we also not reap the whirlwind of war . . . ? If the wrath of Almighty God has mounted up against proud, frivolous, adulterous, drunken, Bible-denying, Christ-rejecting, Spirit-resisting America, then how can America escape the judgment of God in a bath of blood . . . ? We may expect all the hell of modern war in America soon." Indeed, radical evangelicals sensed that the hell of war was coming to America.[49]

9

REVIVING AMERICAN EXCEPTIONALISM

HAROLD JOHN OCKENGA HAD FAITH in the United States. "We have a providential position in history," he preached just as the world plunged into war. "Our continent was preserved to incarnate the development of the best civilization. Humanly speaking, it is almost as though God pinned His last hope on America." Like the Puritan divines, Ockenga believed that God had chosen the United States to play a special role in the world; and like his Great War predecessors, he knew that American Christians could speed up or slow down the march toward the apocalypse. With Hitler storming across Europe and Japan penetrating deep into China, the stakes could not have been higher. "The decisions and the course of America," he asserted, "will hasten or defer the collapse of civilization into chaotic barbarism." Although he feared that the United States was ripe for judgment, Armageddon was not inevitable. Building to his conclusion, he asked, "What then is the way out? Will it be with a revival or the rapture? Will it be a triumph for the truth or the tribulation for the world?"[1]

Ockenga was one of the most important and influential fundamentalists of the twentieth century. Tall and imposing, with a bookish look that softened his unwavering confidence, he was one of J. Gresham

Machen's top students at Princeton Theological Seminary. He with-
drew from Princeton in 1929 before finishing his studies to help his
mentor found Westminster Theological Seminary, a school Machen
launched as a conservative alternative to Princeton. In the early 1930s
Ockenga assumed the pastorate of a Presbyterian church in Pittsburgh
while completing a doctorate in philosophy from the University of
Pittsburgh. His dissertation, "Poverty as a Theoretical and Practical
Problem of Government in the Writings of Jeremy Bentham and the
Marxian Alternative," was a carefully crafted work. Despite Ockenga's
hostility to the New Deal, he mostly kept current events out of the
manuscript. In 1936, the minister left Pittsburgh for Boston, where he
accepted a call to become the pastor of the Park Street Congregational
Church. From the pulpit of the famous and historic church located on
the Boston Common where the young William Lloyd Garrison had
first railed against slavery, Ockenga played a critical role in reshaping
the trajectory of American fundamentalism. He eventually served as
the first president of the National Association of Evangelicals, as the
first president of Fuller Theological Seminary, and with Billy Graham
as a cofounder of the periodical *Christianity Today*.

As Ockenga and his fellow believers watched the world's most horrific war unfolding before them, they had to reconcile their apocalyptic
beliefs with their commitment to their nation. How do you support the
American military effort while preaching Armageddon? Some apocalyptic groups, such as the pacifistic, nonvoting Jehovah's Witnesses, repudiated all forms of violence. But fundamentalists had no intention of
playing the role of minority exiles; they wanted access to the mainstream of American life. In fact, they wanted to guide the mainstream.
Radical evangelicals continued to expect an imminent rapture and they
saw the signs of the times appearing all around them. But as the war
evolved, their emphases shifted as their national identity began to compete with their religious identity. Premillennialists had long believed
that immediately after the battle of Armageddon, God would assess not
just the faith of individuals but also the righteousness of nations. However, they had not yet spent much time working out what it meant for
God to judge individual countries. World War II–era fundamentalists,
in contrast, used Jesus's promise in Matthew 25:31–33 to justify building a tighter relationship with their nation: "When the Son of man shall

The bookish intellectual Harold John Ockenga played an unparalleled role in the
transformation of fundamentalism. As the pastor of Boston's historic Park Street
Church, the first president of the National Association of Evangelicals, the first
president of Fuller Theological Seminary, and a cofounder of the periodical
Christianity Today, he left his imprint on each of the major institutions of modern
American evangelicalism.

Courtesy of Fuller Theological Seminary.

come in his glory . . . before him shall be gathered all nations: and he
shall separate them one from another, as a shepherd divideth his sheep
from the goats." The faithful wanted Jesus to count the United States
among the sheep. As a result, their sense of themselves as aliens and
strangers in a foreign land gave way to a revived nationalist theology.
They still believed in an inevitable apocalypse, but like nineteenth-
century evangelicals, they also trusted that as Christians occupied the
United States, they might reform their nation along godly lines. They
offered their fellow citizens both a carrot and a stick. If Americans embraced the religion, politics, and values of fundamentalism, God might
delay Armageddon; and when the apocalypse did come, God might
spare the United States from his wrath. But if the nation continued in
religious apostasy, judgment would soon fall hard upon them.

   World War II marked a critical point in the evolution of American
religion. Fundamentalists' lack of patriotism during World War I and
their skepticism of the American state during the 1930s limited their
social and political power. World War II provided an opportunity for redemption. Over the course of the conflict, the faithful reversed roles with
their theologically liberal counterparts. Fundamentalists became the voices
of patriotism and American exceptionalism, while liberals more often
criticized American intervention abroad and the violent tactics of total
war. For radical evangelicals, this war, more than any other, represented
evil's rise to unprecedented heights, which justified their efforts to combat it. They routinely described the conflict as one of Christ versus Antichrist. By the end of the fight fundamentalists had done what just a few
years earlier had seemed almost unthinkable—they had baptized Christian fundamentalism in the waters of patriotic Americanism. For the rest
of the century they positioned themselves as the legitimate guardians
of the nation. Rather than living as dissidents and exiles simply buying
time until the rapture, they sought to protect the United States from
divine judgment—if the American people would only listen. This shift,
subtle as it was at the time, laid the groundwork for evangelicals' post–
World War II ascension into an integral position in American life.[2]

During the 1930s, Congress passed a series of neutrality acts intended
to keep the United States free from the kinds of entanglements that

had drawn the nation into World War I. Legislators stipulated that when the president recognized a foreign war, certain restrictions would automatically go into effect: Americans could not sail on belligerent ships, sell or transport munitions to warring nations, or make loans to a country at war. As a result, while totalitarian leaders built tremendous military machines, the United States refused to supply weaker nations with the goods necessary for their defense. Public debate over neutrality gave fundamentalists another opportunity to explain and defend the ways their beliefs intersected with their citizenship.

Most fundamentalists supported the neutrality acts, hoping that they would save the United States from another devastating conflict. But as events in Europe looked increasingly ominous, a few leaders called for American intervention. "I hope you will isolate Germany," Mark Matthews wrote the president in the wake of Munich, "put a boycott around her, quarantine her, and make her eat her own hatred and malice." He called the neutrality acts "infernal" and "the biggest piece of legal bunk that was ever put on the statute books." He also encouraged the president to send the navy into Alaskan waters to intimidate the Japanese. "We may have to fight Japan sooner or later, and sooner perhaps than some people think." He wanted the president to make "no compromise with those brutes." Nelson Bell's experience as a missionary challenged his isolationist tendencies as well. When Japan invaded China, Bell complained that the US government was impotent. "Pacifism, which is a symptom of moral degeneration, has done its evil work at home and we are not willing to fight, even for the right." In his annual Christmas letter to friends and supporters, the doctor responded from China to totalitarian aggression by chastising the United States. "No nation lives to itself and no nation dies to itself. . . . If there are international gangsters, there is only one way to deal with them." That he shared these sentiments in a public letter illustrates his anger at the United States and the depth of his sympathies with the people among whom he was living.[3]

As the war spread in Europe and Asia, fundamentalists continued to wrestle with their long-standing isolationist convictions. They did not always agree on the appropriate American response to events abroad. In the first wave of sermons delivered shortly after Hitler invaded Poland, many advocated continued American neutrality, reflecting the

majority American viewpoint at the time. Ockenga defended isolationism in a series of "emergency" sermons while telling his congregation and radio audience that "the end time has begun." The men and
women who heard Ockenga's messages, however, were not as convinced as their minister about the righteousness of American neutrality.
"It is to be deplored," one man wrote the Boston minister, that "the
people of these United States should be so obsessed with the idea of
isolationism," which "in my heart I feel God hates." Another called for
repeal of the neutrality acts, assuming that the United States would
eventually be in the fight anyway. "We are safe from these forces only
so long as our democratic european neighbors are safe." A third correspondent believed that Ockenga was not isolationist enough. Frustrated by the minister's advocacy of a strong military for defensive purposes, he wrote, "you leave me bewildered when I compare what you
say with what Christ says. . . . The Christian who really believes in
Christ and puts his trust in God doesn't resort to force of arms."[4]

As clerics like Ockenga preached caution, others argued for intervention. Their actions revealed the move under way among some fundamentalists to integrate their faith with support for expanding American power and influence abroad as the world approached Armageddon.
J. Frank Norris applauded Roosevelt's efforts in 1939 to convince Congress to loosen the neutrality acts. "After traveling 32,000 miles around
the world and seeing the conditions in different countries first hand,"
he telegraphed the president, "I have reversed my position and am one
hundred percent for repeal of the embargo on arms." He worried that
"the present neutrality law makes America the ally of this atheistic totalitarian despotism." Keith Brooks believed that "no enlightened
Christian can be neutral. If ever the forces of darkness were arrayed
against the forces of light, it is in our day." Others feared that neutrality
put the United States at risk. "If our nation does not take more effective measures before it is too late," Bell cautioned, "we may have to
face an enlarged Germany alone too." Donald Grey Barnhouse criticized isolationists, including Charles Lindbergh and members of the
America First Committee, for undermining the security of the nation.
He called them "true American appeasers" and warned that a negotiated peace with Germany was dangerous for Europe and would ultimately wreak havoc on the United States.[5]

One of fundamentalists' greatest fears about the United States entering the conflict was that FDR would use it as yet another opportunity
to boost executive power. "America would be especially endangered to
enter war," John R. Rice preached just as France began to fall, "under
a regime that trends toward dictatorship and socialism as does the New
Deal." "The moment America goes to war," Dan Gilbert fretted, "democracy shall be abolished." For many fundamentalists, the conflict
presented the president with yet another opportunity to undermine the
free enterprise system as well as to move the nation further down the
road toward the government of the Antichrist. Fundamentalists had
high expectations for the United States, believing that their nation
could potentially serve as a check against the amassing forces of the
Antichrist. However, with Franklin Roosevelt as commander-in-chief
they were not sure that this was possible.[6]

Despite growing American material support, by late 1940 the Allied
powers teetered on the verge of defeat. Hitler controlled much of western Europe and England was on the defensive. Prime Minister Winston Churchill pleaded with FDR for more US aid. Roosevelt had
been cautiously moving the country away from neutrality; with his
reelection now secure, he was finally prepared to commit fully to helping the Allies defeat the Axis powers. On December 29 he informed
the American people during a "fireside chat" over the radio that the
stakes could not be higher. "Never before since Jamestown and
Plymouth Rock," he solemnly began, "has our American civilization been in such danger as now." Then he laid out the consequences
of an Axis victory. "If Great Britain goes down," he warned, "the
Axis powers will control the continents of Europe, Asia, Africa, Aus-
tralasia, and the high seas—and they will be in a position to bring
enormous military and naval resources against this hemisphere. It is
no exaggeration to say that all of us, in all the Americas, would be
living at the point of a gun." Then, reaching the climax of the speech,
he delivered one of the illustrative phrases that came to define the
war. The United States, he boldly asserted, "must be the great arsenal
of democracy."[7]

A week later, Roosevelt went to the Capitol to deliver his annual State
of the Union address. In this historic speech, he laid out his vision of
what an Allied victory would accomplish. "We look forward to a world,"

he pledged, "founded upon four essential human freedoms." He identified them as the freedoms of speech and religion and from want and fear. He promised Congress that he was offering "no vision of a distant millennium. It is a definite basis for a kind of world attainable in our own time and generation." Roosevelt, like Wilson before him, wanted to remake the world in the image of the United States. "Apparently," Gilbert sarcastically quipped, "our nation is supposed to seek to function in the stead of Christ, and to establish that utopian kingdom on earth which He Himself alone can create." Soon, however, many fundamentalists reconciled FDR's global vision with their own millennial dreams.[8]

Roosevelt's call to make the United States the arsenal of democracy was eventually codified in the Lend-Lease Bill, which Congress passed in March 1941 after vigorous debate. The bill set generous terms by which the United States could provision the victims of Axis aggression. Ockenga believed that the new bill constituted American entry into the conflict. "We, the people," he preached, "will now blindly follow step by step to total war." In part the controversy over Lend-Lease had to do with FDR's decision to supply the Soviet Union. Many American religious leaders were deeply troubled by the lack of religious freedom in the USSR, and fundamentalists were worried as well that the Soviets were interested not just in defeating Hitler but also in fomenting a communist revolution in the United States. "Our military alliance with Russia," Ockenga warned, "has made respectable adherence to red social philosophy. Communistic influence has permeated this nation to a degree thought unbelievable." But Barnhouse, unlike many of his fundamentalist allies, supported FDR's policy. "Any true Good Samaritan," he wrote, "should realize that there are moral principles involved and without compromise with the bully or the thief should furnish clubs to the man of principles and to the criminal who is fighting the bully."[9]

As the United States inched toward war, fundamentalists' conviction that they stood at the threshold of Armageddon intensified. Charles Fuller announced on the *Old Fashioned Revival Hour* that "the next 5 or 6 broadcasts will be among the most important we have ever given." Thousands, he explained, "are asking for further light, information on prophecy—what the Bible has to say." The *Sunday School Times* reprinted a "Guide to Be Used after the Rapture," which explained to those left behind how to navigate the tribulation. Arno Gaebelein summed up the changing world scene in *Our Hope* just days before the United States entered the war. "We are witnessing the most startling preparations for the tragic events with which our present age and the Times of the Gentiles close according to Bible Prophecy." The faithful sensed that international events were rapidly moving the world to the precipice of Armageddon.[10]

On Sunday morning, December 7, 1941, Japanese fighter planes dispatched from aircraft carriers hidden in the vast Pacific surprised the United States by bombing the American naval base at Pearl Harbor, Hawaii. Enemy planes damaged or destroyed much of the western fleet, and three thousand Americans lost their lives. "A date," Roosevelt proclaimed the next day, "which will live in infamy."[11]

Fundamentalists responded to the attack, like the rest of the American public, with a combination of shock and outrage. "War declared against Japan today," Ironside recorded in his diary, "Much intense excitement but suppressed. All America behind the president." As the war progressed fundamentalists carefully distinguished their criticisms of New Deal liberalism from FDR's role as commander-in-chief. "You need not take sides for the Democratic Party nor for the New Deal's domestic policy," John Rice explained. "You need not be for boondoggling, for unlimited relief, for radicalism in government, for the attacks on business, for packing the Supreme Court, for giving way too much to radical labor leaders." But, he concluded, Roosevelt still deserved their support in prosecuting the war. The cover of *King's Business* summed up the state of American fundamentalism. It depicted an American flag being raised over Pearl Harbor. Underneath it appeared a poem entitled "America—Remember!"

> Though tempests toss the Stars and Stripes,
> And rock the ship of state,
> God will not leave America
> Abandoned to her fate,
> Unless America leaves God.
> He knows, He hears, He sees:
> Oh, seek His face . . . They, only, stand
> Who fall upon their knees.

The opening of World War II seemed to verify fundamentalists' decades-old predictions. The restoration of the Roman Empire, the ascension of Russia, the growing power of Japan, the return of Jews to Palestine, and finally the start of a global war convinced fundamentalists that they alone understood the past, the present, and the future.

Sunday School Times, November 25, 1939, cover.

The poem indicated how far the Los Angeles–based fundamentalists had moved since World War I. During the 1910s they had questioned overt displays of patriotism and sometimes criticized those who waved the flag. Now they rallied behind the Stars and Stripes and printed hypernationalist magazine covers that linked God with American exceptionalism. World War II, they believed, was theirs to win.[12]

As fundamentalists aligned the latest news with biblical prophecy, some suggested that the Bible foreshadowed Japan's growing global prominence. The New Testament book of Revelation, Gilbert contended, refers "plainly and unmistakably to Japan." He argued that John's reference to the "kings of the east" should be literally translated "the kings who are from the rising of the sun," which "must mean Japan—the nation internationally known as 'the Land of the Rising Sun.'" According to this reading, "Satan has doubtless fired the Japs with a 'victory vision' of the yellow hordes overrunning Western (European) civilization" and Christendom. Young fundamentalist theologian John Walvoord summed up the premillennial viewpoint. The "awakening" of Asia, he wrote, and "the increasing tempo of world events and the constantly narrowing frontiers of the world all point to the climatic events prophesied in the Scriptures for the days preceding the return of the Lord."[13]

The Japanese attack and German declaration of war encouraged fundamentalists to ask whether God was trying to send the United States a message. They had long believed that the Almighty rewarded and punished nations based on their loyalty to him. And Americans hadn't been very loyal lately. Radical evangelicals offered numerous critiques of their nation as they sought to understand where the United States had gone so wrong. Some thought that the nation had abandoned its supposed Christian foundations. "God," Jewish convert Hyman Appelman harangued in Pershing Square in Los Angeles, "is using Hitler to remind America of the religion of the Pilgrim Fathers, the founders of this marvelous land of ours." Others worried that Americans had erred in looking to the false panacea of the New Deal for salvation. Atlantic City fundamentalist Clarence Mason called the onset of the depression God's effort to awaken the United States to its sins. Americans, however, did not listen. Instead of repenting they "went on to greater sin" in voting in the New Deal, repealing Prohibition, destroying crops, trying to "spend ourselves rich" while running up the "greatest national debt in our history," and "playing politics with human suffering." Because of each of these godless policies, the nation had received its just deserts. "By this tragedy God tried to shock America into a recognition of her sinful complacency and unrepentant pride. . . . If America does not see God's hand in Pearl Harbor," Mason concluded, "I tremble for us." Fundamentalists also continued to wonder if God was angry over the nation's indifference to the plight of the Chinese. "How wicked the Japanese are!" John Rice preached in a biting, sarcastic invective. "We sold them millions of pounds of scrap iron with which to make bombs and guns and ammunition and tanks and warships; but we had a clear understanding that they were to kill helpless Chinese with them." But the Japanese had not upheld their side of the bargain. Instead they began "to kill Americans with our own scrap iron!"[14]

Others saw in the nation's social sins the cause of God's wrath. African-American Charles Barbour believed that discrimination had provoked the Almighty. "Our present civilization cannot survive and ought not survive as it is," he wrote in the *Chicago Defender*. "Sometimes catastrophe is a better teacher than anything else. The Negro minister's task at such a time as this is to prepare black people for world leadership." The time had come for white Americans to atone for their sins of racial injustice. Meanwhile Dan Gilbert identified abortion as a significant sign that God's judgment and the end of time was rapidly approaching. "The violence practiced by the Japs and Nazis against helpless prisoners is horrible and fiendish," Gilbert wrote. "But there is a kind of violence which is even more appalling." It is a kind of violence not "practiced against foreign enemies, but against one's own flesh and blood . . . against unborn babies—the most helpless of all living things. . . . For every three American women," he summarized, "who became mothers, one American woman became a murderess!" Such behavior, he believed, had outraged God and brought war to the nation's shores.[15]

With divine judgment seemingly falling on the United States, fundamentalists debated how best to respond to wartime mobilization. During World War I, religious liberals had used fundamentalists' lack of involvement in the war effort to paint the movement as subversive and un-American. The faithful viewed World War II, in contrast, as a much clearer battle between good and evil, righteousness and unrighteousness. The increasing intersections of fundamentalists' theology with their political concerns, combined with the perception that World War II was preparing the world for Armageddon, made it easier for radical evangelicals to commit to the fight. Nevertheless, they still struggled to reach a consensus on Christians' duty to government in wartime.

As war raged in Europe in the late 1930s, some fundamentalists still adhered to pacifism. Bauman believed that his denomination, the Brethren, should not compromise its long pacifist tradition. When Congress instituted the Selective Service Act in 1940, he counseled fellow believers to register as conscientious objectors. Charles Mason of the Church of God in Christ telegrammed Roosevelt to clarify the position of his movement. "We hereby and herewith declare our loyalty to the President of the U.S.A.," he began. But then came the rub. "We believe the shedding of human blood or taking of human lives to be contrary to the teaching of Jesus Christ; and as a body we are adverse to war in all its various forms." This African-American religious leader's position once again earned him the scrutiny of the FBI. Federal agents questioned why numerous conscientious objectors had listed Mason as a reference and feared that he might be "engaged" in "activities inimical to the best interests of the United States." Rice also took a surprisingly cautious position on the question of Christians' military obligations. "I advise every boy to stay out of the army and navy even in peace time unless conscripted. If drafted by the government, I advise young men to seek non-combatant work. If conscience will not allow one to fight, then follow conscience and serve God at any cost." However, he reminded followers that George Washington, Robert E. Lee, and Abraham Lincoln proved that one could be a soldier and a good Christian, and further warned that Christians should never join "such unchristian elements as . . . pacifist organizations." Fundamentalists had come to see the nation's leading pacifist groups as beacons for theologically liberal postmillennial scheming and communist subterfuge.[16]

Once the United States entered the war, most of those fundamentalists who had expressed qualms about combat duty reversed positions, while those from peace traditions went mute. Rice believed that there was only one appropriate response to Pearl Harbor—bloody revenge. Aimee McPherson's views shifted as well. In the 1930s her denominational bylaws encouraged conscientious objection. But in response to the Japanese attack, she asked the Foursquare board of directors to strike the article supporting freedom of conscience from the denomination's rules. An aide explained that McPherson believed that "this is a war of Christ against anti-christ." She expected her followers to take up arms and fight for the United States.[17]

In moving away from pacifism, Rice and McPherson joined the fundamentalist majority. Few of the faithful had any patience for conscientious objectors during this war. "Certainly our New Testament does not teach believers to be slackers," Brooks insisted, "when their government calls upon them to defend their homes and country." Then he impugned the motives of pacifists. "It is not for us to say," he smirked, "which of these may be unconsciously seeking in Scripture something to justify a cowardly quirk in their own hearts." Gaebelein called for an unapologetic, aggressive response to Pearl Harbor. "Our country has been ruthlessly and viciously attacked by a heathen nation." He called "so-called *Christian objectors*" "either cowards or shallow thinkers or both." That the rapture and tribulation were imminent, he explained, "does not mean that true Christians have no present responsibilities."[18]

Some fundamentalist leaders directly addressed the issue of serving under a seemingly secular state. *Moody Monthly* ran numerous articles supporting conscription and arguing that Christians had a biblically sanctioned obligation to serve in the military. But the editors, taking a jab at the New Deal, asked the commander-in-chief to clarify the purpose to which he was sending soldiers into battle. "Is it actually for the America of our fathers, or is it for the America of the experimenters? Are the specifications for the America of tomorrow to be taken from Washington, Lincoln, and Jefferson, or from Stalin and Marx?" Nelson Bell insisted that the only way to fight the fascist threat was to employ some of the enemies' tactics. Despite his fears of New Deal authoritarianism, he grumbled that American leaders gave the people "too much latitude." Congress, he suggested, should require compulsory service. The Axis had the advantage of forcing citizens to do anything necessary to win the war whether the citizens "like it or not." Ockenga believed that Paul's claim in Romans 13 that God had ordained the state was all the justification Christians needed to serve. "In a matter of war we must admit that the ministers of the State become our conscience before God. What the rulers decree we must obey. We do not have the right to sit in judgment upon whether this is a righteous or an unrighteous war. It is simply ours to obey." Ockenga's willful call for Christian submission to the state revealed yet again a paradox in the fundamentalist creed. Despite fundamentalists' criticism of New Deal policies, they remained willing to support the state when its actions aligned with their convictions and worldview. Ensuring that the state acted in their interests animated their end-times politics.[19]

As the conflict continued, some Americans raised questions about the tactics required to wage total war. A group of liberal clergymen that included Harry Emerson Fosdick issued a statement protesting the "carnival of death" that the American military had unleashed on German cities. In a symbol of how far things had come since World War I—when the modernists were the war-mongering crusaders and fundamentalists were the aloof peacemakers—Ockenga published a letter in the *New York Times* defending firebombing. The Boston minister returned to Paul's assertion in Romans 13 to justify the terror American and British planes unleashed on civilian populations. "We protestants repudiate the un-American pacifism of Dr. Fosdick and associates," he opined. "Protestant Christian patriotism endorses and supports the use of force to free the world of the menace of German militarism and Japanese barbarism. We want the men at arms to know that the church is praying for their complete victory." Radical evangelicals wanted the American public, the government, and the military to understand that they, not their liberal counterparts, were the true citizens and patriots.[20]

As fundamentalists struggled with the many ways the war affected their lives, they sought to discern God's will in the conflict. All around them patriotism had soared to new heights. Irving Berlin's song "God Bless America" and Frank Loesser's "Praise the Lord and Pass the Ammunition"—both huge hits—linked the United States' war effort with God's aims. Nevertheless, some fundamentalists remained cautious about claiming the Almighty as their ally in the fight; and some even continued to dispute the idea that the United States was a Christian nation. "There isn't such a thing as a Christian nation," *Moody Monthly* editorialized. "Nor can there be—certainly not in this age. . . . God hears a nation not because it is more righteous but because it is less unrighteous." An Atlanta Baptist invoked Berlin's song to chastise Americans for misunderstanding their relationship to the Divine. "God Bless America? America Bless God!" he preached. "Only a return to the 'Faith of our Fathers' from the debauchery of our times will witness God's blessing upon America." Barnhouse agreed. "We would lose all respect for a God who would bless such an America as that in which we are living today." When Bauman referred to the United States as a Christian nation, he heard from gadfly Arthur Phelps, who once again subtly attacked the tight relationship between fundamentalism and men of wealth. "There has never been a political form of government in this world over which Satan was *not* the 'prince' except that of David and his followers, has there? . . . You seem to think that because the writers of our constitution were men of brains and culture and in good reasonable financial circumstances and were church members that that made this government a Christian nation. I beg to differ with that conclusion." Yet as the war progressed more and more fundamentalists adopted the position of Bauman rather than that of Phelps. They came to believe in a United States that God blessed and that blessed God.[21]

While fundamentalists debated the United States' Christian foundations and pondered the judgments of the divine, they failed to recognize American racism as a possible source of God's anger. During the war African Americans pledged themselves to a "Double-V" campaign; they wanted to secure victory over fascism abroad and over racism at home. Although various African-American church leaders joined the Double-V campaign, white fundamentalists ignored it. They did not see racism or segregation as signs of injustice or as sins that required their penance.

Nor did fundamentalists show much sympathy for the plight of Japanese Americans. In the aftermath of Pearl Harbor, many white Americans living on the West Coast worried that Japanese immigrants and/or Japanese-American citizens might help orchestrate an enemy invasion. The president and military leaders agreed. Roosevelt signed Executive Order 9066, which gave the army the authority to relocate those people deemed a threat to assembly centers located away from the coast. In implementing the order, the military transferred over one hundred thousand Japanese and Japanese Americans into internment camps sprinkled around the western United States. Fundamentalists, like the vast majority of other white Americans living in the West, generally supported Japanese internment—even when the internees were fellow fundamentalists. *King's Business* printed a positive account of the assembly center at the Santa Anita, California, racetrack along with a letter from a Bible Institute of Los Angeles student who had been relocated there. "Although this Institute student has found his formal education for Christian service interrupted," the editors acknowledged, "there has opened to him a unique field of opportunity." The student wrote to school administrators about the many occasions he found for ministering to his fellow internees. His account of the camp was almost entirely positive (in contrast to what we know from other sources about the deplorable conditions of the camp). Despite the writer's admission of homesickness, fundamentalists did not protest on behalf of him or any other interned Christians.[22]

McPherson supported the government policy as well. She responded to discussions about shutting down the camps in 1943 with a telegram to state leaders. "We know positively that these Japs will carry on extensive and organized sabotage. . . . We know the treachery of the Japanese. . . . The greatest possible mistake that could be made at this time by our Government would be to force these Japs back upon the people of the Pacific Coast. It will incense the people and create riots and even bloodshed. We earnestly pray," she concluded, "that they will not be freed." They were not. The tragedy of war reinforced for many fundamentalists the xenophobia that had characterized the movement since its beginning. The faithful remained on guard against those who seemed different, both in terms of religion and ethnicity. They constantly guarded against the enemies and aliens in their midst who might serve as tools of the Antichrist.[23]

The US entry into the war provided substantial new ammunition for fundamentalists' prophetic analysis and speculation. "The nations have

gone goose-stepping toward Armageddon ever since 1914," Bauman
preached. "It would seem that it is about time for their arrival on that
fateful spot." Assemblies of God leader J. Roswell Flower confided to a
friend that the war will be "followed by a period of peace during which
the anti-Christ will appear as the superman to solve the problems of
the world." Members of the small African-American denomination
United Holy Church of America also believed that the war marked the
end of the era. "We as a part of the great body of Christ firmly believe
that the signs of the times point toward the close of the 'Times of the
Gentiles,' and that the return of the Lord may be expected at any moment." The start of the war in Europe had excited fundamentalists'
hopes that the book of Revelation was coming to life before their very
eyes, but nothing could match the intensity of American involvement
in the conflict. Fundamentalists could now feel and participate in—not
just read about—the epic battle of the ages.[24]

That premillennialists' expectations had been wrong before did not
dissuade these fundamentalists. "In the past there have been those who
have criticized believers in the return of Christ on the ground that
similar believers in other centuries have thought that His coming was
near, when history has proven that it was not near," Barnhouse acknowledged. "To them we reply that their historical sense should show
them that never in history has the stage been set as it is set at the present
time." Little did he realize that hidden below the stage was a series of
trap doors that would wreak havoc on fundamentalist predictions.[25]

The first had opened on June 22, 1941, when Hitler had turned on
his Soviet allies and launched an invasion of Russian territory. Although Americans were wary of Stalin, they saw Hitler's eastern offensive as proof of his insatiable expansionist aims, which made their
neutrality all the more difficult to maintain. Roosevelt opened the
cupboards of the "arsenal of democracy" to the world's most powerful
communist—and explicitly atheist—nation. The US-USSR pact substantially undermined fundamentalists' expectations about an end-
times Germany-Russia/Gomer-Magog alliance.

Many fundamentalists were angry over FDR's willingness to work
with Stalin. In Bell's last letter to his mother as he and his family were
en route from China back to the United States, he wrote that Hitler's
attack on the Soviet Union was "amazing and very dangerous. We in

America," he wrote, "must let them fight it out and under no conditions help Russia." Bauman had even stronger feelings. "We have forsaken God," he lamented, "and have wandered far from the landmarks that our fathers placed." He believed that "it would be better for America to go down alone fighting a glorious fight to preserve the political and spiritual faiths of our fathers than to live and be so conscienceless as to wink at the crimes of Russia." Nevertheless, he saw substantial meaning in the unfolding events. "The way the world is going just now," he told a friend, "I am inclined to doubt very much whether the Saints will be upon the earth when the next Christmas rolls around."[26]

The shifting alliances forced Christian publishers to proceed cautiously. In early 1942 the *Sunday School Times* had a new series of articles in development that discussed Russia's role in prophecy, but once the United States allied with the Soviet Union, the editor decided that political realism trumped prophetic speculation. "After prayerful consideration," he explained in private correspondence, the series was going on hold. *Moody Monthly* responded in similar fashion by backing off of its Magog-Gomer equation. In response to a question from a reader, the editors concluded, "the differences of opinion, and the rapidly shifting scenes and course of events today, make exact prediction and location a precarious matter." Fundamentalists had never before thought that the meaning of Magog was unclear; the changing dynamics of the war, however, forced them to read their Bibles with greater caution.[27]

The fallout from the German-Soviet break represented one of many interpretive challenges premillennialists faced during the war. For years fundamentalists had believed that nations were lining up for Armageddon just as Daniel, Ezekiel, and Revelation had predicted. But as the geopolitical situation evolved, fundamentalists struggled to align the prophetic plan with reality. Over time the list of fundamentalists' errant prophecies snowballed. A full-page ad that ran in the *Sunday School Times* shortly after the war began in Europe best encapsulated the dangers of premillennial prognostication. The purpose of the ad was to promote a new series of forthcoming articles on prophecy and the war. Every one of the advertised articles proved to be dead wrong. Titles included "Why Russia Had to Break with Britain and Join Germany," "Why Italy Must Break with Germany and Join Britain,"

"Why the Roman Empire Must Be Revived," "Why Palestine Will Be Coveted by the Nations," "Britain's Break with the Jews and Italy's Opportunity," "Why the Final War Must Head Up in Armageddon," and finally, "Why the Rapture of the Church Must Be Very Near." Russia allied with Britain; Italy stayed with Hitler but became a second-tier player in the war; the Roman Empire never resurrected; Palestine did not become an object of colonial rivalry; and Britain did not turn on the Jews. The twists and turns of the war brought victory to the United States but seriously challenged fundamentalists' interpretations of prophecy. As the future looked increasingly bright for the Allies, fundamentalists had to confront their errors.[28]

Premillennialists' greatest mistake had been placing so much importance on Mussolini. Many had viewed him as the Antichrist's predecessor, if not the Antichrist himself. Yet by 1941 most of the world recognized that the Italians had overplayed their hand. The British were driving back the fascists in North Africa and the Greeks had resiliently fought an Italian invasion. Il Duce evolved quickly from the potential beast of Revelation into Hitler's weak-kneed lackey. Gaebelein stubbornly refused to acknowledge how he had fostered false hopes; instead he denounced others for doing the same. "It is through confusion . . . through date-setting . . . through calling certain present-day actors in world history the Antichrist, etc.," that prophecy teachers bring "the Word of God into disrepute." Bauman, who had continued to assert in books, magazines, and sermons that the Roman Empire was ascending, kept faith in Mussolini longer than most. "Just now," he wrote a friend, "people may be questioning my position with regard to Mussolini." "May it not be," he later suggested, "that the critics are a little premature in their criticism?" Apparently not. A few fundamentalists later joked about the extremes to which prophetic speculation had gone. *Moody Monthly* editors, for example, reprinted a story making the rounds in the 1940s. "One prominent Bible teacher, just after the inglorious death of Mussolini, was asked to bring four addresses on prophecy at a Bible conference. He is said to have wired, 'Cannot come; I have only two addresses left.' "[29]

For the most part, however, fundamentalists did not acknowledge how much they had erred. Because they had carefully avoided setting specific dates for Christ's return, and because they routinely acknowledged that their speculation was just that, they left themselves an out. They could keep expectations of an immanent rapture high without being pinned down as false prophets. If the return of Christ was not around the next corner, it was always behind the corner after that. This was the genius of premillennialism. Like the faithful virgins in Jesus's parable in Matthew 25 who had properly prepared for the return of the bridegroom, fundamentalists were always ready.

As the war crisis deepened, radical evangelicals believed that God had prepared them for such a time as this. Judgment was coming, but the United States could be spared if the American people humbled themselves and sought the Almighty. Fundamentalists found that focusing on the betterment of the nation in anticipation of Jesus's return gave them a sense of stability and a clear focus when apocalyptic predictions went awry. "The United States of America," Ockenga preached, "has been assigned a destiny comparable to that of ancient Israel which was favored, preserved, endowed, guided and used of God." Whether Americans would be faithful to that destiny was their choice. "Two ways" lie "open before us," Ockenga continued. "One is the road of the rescue of western civilization by a re-emphasis on and revival of evangelical Christianity. The other is a return to the Dark Ages of heathendom."[30]

Fundamentalists like Ockenga perfected the myth that their nation's historic success could be traced to its unique godly origins, a belief that grew increasingly popular over the course of the war. Moody dean Will Houghton called for a return to the Declaration of Independence and the Constitution and reminded fellow believers that Christian men and women had founded the United States on Christian principles. "The Church," Lutheran minister Oscar Hanson preached, "is the mother of freedom. The Church has given meaning to our Stars and Stripes. Read American history. God's Word and the Church of Jesus Christ are woven into the very foundations of American history." The faithful came to believe that they not only had a monopoly over the proper interpretation of the scriptures but also truly understood the Christian origins of the United States' sacred documents. They saw a return to New Testament faith combined with a resurrection of the

ideals of the American founders as the remedy for the world's ills. All
they needed was to mobilize the faithful to bring the message home to
all Americans.[31]

In 1940, Ralph T. Davis, a missionary executive concerned about
the potential impact of the military draft on overseas evangelistic work,
approached leaders around the country about creating a new fundamentalist lobby. "Insidious forces," he wrote, "are at work against us and
we question whether we are awake to the probable consequences of
their activities." Decades earlier, he explained, liberal-led Protestants
had organized the Federal Council of Churches to represent their interests to the government. Davis believed that it was well past time for
fundamentalists to do the same. "The functions of the proposed council," he suggested, "should be to deal with problems which are common to us all. Perhaps the headquarters should be located in Washington." Davis was not advocating another evangelistic society; he wanted
to shape the grassroots fundamentalist movement into a mainstream
political organization with its own lobby to represent its interests in the
nation's capital. Religious leaders sensed that despite their fears of cen-
tralized control, the only way to deal with the evolving New Deal state
was to centralize fundamentalist efforts—to fight fire with fire. Working as disparate individuals had simply not achieved the results they
wanted.[32]

Davis turned to J. Elwin Wright to help him build what he initially
called a "Council of Fundamentalist Protestants." Wright was a smart
choice. In 1929 he had established the New England Fellowship, a
loosely knit organization that united various Protestant churches for
fellowship and evangelism in a region dominated by Catholics and
Unitarians. Like other fundamentalists, Wright wove together his
political and religious views, which he expressed in criticism of the
Federal Council. He believed that it had allied with "politically radical, anticapitalistic, and even communistic" forces. "The weight of its
influence," he summarized, "is on the side of labor as against manage-
ment, government ownership as against private industry, paternalism as
against free enterprise, radical socialism as against the American democratic system of the past." Wright wanted to create a religious-political
alternative to the Federal Council that countered the liberal view of
the state and of the general welfare with a decidedly conservative

thrust. Thrilled by Davis's proposal, he pledged to help. Together they began recruiting the nation's leading fundamentalists to mobilize intellectual and material resources as well as to direct their energies toward common goals.[33]

Davis and Wright's plan initially provoked some mild resistance. William Bell Riley, for example, expressed doubts about its purpose and wondered if it would duplicate the languishing World's Christian Fundamentals Association. His questions gave Davis the opportunity to make even more explicit the political nature of the group he had envisioned. "We feel that the greatest need is for some common meeting ground for representation to government where legal matters may be handled as they concern one endeavor or another of the evangelical forces." Riley was persuaded and agreed that a new organization was needed to exercise "righteous influence in government affairs."[34]

Others, however, proved harder to convince. Paul Fischer, secretary of the Christian Business Men's Committee International, invoked premillennial arguments about the last days and explained, "the early church paid little attention to the political implications of their contacts with civil government." When Christians eventually "began to claim civil rights and the church began to make its influence felt politically," he warned, "a period of spiritual decay set in." Organizing with other Christian businessmen for financial gain was apparently not, in contrast, contrary to the teachings of the early church. Lutheran minister John Brenner agreed with Fischer's theological premises. "To introduce an 'evangelical bloc' into the political and economic affairs of our nation would lead to internal dissensions and finally to the loss of our freedom of religion."[35]

Despite these concerns, few leaders of the mainstream fundamentalist network spurned politics. In 1942 the most powerful and influential white fundamentalist men in the nation, including William Ward Ayer, L. Nelson Bell, John Bradbury, Lewis Sperry Chafer, Percy Crawford, William Culbertson, Charles Fuller, Frank Gaebelein (coeditor of *Our Hope* and son of Arno), Dan Gilbert, Will Houghton, H. A. Ironside, Bob Jones, Harold J. Ockenga, Harry Rimmer, Paul Rood, Bob Shuler, J. Roswell Flower, and many others descended on St. Louis to organize the National Association of Evangelicals for United Action (NAE). Historians have traditionally viewed the NAE as the first step in the reconstruction of a new, modern evangelicalism. Rather than a new beginning, however, it more accurately represented the logical culmination of decades of hard work.

Leaders' shift in language from "Fundamentalist Council" to "National Association of Evangelicals" was intentional. Replacing the label "fundamentalist" with the more historic "evangelical" demonstrated the seriousness of their efforts to relaunch their movement and craft a new public image free from the negative associations that had dogged them since the Scopes trial. That pentecostals ranked among the leaders of the group further demonstrated how much had changed in the previous decades. Many fundamentalists now accepted pentecostals, whom they had once considered tongues-speaking, chandelier-swinging, faith-healing radicals, as part of mainstream American evangelicalism. As long as pentecostals kept their bums in their pews, their jaws locked, and their hands to themselves, they were welcomed.

In their effort to cast as wide a net as possible, NAE leaders, most of who were premillennialists, intentionally downplayed issues of doctrine. The group adopted a generic statement of faith that affirmed evangelical Christianity without broaching the specific issues that had long separated various fundamentalists from one another and from their pentecostal brothers and sisters. They chose to take no official position on premillennialism—a wise move, in light of their intention to include a broad array of denominations and their growing awareness that geopolitical events had not aligned as they had expected. They hoped to distinguish the new evangelicalism represented by the NAE from the radical apocalyptic theology that had given birth to it. Nevertheless, apocalypticism continued to shape much of their ideology and remained a prominent feature of the evolving movement.

The group was overwhelmingly white and male but did not take explicit positions on women's roles or race. Nevertheless, leaders' positions were clear and consistent with those of the past. "You see," recalled Elizabeth Morrell Evans, who recorded minutes for the new organization, the "NAE was for the men," although "some of us single girls" helped as secretaries and planners. De facto racial segregation prevailed as well. The all-white organizers made little effort to recruit African Americans as they established a new evangelical front. The inclusion of vocal segregationists among the leadership and the courting of explicitly segregated denominations guaranteed that African Americans were not welcome. Eventually African Americans organized their own National Black Evangelical Association.[36]

Wright opened the inaugural NAE meeting by explaining the reasons they had assembled. "We are here met in conference . . . to find common ground upon which we may stand in our fight against evil forces, to provide protective measures against the dictatorship of either government or ecclesiastical combinations in restraint of religious liberty, and to seek ways and means of carrying on for Christ unitedly and aggressively." Fundamentalist leaders wanted to organize the nation's conservative Protestant churches in order to develop better relations with the government; to strategize for more control over radio airwaves; to foster better public relations; and to evangelize more effectively. The group also pledged its total commitment to the preservation of the separation of church and state, which essentially meant that they hoped to squelch any and all Catholic intrigue.[37]

Ockenga served as the NAE's first president. Long before Richard M. Nixon discovered the "silent majority," Ockenga rallied what he called "the unvoiced multitudes" to action. His keynote address at the conference, representing the decades-long cross-fertilization of conservative political ideology, free market economics, and fundamentalist theology, helped give modern American evangelicalism its identity. He began his sermon with an allusion to Armageddon, warning, "I see on the horizon ominous clouds of battle which spell annihilation unless we are willing to run in a pack. . . . This is the time, the day for the offensive." He then went on to identify those clouds. The first was Roman Catholicism, "a power which cannot be successfully resisted." Second was theological liberalism, which produced the "great poison" dominating the American education system. Third was secularism, represented by the "disintegration of Christianity" and the "break-up of the moral fibre [sic] of the American people." Because evangelicals had not sufficiently challenged Catholicism, liberalism, and secularism, there was a fourth issue that needed to be confronted—the growth of government under the New Deal. "A revolution has taken place in our nation," he explained. "Whenever the major part of the business of the nation is being done by the government rather than by private interest, capitalism ceases its functioning." He would later identify this evil as "statism." Under Franklin Roosevelt and the New Deal the federal government, Ockenga asserted, had become a direct threat to true Christianity.[38]

After Ockenga finished his sermon, William Ward Ayer reiterated many of the same themes. "The inroads of wild socialistic theories," he preached, "through the power of organized minorities in government are creating a cancerous condition in America." Radicals entrenched "in high places in our government life," working with other administration authorities, "smear any who call attention to these cancerous adhesions to our body politic." But uniting together offered a solution. "It is not boasting to declare that evangelical Christianity has the America of our forefathers to save. . . . Millions of evangelical Christians, if they had a common voice and a common meeting place, would exercise under God an influence that would save American democracy." Ayer meant what he said. Fundamentalists-turned-evangelicals truly believed that in uniting, they could drive out all who threatened them and answer God's call to save their nation.[39]

The evangelicals who constituted the core of the NAE, such as Ayer and Ockenga, believed that God had chosen them to serve as the guardians of the nation. This was their country founded on Christian principles, divinely chosen by God to bring revival to the world in these last days. They appealed to the Puritans and the nation's founders, arguing that because many churches and denominations had fallen away from the true faith, and political leaders had driven the country in secular and communist directions, they had a God-given responsibility to restore authentic Christianity to America. Convinced that God had chosen them to lead the fight against the impending apocalypse, they redoubled their efforts to inject Christian ideas into politics and government, to restore the nation's standing in God's eyes before it was too late. They gave Americans a clear choice—return to God or face his wrath.

Despite their confidence and determination, NAE leaders proved unable to bring all white fundamentalists under their tent. At the same time that Wright was organizing the NAE, Carl McIntire, a fiery, tyrannical preacher who had studied with Ockenga under Machen in the late 1920s, simultaneously launched the "American Council of Christian Churches." He called fundamentalists to separate from mainstream culture and to assume hard-line, uncompromising positions. He insisted that American Council members not affiliate with any denomination aligned with the Federal Council. The separatist mentality at the heart of the American Council contradicted the views of NAE leaders, who believed that the choice to work for reform within a denomination or to abandon it should be left up to individual ministers and churches. Efforts to unite the two organizations proved futile. Over time the American Council came to represent the polemical far right of the fundamentalist movement while the much larger and more effective NAE engaged with the broader culture and crafted partnerships with like-minded allies. Despite differences in strategy, both groups had much in common. They appealed to Americans of all economic classes and regions, they attracted the support of various politicians and business leaders, and they shared a common suspicion of the Federal Council of Churches and its successor, the National Council of Churches, which they feared could serve as a tool of the Antichrist in the last days to spread false religion.

In part, the break with the irascible McIntire benefited the NAE. Its leaders wanted to move past fundamentalism's cantankerous and divisive past and instead to present a respectable image to the public. But this was easier said than done. They opted to excise not just hotheads like McIntire but also some of their more embarrassing potential partners. A case in point was the NAE's treatment of Aimee Semple McPherson and her thriving denomination, the International Church of the Foursquare Gospel. Ockenga had initially sent the Foursquare board of directors a telegram promising their "acceptance" into the organization. But despite such promises, the NAE stalled on admitting McPherson's organization to fellowship. The NAE was feeling pressure about the substantial number of pentecostal groups that had joined. Leaders also feared that affiliating with the Foursquare church would provoke negative publicity. The Assemblies of God's Ernest Williams explained that his reservations about Foursquare had to do with "some things that had taken place in the life of the little woman"—especially McPherson's 1926 sex scandal, among a handful of other very public controversies. These events did not sit well with the male leadership of the NAE, who were seeking public respectability, not an unwanted lightning rod for controversy. McPherson died in 1944, and in 1952 the new male leaders of the Foursquare denomination reapplied for membership. This time their application was accepted. For decades to come, the NAE consistently served as the face of a male-dominated, respectable, mostly irenic, white evangelicalism.[40]

By 1944 the tide of the war had turned. The US navy was making good progress in the Pacific and the Allies under the command of General Dwight D. Eisenhower were preparing to open a western front in Europe with an invasion across the English Channel. Unwilling to relinquish his office, Roosevelt announced that he would seek a fourth term despite his declining health. Evangelicals again came out swinging against the incumbent. Ockenga believed that FDR's disregard for "evangelical Christianity," "free enterprise," and "representative democracy" had undermined the "American way of life." Ockenga linked the president to supposed last-days signs of immorality. The president's perceived inaction on growing sexual licentiousness in the forms of "homosexuality, fornication and adultery" and Eleanor Roosevelt's support of interracial marriage meant that it was past time for a new leader to "clean house at Washington." During the campaign *Moody Monthly* reiterated its long list of anti-FDR grievances. The editors blamed the president for providing young soldiers with easy access to alcohol, repeated tired accusations of his communist inclinations, and critiqued his character. Brooks framed the election as a referendum on the free market. He claimed that he was being "faithful" to his readers in dealing "with the question of whether or not we want a socialistic America." Rice reminded readers of the *Sword of the Lord* that over the previous decade the New Deal had grown more radical than the radicals. "Socialists and Communists now follow the New Deal," he preached. "They do not try to stay ahead of it." He called his "vote against the New Deal" a "vote against immorality and a vote for righteousness; a vote against irreligion and for Christianity."[41]

Despite evangelicals' efforts, Americans elected FDR a fourth time. Ironside once again returned to his diary to record the result. He could have been speaking for the movement as a whole. "As usual," he grudgingly recorded, "I was on the wrong side."[42]

Just a few months later, on April 12, 1945, Franklin Roosevelt died of a cerebral hemorrhage. Vice President Harry S. Truman assumed the presidency and took charge of wrapping up the war. The next month Germany surrendered and the battle for Europe was finished. Americans poured into the streets to celebrate V-E Day. But the war was not yet over. As American soldiers, sailors, and marines slowly hopped from island to island across the Pacific moving ever closer to Japan, the new president had a decision to make. American scientists and their allies had created a secret weapon unlike anything that the world had ever known. On July 16, 1945, while Truman negotiated the terms of postwar reconstruction with Soviet and British leaders in Potsdam, he learned that the US military had successfully tested an atomic bomb in the New Mexican desert. He believed that to deploy the bomb against Japan rather than launch a ground invasion would substantially reduce the number of American casualties, likely speed the end of the war, and keep the Soviets out of the Pacific. For the commander-in-chief the decision to use the bomb was an easy one. After all, United States leaders had not invested billions of dollars in the Manhattan Project to build a weapon that they did not plan to deploy. On August 6, 1945, the United States dropped an atomic bomb on Hiroshima, Japan; on August 9, American aviators detonated a second atomic bomb over Nagasaki. Hundreds of thousands of Japanese civilians were killed. The next day, Japan began negotiating a surrender, which the United States formally accepted on September 2, 1945. The war was finally over.

Truman credited God for the bomb. "We thank God that it has come to us," the president told the American people, "instead of to our enemies; and we pray that He may guide us to use it in His ways and for His purposes." Evangelicals too saw atomic power as a gift from the Almighty. Like the vast majority of Americans desensitized by the brutalities of the war and still smarting over Pearl Harbor, they had few qualms about the use of the bomb. *King's Business* described it as "a work of God," while Clarence Benson saw the bomb's use as a fitting end to this war of "religion." "The conflict," he opined, "between these two unconquered nations was a battle of the gods. God accepted the challenge and placed in the hands of His people the mysterious weapon which was to bring overwhelming devastation without the loss of a

single American." *Moody Monthly,* however, raised a mild note of caution. The editors praised Truman but expressed some anxiety over the
bomb's power. "Where do we go from here? It shortened this war, and
something has been gained temporarily. But what will it do to the next
war?" The bomb had a substantial impact on Barnhouse as well. In a
sermon delivered on the day he heard the news of the bomb, he acknowledged that it had transformed his thinking. Although he feared
that the Soviets would soon have their own atomic weapons, he felt
positive about its development, which even forced him to reassess his
opinion of FDR. "I now believe that history, if there is much more of
it left, will chiefly remember Mr. Roosevelt for his greatest feat." Liberal religious leaders, in contrast, lamented the use of the bomb. As
they had differed with evangelicals over the tactics of total war, so too
did they differ over the president's decision to use atomic weapons.[43]

The end of World War II forced evangelicals to recast their positions. While they had interpreted the war and its devastating affects as
the vindication of their end-times speculation, they now invoked American victory as a sign of God's last-days benevolence and prophecy's
fulfillment. God was giving them more time to complete their work.
After the "terrifying demonstration of man's most deadly weapon, the
Lord has suddenly brought peace," *King's Business* summarized. "Why
peace? There is but one answer, and that is that God is giving the
Church of Jesus Christ another—the last—chance." Indeed, as American evangelicals emerged from the worst war the world had ever witnessed, they believed that they had yet one last chance to return the
nation to its godly foundations and to bring revival. But as they grew
more aware of the potential of atomic weapons to destroy the earth and
sensed a cold war developing on the horizon, their faith in the coming
apocalypse was renewed. This time, Jesus really had to be coming.[44]

10

BECOMING COLD WARRIORS FOR CHRIST

IN 1947 CARL F. H. HENRY published a major critique of American fundamentalism and laid out a new agenda for the future. "For the first
protracted period in its history," he asserted in *The Uneasy Conscience of
Modern Fundamentalism,* "evangelical Christianity stands divorced from
the great social reform movements." For Henry, this was unconscio-
nable. "Modern Fundamentalism," he lamented, "does not explicitly
sketch the social implications of its message for the non-Christian
world; it does not challenge the injustices of the totalitarianisms, the
secularisms of modern education, the evils of racial hatred, the wrongs
of current labor-management relations, the inadequate bases of international dealings. It has ceased to challenge Caesar and Rome." Fundamentalists, he believed, had withdrawn into their churches and Bible
institutes while the world changed around them. "The apostolic Gospel . . . stands divorced from a passion to right the world. The Christian social imperative is today in the hands of those who understand it
in sub-Christian terms."[1]

Henry believed that a misuse of premillennialism was partly to
blame. Fundamentalists' focus on the dire conditions around them,
he bemoaned, had encouraged the faithful to take "a world-changing

message" and reduce it to one focused only on "isolated individuals."
"The Gospel of hope," he continued, "coupled with a prophetic despair
has posed, during the past two generations, a problem which Fundamentalism was unable satisfactorily to resolve." As Social Gospel liberals launched "a vigorous attack on great social evils of the modern
world" fundamentalists waited for Armageddon. They had failed "to
work out a positive message" but instead took "further refuge in a despairing view of world history that cut off the pertinence of evangelicalism to the modern global crisis." Henry called for a reenergized
Christianity that offered "a formula for a new world mind with spiritual ends, involving evangelical affirmations in political, economic, so-
ciological, and educational realms, local and international. The re-
demptive message has implications for all of life," he concluded, while
"a truncated life results from a truncated message." He believed that
fundamentalists' obsession with identifying the Antichrist and insistent
predictions about a global cataclysm had overshadowed the message of
salvation. They had become so obsessed with the evils of this world
that they had failed to place sufficient attention on the remedy—a saving faith in Jesus Christ that guaranteed a glorious, eternal life in the
millennial kingdom. In this manifesto Henry was calling for not only
a change in theology but a change in tone, emphasis, and tactics.[2]

Henry, who was more likely to be mistaken for an out-of-shape former college linebacker than an influential theologian, spent his career
trying to restructure what he saw as fundamentalism's truncated message. Born in New York to German immigrants, he attended Wheaton
College in the early 1940s with Billy Graham. He later earned a doctorate from Boston University. He served on the founding faculty at
Fuller Theological Seminary and as the first editor of Christianity Today. At the time of his death in 2003, the New York Times called the
tall, prickly conservative the "brain" of the evangelical movement.
Since the publication of The Uneasy Conscience historians and evangelicals have been seduced by Henry's vision of the past and his call for a
new, culturally engaged evangelicalism.[3]

But Henry did bad history. He mischaracterized pre–World War II
fundamentalism in order to give his generation a fresh start and a clean
slate in the postwar period. Although his anticommunist sensibilities,
conservative politics, apocalyptic premillennialism, and vision for rebuilding the evangelical movement had much more in common with

interwar fundamentalism than he ever acknowledged, he tried to disavow the past. He minimized fundamentalists' intense interwar political activism and sought to disown all of the failed prophecy, ugly racism, and embarrassing internal squabbles of the interwar years. Beginning with the launch of the National Association of Evangelicals (NAE) in 1942 and continuing over the next decade and a half, radical evangelicals crafted a culturally savvy, professional movement. A new generation—along with important players from the previous generation—sanded down fundamentalism's rough edges and relegated its most colorful characters to the sidelines. Henry, along with Harold Ockenga, L. Nelson Bell, Charles Fuller, Billy Graham, and others transformed fundamentalism from a dispersed, decentralized movement into one carefully directed by a powerful and culturally influential white male elite.

The postwar generation of evangelical leaders had a clear sense of what "occupying" until Jesus's return meant for their lives, their movement, and especially their nation. The apocalyptic implications of the atomic bomb, combined with the increasingly intense Cold War, provided an ideal opportunity for fundamentalists-turned-evangelicals to relate their faith to the concerns of their communities. Americans knew that an epic battle of good and evil, right and wrong, was in the offing. While they longed for a future of peace and prosperity, they understood that an atheistic Soviet Union, nuclear weapons, and global devastation threatened on the horizon. Evangelicals helped Americans make sense of this postwar world by aligning it with their apocalyptic visions of imminent violence, horrific persecution, and world war.

Repudiating decades of American isolationism, evangelical leaders admonished their national representatives to assume unilateral global leadership and to reconstruct the world in the image of a supposedly Christian America. Their vision of expanding US power paralleled that of publisher Henry Luce. In dubbing the twentieth the "American Century," Luce called on Americans to "accept wholeheartedly our duty and our opportunity as the most powerful and vital nation in the world" and "to exert upon the world the full impact of our influence." Evangelicals wanted to do exactly that. While Luce and evangelicals had somewhat different visions of the ends to which they were working, it is no coincidence that the unfolding of the American Century paralleled the rise of modern American evangelicalism. The publisher and evangelicals both blended faith with country and demanded that the

United States take a new, bold, and preeminent place on the world stage. Atomic weapons, the birth of Israel, the rise of the UN, and the developing Cold War all helped make the American Century the century of apocalyptic politics as well. Evangelicals offered Americans redemption through faith in their nation and in the power of Christianity.[4]

The end of World War II provided new opportunities for the growing evangelical movement. Rather than reflect on how their wartime prophetic expectations had gone awry, evangelicals turned to aligning new weapons and geopolitical alliances with their vision of the end of days. Hiroshima and Nagasaki convinced radical evangelicals that even if they did not know when the world was going to end, they now knew how it would end. 2 Peter 3:10 reads, "but the day of the Lord will come as a thief in the night; in the which the heavens shall pass away with a great noise, and the elements shall melt with fervent heat, the earth also and the works that are therein shall be burned up." As early as 1929 *King's Business* had cited this passage in a discussion of the potential of the atom as a source of unimaginable energy. "Perhaps," the editors noted, the "great world cataclysm" predicted by Peter "will be accomplished by the release of atomic power."[5]

Almost as soon as the US army detonated "Little Boy" over Japan, prophetic speculation began anew. Like most Americans, evangelicals did not lament the number of causalities the bomb produced. Instead, they celebrated victory and moved quickly to analyzing how atomic weapons represented another key piece in the prophetic puzzle. The *Sunday School Times* ran a letter from a minister who cited multiple passages to demonstrate that the biblical prophets had anticipated the powerful new weapon. The editors confessed that these "signs of the times," dark as they may be, renewed their faith in Jesus's imminent return. Robert Fischer, a Christian chemist who had worked on the Manhattan Project and later a professor at the University of Indiana, admonished Christians that the time was short and encouraged them to renew their focus on missions. In a popular booklet, *The Atomic Bomb and the Word of God,* Wilbur Smith explained that the 2 Peter text, "without the slightest straining . . . or any forcing of its meaning," made clear that the atomic bomb was God's tool for the "final conflagration." Now that humans had the capacity to obliterate the earth, he argued, God had to be planning to intervene soon.[6]

The detonation of atomic weapons at the end of World War II renewed evangelicals'
faith that they were living in the end times. With first the United States and then
the Soviet Union acquiring the capacity to destroy the earth, evangelicals believed
that the rapture of true Christians had to be imminent.

Wilbur M. Smith, *The Atomic Bomb and the Word of God* (Chicago: Moody Press, 1945), cover.

Following the Moody professor's lead, American evangelicals speculated that atomic weapons would soon force God to bring history to an end. But as long as only the United States had the bomb, most saw little risk of humanity destroying itself. The faithful understood, however, that if or when the bomb fell into the hands of the United States' rivals, the train to Armageddon would accelerate. No enemy loomed larger at the time than the Soviet Union. In the late 1940s evangelicals, journalists, and government officials alike worried that Stalin would develop atomic weapons and soon thereafter strike the United States. The Soviets' successful test of an atomic weapon in 1949 confirmed their worst fears. With a nod to old speculation about "Magog," *King's Business* editors interpreted the news as "another step in the advance of Russia toward the goal of this Northern Confederacy." Meanwhile, Lowell Blanchard and the Valley Trio translated premillennial ideas into pop culture. They recorded "Jesus Hits Like an Atom Bomb" (1950), fretting that "Everybody's worried 'bout the Atomic Bomb, but nobody's worried 'bout the day my Lord will come when He'll hit—Great God Almighty—like an Atom Bomb when He comes, when He comes."[7]

Although evangelical leaders feared the growing power of the Russians, some relished the fact that the bomb had made apocalyptic expectations part of mainstream American life. Los Angeles pastor Frank Lindgren claimed that the bomb had forced American elites to grapple with what "we 'illiterate fundamentalists'" had been saying for years. Louis Bauman made a similar point in his last series of articles on prophecy before his death in 1950. "Dark indeed are the prognostications of our generation of statesmen, scientists, modernists and men of war," he wrote. "The super-optimists of a few years ago have become the super-pessimists of today." Smith summarized how radically things had changed since he had attended his first prophecy conference in 1914. At that time, fundamentalist doomsayers represented a small minority. In the late 1940s, in contrast, secular authorities, even more than evangelicals, were preaching imminent ruin. "Today," he observed in *Moody Monthly,* "the unbelieving world unites in testifying that we are in an hour of dire crisis—not only an hour of possible, impending calamities, but it would seem on the very verge of the eclipse of civilization and the destruction of humanity." Indeed, the premillennial message of imminent destructions resonated with Americans in new ways.[8]

Doom-and-gloom theology even became a prominent theme in the work of some liberal Protestants. Harris Franklin Roll, an influential critic of fundamentalism in the late 1910s, acknowledged in the *Christian Century* that "the First World War brought a marked revival of belief in the imminent second coming of Christ" (which he had vehemently denounced at the time), but World War II produced "a new apocalypticism." Indeed, in the late 1940s postmillennial optimism yielded to a revised expression of liberal Protestantism that some adherents dubbed neoorthodoxy. It grew out of the work of Karl Barth, Reinhold Niebuhr, and Paul Tillich and came to animate central tenets of midcentury political liberalism. As Americans tried to make sense of the wartime carnage, human depravity and original sin became topics of regular conversation not just among evangelicals but also among the nation's leading liberal theologians. Evangelicals accurately sensed that American culture had taken a dark turn. Popular music, movies, literature, and the arts all testified to the fact that in the post-Holocaust, post-Hiroshima world their fellow citizens had embraced apocalypticism in new and profound ways. The whole world now truly understood that the end might be near.[9]

Many African-American evangelicals saw atomic weapons in the same prophetic terms as their white counterparts. Evangelist James Webb, however, saw things differently. He continued to believe that the war served as God's judgment on humanity for its sins and that the Almighty would soon overturn global racial hierarchies. "As long as governments have imperialism policies that make economic slaves of the people that they rule over," he opined, "God will lead them into war." Reiterating the message he had been preaching since the 1920s, he explained to a reporter, "God has prepared a colored man to conquer the coming War No. III. He rocked in the Black Man's cradle in Africa. All according to Biblical history and prophecy." As African Americans, inspired by gains made during the war, lobbied for their civil rights, their reading of the Bible, the signs of the times, and the sins of humanity continued to differ in substantial ways from those of their white counterparts.[10]

The atomic bomb was not the only new sign of the times invigorating evangelicals. Roosevelt had hoped that World War II would end differently from World War I and that American isolationism would truly be history. Rather than allowing the United States to withdraw once again from the rest of the world upon the war's conclusion, the president laid the foundations for a new international peacekeeping organization—a revived, refined league of nations—in which he guaranteed that the United States would play a central role. Just two weeks after the president's death, the inaugural United Nations conference opened in San Francisco, where representatives from fifty nations drew up a charter intended to foster international cooperation and prevent future wars. For evangelicals, however, the establishment of the UN, like that of the League of Nations before it, confirmed their belief that increasing internationalism represented one more step on the road to the Antichrist. The UN, they speculated, could potentially serve as a tool for the devil to use to assert his power over the world's nations.

As global leaders worked to establish an effective UN, evangelicals condemned their efforts. "Whatever clever foreign diplomats or bungling American politicians may tell us," *Moody* editors wrote, "we help the world best by guarding our own interests." Returning to the classic American anti-entanglement mantra, they counseled national leaders to "keep America out of the pest house of European diplomacy." Riley, near the end of his life, called UN internationalism a tool for paving the way to the Antichrist. Influential African-American minister and radio broadcaster R. C. Lawson predicted that the new international organization would ultimately facilitate "the Ten-Toe Kingdom of Daniel headed by the anti-Christ." Bauman called the United Nations "the world's first attempt to establish an 'international organization' with the power of a world-government since Caesar ruled the earth. Divine revelation," he solemnly concluded, "plainly reveals that it will be the last." Their sentiments appealed not only to evangelicals but also to those Americans who still believed that it was possible for the United States to return to a position of isolation from European affairs. Evangelicals' claim that the Bible was on the side of American independence proved attractive to many people in the wake of the war.[11]

Once UN delegates published their charter, evangelicals complained that it did not include any references to God. The religious diversity of the UN member nations meant nothing to them. "It is our profound conviction," *King's Business* editorialized, that delegates could have found a way "at least to acknowledge their dependence upon God in their own way." Dan Gilbert grumbled that the initial UN meetings did not open with prayer and he too lamented that delegates opted not to include any references to God in the founding documents. The UN had taken a clear position, he argued, for atheism and the Soviet Union and against Christianity. He called on "Christian Americans" to "let their members of Congress know that they oppose the use of tax-funds of the American people to finance this Christ-rejecting, God-dishonoring propaganda arm of Antichrist." While he recognized that effective postwar missions work required international cooperation, spreading the gospel abroad fell second to protecting faith in the United States. "Regardless of what course other nations are determined to take," he asserted, "we are resolved to occupy America for Christ until He comes." Leaders like Gilbert were continuing to craft an absolutist politics that framed evangelicals' positions as the only righteous ones, while simultaneously implying that those who disagreed with them were inadvertently serving as pawns of Satan.[12]

The growing Jewish-Palestinian conflict and ultimately the creation of the state of Israel provided evangelicals with still more evidence of Armageddon's imminence. The Holocaust fostered worldwide sympathy for the plight of Jews and amplified calls for a permanent homeland. But local Muslims in Palestine did not want their Jewish neighbors to erect a new nation. Evangelicals coupled their view of the conflict in the Middle East with their understanding of global Islam. The faithful generally loathed Muslims and they had long seen Islam as an emerging threat. A 1918 *Christian Workers* cover, which depicted a menacing-looking man planting the flag of Islam in the heart of the African continent, illustrated their views. The caption read "The Moslem Menace, Shall we let him have it?" The next year the magazine ran a cartoon of Mohammed encouraging a Unitarian to trim the deity of Christ, the atonement, and the second coming out of the Bible. The prophet says, "Go right on, my friend; that's fine! Just what I've been doing these many centuries."[13]

During the interwar, British-mandate period, fundamentalists' fear of Islam, combined with their long-standing Zionism, guaranteed that they would side with the Jews in the growing conflict over territory. After visiting the Holy Land, Frank Norris bragged that Jews would soon displace Arabs as the "white man" had displaced the "American

Indian." "The Jew is industrious, the Arab lazy; the Jew is progressive, the Arab is only half civilized." Keith Brooks accused Arabs of "squatting" on Jewish land. "The Arab and the Moslem world is not only anti-Semitic," he concluded, "but is out and out anti-Christ." When in 1939 British leaders proposed the creation of separate Palestinian and Jewish states rather than a single Jewish nation, Neville Chamberlain received a strongly worded letter from Mark Matthews. "You have no authority to take Palestine away from the Jews. God has decreed that it shall be delivered to them."[14]

In the aftermath of the war, evangelicals' Zionist hopes intensified. "Believers in God's sure word of prophecy," *Sunday School Times* opined on its front page, "cannot help feeling a thrill as they see the increasingly prominent place that Palestine is taking in world affairs." Jewish Presbyterian Aaron Kligerman argued that Arabs had no legitimate claim to the Holy Land. "The peculiar Book, the peculiar people and the peculiar land," he argued in reference to the Bible, Jews, and Palestine, "must always be viewed together. What God has put together let no man, be he theologian or politician, put asunder." Ockenga acknowledged that from a purely political or international perspective, one could make a compelling case for either Palestinian or Jewish rights to the land. But "the Biblical view-point" settled the question. "God did not give it to the Arabs, but gave it to Israel." Gilbert believed that Americans had to decide just one thing in the Jewish-Palestinian debate—would they side with God or with the devil? "Only woe and disaster can come upon any nation which obstructs the program of God." Evangelicals' understanding of the Bible and prophecy assured them that to challenge Zionist designs on the Middle East was to challenge God. With the Almighty on their side, there was no question of the correct path to follow.[15]

In 1947, frustrated British leaders turned control of Palestine over to the new UN. The UN, in turn, proposed partitioning Palestine into Jewish and Arab states. While Jewish leaders in Palestine supported the proposal, Arab nations around the Middle East squelched it. Once the British started pulling out of the region, violence ensued. Jews and Palestinians began killing each other, forcing Palestinians to flee Jewish-majority areas. On May 14, 1948, a triumphant David Ben-Gurion announced the creation of the state of Israel.

The declaration of Israeli statehood and its immediate recognition by President Truman thrilled evangelicals. "Do you realize what this means?" Bible Institute of Los Angeles professor Louis Talbot asked on his radio program. "This could be the beginning of that train of events which will not end until the Lord Jesus Christ Himself returns and sets up the everlasting Kingdom." The editor of the *Pentecostal Evangel* enthusiastically told readers that events in the Middle East were aligning so closely with biblical prophecy that "we may well wonder whether we are awake or . . . merely having a very exciting dream." *King's Business* called the rise of Israel "the greatest piece of prophetic news that has appeared in the twentieth century." Once again, evangelicals' prophetic expectations seemed to match world events. Over the next couple of decades the faithful often returned to the 1948 creation of Israel as the principal event that validated their prophecy and marked the beginning of the end.[16]

Despite all of evangelicals' talk of a new engagement with their communities, their politics had changed very little over the years. The birth of the new evangelicalism had given more explicit direction and power to the political and economic conservatism that had characterized the fundamentalist movement since the era of the first Red Scare. In the post–World War II years evangelicals continued to champion states' rights and free market economics while identifying New Deal liberalism as Satan's vehicle for preparing the United States for Antichrist rule. Thus they tended to frown on progressive social and economic measures pursued by the state and favored instead individual self-help and faith in God's sovereignty and care. Their uncompromising politics appealed to wide numbers of Americans who felt left behind by their government or troubled by its seemingly unending growth and power.

Evangelicals drew on the work of popular and influential secular conservative theorists, such as Friedrich Hayek, to broaden their criticism of modern liberalism. "We are well on our way," Los Angeles minister Roy Laurin argued, "to the establishment of a *welfare state* which in relation to the essential genius of our country could well be a

farewell state. . . . Welfare states always *lead to slave states.*" Ockenga linked
Christianity to economics. "You cannot," he fretted, "divorce the
church and the Gospel from the forms of political economy in which
those things are either ministered or preached." He worried that "more
and more the viewpoint in America is toward the socialistic or the
welfare state," which had "no place" in the Bible. Carl McIntire published a long book arguing that the Bible "teaches private enterprise
and the capitalist system . . . as the very foundation structure of society
itself." He claimed that the liberal challenge to free markets "partakes
of all the aggravated complications of the conflict of the ages: tyranny
versus freedom, darkness versus light, error versus truth, Satan versus
Christ." Evangelicals' penchant for viewing the world in absolutist,
Manichean terms continued to define their movement. In taking such
clear positions, they claimed with certainty that they had the truth on
their side that would bring redemption for all sins. They also widened
their appeal. By drawing from nonevangelical theorists, they were
hoping to make inroads into the traditional right.[17]

Evangelicals' sanctification of the free market bolstered their antilabor sentiments. They joined business leaders and political conservatives
who in the immediate postwar period sought to roll back the concessions they had made to organized labor during the conflict. John R.
Rice repeatedly preached against the Congress of Industrial Organizations and complained that the government had "clearly" sided with the
"crooked labor boss" against the interests of workers. McIntire pronounced the "ungodliness exercised by the union leaders . . . far worse
than the ungodliness of the exploiter-capitalist." Evangelist W. O. H.
Garman worried that "ruthless, lawless, irresponsible labor unions are
imperiling the nation, tyrannizing the public and compelling workers,
Christians in particular, to violate their consciences and convictions."
Moody Monthly generally discouraged workers from joining the labor
movement. "What the agitator fails to tell the worker," the editors insisted, "is that under state socialism . . . the worker becomes a serf. We
take editorial space to write these things because we believe America
has unnumbered enemies within her gates seeking to destroy the
American system." For evangelicals, enemies lurked abroad and at home.
Their apocalypticism continued to foster a fear of those who differed
from them and who looked to competing sources of authority.[18]

As the economy sputtered in the transition from war back to peace, workers launched a new wave of strikes. While most fundamentalists agreed with Keith Brooks's argument that "we are reaping what the New Deal has sown," Washington state minister Howard Lehn had a different take. In the pages of *Moody Monthly* he confessed that although he used to have "a strong antilabor union attitude," his "close study of the labor union, its methods and its contribution to the working man caused a complete revision." He called on Christians to recognize workers' right to organize, bargain collectively, and strike.[19]

Lehn did not, however, have the last word. A few months later the evangelical periodical ran a correction in the form of an article by wealthy manufacturer and Moody Bible Institute trustee Maxey Jarman. The renowned evangelical shoe tycoon described union leaders as mostly self-serving, unscrupulous, and communist. He insisted that the collective bargaining process "should never be resorted to," he challenged the legality of the right to strike, and he alleged that unions "thrive on strife." So what should a Christian do if he or she faces problems at work? Join a union? Never, according to Jarman. Instead, "that person must take his problems to God in prayer . . . and I believe the Lord will provide a means of taking care of that man's problems, if he is a child of God." If God does not respond to the worker, he continued, "it is time to examine our lives to see what keeps us from having God's help in meeting the problems of life." His message was clear—if a person had trouble at work, his or her own sin must be the cause. From his corporate perch Jarman admonished ministers like Lehn to stay out of the business of the economy. "Our responsibility," he concluded, "is not to reform the world but it is to reach the individual with the gospel of Christ, to help him take care of his own individual problems." By offering support for both individuals' souls and their soles, he demonstrated how seamlessly creative evangelical leaders could blend their own market interests with their spiritual ideals.[20]

In the postwar years evangelicals remained as divided by race as ever, which continued at times to play out along eschatological lines. African-American Christians, inspired by the Double V campaign that had sought victory over fascism abroad and racism at home, persistently fought for their civil rights. Some integrated critiques of American segregation and race prejudice into their premillennial understandings of the future. R. C. Lawson, who identified racism as "the greatest evil in this world," spent decades seeking to discern signs of the times. In a characteristic postwar sermon the Harlem minister moved from insisting that "on every hand the stage is being set for Armageddon" to a critique of the "white complex" of the Christian church. Despite his conviction that history was approaching its denouement, he nevertheless called for Christians to "awake to a sense of their responsibility and fight the hydra-headed monster of prejudice, and all its attendant evils— economic exploitation, lynching, Jim-crow cars and Jim-crow churches, slum housing, etc."[21]

Oblivious to such pleas, white evangelicals paid little attention to these issues. Their racial views, like their economic views, continued to mirror those of their prewar predecessors. In the late 1940s the *Sunday School Times* offered a "lesson" to young people on race and race prejudice. The author, John W. Lane, Jr., discouraged Christians from misreading Acts 17:26 (And God "hath made of one blood all nations of men for to dwell on all the face of the earth, and hath determined the times before appointed, and the bounds of their habitation") as a justification for integration. The author argued that the Almighty had intended for the races to remain separate and that racial intermingling had "upset God's design" and produced racial turmoil. "In the majority of cases people of the various races of this earth would be far happier," he advised young readers, "living among their own kind and in their own places, as evidently God intended, than they can be, mixed up among the other races of the world." Although Christians had an obligation to treat all people as equal in God's eyes, Lane concluded, "the Christian should feel no obligation to let down the barriers set by propriety and custom in the matter of intermarriage with those of other races." "The Scriptures," he wrote in another lesson for young people, "carry no directive to the church to campaign for social or economic equity among the races."[22]

White evangelicals' long-standing antistatism reinforced their reluctance to act on racial issues or to support the nascent civil rights movement. They remained highly suspicious of any attempt by the federal government to encourage integration as socialist and suspect. In the late 1940s the NAE editorialized against Truman's effort to create a permanent Fair Employment Practices Commission. They claimed that such a move by Congress would "open the floodgates to a score of un-American practices" and "encourage rule by minorities." Once again, evangelicals' sense of besiegement came to the fore. Government by anything other than white Protestant males who lived up to evangelicals' theological litmus tests proved threatening.[23]

Over the next few years, evangelicals shifted from primarily criticizing the power of the executive branch to grousing about the actions of the judicial branch. They increasingly blamed the courts for undermining American freedoms and they particularly loathed the ways the US Supreme Court intervened in the civil rights struggle. Nelson Bell published a tract denouncing the 1954 *Brown v. Board* decision that mandated the racial integration of public schools. The Supreme Court frustrated Dan Gilbert as well, who claimed that its actions had worsened racial tensions. "The Supreme Court has created new and bitter divisions between our people," he harangued. "It has embittered and intensified racial and sectional conflict." A southern evangelist even called racial integration "another stepping stone toward the gross immorality and lawlessness that will be characteristic of the last days, just preceding the Return of the Lord Jesus Christ." For all of white evangelicals' talk about a new engagement with culture, they continued to be slaves to the old prejudices of fundamentalism. When men like Carl Henry denounced evangelicals' failure to stand up to race prejudice, he was primarily referring to Hitler's treatment of Jews, not white Americans' treatment of African Americans.[24]

Evangelicals' fears of the welfare state and civil rights and their concerns about the power of labor had direct political implications. Like their 1930s-era fundamentalist predecessors, they drew on their faith to justify their battle against political liberalism. Wheaton College historian C. Gregg Singer, who had earned a PhD from the University of Pennsylvania, called for an evangelical "awakening" to reclaim the state for God. Comparing the allegedly secular and internationalist Roosevelt and Truman administrations to Nazi Germany, he warned Christians that they would have to conform "to a totalitarian regime" if they did not act. Rather than acknowledge that fundamentalists had been politically active but ineffectual in the Progressive and New Deal eras, he perpetuated the dubious postwar myth that earlier generations had been indifferent to politics. "Unless Christians reverse sharply and quickly the predominant attitude of the past seventy-five years," he warned, "they may expect the rise of a political hierarchy distinctly hostile to the Church and all forms of Christian activity." Ministers and professors like Singer feared that they held a precarious position in American society and that at any moment the government might eradicate their liberties if they did not mobilize to prevent it. They continued to see the world as "us" against "them." Their ideas appealed to Americans in many different walks of life who found evangelicals' bold and confident articulation of a Christian politics of action attractive. The faithful offered white Americans a plan for holding on to power that they feared they were losing in the face of growing pluralism, secularism, and diversity.[25]

Most white evangelicals believed that protecting their freedom and engaging in politics meant working against Truman's efforts to expand the New Deal state. Roosevelt had initially hoped that the Social Security Act would cover Americans' health care. When he realized, however, that a health care initiative would not survive Congress, he dropped the idea. After the war, Truman resurrected it, proposing a comprehensive national health care plan. Evangelicals deplored the proposal. "Socialized medicine," McIntire ranted, "is nothing more than the totalitarian principle at work in the medical world." Brooks called Truman's plan "Communist-conceived" and "another chapter in the plan for socializing America." He believed that Truman's proposal anticipated the tactics of the coming "world dictator" who "will proceed to power by these very means." Evangelical spokesmen expected Americans to provide for their own health care and they trusted that the Great Physician would always have appointments available.[26]

To many Americans, evangelicals' political philosophy seemed heartless and cruel. After all, how could religious leaders of all people seemingly oppose policies that would save the lives of the poorest and most defenseless Americans? But evangelicals did not see it this way. They argued that government-run programs offered little more than oppressive bureaucracies. They believed that the true means of helping those most in need was through the efforts of private doctors working in conjunction with church groups. If doctors and local government oversaw community health care, Truman's opponents argued, individuals would receive far better and more efficient care than they could ever receive through mammoth programs run by the federal government. For evangelicals, opposing national health care was both ideological, in that they did not want to see the power of the state expand, and practical, in that they believed that private health care better served the American people. Their ability to link what they described as the old-time Christian faith to modern conservative politics drew substantial support. While apocalypticism drove evangelicals' thirst for action, the politics that grew out of their work appealed to many different kinds of Americans. Evangelicals' ability to seamlessly integrate faith with a conservative brand of politics helps explain why the movement expanded so rapidly in the Cold War era.

In 1948 Republicans nominated Thomas Dewey to run against Truman. The polls leading right up to the election indicated that Dewey would easily beat the Democratic incumbent. But to the surprise of most Americans, the election was an unexpected triumph for Truman. As usual, evangelical leaders shared their frustrations with the faithful. Bauman, initially astonished by the results, realized that he should not have been. He believed that the president's support of the newly formed Jewish state had earned him tremendous favor from God. The Almighty, he wrote, "could hardly do other than bless the man who so courageously acted." But Bauman's optimistic appraisal did not last long. "In this time for the Gentile sunset . . . liberalism, Laodicean [i.e. lukewarm] democracy, Socialism, Communism and every other what not of the leftists, is going to be in the saddle. . . . Had we paid more attention to the prophets and less to political prognosticators," he concluded, "we should have known that the party that has, and does, stand most strongly for economic controls, for government control of prices—of buying and selling—is the government that will sit on the throne as the midnight hour approaches." Brooks speculated that the Truman victory signified that "the socialistic trend . . . is now given new impetus." Although Norris was also disappointed, he confided to a businessman friend, "the day is not far distant when the old solid South and the conservative North will join together to save America." Indeed, the multigenerational work of fundamentalists and evangelicals like Norris helped lay the foundations for what eventually proved to be a major political realignment. While the Texas Tornado had often misread the signs of the times, he correctly anticipated the rise of the Sunbelt. Millions of white Americans, from Florida to Texas to California, saw in evangelicalism an attractive faith that also spoke to their political ideals.[27]

The Cold War inspired in evangelicals a renewed sense of urgency and stimulated Americans' apocalyptic fears. In 1946 George Kennan, a US diplomat stationed in Russian, predicted that conflict with the USSR was inevitable. "We have here," he concluded, "a political force committed fanatically to the belief that with US there can be no permanent modus vivendi, that it is desirable and necessary that the internal harmony of our society be disrupted, our traditional way of life be destroyed, the international authority of our state be broken." He recommended that American policy-makers "confront the Russians with unalterable counter-force at every point where they show signs of encroaching upon the interests of a peaceful and stable world." Winston Churchill put Kennan's beliefs into words that average Americans could easily understand. He warned an audience in Fulton, Missouri, that "an iron curtain has descended across the Continent" of Europe. Cold War–era Americans, like radical evangelicals, believed that evil lurked all around them and they were engaged in an ongoing war against the forces of evil that could well end at Armageddon.[28]

Over a half century of premillennial speculation prepared evangelicals to interpret the Cold War in apocalyptic terms. How they understood their role, and the role of their nation, however, was shaped as much by their World War II experiences as by traditional premillennial thought. During the war they had transformed from staunch isolationists into advocates of aggressive, American global leadership. They called on the United States to fight evil and to spread freedom and godly rule abroad in order to combat atheistic communism and bring spiritual revival before the final judgment.

While Christians throughout American history had often worked with political leaders to export Bibles, Christianity, and "civilization" to the rest of the world, radical evangelicals in the 1920s and 1930s saw themselves in competition with the state. They believed that the federal government was hostile to their interests and could accomplish little of lasting value. During World War II, however, their position evolved. Reviving the ideas of their nineteenth-century predecessors, evangelicals came to recognize the possibilities of Christianity walking hand in hand with the American government to redeem other peoples and other nations through the export of democracy, free markets, and the Christian faith. While they continued to disagree with Truman's domestic policies, they shared much of his Cold War vision for the world. Truman, followed by Dwight D. Eisenhower, used the bully pulpit to encourage the revitalization of faith as an alternative to "godless" communism. During the 1950s political leaders saw Christian revival as a core part of the United States' global Cold War strategy. While the faithful remained steadfastly opposed to modern political liberalism and global organizations like the UN, their advocacy of the United States as a unilateral but interventionist world leader, rooted in their belief that America was at heart a Christian nation, reinforced Truman and Eisenhower's vision for the globe and came to characterize postwar evangelical foreign policy.

As Cold War tensions rose, evangelicals returned again and again to the scriptures. While fundamentalists had spent the 1930s fretting over Mussolini and the restoration of the Roman Empire, they spent the 1940s and 1950s obsessed with Stalin and the Soviet Union. Russia had long played an important role in prophetic speculation and the Cold War simply reaffirmed the USSR's last-days significance. "There is no country in all the world," Talbot observed, "more autocratic than the Union of Soviet Socialist Republics, governed by its man of cold steel, Stalin. . . . And this is exactly in fulfillment of the prophecy of this Scripture." Wilbur Smith penned a new, up-to-date series of articles on prophecy for the *Sunday School Times*. A widely circulated ad for the articles asked readers to identify which world leader—Napoleon, Hitler, Mussolini, or Stalin—was the coming "World Dictator." The only possible answer had to be Uncle Joe—the one guy in the picture who was still alive and in power.[29]

Evangelicals continued to monitor the Cold War actions of the Catholic Church as well, looking for the pope's fingerprints in domestic politics and on international events. Truman, however, shared none of their anti-Romanist, Whore-of-Babylon fears. In his effort to contain the Soviets, he sought to build bridges to the Roman Catholic Church.

Despite the misgivings of Protestant ministers from across the theological spectrum, he viewed the Vatican as a powerful ally that could
help him unify Catholics, Protestants, Eastern Orthodox, and other
people of faith in the global war against communism. To that end he
planned to dispatch a permanent ambassador to the Vatican. Evangelicals around the country decried the president's proposal.[30]

As evangelicals' fears of Roman Catholic influence grew, Norris
proved to be a surprising exception. Despite his long history of rabid
anti-Catholicism, he believed that the Catholic Church could serve as
an important Cold War ally. "I am tremendously encouraged," he
wrote M. E. Coyle, a Catholic friend and General Motors executive,
"over the awakening that increases throughout the country on the
menace of Communism. A most peculiar and yet a natural thing has
occurred, namely, the Fundamentalists and Roman Catholics are finding themselves allies against a common foe." He even brought Coyle a
rosary from Rome, a surprising move for a preacher who had previously killed a man in defense of his anti-Catholic views. The rosary,
however, came with a catch. Norris was busy at the time trying to
shake down his Catholic ally for a new car, a Buick Roadmaster coupe,
which he hoped Coyle could charge to "advertising." Coyle called the
request "clearly out of order." This evangelical–Catholic alliance would
have to wait. Norris later bragged to Eisenhower that Chrysler executives had given him five cars over the previous decades; apparently
their "advertising" budget was more generous.[31]

In 1950, the Cold War turned hot on the Korean peninsula. At the
end of World War II, the Allies had divided the former Japanese colony
into two, with Soviets controlling the North and Americans the South.
Despite Koreans' hopes of a peaceful reunification, the governments in
Seoul and Pyongyang remained deeply divided. When the North Koreans moved into the South in an attempt to force reunification in 1950
under a procommunist regime, Truman sprung into action. He deployed General Douglas MacArthur and thousands of American troops
back to Korea under the auspices of UN "police action." Just five years
after V-J Day, the United States was at war again in Asia.

Evangelicals responded to news of the hostilities with prophecy analysis. "I have been spending much of my time in private study devoted to
Bible prophecy," up-and-coming evangelist Billy Graham announced

on his national radio broadcast. "There are strong indications in the Bible that in the last days a great sinister anti-Christian movement will arise. At this moment it appears that communism has all the earmarks of this great anti-Christian movement." Korea, Ockenga worried, "is most certainly the prelude to and the first annunciation" of World War III.[32]

Already furious with Truman over the presumed "loss" of China to communism, evangelicals used Korea as an opportunity to express their frustrations. Brooks criticized Truman's "inadequate" leadership; Norris, in a stirring sermon that demonstrated that he had not lost any of his rancor over the years, predicted that the skirmish would not "end with Korea" but would include China and then Russia. Why? Because "we have been betrayed. We have been betrayed by our own government." Ockenga blamed Truman for letting the situation unfold as it had and again fretted that the supposed sins of the United States, including drink, promiscuity, and homosexuality, had invoked God's wrath.[33]

Fears of the Soviet Union and anger over Korea inspired evangelicals to enlist in the growing anticommunist movement. The NAE instructed laypeople to watch for signs of subversion, boycott leftist entertainers, join anticommunist groups, and vote for conservative candidates. Many evangelicals supported leading anticommunist rabble-rousers such as Australian evangelical Fred C. Schwarz. His wildly popular Christian Anti-Communist Crusade attracted hundreds of thousands of followers who praised its blend of faith and politics. He told all who would listen, "I believe in God and His love, Christ and His redemption, and the great commission to go into all the world and preach the gospel. Communism is the enemy of God and of Christ and His gospel. These two facts have motivated me to do everything within my power to stay the advance of communism." Others still praised the House Un-American Activities Committee and men like Senators Joseph McCarthy and Richard Nixon for their efforts to root out subversives. "While nobody likes a watchdog," Graham acknowledged, "I thank God for men who, in the face of public denouncement and ridicule, go loyally on in their work of exposing the pinks, the lavenders, and the reds who have sought refuge beneath the wings of the American eagle." Like his predecessors, Graham worried as much about subversives within as enemies without, which encouraged evangelicals' besiegement mentality. The faithful hoped that as the United States executed an aggressive, Cold War foreign policy, some of their own would play leading roles. Ockenga called on fellow believers to get involved "in world leadership. Evangelicals," he emphasized, "should be thrust into political, diplomatic, military posts of responsibility and leadership." For the next few generations, evangelicals would make this call a reality by assuming important posts in Washington and around the globe.[34]

In the immediate postwar period, radical evangelicals engaged in significant introspection and a bit of self-flagellation as they aspired to greater social and political influence. In the nineteenth century, evangelicals had often served in important positions in government and the economy—they had substantial influence on the nation, helping shape everything from what teachers emphasized in schoolrooms to what foreign policies the White House pursued. Postwar evangelicals hoped to do the same.

Carl Henry's critique of fundamentalism in *The Uneasy Conscience* represented just one of many calls for reform. "An appalling impotence has crept over the Protestant Church in America," Manhattan minister William Ward Ayer lamented. Fundamentalists "doggedly, and sometimes cantankerously, cling to our complete Victorianism of thought and language," while the secular world "looks at us, smiles at our naiveté—and goes about capturing the masses." He called on his coreligionists to "face the fact" that "God's people are in the main backward." Smith groused that in "the last one hundred years, evangelical Christianity has suffered tragic defeat, and is being beaten back in almost every important area which once it occupied." While he interpreted this as in part the fulfillment of last-days prophecy, he did not believe that premillennialism required Christians to abandon secular society. "The purpose of the church's warfare," he wrote quoting G. Campbell Morgan, "is the capture of the inspirational centers of human life . . . to create opinion; to capture the thinking of men, and compel it to the thinking of Christ." In a blunt *Christian Life* article—"Can Fundamentalism Win in America?"—Ockenga wrote, "fundamentalism watches the struggle for power" between the "big three of Modernism, Catholicism and Secularism, and wistfully wishes for some magic to transform itself from a pigmy into a giant." He called for a "progressive fundamentalism with an ethical message" that would bring the evangelical message to Americans from every walk of life.[35]

The popular minister's call to reimagine fundamentalism did not mean that he had lost faith in a premillennial rapture. Ockenga had long defended the seeming contradiction between apocalypticism and politics by insisting, "we labor as though Christ would not come for a millennium. We live as though he were to come to-night." This was a message he preached over and over again. "A belief in the second coming of the Lord Jesus Christ should not make one fatalistic in social problems," he admonished his congregation. "This attitude that the world is going to the devil and therefore we can do nothing about it is quite contrary to Christian ethics and doctrine. . . . It is the Christian's duty to occupy till Christ comes. This means that we shall be engaged in humanitarian activity as well as evangelism and missions." For Ockenga and many like him, faith in the soon-coming Christ provided tremendous incentive for action.[36]

Ockenga's *Christian Life* article and the vision it expressed for the evangelical movement sparked substantial controversy. The magazine received a flood of responses, many of which criticized the NAE president. "Does he advocate that the Church of Jesus Christ go into politics?" one asked. "If he does, I would like to know chapter and verse for such authority." Others saw the question "Can fundamentalism win in America?" as a repudiation of premillennialism. "Frankly," Ironside wrote, "I do not think any ism, no matter how orthodox, will ever win America. The apostasy, I believe, has set in for good." But Ockenga stood firm. "The judgment of history on fundamentalism," he preached, "is that it has failed."[37]

In shaping a new evangelicalism, men like Ayer, Smith, Henry, and Ockenga assumed that the United States had always been a Christian nation and that God wanted radical evangelicals to return it to its roots. They believed that at its origins, the United States had been governed by biblical principles and that their mission was to lead it back to its righteous foundations. Billy Graham, who shared their aspirations, masterfully invoked this imagined past. "Our country," he insisted, "was founded upon a supernaturalistic concept—a belief in God and a belief in the book we call the Bible. . . . Our forefathers meant that this country was to be established as a Christian nation." As such, only godly men in tune with God's plan for the ages should rule it.[38]

Evangelicals' vision of the nation's history and future resonated with millions of Americans. During the Cold War, attendance at churches and synagogues skyrocketed, enrollment at seminaries surged, and construction of new houses of worship boomed. According to polling data from the period, the percentage of Americans who claimed church affiliation reached an all-time high of 69 percent in 1960. Even the president fell under the spell of revivalism. In 1954 Dwight D. Eisenhower famously declared, "our government makes no sense unless it is founded on a deeply felt religious faith—and I don't care what it is" (he went on to acknowledge that in the United States it was Christianity). Such declarations tapped into a deep American tradition of "civil religion" that dated back to the Puritans. Many Americans believed that the United States—like ancient Israel—was a particularly religious nation that had been divinely chosen by God to play a major part in his plan for the ongoing redemption of the world. They believed that God had destined the United States to bring Christian economic, political, and religious values to the rest of the world. This ideology melded perfectly with the Cold War. Congress's addition of the phrase "under God" to the Pledge of Allegiance in 1954 to distinguish it from the "atheist" pledges of communist countries and Congress's 1956 elevation of "In God We Trust" to the national motto further demonstrated the hold of civil religion on the American consciousness in this period. Fears of atheistic communism and a powerful Soviet empire encouraged politicians, evangelicals, and the American people all to see the world in similar ways.[39]

While evangelical leaders framed their call for cultural engagement and action as something new, their agenda did not differ much from that of fundamentalists in the interwar period. The faithful had long labored to bring their beliefs into American civic life. However, two substantial differences set the periods apart. First, the rise of New Deal liberalism had profoundly changed the stakes. Evangelicals now faced what they perceived as a secular, hostile, all-powerful state whose social and political policies appeared to threaten religious liberty. Second, the revolution in communications gave the faithful new and innovative ways to organize, coordinate, and disseminate their message to broader constituencies. Their skill at tapping into American apocalyptic angst in the 1950s and 1960s facilitated the rapid acceleration of the movement.

Committed to making the movement as effective as possible, some evangelical leaders aspired to have greater influence in the realm of ideas—they wanted to make a scholarly and rational case for the evangelical faith. They recognized that the interwar fundamentalist passion for missions in the context of an imminent rapture had produced a generation of believers who knew their English Bibles inside and out, but not much more. Arno Gaebelein's son, Frank, who had earned degrees from New York University and Harvard, confided to Wilbur Smith, "the intellectual poverty of most of modern fundamentalism is disturbing." Smith agreed. In fact, he was already helping Charles Fuller lay the foundations for revolutionizing the evangelical mind.[40]

In 1946 Charles Fuller decided to organize a new Christian school to focus on missions and evangelism. Such a school was essential, he believed, for building the intellectually sophisticated, culturally relevant faith that many evangelicals longed for. Fuller's radio program, the *Old Fashioned Revival Hour,* had represented evangelicals extremely well. The broadcasting pioneer had embraced the latest technologies and employed the most talented staff to create one of the nation's most popular radio programs. He expected his school to have an equally important and perhaps more lasting impact. He reached out to Ockenga and Wilbur Smith with his plans. Both were intrigued, but Ockenga told Fuller that evangelicals needed a center for top-notch graduate training rather than another Bible institute. The radio evangelist agreed and Fuller Theological Seminary (named for Charles's dad) was born. Ockenga agreed to serve as the founding president. The initial faculty included Everett Harrison, with a PhD from the University of Pennsylvania, Carl Henry, with a PhD from Boston University, Harold Lindsell, who held a doctorate in history from New York University, and Smith. The latter had by far the least prestigious academic pedigree of the bunch and had never earned a degree—not even from high school. But he offered more than a diploma. His father, a wealthy businessman and produce wholesaler, had contributed to the development of MBI and had helped Lyman Stewart oversee the publication of the *Fundamentals.* Wilbur had long used his father's money to collect rare books in many areas of literature and theology and he brought to the school an extensive and valuable library. The entire Fuller faculty ascribed to premillennialism, a point of doctrine that they codified in the school's founding statement of faith.[41]

In 1947, Fuller Theological Seminary opened in the beautiful Los Angeles suburb of Pasadena. Once again, fundamentalists-turned-evangelicals counted on deep pockets to make their work a success. A trust created by wealth derived from the Fuller family's orange groves covered the initial expenses. Numerous wealthy executives, such as Herbert J. Taylor and later C. Davis Weyerhaeuser, served on the board of trustees. Lavish faculty offices located on a palm-tree-lined estate in a tony neighborhood sent a clear message—this was no fly-by-night Bible institute. Consistent with traditional evangelical views, the founders did not initially let women enroll in the school. Soon, however, women persuaded the board that seminary training was essential for their gender-appropriate work in Christian education and on the mission field.

At the inaugural convocation Ockenga explained the founders' vision for the school. Speaking before a packed Pasadena Civic Auditorium audience on the "challenge to the Christian culture of the West," he offered a brief survey of the rise and fall of Western Christendom. "The time is shorter than you think," he repeatedly warned while reminding the assembled students that Jesus had required them to "occupy" until he returned. He called on them to rethink and restate "the fundamental thesis and principles of a western culture. . . . We need," he continued, "to rebuild the foundations and to restore the breaches." His impassioned message encapsulated his life's work and his commitment to shore up white Christian culture against the forces of secularism, socialism, and moral decadence. He reiterated the premillennial sense of urgency to act before it was too late while calling on the next generation of evangelicals to reclaim the culture—and the world—for Jesus. Responding to Ockenga's challenge would define the mission and trajectory of evangelicalism for generations to come.[42]

By the mid-1950s, white evangelicals had an advocacy group in the NAE, a professional graduate training school in Fuller Seminary, and a new generation of media savvy, charismatic, smart ministers and evangelists dedicated to expanding the movement into the broader culture. But they did not have a consistent platform for reaching other religious

In the postwar era, a group of ambitious evangelicals worked to strengthen the intellectual basis of their movement through a new institution, Fuller Theological Seminary. Pictured here on the new seminary campus (left to right) are Harold Ockenga, Charles Fuller, Everett Harrison, Harold Lindsell, Wilbur Smith, Arnold Grunigen, and Carl Henry.
Courtesy of Fuller Theological Seminary.

leaders or the general public with their views. Billy Graham believed that a new magazine could meet this need. To that end he helped found *Christianity Today,* which has been the magazine of record for the evangelical movement ever since. Essentially Graham wanted to do for evangelicalism what the *Christian Century* had long done for liberal Protestantism. He hoped that the magazine would "restore intellectual respectability and spiritual impact to evangelical Christianity" and serve as yet another means of distancing evangelicalism from the negative stereotypes of anti-intellectualism and detachment that dogged it. "Instead of using the stick of denunciation and criticism," he recalled, the magazine would "present a positive and constructive program" and would "lead and love rather than vilify, criticize, and beat. Conservative Christians," he explained, "had failed with the big stick approach; now it was time to take a more gentle and loving direction."[43]

Ockenga, Henry, and L. Nelson Bell (who was now Graham's father-in-law and a close confidante) quickly jumped on board the evangelist's project. Ockenga agreed to serve as chairman of the board and Henry accepted the position of editor. They solicited articles from prominent white evangelicals in North America and Europe, as well as from the nation's leading political conservatives, such as J. Edgar Hoover and Russell Kirk. Although the magazine occasionally ran articles by women, its editors and authors consistently toed the traditional evangelical line in terms of gender relations and most often treated women in practice as subordinate to men.[44]

Contributors often boasted PhDs or ThDs from top-tier American and European universities. Editors listed their degrees to highlight evangelicals' efforts to take the intellect seriously. Over time the magazine delivered what it promised, providing a respectable forum for broadly defined evangelical discussion and debate. Taking a page out of Lyman Stewart's book, the magazine's founders initially distributed their product to over one hundred thousand clergy and church leaders free of charge. It immediately became the most significant voice of modern evangelicalism. By 1967 *Christianity Today* boasted 148,900 paid subscribers compared to the *Christian Century*'s 37,500. Today the magazine claims six hundred thousand print readers in addition to millions more who follow the magazine through its website.[45]

Once Graham set the magazine plan in motion, he and his team began recruiting financiers. Radical evangelicals had always had close ties to business leaders, from John Wanamaker to Henry Crowell to Lyman Stewart, with whom they shared a deep faith in the free market. Things were no different in the postwar period. Graham explained his vision for *Christianity Today* to staunch conservative oilman J. Howard Pew and shoe tycoon Maxey Jarman. Pew had long channeled his vast wealth through religious leaders to try and push the country to the right. In the 1930s and 1940s he worked with theologically liberal but politically conservative ministers, including James Fifield, Jr., and Norman Vincent Peale, but in the 1950s he sensed that evangelicalism rep-

resented the next valuable reserve that if properly drilled would produce a gusher. Economics, not theology, mattered most to Pew, and he
used whomever he could to validate his free market agenda through
the language of Christianity.[46]

In supporting the magazine, Pew knew exactly what he was paying
for. Rather than "making Christians out of people," he explained in a
fundraising letter to potential fellow investors, "many ministers" lobbied Washington "to obtain more laws to make more people subject to
more government controls." Changing the perspectives of such ministers served as the oil baron's primary goal. He charged that using the
"Welfare State" even in the service of humanitarian ideals was inde-
fensible. He feared that ministers' compassion for the poor blinded
them to the hazards posed by New Deal liberalism, which "will inevitably lead us into Communism." For Pew, *Christianity Today* offered the
solution to this problem. "For many years now," he advised potential
donors, "most" religious leaders and publications had been "slanted toward the left; so that there has been little opportunity for the ministers
to have access either to scholarly theological literature or sound literature dealing with our social and economic philosophy. To fill this gap,"
he concluded, "Dr. Bell, Dr. Ockenga, Billy Graham, and I met together three years ago; and as a result . . . CHRISTIANITY TODAY
was incorporated." Pew hoped that the magazine could help push ministers to the right and persuade their congregations to move with them.[47]

The founders of the magazine quickly discovered that running a
publication primarily with private funds rather than advertising and
subscription revenue had unique challenges. Keeping the books balanced meant keeping the donors happy. Pew, in particular, knew exactly what economic and political philosophies the magazine should
preach and he did not want it to deviate. While his values usually
aligned with those of the board of directors, his strong opinions sometimes caused problems for the magazine's editors, who had hoped in
the spirit of the new evangelicalism to use the magazine to present a
thoughtful range of opinions on controversial issues. Pew's efforts to
shape the magazine and Bell and Graham's desire to keep Pew's check-
book open occasionally infuriated Henry. At one point the editor sent
an impassioned memo to Bell about Pew's interference, vowing, "I'm

not going to ruin C.T.'s opportunities. Let somebody else do it." But for the most part the editors accommodated Pew.[48]

Christianity Today proved to be an ideal venue for promoting evangelicals' efforts to bring Christian revival to the United States, remind the nation of its Christian foundations, and promote a political conservatism that exalted individual faith, free markets, and antistatism. Their politics indirectly (and sometimes directly) discouraged attempts to challenge the subordinate status of women and racial and ethnic minorities in American society. In choosing to locate the magazine's offices in Washington, D.C., the founders made their goals explicit. "The editors," Henry explained in the inaugural issue, "daily look down Pennsylvania Avenue and glimpse the White House, Blair House, and other strategic centers of national life. Thus CHRISTIANITY TODAY is a symbol of the place of the evangelical witness in the life of a republic." In a letter to the board of directors Henry made the periodical's political presuppositions clear. "The magazine is committed to neither party, but it is committed to specific principles." He identified those principles as limited government, the free enterprise system, and church-state separation, the last of which was code for keeping Catholics from gaining any advantages. The editors consistently decried "Big Government" (always capitalized) and in a regular column Bell routinely waved the flag of antistatism. "A new generation has emerged," he lamented in one representative piece, "a generation which values security more than freedom, ease more than hard work, pleasure more than application, entertainment more than enterprise. Worst of all we live in a time when millions think the government owes them a living—one of the most damning philosophies men ever had." Henry too routinely criticized the welfare state, arguing that it had assumed the role the church should fulfill. He did, however, occasionally provide space for dissenting opinions.[49]

A decade into the magazine's run, its politics continued to reflect the conservative ideals of its founders and financiers. Historian William G. McLoughlin wrote at the time that evangelicals were "deeply committed to nationalistic, laissez-faire ultraconservatism." They "equate Christianity with 'the American way of life' as defined by the National Association of Manufacturers; they are hysterically anti-Communist in foreign policy and totally opposed to any extension of the Welfare

State in domestic policy." McLoughlin's purpose in profiling the group was to alert the broader public that they needed to take the evangelical movement seriously as a political force. "The United States now has a permanent, powerful, and respectable ultra-right wing in its political spectrum," he concluded. "The new evangelicals are the spiritual hard-core of the radical right." The magazine's editors basically agreed with McLoughlin's characterization. In an article subtitled "For the Right— Not 'On the Right,'" they "admitted that there is some truth" to the Brown University historian's characterization of the movement. How-ever, in a chicken-or-the-egg dissent from McLoughlin, they argued that rather than conservative politics shaping their faith, the true ap-plication of Christianity produced their conservative politics. But they did not doubt that hard right conservative politics and evangelical faith were mutually reinforcing, which proved to be essential to the move-ment's growth and appeal.[50]

While the magazine's editors took prophecy seriously, they presented a broad range of views in the articles they chose to print. In 1958, for example, the magazine ran a series on the coming millennium with contributions from George Eldon Ladd, John F. Walvoord, Loraine Boettner, and W. J. Grier. Each man defended a different position on eschatology. Walvoord's classic premillennialism appeared as only one option among many from which evangelicals could faithfully choose. But in one of the same issues the editors showed their hand by running a piece by A. W. Tozer. "The pendulum has swung from too much prophecy to too little," the popular minister and writer lamented, "and that just when we most need the sobering word of the prophet to keep us calm and sane amid the crash of worlds." Henry repeated and ex-panded on Tozer's point shortly thereafter. "No good reason exists for a failure to discern the sure hand of God in current events," he wrote. "No generation in history has seen such swift propaganda advances as ours toward World Government, a theme on which Revelation 13 has much to offer. For the first time since the Old Testament era, nations of the ancient biblical world are crowding the front-page headlines of the world press." Evangelicals, he believed, needed to herald this message. "The far-flung lines between the Soviet and the Free World are drawn near Armageddon itself. . . . World events are too awesome to leave the subject of Bible prophecy to Jehovah's Witnesses and the fanatics."

Although *Christianity Today's* tone was far more temperate and less dogmatic than that of the popular fundamentalist magazines that appeared between the world wars, the editors regularly engaged with premillennial prophecy, especially in their "interpretation of the news" columns. Evangelicals' apocalyptic sensibilities continued to motivate them to call for action and to shape their understandings of the state, reform movements, national politics, and world events.[51]

White evangelical leaders' efforts to rebrand their movement in the post–World War II era signaled a new determination to take seriously Jesus's admonition to occupy until he returned. The destruction caused by the war and the untold horrors it had opened made their end-days prophecies all the more significant and pressing. It gave their faith a new sense of moral certitude and authority and made apocalyptic predictions seem more and more legitimate.

Shortly after organizing, the NAE sent Clyde W. Taylor to Washington, D.C., to open an office in the Capitol, where he spent the next forty years lobbying for evangelicals. "We are seeing the gradual awakening of Protestantism," he wrote in an annual report in 1948, "and many of its activities are centering in Washington. . . . Senators and Representatives are becoming very much aware that great religious forces are active." Symbolizing how effective their strategy had become, in 1953 the NAE presented President Dwight D. Eisenhower and Vice President Richard Nixon with a "Declaration of Seven Divine Freedoms," which the president and vice president signed in an elaborate ceremony celebrating the Fourth of July. This event marked the beginning of the NAE's "March of Freedom" campaign, a movement to "sponsor and promote a nationwide, non-sectarian religious and educational campaign to re-emphasize the fact that good citizenship and freedom depend upon faith in God." In this identification of country and Christianity, postwar evangelicals and secular politicians alike, echoing American Puritans before them, celebrated their nation not as another Babylon but as the City upon the Hill.[52]

Evangelicals' political efforts hinted at the success that was to come. In 1958 the *Christian Century* profiled the "fundamentalist renaissance," citing the proliferation of serious evangelical theologians, the rise of

Christianity Today, the success of revivalists, and the influence of Fuller Seminary as evidence that changes in American religious life were under way. "It is no longer proper," Arnold W. Hearn wrote, "to view fundamentalism exclusively in terms of the stereotypes which emerged during the period of bitterest controversy following World War I." He went on to list the many ways evangelicals were contributing to the revitalization of the church and society. Uneasy conscience or not, evangelicals were well on their way to recapturing a significant chunk of Western civilization. Little did they realize that rather than facing Judgment Day, they were on the verge of their greatest revival yet. A young man from North Carolina was positioned to reshape evangelical Christianity and to change the world—at least until it arrived at Armageddon.[53]

11

APOCALYPSE NOW

ON SEPTEMBER 23, 1949, President Harry Truman revealed to the world that the Soviet Union had conducted a successful test of an atomic bomb. Two days later, a handsome, lanky, thirty-one-year-old evangelist stepped up to the podium in a makeshift tabernacle erected on a vacant lot in southern California. "I think that we are living at a time in world history when God is giving us a desperate choice, a choice of either revival or judgment," the preacher blustered in a southern twang. "There is no alternative! . . . God Almighty is going to bring judgment upon this city unless people repent and believe—unless God sends an old-fashioned, heaven-sent, Holy Ghost revival."[1]

The young Billy Graham warned the sixty-five hundred people who had packed into the revival tent that now was the time for salvation. "Across Europe at this very hour there is stark naked fear among the people, for we all realize that war is much closer than we ever dreamed," he warned. "Russia has now exploded an atomic bomb. An arms race . . . is driving us madly towards destruction! . . . I am persuaded that time is desperately short!" But he did not despair. Throughout Graham's career he reminded his listeners of God's promise to the Hebrews in 2 Chronicles 7:14, "if my people, which are called by my name, shall humble themselves, and pray, and seek my face, and turn from their wicked ways; then will I hear from heaven, and will forgive their sin, and will heal their land." Like most other fundamentalists and evangelicals, Graham did not just see this verse as a promise to ancient Israel. He also believed it applied to the modern United States. Judgment was coming, but it was never too late to repent and find redemption.[2]

Graham's ascension into the center of American religious life marked a new point in the history of modern evangelicalism. Graham's maturation in the faith, unlike that of Ockenga, Ayer, Smith, Fuller, and the many other religious leaders scarred by the fundamentalist controversies and errant prophecies of the depression era, occurred during World War II. He was a product of the new evangelicalism that sought to find better ways to appeal to outsiders rather than the old fundamentalism that too often produced ugly internecine squabbles. He masterfully integrated the apocalyptic theology of his predecessors with the irenic disposition and respectability of the new evangelicals. He never doubted that faith and American nationalism walked hand in hand and he believed that God had selected the United States to help prepare the world for the coming judgment. Advising presidents, meeting with foreign leaders, and counseling political policy-makers, he achieved the influence that the faithful had long prayed for. As Graham came to represent the public face of evangelicalism, he demonstrated that efforts to rebrand the fundamentalist movement had been a stunning success.

But Graham's was not the only voice of postwar evangelicalism. No matter how hard movement leaders tried to rein in premillennial speculation and to present their faith as a constructive, respectable alternative to liberal Protestantism, the faithful continued to devour the most daring and radical expressions of apocalypticism. The civil rights movement, Vietnam, the Cold War, and the 1970s oil crisis inspired visions of disaster and doom among a new crop of evangelical writers. These men and women provided a populist, grassroots challenge to the increasingly staid evangelicalism of the second half of the twentieth century. The onslaught of wars and revolution and of gender- and race-related upheavals left many Americans fearful. They found solace in placing faith in sources of traditional authority and in promises of salvation from the cataclysm that was to come. While postwar evangelicals

Billy Graham masterfully blended the apocalyptic urgency of interwar fundamentalism
with the respectability of postwar evangelicalism. As a young evangelist, Graham
consistently heralded the imminent second coming of Christ.
   September 19, 1951, *Los Angeles Examiner* Collection. Courtesy of Special Collections,
   Doheny Memorial Library, University of Southern California.

did not draw on premillennialism as often or as rigorously as earlier
fundamentalists to interpret their lives or to make sense of global
events, it continued to have dramatic appeal and provide moral solace
for growing numbers of people.

Graham never doubted that the time was nigh. Although he believed,
like so many others, that the specifics of biblical prophecy were vague
enough to guarantee vigorous debate, he made apocalypticism a central component of his ministry throughout his entire career; the second
coming was one of the topics that most animated him. His invocation
of apocalypticism served to instill in followers a belief that time counted
and that it mattered how they spent their lives. "Fifty years ago," he
explained early in his career, "a few evangelical ministers preached that

Jesus is coming and, although their audiences listened with interest, few thought that their beliefs would ever find wide acceptance among the religious and secular leaders of the world." But in the wake of the world wars, the Great Depression, and the hydrogen bomb, things had changed. "A doctrine," he effused, "which was written off fifty years ago as irrelevant, inconsistent and impossible had become the great hope of the church in the middle of the twentieth century." He recognized that apocalyptic fears were playing a role in global politics. "Many world leaders," he insisted, "are consciously aware that we are on the brink of a world catastrophe and impending judgment." His goal, however, was to instill hope. With Jesus, the men and women attending his crusades, reading his books, or listening to him on TV or radio could find salvation.[3]

During Graham's evangelistic crusades, he routinely warned that Jesus would soon return to separate the sheep from the goats. At a 1950 southern California revival he confessed that his calculations regarding the rapture's imminence had been evolving. "I'm revising my figures," he explained. "Last year in Los Angeles I thought we had at least five years, now it looks like just two years—and then the end." While neither Graham's pistachio-colored suit nor the sins of humanity brought down God's immediate wrath, his message did not change. "We do not know whether we have one year, two years, five years, or ten years," he preached a few years later. "But one thing is certain—there is a feeling in the air that something is about to happen. Men sense that they are rushing madly toward a climactic point in history." Shortly after the Soviets' launch of *Sputnik* in 1957, Graham again defended his apocalyptic sensibilities. "The Church," he told a national radio audience, "has all but lost its emphasis on this thrilling doctrine which is so clearly taught in the New Testament. I know that some have gone over-board and twisted and distorted the prophecies. I realize that many have foolishly set dates. . . . But the truth is that the Church has been most effective in the world when she has lived in momentary expectancy of the return of Christ." Graham understood that premillennialism was much more than an abstract doctrine; it invigorated faith and inspired action that would hasten redemption in a sinful world. "The Church," he urged, "must re-discover this great doctrine which is so clearly and amply taught in the Bible."[4]

In the 1950s and early 1960s, Graham became evangelicalism's great-est booster. He worked closely with Henry, Ockenga, Fuller, and oth-ers through institutions like Fuller Seminary, *Christianity Today,* and his own Billy Graham Evangelistic Association to build the movement. He embodied its most distinctive characteristics. He waged a relentless fight against communism and masterfully evaluated and shared with his radio and crusade audiences the foreboding signs of the times and their relationship to Armageddon. In 1965 he put his ideas into print in *World Aflame,* a powerful, apocalyptic diagnosis of the era that tied to-gether the many themes of his work up to that point.

World Aflame illustrated Graham's positions—and those of white evangelicals more generally—on the great social and political issues of the day. Graham opened the book by recounting the detonation of the first atomic bomb in July 1945. "From that day on our world has not been the same," he wrote. "We entered a new era of history—perhaps the last era." But for Graham this was good news. Armageddon, he assured readers, will bring ultimate redemption. "The salvation of society . . . will come about by the powers and forces released by the apocalyptic return of Jesus Christ." This did not mean, however, that evangelicals should not work for society's betterment; in fact despite Graham's deep-seated antistatism he supported his friend Lyndon Johnson's War on Poverty. Such strange contradictions never fazed this pragmatic evangelist, whose desire to be close to those in power some-times trumped his political principles.[5]

Like each of his premillennial predecessors, Graham argued in *World Aflame* that certain signs would mark the approach of the last days. "Today," he wrote, "it would seem that those signs are indeed converg-ing for the first time since Christ ascended into heaven." They included hydrogen bombs, the population explosion, increasing crime, sexual perversion, homosexuality, immorality, dependence on pills and alco-hol, political turmoil, and a lack of true faith. The most controversial movements of the day, such as feminism, civil rights, and the battle against communism, served as additional signs. Graham's work illus-trates how evangelicals in the 1960s understood the dramatic changes afoot, as well as how premillennialism continued to shape the ways the faithful apprehended the world in which they lived.[6]

The escalating war in Vietnam provided context for *World Aflame*. Graham supported the war but rather than deal directly with the divisive conflict in Southeast Asia he focused on the growing global communist threat. "God," he wrote, "may be using Communism as a judgment upon the West. The sins of the West are now so great that judgment is inevitable, unless there is national repentance." Although Graham hoped for an American victory against North Vietnam, he did not believe that the world's battles would be resolved in this age. "We cannot have permanent peace until hearts are changed," he admonished the North Carolina legislature at the height of the Vietnam conflict. And those hearts would not change until "man stands at Armageddon— which could happen in this century—with atomic bombs ready to burst, and God intervenes, and Jesus Christ comes back to this world and sits on the throne and rules the world." Premillennial apocalypticism remained central to the evangelical creed. Graham saw it as the message of the hour not just for Christians but also for the nation's political leaders.[7]

Like Graham, most evangelicals saw the Vietnam War as an essential part of the campaign against communism and atheism. Articles in *Christianity Today* regularly reinforced believers' faith in their nation's righteousness in leading the battle against global communism. So did the sermons of evangelical leaders like Ockenga. "As a Christian," the Boston minister preached, "I believe we must stand against Communism in southeast Asia." He wrote President Johnson in 1966 to complain about the administration's "hesitancy to pursue the war to a victorious conclusion" and "willingness to let the war drag on for years." Instead Ockenga called on the nation to "fight to win the war and thus to end it" using "whatever weapons and fire power necessary to win." He expressed similar views in a letter to a Park Street congregant serving in Vietnam. "I want you also to know that I stand with you 100% in the cause for which you are fighting," he explained. "Be assured that we at home oppose any of the beatnik attitudes on the part of students, or the pacifist attitude on the part of preachers, or the compromising views of politicians." His words illustrated the continuing development of an absolutist evangelical politics that had no tolerance for compromise or for seeking consensus.[8]

Ockenga, like Graham, believed that larger forces were at work in the conflict in Southeast Asia. In the spring of 1967, he delivered a sermon titled "Vietnam, World War III and the Second Coming." He interpreted the campaign against communism and Arab mobilization against Israel (which would lead to the Six-Day War just a few weeks later) as the first acts of World War III. "It is time," he preached, "to renew our knowledge and faith" in the imminent return of Christ. "It used to be a pious hope; now it comes to the place where we begin to see it as a great reality."[9]

The American catastrophe in Vietnam forced all Americans to question the future of their country. Was the United States truly a chosen nation to lead the world or was it just one corrupt nation-state among many? Evangelicals also had to ask themselves if God wanted the United States to serve as the vehicle for launching a final, last-days revival or if it was already too late? Evangelicals' assessment of the global battle under way between good and evil offered Americans answers that made sense out of their seeming impotence; the faithful provided hope in an era of chaos and despair. The war, which had done so much to divide Americans, provided evangelicals with the opportunity to pledge again their loyalty to their nation and to the United States' mission in the world. Their appeals to God and country continued to resonate with the many Americans disillusioned by the rapid changes of the time.

While Vietnam and the Cold War kept evangelicals alert to events around the globe, both the growing feminist movement and the ongoing battle for civil rights occupied much of their attention at home. Graham wrote *World Aflame* just as the second wave of feminism was gaining traction. His response to changes in American home life revealed the way challenges to traditional gender roles made most white evangelicals uncomfortable. "Our homes," Graham explained, "have suffered. Divorce has grown to epidemic proportions. When the morals of society are upset, the family is the first to suffer. The home is the basic unit of our society, and a nation is only as strong as her homes."[10]

Graham had long feared that women's efforts to move into new spheres had hastened the breakdown of the culture. Too many women, he lamented in the 1950s, "are wearing the trousers in the family" despite the biblical principle "that the husband be the head of the house." Nevertheless, Graham believed that God had still given women important responsibilities to fulfill. "The Bible," he explained, "teaches that the wife is to make the home as happy as possible . . . as near like heaven as possible." In case Graham's biblical exposition went over the heads of those he hoped to reach, he offered women some practical suggestions for serving their husbands. "You can keep the house clean and in order, you can prepare his favorite dishes and have the meals on time. . . . Consider, too, that any slovenliness or carelessness in your dress or personal appearance and cleanliness will naturally lessen the admiration and love your husband has for you." Ruth Bell Graham agreed with her beau. "I just don't approve of the working wife," she told a reporter.[11]

The Grahams' perspective revealed how little traditional views had changed since the 1920s. For most evangelicals, men and women still had absolute roles to fulfill; any violation of those roles sparked turmoil on the domestic front and angered God. The men who crafted postwar evangelicalism believed that while women could contribute to the movement as missionaries and in Christian education, gender roles remained absolute. God had designated men to serve as leaders in both the church and the family. As a result, women's impact on the trajectory of midcentury evangelicalism was usually subtle and indirect. In some cases women created their own gender-segregated institutions and auxiliaries where they could organize as they saw fit and influence the movement without directly challenging male authority. However, a few did confront the patriarchal nature of evangelicalism. Ruth A. Schmidt, a State University of New York professor, took to the pages of *Christianity Today* to lament her "second-class citizenship" in the modern evangelical church. She believed that Christians' views of gender represented their acquiescence to the dominant culture around them rather than what she saw as the liberating message of Jesus.[12]

Although feminism proved to be the greater threat to evangelicals in the long run, during the mid-1960s the civil rights movement provoked more substantial commentary and analysis. In *World Aflame* and throughout his ministry Graham promoted the long-standing evangelical view that only through changing the hearts of individuals would enduring racial justice be achieved. Government policies and legislation could not do it. "There is only one possible solution to the race problem," he insisted, "and that is a vital personal experience with Jesus Christ on the part of both races." No matter how hard civil rights activists worked, Graham did not believe that they could succeed apart from Jesus. "Until we come to recognize Him as the Prince of Peace and receive His love in our hearts," he predicted, "the racial tensions will increase, racial demands will become more militant, and a great deal of blood will be shed." While legislation might help, only those men and women whose lives overflowed with Christ's compassion could ultimately save the world from racism and race war. Moral reform, evangelicals believed, always had to precede political reform.[13]

Articles and editorials appearing in *Christianity Today* illustrated evangelicals' ambivalence toward the ongoing civil rights movement. In an early piece New Testament scholar E. Earle Ellis defended segregation, criticized the Warren Court, and denounced those who linked "forced" integration with the Christian faith. Touting the alleged benefits of segregation, he claimed that it had "the potential to develop into a partnership of mutual respect" that could "never arise from a judicial force bill which is intolerable to one of the groups." Following Ellis's article the editors defined their own position. "Forced integration," they wrote, "is as contrary to Christian principles as is forced segregation. The reliance on pressure rather than on persuasion has resulted in a marked increase of racial tensions in some areas." They did insist, however, that churches should always be open to all people. *Christianity Today*'s chairman of the board Ockenga had a slightly more nuanced position. While he believed that public spaces and public institutions should be integrated, he also maintained that private businesses had the right to decide whom they would serve.[14]

In 1959, *Christianity Today*'s editors laid out the case for what they called an "evangelical moderate" position. In reality, they defended the status quo, which they paired with the hope that racism and segregation would die natural deaths. They grounded their opposition to the civil rights movement in their criticism of the state, which allowed them to claim to support civil rights in principle without supporting the mechanisms that would actually make those rights a reality. "In the churches," the editors wrote, "a tide of anxiety has risen" over integrationists' "veiled approval of Big Government that enlarges Federal controls, promotes the welfare state, and relies more and more on legislated morality." They continued, however, to advocate legislated morality on issues like alcohol consumption, same-sex relationships, and

divorce. The debate over integration, they argued, had to be understood in "a context of debate far broader than the sin of race prejudice;
it becomes a battleground where conflicting social philosophies
maneuver for position." They fretted that behind the civil rights movement lay a "quasi-socialistic political philosophy" bent on undermining "limited government and States' rights." These editors' insistence
that the real "issue at stake" was "Big Government more than the Ex-
iled Negro" provided them with convenient cover for decades of prejudice, segregation, and indifference, as well as justification for continuing inaction.[15]

Other evangelical leaders expressed less veiled criticism of the civil
rights movement. Dan Gilbert identified civil rights activists as the
"rabble rousers" that Daniel had prophesied for the end times. "The
self-proclaimed bleeding hearts of the 'civil rights crusades' obviously
have no real regard for the colored people," he fumed. "Their sole purpose is to keep agitating the civil rights crusades, keep stirring up bitterness and hatred, so that a large bloc of voters can be blindly steered
by prejudice." He stubbornly refused to recognize racial injustice as
both a reality and a challenge to the faith that he claimed. Instead, he
attributed African Americans' quest for rights to the activities of subversive and threatening outside forces.[16]

But prophecy could cut both ways. African-American pentecostal
minister and premillennialist Smallwood Williams blended a lifetime
of racial activism with radical Christianity. He had long supported
activist groups such as the Congress of Racial Equality, and he praised
the work of those presidents, including FDR, Kennedy, and Johnson,
who used the state to promote racial justice. When white evangelicals
lined up against civil rights legislation in the 1960s he preached a sermon on the "signs of the times" and warned his congregation to "look
up . . . for the outlook is dark." He interpreted white resistance to
black calls for justice and equality as examples of last-days religious
apostasy. That white evangelicals could be so myopic, Smallwood believed, could only mean that the devil had captured them.[17]

A young and ambitious preacher from Lynchburg, Virginia, may
have been among those white critics of civil rights that Smallwood had
in mind. Typical of most white southern evangelicals, Jerry Falwell
supported the South's autonomy when it came to issues of race. In 1964

President Johnson asked clergy across the nation to support a new civil rights bill. Falwell, like many other socially conservative ministers, did not give the president his endorsement. "It is a terrible violation of human and private property rights," Falwell claimed. "It should be considered civil wrongs rather than civil rights." On a seemingly routine Sunday morning the following year, Falwell preached what became one of the most famous (or infamous) sermons of his career in response to the march of Martin Luther King, Jr., in Selma, Alabama. Falwell began by reminding the men and women at Thomas Road Baptist Church that their citizenship resided in heaven, not on earth. "Preachers," he declared, "are not called to be politicians but to be soul winners. . . . If as much effort could be put into winning people to Jesus Christ across the land as is being exerted in the present civil rights movement, America would be turned upside down for God."[18]

Little did Falwell know that a handful of white evangelicals were marching with King in Selma. Among them was Bruce Crappuchettes, a Wheaton graduate and Fuller Seminary student, who left Southern California for Alabama in an effort to live the full truth of the gospel he embraced. On his return to Los Angeles, Crappuchettes described on the pages of the Fuller student newspaper his firsthand encounter with the "spiritual depth" of the civil rights movement and praised its leaders' "deep commitment" to God. For this seminarian, marching for social justice and civil rights in Selma represented Jesus's call for his followers to love one another. Frank Gaebelein marched as well. He had gone to Selma to cover the event for *Christianity Today,* but feeling the "righteousness of the march" he ended up evolving from dispassionate journalist into enthusiastic participant.[19]

Although the number of white evangelicals in the civil rights movement was small, their participation illustrated the ways some believers were starting to challenge the preconceptions of their predecessors. Younger evangelicals in particular demonstrated more openness to civil rights than most of their pastors and teachers. The college campus–based parachurch organization InterVarsity Christian Fellowship published a nationally distributed magazine for Christian students that routinely included articles by African-American evangelicals who linked civil rights with the gospel and advocated an end to Christian racism. Meanwhile, northern and western evangelical schools had started to hire people of color for their faculties, some of who helped students see beyond the perspectives of their families. The future held some hope.

Although Graham believed that racial turmoil would ultimately end only at the foot of the Cross, he too had more sympathy for civil rights activists than did his father-in-law or ministers like Falwell. Despite facing substantial opposition from other white Christians, he famously integrated his southern crusades, and he brought African-American ministers onto his staff. For Graham the move was both theologically correct and good politics in the Cold War context. "After traveling all over the world," he wrote, "I am convinced that one of the greatest black eyes to American prestige abroad is our racial problem in this country." He befriended Martin Luther King, Jr., and invited him to give an invocation at his famous 1957 Manhattan crusade. But over time Graham cooled to the movement, concluding that leaders like King had pushed too hard. In 1963, within days of the publication of King's famous "Letter from a Birmingham Jail," Graham told reporters that the Southern Christian Leadership Conference founder should "put the brakes on a little bit." The evangelist did not believe that the increasingly dramatic and confrontational civil disobedience practiced by activists was wise or biblically justifiable. Yet he also did what he believed was right to support the movement. A few months after white supremacists lobbed a bomb into a church in Birmingham, Alabama, killing four young African-American girls, Graham—in the face of death threats to him and to the African-American ministers working with him—held what may have been the largest integrated meeting in Alabama. Thirty-five thousand whites and blacks defied convention and worshipped in a football stadium together on Easter morning, standing shoulder-to-shoulder. At the meeting Graham called for a "spiritual awakening throughout America that would end hate and prejudice."[20]

As King's fraught relationship with Graham revealed, the civil rights leader provided a serious challenge to evangelicals. On the one hand he was a brilliant minister who knew how to harness the power of Jesus's words. His rhetoric and ideas resonated powerfully with evangelical audiences. On the other hand King's theology harked back to the old Social Gospel and aligned much more closely with the Protestant liberalism that the rights leader had encountered as a student at Boston

University than the evangelicalism of his father's Baptist church. As King grew in popularity and influence, evangelicals like Graham recognized the value in aligning with the black leader, at least on the principles of civil rights, even as they disagreed on his confrontational tactics. King had so masterfully linked the African-American crusade for justice with the Christian faith that evangelicals could not ignore him.

While King called on all Christians to live up to the words of Jesus, a handful of African-American evangelicals more directly challenged the hypocrisy of their white brothers and sisters in the faith. In 1959 Detroit youth minister William Pannell condemned white evangelicals' racism and exclusionary practices. "The Negro is scarcely represented within the Bible-buttressed enclosure of the evangelical church," he lamented. Nor were they present at Bible conferences, at Sunday school conventions, or "at national gatherings of evangelicals in plush hotels" (the last line was a swipe at the NAE). Christian college and Bible institute administrators, Pannell continued, forced the few African Americans they enrolled to find housing off campus rather than integrate dorms. The white evangelical press had done no better in building relationships with black Christians. "When the question of race relations arises among evangelicals (and it rarely does)," he wryly observed, "the Negro is absent." Meanwhile, when the white evangelical is confronted with the injustices black Americans experienced, he "has been known to tremble slightly and to mumble nonsense about inter-marriage, a basic fear he never seems able to surmount." "But why," Pannell asked, "is the Negro treated thus?" For the young minister, white evangelicals' racial views exposed the point where their "creed and conduct part company." Should this continue, Pannell concluded, white evangelicals might someday find themselves in an "integrated hell."[21]

As the struggle for civil rights gained steam, many African-American evangelicals linked their faith with the movement rather than the church. Presbyterian minister C. Herbert Oliver claimed that the fight for justice was "built upon Christian foundations" and consistent with "the Declaration of Independence, the Bill of Rights, the Ten Commandments and the Golden Rule." He praised the sit-ins and warned Christians that "the gospel can never be spread, nor can the injustice of man be remedied when we use prayer as an excuse for doing absolutely nothing." He was particularly critical of segregated churches, where he claimed not even Jesus would be welcome. "The hardest task," he wrote, "and most thankless role of the Christian called Negro will be to make God's love known to those who profess most strongly to know it" (i.e. white Christians). He concluded by identifying the rights movement as "God-given" and called it the responsibility of "the Christian called Negro" to demonstrate "forever the glorious truth that in God's sight no flesh shall glory."[22]

Another prominent black evangelist, Tom Skinner, consistently blended rights activism with traditional Christian evangelical theology throughout the 1960s. The *New York Times* compared Skinner, who claimed to have been a member of a notorious street gang prior to his conversion, to Billy Graham. He later served as the chaplain for Washington, D.C.'s professional football franchise. He drew on American history, the Black Power movement, and the vernacular of urban America to critique the racism of white evangelicalism. His confrontational tactics and sermons were a hit with many evangelical students of all races, but they made white church leaders uncomfortable. He was thrown off Christian radio stations in the late 1960s for his criticisms of political and business leaders, while the NAE's Clyde Taylor complained that he was a little "too hepped" on race issues. But he persisted.[23]

Skinner's ideology was best expressed in a sermon he delivered before college students at InterVarsity's 1970 convention at the University of Illinois campus in Urbana. After summarizing the long history of African-American repression in the United States, he turned to the intersection of contemporary religious and political issues. He criticized white evangelicals who claimed that Jesus was the answer to African Americans' problems while never daring to set foot in a black neighborhood. In contrast, he praised the work of black nationalists, whom he called witnesses for God. "It was not the evangelical who came and taught us our worth and dignity as black men," he explained. "It was not the Bible-believing fundamentalist who stood up and told us that black was beautiful. It was not the evangelical who preached to us that we should stand on our two feet and be men, be proud that black was beautiful and that God could work his life out through our redeemed blackness. Rather, it took Malcolm X, Stokely Carmichael, Rap Brown and the Brothers to declare to us our dignity." Then he turned to politics. He interpreted calls for "law and order" as code for maintaining white power and he called police "nothing more than the occupational force present in the black community for the purpose of maintaining the interests of white society." On the bugaboo of intermarriage he quipped, "I do not know where white people get the idea that they are so utterly attractive that black people are just dying to marry them." Moving to what was perhaps the most controversial part of the sermon, Skinner denounced Christian nationalism. "I as a black Christian have to renounce Americanism. I have to renounce any attempt to wed Jesus Christ off to the American system," he preached. "I disassociate myself from any argument that says a vote for America is a vote for God. I disassociate myself from any argument that says God is on our side. I disassociate myself from any argument, which says that God sends troops to Asia, that God is a capitalist, that God is a militarist, that God is the worker behind our system." He ended the sermon declaring, "the liberator has come." It was a testament to Skinner's unique influence that Jesse Jackson, Maya Angelou, Betty Shabazz (Malcolm X's widow), and Louis Farrakhan, along with many prominent evangelicals, attended his funeral.[24]

Like Oliver and Skinner, most black evangelical civil rights activists were disappointed that their white brothers and sisters did not more fully embrace the movement. Andrew Young succinctly clarified the distinction he saw between white and black evangelicalism in the midst of the struggle. "Ours," he wrote, "was an evangelical freedom movement that identified salvation with not just one's personal relationship with God, but a new relationship between people black and white." John Perkins, who returned in 1960 from southern California to the Deep South to build evangelicalism among African Americans, summed up what many felt. "I do not understand," he lamented "why so many evangelicals find a sense of commitment to civil rights and to Jesus Christ an 'either-or' proposition. . . . The evangelical church—whose basic theology is the same as mine—had not gone on to preach the *whole* gospel." He included blacks along with whites in this critique, believing that his fellow African-American evangelicals had not done enough for civil rights.[25]

During the late 1960s and early 1970s, some white evangelicals finally started to see the light. A group of leaders, black and white, male and female, met together at a Chicago YMCA in 1973 to discuss the future of evangelicalism. They believed that the faithful had still not properly defined their relationship to the rest of the world. Out of their discussions came the Chicago Declaration of Evangelical Social Concern and the launch of a new group, Evangelicals for Social Action. The declaration touched on the many social issues of that generation. "We acknowledge that God requires justice," the declaration read, "but we have not proclaimed or demonstrated his justice to an unjust American society." Turning to race, they continued, "we deplore the historic involvement of the church in America with racism and the conspicuous responsibility of the evangelical community for perpetuating the personal attitudes and institutional structures that have divided the body of Christ along color lines. Further, we have failed to condemn the exploitation of racism at home and abroad by our economic system." What they did not affirm was that the state could play an important role in reducing racism—an issue on which they remained divided. White signatories included Frank Gaebelein, Carl Henry, and Henry's son and future Republican congressman Paul Henry. Jim Wallis also signed the declaration; he would soon become the best known leader of the evangelical left. African-American signers included John Perkins and William Pannell. The following year, Pannell became the first African American to join the faculty at Fuller Seminary.[26]

Another signatory was Chicago minister Clarence Hilliard, a preacher-activist who became one of the first black leaders of the NAE. In 1976 he published an article in *Christianity Today* titled "Down with the Honky Christ—Up with the Funky Jesus." He explained that "funky" and "honky" "pinpoint the problem I see in traditional evangelical circles, black or white. We and our leaders have been preaching a honky Christ to a world hungry for the funky Jesus of the Bible. The honky Christ stands with the status quo, the funky Jesus moves apart from the ruling religious system. Jesus stood with and for the poor and oppressed and disinherited. He came for the sick and needy." As evangelicals grew in power and prestige, some within the movement began to see how they had been complicit in maintaining exploitative power hierarchies. While *Christianity Today* did not always welcome the liberation message expressed by black leaders such as Hilliard, that the editors ran this piece shows how far they had come in the twenty years since they founded the magazine.[27]

In addition to raising issues of race and poverty, the Chicago Declaration of Evangelical Social Concern called for a rethinking of the evangelical movement's historic treatment of women. "We acknowledge," the Declaration read, "that we have encouraged men to prideful domination and women to irresponsible passivity. So we call both men and women to mutual submission and active discipleship." Out of Evangelicals for Social Action came the Evangelical Women's Caucus, which challenged the hierarchical views so deeply embedded in evangelicalism. The conference and the declaration, with its attention to issues of race and gender, marked the rise of a progressive wing within evangelicalism. This wing's impact on the evangelical movement as a whole, however, has remained relatively limited. The number of activists working in progressive evangelical organizations has never been large and they have not built the kinds of successful alliances with wealthy benefactors that helped finance the work of their more conservative counterparts. The socially and politically conservative white male leaders who have controlled the major evangelical institutions and media outlets have masterfully quashed most dissent and maintained their position as the representatives of evangelicalism writ large.[28]

Graham's *World Aflame* reflected and anticipated the substantial changes under way that came to define the 1960s. The ongoing Cold War, the assassination of a president and then a civil rights icon, the quagmire in Vietnam, student rebellions, the sexual revolution, and the free speech, Black Power, and feminist movements, all shaped a world that to many Americans truly looked out of control. As they struggled to understand the turmoil of the era, evangelicalism offered them hope in this world and especially in the next. The ongoing cultural revolution could only mean that the last days had begun and that paradise was just around the corner.

As the 1960s came to an end, the world still seemed aflame. American youth living on the margins of the evangelical movement experienced a premillennial-infused Jesus explosion. Tens of thousands of young people disillusioned with sex and drugs turned to the "first hippie" to find meaning in their lives. They blended the counterculture's criticism of mainstream American society with a call for a return to a radical, New Testament–type Christianity. Disgusted by the consumerism at the heart of American life and the complacency of their nation's churches, they built alternative communities. They had long hair and unkempt beards, wore beads and bell-bottoms, wandered cities and beaches barefoot or in sandals, and talked about being stoned on Jesus. Dubbed "Jesus people," they rejected the trappings and demands of the modern world and looked forward to a post-Armageddon Christian utopia.

Believing that the rise of the Jesus people jibed with last-days prophecy, Graham tackled the movement in 1971 with *The Jesus Generation*. He peppered his new book with hip language, groovy advice, and references to Jack Kerouac, Bob Dylan, the Beatles, Erich Fromm, and Paul Ehrlich. He confided to readers that he had attended youth festivals, concerts, and even love-ins incognito to study the problems of America's young people. What he saw among the Jesus people impressed him. He praised their "reemphasis on the Second Coming of Jesus Christ" as a sign of their authenticity. He also applauded their antistatist political sensitivities. "These young people," he wrote, "don't put much stock in the old slogans of the New Deal, the Fair Deal, the New Frontier, and the Great Society. They believe that utopia will arrive only when Jesus returns. Thus these young people are on sound Biblical ground." The Jesus people were making inroads into the broader youth culture at the time and Graham hoped to do the same. He used the book to try to reach those youth who had not yet embraced Jesus—those experiencing "bad vibes"—through chapters entitled "generation gap," "hang-ups," "copping out," "turning on," "getting high," "we wanna revolution," and "Jesus Christ Superstar." "Jesus Christ," he assured readers, "was the greatest revolutionary" of all times in the truest sense.[29]

Graham ended the book with a recap of premillennial theology and an overview of the many signs that confirmed that the last days were upon them. They included the usual suspects—false messiahs, wars and rumors of war, famines, overpopulation, earthquakes, lawlessness, and sexual immorality. Then he turned to geopolitical events, resurrecting the classic fundamentalist tropes. The creation of Israel was "the most certain sign of all," the rise of Russia fulfilled Ezekiel's prophecy, and Revelation's reference to "the kings of the East" foreshadowed the growing clout of Japan and China. "All of the above signs," he concluded, "seem to be converging for the first time in history. . . . This is *good* news!" Offering readers the choice of reward or punishment, he

Fundamentalists and evangelicals always made full use of various forms of mass media. Here Billy Graham takes to the television to warn the nation of the coming apocalypse.

 Courtesy of the Billy Graham Evangelistic Association.

Are the last days almost here?

Tune in for Billy Graham's vital message — "When Will the Last Days Come?"

BILLY GRAHAM TV SPECIAL

TONIGHT 7:00   CH 15

promised, "Christ will take all of us who have put our trust in Him to heaven before the earth suffers the apocalyptic woes that are described in detail in the Book of Revelation." This was a message that resonated powerfully among the Jesus people.[30]

The rise of the Jesus people represented a substantial shift in American culture. In the 1960s many Americans questioned pervading assumptions about mainstream cultural norms, sources of traditional authority, and religion. At precisely the same moment that evangelical leaders were trying to consolidate their authority, a new generation of believers rejected institutional faiths of all kinds. The well-orchestrated efforts of Graham, Ockenga, Fuller, and Henry to expand the power and prestige of evangelicalism did not mean that they could control the direction the movement would take. Nowhere was this clearer than in a new surge of interest in the apocalypse.

Despite evangelical leaders' careful efforts to make their faith more reasonable and respectable, laypeople for over one hundred years flocked to doomsday radicals. Those preachers, writers, and evangelists bold enough to name names, offer dates, and make specific predictions about the end of the world earned their attention and their dollars. Hundreds of evangelicals fueled apocalypticism through books, tracts, and sermons. Many also continued to advocate premillennialism on the pages of the old fundamentalist magazines like *King's Business* (until it ceased publication in 1970) and *Moody Monthly* (which continued publishing until 2003). The certainty and authority conveyed by an apocalyptic faith in an imminent Armageddon drew substantial numbers of followers.

In the 1970s no one tapped into evangelicals' fascination with Armageddon better than the heavily mustachioed Hal Lindsey. Lindsey had worked as a Mississippi River tugboat captain before attending Dallas Theological Seminary. After graduating he moved to California, where he joined the popular college organization Campus Crusade for Christ and began ministering to students at the University of California, Los Angeles. In 1970 he published *The Late Great Planet Earth,* which represented in part a rehashing of the many prophecies that had long mesmerized other premillennialists. The global influence of the USSR and China served as important markers of the times, as did the increasing power of Arab nations and the creation of the European Common Market. More than anything else, however, Israel occupied the center of Lindsey's analysis. He believed that as the world moved toward the battle of Armageddon, three events would occur. "First," he wrote, "the Jewish nation would be reborn in the land of Palestine. Secondly, the Jews would repossess old Jerusalem and the sacred sites. Thirdly, they would rebuild their ancient temple of worship upon its historical site." The first of these steps had been accomplished in 1948 with the creation of the state of Israel. The second had occurred in 1967 when Israel had captured Jerusalem during the Six-Day War. The final event Lindsey predicted was the reconstruction of the Jewish temple. Many premillennialists believed (and still believe) that the Jewish temple would rise again on the land currently occupied by the Dome of the Rock, a major Muslim holy site. The most radical among them gleefully anticipate the day when this Muslim sacred space is destroyed and even trade stories about secret farms where ranchers are trying to raise pure red heifers in preparation for future temple sacrifices. Modern-day guards assigned to protect the Dome of the Rock are well aware of premillennialists' apocalyptic beliefs. They remain on the lookout for overeager Christians who hope to speed up the destruction of the dome through their own actions.[31]

In *The Late Great Planet Earth* Lindsey offered a rough date for the rapture based on Jesus's promise that when certain signs appeared the "generation" that witnessed them would not "pass till all these things be fulfilled" (Matthew 24:33–34). The "rebirth of Israel," the evangelist informed readers, marked the fulfillment of this prophecy. "A generation in the Bible," Lindsey continued, "is something like forty years. If this is a correct deduction, then within forty years or so of 1948, all these things could take place." The church was now on the clock. Lindsey expected the rapture to happen by 1988 (*Late Great* is still in print and has not been updated or revised).[32]

The book, filled with silly puns for chapter titles and subtitles including "Russia is A Gog," "Scarlet O'Harlot," and "Sheik to Sheik," became the best-selling nonfiction book of the 1970s, with seven and a half million copies sold in its first decade and nearly twenty million copies in print today. In 1979, Orson Welles narrated a popular film version of *The Late Great Planet Earth*. The broad reception of Lindsey's work reveals how premillennialism's influence continued to grow in the second half of the twentieth century, as well as the ways the many crises of the era, ranging from environmental fears, overpopulation, and Vietnam to nuclear annihilation, all made apocalyptic evangelicalism palatable to the broader American public. The success of the book opened many doors for Lindsey, who did consulting work on global politics for both the Pentagon and the Israeli government, giving him establishment cachet. It also gave him a platform for expressing his political views. Like so many other premillennialists, Lindsey was (and is) a staunch conservative. He has since written many more books on the coming apocalypse and claims to have more than forty million copies in print.[33]

Over the next few years, eager premillennialists followed Lindsey's lead. They kept readers up-to-date with analyses of the unremitting global turmoil and chaos that defined the 1970s. In 1972 San Diego minister Tim LaHaye laid out an argument for an imminent second coming. "I believe the Bible teaches that we are already living in the beginning of the end," he wrote in his aptly titled book *The Beginning*

Americans purchased more copies of Hal Lindsey's *Late Great Planet Earth* in the 1970s than any other nonfiction book, illustrating their ever-growing interest in evangelical apocalypticism. The success of the book inspired a popular 1979 documentary narrated by Orson Welles.

Courtesy of the Everett Collection.

of the End. "See if you agree." The minister cited wars, rumors of wars, global travel, increased knowledge, growing labor-capital conflicts, homosexuality, Israel's statehood, and the creation of the UN to support his thesis. But he also included some more original signs that reflected the concerns of the era, such as the relatively new phenomenon of Satanism and the rise of "scoffers" who denied young-earth creationism. LaHaye agreed with Lindsey that the generation who would experience the rapture was already on earth, but his calculations differed. The gaunt minister argued that Jesus had identified World War I, not the creation of Israel, as the start of the last days. "The Austrian declaration of war," LaHaye wrote, "began to fulfill *the sign* of the end of the age as given by our Lord." The rapture, he concluded, would have to occur before those men and women alive when the war began had all died. "If you think the above teachings indicate that time is short," he concluded, "you are right."[34]

Two years later John F. Walvoord published *Armageddon, Oil and the Middle East Crisis,* which marked a new phase in end-times prognostication. The Dallas Theological Seminary president, who had long blended analysis of biblical predictions with world events, tackled the swiftly evolving geopolitics of the era. He allocated far more attention to the place of Arab and Persian nations in prophecy than any of his predecessors, demonstrating how the Middle East was rapidly moving to the center of evangelicals' attention. His work illustrated how dramatically evangelicals' expectations were evolving in conjunction with the times. Living amid the rise of the Organization of the Petroleum Exporting Countries, a severe energy crisis, and long gas station lines, Walvoord thought he knew where global events were headed. He predicted that Arab and European nations would soon establish an Antichrist-led cartel that would regulate the rise and fall of national currencies, control world trade, manage the world's energy reserves, and "eclipse the power of both Russia and the United States."[35]

In making this argument, Walvoord answered a question that had long troubled premillennialists. The faithful knew that in the last days four great confederacies would descend on the Middle East to wage the battle of Armageddon, but they had never understood how or why this would happen. The growing significance of and conflict over Middle Eastern oil finally helped them see how the final conflict could unfold.

"The prophetic significance of this rise in power in the Middle East is tremendous," Walvood concluded, "and from a biblical standpoint it is the most dramatic evidence that the world scene is shaping up for Armageddon."[36]

The apocalyptic messages conveyed by evangelical writers and preachers found another innovative expression through a new medium. In 1972 the Armageddon-themed film *A Thief in the Night* opened to audiences around the nation. By that time evangelicals had made their peace with the medium of film, following the lead of pioneers like Billy Graham who had developed his own successful production company. *Thief* scared a generation of teenagers into preparing for the rapture. The film focuses on a young woman who despite her nominal Christianity discovers that the rapture has occurred and that she has been left behind. She remembers enough of her Sunday school lessons, however, to be suspicious of the new global leader and his UN-based organization, UNITE (United Nations Imperium of Total Emergency). When he requires everyone to take a mark of three rows of "0110" (the binary code for 6, which produces a not-so-subtle 666) to demonstrate their loyalty to the new one-world government, she refuses. The rest of the film follows her efforts to survive as UNITE agents track and chase her in windowless 1970s vans.

The low-budget film has become a cult classic, reportedly seen by over three hundred million people. But the producers of *Thief* and its three sequels wanted to do more than simply entertain audiences. They claimed that the films sparked thousands of conversions. They also published *Finding God in the Final Days,* a study guide that offered proof texts to support the major plot points of the film. The book warned readers that the rise of the real-life Antichrist was looming.[37]

A Thief in the Night not only marked a significant achievement in evangelical film production, it also introduced new audiences to the emerging genre of Christian rock music. Larry Norman's track "I Wish We'd All Been Ready" haunts the film. Swelling violins add a sense of impending doom, as does the melancholy sound of the vocals. The lyrics read:

Life was filled with guns and war,
And everyone got trampled on the floor,
I wish we'd all been ready

Children died, the days grew cold,
A piece of bread could buy a bag of gold,
I wish we'd all been ready,
There's no time to change your mind,
The Son has come and you've been left behind.
A man and wife asleep in bed,
She hears a noise and turns her head, he's gone,
I wish we'd all been ready,
Two men walking up a hill,
One disappears and one's left standing still,
I wish we'd all been ready,
There's no time to change your mind,
The Son has come and you've been left behind.
Life was filled with guns and war,
And everyone got trampled on the floor,
I wish we'd all been ready,
Children died, the days grew cold,
A piece of bread could buy a bag of gold,
I wish we'd all been ready,
There's no time to change your mind,
How could you have been so blind,
The Father spoke, the demons dined,
The Son has come and you've been left behind.
You've been left behind
You've been left behind
You've been left behind
You've been left behind[38]

The success of books by Graham, Lindsey, LaHaye, and Walvoord, and hundreds of other similar works, films like *A Thief in the Night,* its sequels and imitators, and the music of artists like Larry Norman, demonstrated how in the 1970s innovative evangelicals spread the classic apocalyptic message through multiple platforms. Their work resonated with a new generation of young Christians who straddled the divide between the increasingly mainstream and button-downed evangelicalism of their parents and the youth revolution under way at the time. For these baby boomers, faith in the imminent return of Christ inspired hope in a world that seemed more than ever to be careening toward Armageddon. It also provided adherents with secret knowledge and insight into the past, the present, and the time to come. Despite the chaos surrounding them, their faith guaranteed them a secure and glorious future. Their faith also moved them to action. After all, Jesus would soon come back in judgment.

The revival of apocalypticism revealed fissures within evangelicalism. At precisely the same time that elite, highly credentialed leaders like Henry and Ockenga were downplaying radical apocalypticism in order to create a respectable movement that could exercise serious influence in national and global politics, populist ministers like Lindsey and LaHaye, as well as more respectable theologians like Walvoord, reconnected evangelicalism with the kinds of strident apocalypticism that hark back to the 1930s. Graham meanwhile masterfully straddled both worlds. From the 1970s on, evangelicalism evolved along multiple, sometimes overlapping tracks. Powerful, articulate, reputable white men who worked to give evangelicalism mainstream credibility through institutions like Fuller Seminary and publications like *Christianity Today* ran on one; uninhibited, hard-core, premillennial populists, whose work demonstrated that evangelicals could never truly separate from the apocalyptic theology that had birthed their movement, ran on another; and progressive-minded evangelicals like those who had organized Evangelicals for Social Action ran on a third. Although white evangelicals on all three tracks were starting to work with some African Americans, for the most part black evangelicals continued to labor through their own ministries and institutions on yet another track. They had little incentive for partnering with the white evangelicals who had for so long privileged race over theology.

Unlike race, however, social class and region of birth continued to have little influence on who would and would not embrace the radical apocalypticism of modern evangelicalism. Millions of men and women, from the depressed factories of the urban rust belt to the rural oil fields of west Texas to the upper-middle-class tech-boom suburbs of southern California longed for the second coming. There were (and are) no easy ways to predict along class or regional lines who would and would not embrace a theology of doom. Apocalypticism has provided millions of Americans with a powerful lens through which to make sense of difficult and challenging eras.

Although Billy Graham, representatives from *Christianity Today* and Fuller Seminary, and a host of other leaders and institutions claimed that the evangelicalism of the Cold War was substantially different from the fundamentalism of the 1930s, evangelicals' political ideals remained consistent with past generations. Their obsession with Armageddon continued to foster an attractive, determined, strident, uncompromising politics, a politics that became clearer than ever in the late 1970s.

The faithful had long championed conservative causes and had most often voted Republican. They criticized Roosevelt and Truman, feared Kennedy in 1960, cheered Goldwater in 1964, and many supported Nixon in 1968 and 1972. In 1976 they split their votes between born-again Democrat Jimmy Carter and born-again Republican Gerald Ford. Yet throughout these years they had little influence within either political party. They cast their votes on the basis of the choices that political parties offered them; they had no say in what candidates those parties nominated or in what issues the parties prioritized. This began to change as evangelicals plunged lock, stock, and barrel into the tumultuous world of partisan politics in the late 1970s.

Hal Lindsey, emboldened by the success of *The Late Great Planet Earth,* was pining for action. With the nation mired in economic stagflation and gearing up for a major presidential election, he aspired to recapture the magic of his first book with a new one, *The 1980's: Countdown to Armageddon.* "We are moving," he wrote, "at an ever-accelerating rate of speed into a prophetic countdown. . . . The decade of the 1980's could very well be the last decade of history as we know it." In declaring that the end was imminent, he boldly proclaimed, "WE ARE THE GENERATION" that will witness the end of the age.[39]

The prognosticator's confidence was buoyed by new, last-days evidence. He claimed that the Antichrist was probably already at work somewhere within the parliament of the newly formed European Economic Community (or Common Market) and predicted that credit cards would enable the coming world tyrant to control the world's currency through a "main computer." Following Walvoord's lead, he placed substantial emphasis on Arab and Persian nations as well as on what he called the "Islam revival." Finally, Lindsey interpreted the growing number of alleged UFO sightings and alien abductions as important signs. "It's my opinion that UFOs are real," he acknowledged, "and that there will be a proven 'close encounter of the third kind' soon. And I believe that the source of this phenomenon is some type of alien being of great intelligence and power. . . . Demons will stage a spacecraft landing on earth." In talking about diabolical supercomputers and alien-demons flying UFOs to earth, Lindsey risked undermining the credibility other evangelicals had been working hard to build. But he didn't care. For Lindsey the rapture if not the arrival of little green men was imminent.[40]

The 1980's: Countdown to Armageddon did more than simply mark the imaginative state of popular evangelical apocalypticism at the time. It illustrated in new ways how premillennialism continued to shape evangelical politics. Lindsey believed that American leaders had made one poor decision after another in foreign policy, from handcuffing General Douglas MacArthur in Korea to signing the Strategic Arms Limitations Treaty. The domestic situation was even worse. He despised the "welfare state" and the "socialist" philosophy undergirding it. He insisted that "men and women who don't really believe in capitalism" had long dominated Congress and he relentlessly criticized the national debt. Defense spending, however, was apparently biblical. The Bible "supports building a powerful military force," he insisted, and it "is telling the U.S. to become strong again . . . to use our vast and superior technology to create the world's strongest military power." His sentiments echoed political conservatives' uncompromising faith in America's mission to save the world for God and for capitalism. "If you are a Christian reading this book," Lindsey concluded, "then it is up to you to get involved in preserving this country. True, the Lord could come at any moment, but . . . we should plan our lives as though we will live them out fully." Like so many of his predecessors, Lindsey seamlessly blended apocalypticism with potent conservative activism.[41]

Lindsey's book served as the perfect primer for the 1980 presidential campaign. Since the 1920s, fundamentalists and then evangelicals had made their conservative, antistatist, free market political sympathies clear. However, they had been cautious about affiliating with either political party but rather championed particular policies and particular candidates. As long as the postwar Republican Party shared FDR's multilateral internationalism and supported a moderate, watered-down version of the New Deal state, evangelicals had felt little motivation to organize along purely and explicitly partisan lines. Meanwhile, despite fundamentalists' long-term efforts to decouple the South from the party of Andrew Jackson, many white southerners had remained leery of the GOP well into the 1950s. But as the Democratic Party embraced the civil rights movement, white southerners, regardless of religious affiliation, grew more willing to vote Republican.

By the late 1970s, conservative Republican operatives sensed that if they could organize evangelicals, they could transform American politics. They recognized that the faithful had been disappointed again and again by Democrat Jimmy Carter. Despite the president's own deep evangelical convictions, he had not made evangelicals' social or economic priorities his own. As a committed Baptist who revered the separation of church and state, he did not believe that faith should influence policy. Meanwhile, the controversial social issues of the era, such as feminism, abortion, sex education, gay rights, and the ongoing civil rights movement, pushed many white Christians further to the right. In 1979 a small group of conservative political activists, including Howard Phillips, Paul Weyrich, and Richard Viguerie, began seeking ministers who might help them lure the evangelical masses into the GOP's nets. Jerry Falwell was intrigued. During a meeting Weyrich and Falwell discussed their mutual concerns. "Jerry," Weyrich said, "there is in America a moral majority that agrees about the basic issues. But they aren't organized. They don't have a platform. The media ignore them. Somebody's got to get that moral majority together."[42]

In June 1979 Falwell, Weyrick, and Viguerie incorporated the Moral Majority. The initial board of directors boasted numerous prominent ministers, including Tim LaHaye. Falwell instructed Christians around the nation that they had a threefold mission: to get people saved, to get them baptized, and to get them registered to vote. He believed that if he could push conservative Christians to vote, they would turn back the liberal tide and make themselves heard in the nation. Within a couple of years the Moral Majority claimed to represent nearly seven million people who dedicated themselves to what they identified as prolife, profamily, promoral, pro-Israel, and pro–strong national defense causes. While the organization certainly did not represent all white evangelical Christians, it attracted a substantial number who wanted to make their political voices heard. Through church-based voter registration drives, it succeeded in motivating hundreds of thousands of previously apolitical believers to get to the polls, most often on behalf of the GOP.

Fuller, Ockenga, Henry, and other evangelical leaders, despite their obvious Republican leanings, had been cautious about explicitly hitching their movement to a particular party. Billy Graham was also hesitant, especially after learning in the wake of Watergate, to his deep embarrassment, that the potty-mouthed Richard Nixon had used him for political purposes. Falwell, in contrast, had no such reservations. His actions illustrated how tight the relationship between evangelicalism and conservative politics had become. Although the southern preacher came out of the militant separatist wing of conservative Protestantism that still identified as "fundamentalist," by publically engaging in coalition-based politics, he mostly obliterated the divide between separatist old-guard fundamentalism and the new evangelicalism. Nevertheless, a small number of self-identified fundamentalists criticized Falwell for his move into the public sphere and they tried to maintain their separation from mainstream culture and politics.

In 1980 the memberships of the Moral Majority and the NAE and hundreds of thousands of other white evangelicals discovered in Republican presidential nominee Ronald Reagan a dream candidate who blended apocalyptic rhetoric with criticism of the New Deal state. In fact, Reagan's apocalypticism illustrated how perfectly radical evangelical ideas and rhetoric fit the Cold War context. Evangelicals gave political leaders, policy-makers, and journalists a language for framing the nature of the American mission to the world. The United States seemed to be God's special nation, chosen by him to wage war against the forces of the atheistic, communist legions of the Antichrist.

Reagan never hid how interested he was in evangelical apocalypticism. While premillennialism had little (if any) direct influence on his actual foreign policy, it provided him with the rhetorical tools for mobilizing the American people to wage the Cold War. During the 1970s the California governor discussed *The Late Great Planet Earth* with friends and acquaintances. "For the first time ever," he confided to a state senator, "everything is in place for the battle of Armageddon and the second coming of Christ." Nor did Reagan back down from his apocalyptic views during the 1980 campaign. "We may be the generation," he told televangelist Jim Bakker, "that sees Armageddon." After winning the White House, Reagan made repeated references to the end of days in his diary. "Sometimes I wonder if we are destined to witness

Armageddon," he confided on one page; on another he wrote, "I swear I believe Armageddon is near." He responded to a National Security Council briefing on deteriorating conditions in the Middle East by noting, "Armageddon in the prophecies begins with the gates of Damascus being assailed." Wolf Blitzer, at the time a journalist for the *Jerusalem Post,* best captured Reagan's beliefs. "You know," the president apparently told an Israeli lobbyist, "I turn back to your ancient prophets in the Old Testament and the signs foretelling Armageddon, and I find myself wondering if—if we're the generation that's going to see that come about. I don't know if you've noted any of those prophecies lately, but believe me, they certainly describe the times we're going through."[43]

Reagan's interest in evangelical apocalypticism, combined with the growing influence of the so-called religious right and the publication of yet another Graham premillennial screed entitled *Approaching Hoofbeats: The Four Horsemen of the Apocalypse,* drew the attention of the press. In late 1983 *People* asked the president about his views on Armageddon. This was a story the media could not get enough of. Journalists understood the widespread appeal of apocalyptic ideas to the American public in the midst of escalating Cold War tensions. Reagan noted that he had never discussed the end of the world "publicly." However, he continued, theologians who studied the ancient prophecies in search of signs of Armageddon "have said that never, in the time between the prophecies up until now has there ever been a time in which so many of the prophecies are coming together." While Reagan knew that other generations had incorrectly predicted the second coming, this was different. "There have been times in the past when people thought the end of the world was coming, and so forth," he acknowledged, "but never anything like this." Hoping to get more out of him, the journalists kept prying. "You've mused on it. You've considered it." "Not to the extent of throwing up my hands and saying, 'Well, it's all over,'" he retorted. The generation that witnesses Armageddon "will have to go on doing what they believe is right." While the president was less articulate on theological matters than Billy Graham or Harold Ockenga, he nevertheless perfectly summed up the premillennial paradox and embodied the way many Americans encountered and put to use their apocalyptic faith. Live as though Christ was coming back today; act as if the rapture was a millennium away.[44]

Reagan's apocalypticism troubled a lot of Americans who suspected that his theological convictions were influencing his administration. The president stoked their fears in a 1983 speech before the NAE that seamlessly integrated religion, domestic issues, and foreign policy. In this historic speech, radical evangelicalism and American foreign policy converged. "Freedom," the president began, "prospers when religion is vibrant and the rule of law under God is acknowledged." He insisted that the "Founding Fathers" had passed the First Amendment "to protect churches from government interference. They never intended to construct a wall of hostility between government and the concept of religious belief itself." He denounced secularism and abortion and called for Congress to pass a prayer-in-schools amendment. Then, turning to foreign policy, he directly linked his opposition to a nuclear freeze with his faith in God. The Soviets "must be made to understand we will never compromise our principles and standards. We will never give away our freedom. We will never abandon our belief in God." As he reached the climax of his speech, he famously identified the USSR as the "evil empire." Reagan knew that when it came to aggressively and unapologetically fighting communism, he had no more loyal allies than the evangelical audience hosting him that day. But he also knew that as sure as he was that Armageddon was near, he would do what he could to avoid—not hasten—nuclear annihilation.[45]

During the 1984 campaign, critics worried that the incumbent's apocalyptic views were shaping his Cold War strategies. During a campaign debate with Democratic nominee Walter Mondale, journalists forced Reagan to address again their concerns. "You've been quoted as saying that you do believe, deep down, that we are heading for some kind of biblical Armageddon," NBC News's Marvin Kalb asked. "Your Pentagon and your Secretary of Defense have plans for the United States to fight and prevail in a nuclear war. Do you feel that we are now heading, perhaps, for some kind of nuclear Armageddon? And do you feel that this country and the world could survive that kind of calamity?" Nancy Reagan apparently gasped "Oh, no!" while the president responded, "I think what has been hailed as something I'm supposedly, as President, discussing as principle is the result of just some philosophical discussions with people who are interested in the same things. And that is the prophecies down through the years, the biblical prophecies

Despite President Ronald Reagan's merely nominal religiosity, he had an enduring fascination with evangelical apocalypticism that influenced the ways he described and characterized the Cold War. Here he talks God and politics with Reverend Jerry Falwell in the Oval Office.
Courtesy of the Ronald Reagan Presidential Library, C13442-5A, 3/15/83.

of what would portend the coming of Armageddon and so forth. And the fact that a number of theologians for the last decade or more have believed that this was true, that the prophecies are coming together that portend that." But then he backed down, invoking the traditional evangelical line. "But no one knows whether Armageddon—those prophecies—mean that Armageddon is a thousand years away or day after tomorrow. So I have never seriously warned and said we must plan according to Armageddon."[46]

While Reagan blamed Walter Mondale's presidential campaign aides for raising the issue and confided in his diary that in so doing Mondale revealed that he was "desperate," the *New York Times* had a different take. "It is hard to believe that the President actually allows Armageddon ideology to shape his policies toward the Soviet Union," the editors groused. But they nevertheless remained suspicious. "Yet it was he who first portrayed the Russians as satanic and who keeps on talking about the final battle." Reagan's critics had a hard time understanding that the president's willingness to engage with the Soviets and eventually to negotiate the Intermediate-Range Nuclear Forces Treaty in 1987 was just as much a reflection of his faith in the book of Revelation as his conviction that the end was nigh. Reagan believed in the coming apocalypse; he just did not want to be the president responsible for initiating it. God had called believers to fight the forces of the Antichrist, not to incinerate the world.[47]

Scholars and journalists have debated how seriously Reagan took all aspects of his faith—and he likely did not take faith seriously at all—but there is no doubt that during the 1980s premillennialism became a regular topic of conversation in and around the White House. A century in the making, American evangelical apocalypticism had penetrated the highest echelons of power and provided a discourse through which many Americans understood the global transformations under way at the time.

While Reagan tried to justify the seeming paradox of believing in an imminent apocalypse while working against it, critics routinely pressed evangelicals to do the same thing. In the early 1980s Falwell repeatedly preached on and wrote about an imminent Armageddon while simultaneously overseeing the growth of a powerful political advocacy group. Moral Majority leaders and Falwell aides Ed Dobson and Ed Hindson explained how Falwell and ministers like him balanced premillennialism with activism. "Evangelical Christians," they explained, "believe that we are living in the 'end times' when the world will enter into a series of cataclysmic wars." This did not, however, quench their enthusiasm for political engagement. "The evangelical preachers are in the arena of politics to improve secular society. We are working hard to bring back school prayer, to stop abortion, to improve the schools, to eliminate pornography. . . . The reason we are in politics is that we believe that God created us in order to live fully, to make the world as good a place as we can, to use Christianity as a force for positive change. . . . Our enthusiastic political involvement is proof that we are not among those evangelicals whose apocalyptic views are a pretext for this-worldly despair." Like their predecessors, evangelicals in the 1980s blended doomsday preaching with conservative activism. The success in mobilizing voters behind Reagan while they anticipated the rapture made them one of the most, if not the most, powerful of the multi-issue interest groups in the Republican Party.[48]

As evangelical apocalypticism penetrated the White House, it also became ubiquitous in American culture. Films like *The Omen, Rosemary's Baby,* and hundreds more depicted a cataclysmic end to the world, while the music of popular groups like Megadeath, Iron Maiden, KISS, and many others used evangelical motifs to entertain millions of Americans. Marilyn Manson demonstrated how apocalypticism had influenced his generation through albums like *Antichrist Superstar.* As a teenager, Manson had believed that the Antichrist was already on earth, planning his ascent. "I was thoroughly terrified by the idea of the end of the world and the Antichrist," he recalled, "so I became obsessed with it, watching movies like *The Exorcist* and *The Omen . . .* and the novelized version of the film *A Thief in the Night,* which described very graphically people getting their heads cut off because they hadn't received 666 tattoos on their forehead. . . . It all made the apocalypse seem so real, so tangible, so close." Eventually, like many other musicians and filmmakers, he found a way to transform evangelical fears into pop culture riches. In so doing, Manson demonstrated that no part of American life was immune to Christian apocalypticism. But as rapture talk spread throughout American life the theology that inspired it faced the danger of being trivialized.[49]

Although the Reagan administration did not totally live up to the hopes of evangelicals, in the early 1990s the faithful once again found plenty of new material to analyze in changing global events. Saddam Hussein's invasion of Kuwait and the American response marked a significant turning point in their prophecy analysis. President George H. W. Bush claimed that as he was contemplating his response to Iraqi aggression, Billy Graham told him that Saddam was the "anti-Christ." Although Graham probably did not make such a claim, since Saddam was not the right fit for the evangelist's premillennial theology, Bush found it useful to invoke Graham's well-known apocalypticism to justify his own decisions. Then, as the United States began to pummel Iraq with Scud missiles, reporters again turned to evangelical prophecy experts for their take on the turmoil in the Middle East. Walvoord answered a phone call from one who asked if the world was headed for Armageddon. "Fifty years ago," the Dallas theologian recalled, "skeptics laughed" when he would talk about the coming importance of the Middle East because the region "was insignificant and could never be the center of action." How things had changed. "Now, for the first time, people believe the power that is in the Middle East. They're not laughing today." Indeed, no one was laughing. Evangelical apocalypticism was helping countless Americans make sense of global chaos.[50]

In late 1990 Walvoord quickly rushed out a revised and updated edition of *Armageddon, Oil and the Middle East Crisis*. He eventually sold over two million copies of the book. Seemingly vindicated by the outbreak of war, Walvoord reiterated most of the same arguments he had made in 1974, but he also brought Saddam into the story. "The fact that Babylon, the capital of the ancient Babylonian Empire, was in Iraq," he observed, "gave Hussein the ambition of establishing a new Babylonian Empire with himself in the role of Nebuchadnezzar." With little of interest happening in Rome, evangelicals began looking to the site of ancient Babylon for signs that the Antichrist's kingdom was on the ascent. "The players," Walvoord concluded, "in this new and dangerous game are almost ready. And the game is defined just as the Bible predicted."[51]

The stunning fall of the Soviet Union in 1989 had sparked another round of prophecy analysis. LaHaye counter-intuitively cited its collapse as further evidence that Armageddon had to be imminent. "Ezekiel," he told fellow believers, "prophesied that Russia would lead the Arab world against Israel in the last days. . . . If she is going to fulfill that prophecy, then she will have to go down against Israel very soon or it will be too late." Like the 1940s-era fundamentalists who refused to believe that their expectations about a revived Roman Empire had been so wrong, evangelicals watching the disintegration of the Soviet Union in the early 1990s chose denial rather than acknowledge the way contemporary geopolitical events undermined their long-held expectations. More recently, however, the rise of Vladimir Putin reaffirmed their fears that Russia could again be a nefarious and powerful force in world politics. The idea of the evil empire—of Magog—was never forsaken.[52]

Graham offered Americans watching the collapse of the Soviet Union, the war in the Persian Gulf, and the growing economic recession a new guide for understanding the times. In 1992 he published *Storm Warning,* an updated version of his 1983 *Approaching Hoofbeats: The Four Horsemen of the Apocalypse.* Making sense of what President George H. W. Bush called the "new world order" drove Graham's analysis of geopolitics. "From many points of view," he wrote, "the world seems to be entering a time of peace and calm. But no one should run up the all-clear flags just yet. There is still cause for alarm; there are storms on the horizon." He listed the proliferation of nuclear weapons, the population explosion, famine, civil war, turmoil in the Middle East, and atrocities in Bosnia as signs that despite the end of the Cold War the world was still rapidly descending. The evangelist also fretted about changes at home. The economic recession, the Rodney King riots in Los Angeles, the "plague" of homelessness, the "abortion holocaust," and the "AIDS epidemic" marked the fulfillment of Jesus's end-times prophecies. Graham took on the environmental crisis as well. "The possible death of our planet by some type of ecological suicide is not God's will," he insisted. "We must be responsible stewards." Echoing his approach thirty years earlier to racial segregation, he argued that the solution to environmental problems was primarily in individual choice rather than government action. "The earth will not be saved," he wrote, "by legislation or by compulsion alone but by the responsible concern of men, women, and children who care for God's creation."[53]

The evangelist's position on environmental questions was even more clearly illustrated by a subtle but significant change that appeared in a revised 2010 edition of *Storm Warning.* In 1992 Graham had suggested that if humankind was going to survive, nations needed to stop "manufacturing industries from releasing hazardous chlorofluorocarbons which damage the ozone layer and increase global warming." In the recent version, the phrase "increase global warming" was eliminated from the sentence. Apparently Graham no longer believed that global warming is good science.[54]

Like other evangelicals, Graham in the 1990s blamed many of the problems of the United States on the legacy of the 1960s. "At the bitter end of an era of liberation—women's lib, kids' lib, animal lib, and everything-but-ethics lib—America has apparently been liberated from its moral foundations." But never one to end on a note of despair, Graham counseled his readers against inaction. "We must not feel that we are to sit back and do nothing to fight evil just because some day the four horsemen will come with full and final force upon the earth. Yes, God's final judgment is inevitable, but He alone knows when it is, and until that time we are to learn the lessons of the horseman and act in such a way that God may be pleased to delay His judgment and allow our world the time to hear His Word and turn to Him." Graham continually called unbelievers to faith while he reminded the faithful that they had an obligation to do all that they could before time ran out.[55]

The white male leaders who tried to remake evangelicalism in the postwar period had hoped to avoid repeating the mistakes of interwar fundamentalism. They knew that their predecessors had gotten prophecy wrong so many times in the past that they needed to be very careful about making specific predictions about the future. While movement leaders continued to foster in their followers a premillennial sense of urgency, they tried not to embarrass the movement by making faulty predictions. Responding to the post–Cold War flood of books that sought to situate current events within biblical prophecy, D. Brent Sandy of Liberty University encouraged premillennialists to proceed cautiously. "If our children should ever read the twentieth-century's best-selling books on prophecy," he wrote in *Christianity Today,* "they will learn an important lesson. They will understand, perhaps better than any generation, the perils of trying to make Scripture's prophetic passages fit into the grid of current or expected events." Little did he know that a new series of books by Tim LaHaye would eclipse all previous best-selling Armageddon books and would carry evangelical premillennialism well into the twentieth-first century, making apocalypticism more alluring to Americans than ever.[56]

LaHaye had by the mid-1990s already sold millions of books on prophecy and the Christian life; however, his efforts to write a good book of fiction had proven unsuccessful. He and his agent eventually settled on a plan to have the popular minister pen an outline for a novel on the end times, which writer Jerry Jenkins would transform into a compelling story. The result was *Left Behind,* the first novel in what grew into a sixteen-volume series. The franchise became so successful that the publisher followed up the initial novels with numerous spin-offs, including a forty-book Left Behind series for youth, a run of graphic novels, and another fiction series targeting men and women in the armed forces.[57]

The Left Behind books explain American premillennial eschatology from beginning to end through fiction. The first novel begins with the rapture of all true Christians from the earth and the ensuing chaos. Only the intervention of the UN secretary-general, a good-looking Romanian named Nicolae Carpathia (ironically he has the same name as the boat Mauro was on when the Titanic went down in 1912), brings stability to the global situation. Carpathia, who turns out to be the Antichrist, organizes a one-world government, a one-world currency, and a one-world religion. Meanwhile a small remnant of Christians—a "tribulation force"—does its best to get as many people saved as possible while challenging the works of Carpathia and his henchmen.

The geopolitics of the series closely aligns with traditional premillennial thought. Left Behind begins by focusing on Israel, where a scientist has apparently discovered a new technology that dramatically enhances agricultural production. When Russia—Magog—attacks Israel with the hopes of stealing the technology, God miraculously intervenes to stop the kingdom of the north. Consistent with post–Gulf War premillennialism, Iraq also plays an important role in the series. Carpathia moves the headquarters of the UN to Babylon, where he establishes a new organization, the "Global Community." LaHaye and Jenkins, however, are more cautious than earlier premillennialists about identifying any specific Asian power as the "kings of the east." Rather than interpreting John's words in Revelation as a reference to a real nation, in Left Behind the end-times army from the East is invisible.

The series—like evangelical interpretations of biblical prophecy in general—is not kind to Jews. As more and more Jews convert to Christianity during the tribulation, they take refuge in Petra (where Blackstone hid premillennial tracts in the early twentieth century for just this reason). Although the Antichrist turns on these converts, God protects them. As a result, Carpathia then targets the world's non-Christian Jews, whom he massacres in a new holocaust. The Antichrist then amasses his armies near the valley of Armageddon for one final attack on the Christian and Jewish rebels. But before he can succeed, Christ returns and vanquishes evil.

With over sixty-three million copies in readers' hands, the Left Behind books have become a major cultural phenomenon, garnering royalties exceeding one hundred million dollars for their authors. The books became the best-selling series of novels of the last couple of decades until that other minion of darkness, Harry Potter, surpassed them. The Left Behind franchise spawned a few awful feature-length films, starring outspoken evangelical and former teen heartthrob Kirk Cameron, which were so bad that LaHaye unsuccessfully sued the producers for the damage they did to his franchise. The books also inspired a violent video game, which raised all sorts of objections from evangelicals and others who wondered about the propriety of a game in which Christians get to kill their enemies.[58]

Journalists, policy-makers, and academics have tried to understand and explain the success of the novels as well as to assess their impact on the culture. "In this volatile moment," *Time* claimed, "many people are starting to read the Left Behind books not as novels but as tomorrow's newspapers." Such was the goal of premillennialists since the late nineteenth century. Former secretary of state Madeleine Albright even claimed that the books had affected the United States' international relations. She fretted that the surge in premillennial ideas undermined her ability to work with the UN and destabilized the Middle East peace process. Yet it is clear that most readers of the novels have no idea that the Left Behind authors intended to do anything more than tell a good story.[59]

While LaHaye has never achieved the popular renown of Jerry Falwell or Billy Graham, he embodies all of the trends of post-1970s evangelicalism. He may have even had a more substantial impact on the movement than his more famous colleagues. Just before 9/11, the *Evangelical Studies Bulletin,* published by the Institute for the Study of American Evangelicals at Wheaton College, named him the "most influential American Evangelical of the last 25 years." He began his career as a suburban San Diego pastor and built the Scott Memorial Baptist Church into a thriving congregation; he opened a series of Christian day schools and a Bible college; he helped found the Institute for Creation Research in an effort to bring academic and scientific credibility to creation science; he organized the Pre-Trib Research Center to encourage the study of premillennialism and its implications; he wrote best-selling self-help and marriage books and even a relatively explicit Christian sex primer that sold in the millions; he wrote a series of books in the 1970s and 1980s that helped shape and inspire the rise of the religious right, including two early books criticizing same-sex relationships; he worked with Jerry Falwell to organize the Moral Majority and served on its board of directors; and in 1981 he founded the Council for National Policy, a highly secretive right-wing think tank. Summing up LaHaye's career, the *Evangelical Studies* article concluded: "in so many ways he's someone who was influenced by all the changes swirling around evangelicalism, rose out of the ranks of the movement, and then in turn played a strategic role at key points that have cemented—for good or ill—the direction" the movement "will be taking in the next few decades." LaHaye has left a legacy with which modern evangelicals and their critics will long have to wrestle.[60]

As Americans approached the end of the twentieth century, their apocalyptic expectations continued to grow. The environmental crisis showed no signs of waning, nuclear weapons proliferated, and a supposed millennium bug threatened to shut down computers around the globe and to bring the economy and hundreds of other essential services to a halt. Bill Clinton's extramarital shenanigans and predilection for Oval Office blowjobs convinced the faithful that the days of Sodom had returned. Evangelicals said it would be so.

However, the year 2000 proved to be significant for another reason as well. The faithful helped elect George W. Bush, one of their own, to the presidency. Evangelicals' growing power and success during the Bush administration, combined with the rise of a new generation of believers who felt uncomfortable with the direction the movement had taken, offered the potential to sever apocalypticism from evangelicalism.

But then things changed again. On a cool and sunny late summer morning in September 2001, the actions of a wealthy Saudi terrorist reminded the faithful—and the nation—how close the world might really be to a biblical apocalypse.

EPILOGUE

AMERICAN EVANGELICALISM IS THRIVING in the twenty-first century. While nineteenth-century premillennialists would most likely fail to recognize their spiritual great-grandchildren, white evangelicals have achieved much of what they set out to do since World War II. While they still claim at times to be a persecuted minority, in reorienting their movement and linking their faith with the major social and political issues of the era, they have accomplished more than most ever dreamed possible. Evangelicals have helped to make and break presidential candidates, influenced US foreign policy, and shaped the debates on the most important social and cultural issues of our time. In terms of religion, they have moved from provocative outsiders to consummate insiders. They play important roles in party politics and through their various advocacy groups they have acquired tremendous power at all levels of government. Liberal Christians now often fret about their declining influence while evangelicals see a bright future ahead in both the religious sphere and in every other facet of civic life, in the United States and around the globe. In the last century evangelicals' relentless sense of apocalyptic urgency helped create a movement that now claims almost 30 percent of the US population (Catholics represent about 23 percent and liberal Protestants about 14 percent of the population). Fundamentalists began on the margins of American religious life, where they represented a schismatic alternative to mainstream Christianity; their evangelical descendants now oversee what is arguably the most powerful religious movement in the United States and one of the most powerful around the globe.[1]

As evangelical influence and power has skyrocketed, the faithful have invested more and more time in working toward achieving the kingdom of God in this world rather than in preparing humanity for the next. The result has been a waning emphasis on the imminent second coming of Christ. Some of the most famous evangelical preachers in the nation no longer talk about a soon-coming apocalypse. Despite their premillennial roots, suburban megachurch gurus and best-selling authors such as Joel Osteen, Rick Warren, and T. D. Jakes, to name but three examples, offer therapeutic solutions to life's mundane problems; they do not spend time exploring doomsday scenarios. The evangelical left has also continued to grow since the 1970s. Its leaders encourage followers to engage responsibly with this world rather than to obsess over when (or if) they will be raptured into the next. New movements have emerged out of evangelicalism as well, including the postmodernish, postevangelical "emerging church," which rejects premillennialism, and a revived, staunchly conservative version of postmillennialism called Christian Reconstruction. Nevertheless, apocalyptic premillennialism has succumbed neither to the Antichrist nor to competing theologies. Like a phoenix rising from the ashes, premillennialism reappears whenever tragedy strikes.[2]

No event illustrates this better than the terrorist attacks on the United States of September 11, 2001. As Americans struggled to make sense of the horrific tragedy, some elite evangelical leaders preached caution. *Christianity Today* editors, for example, made few explicit links between the attacks and doomsday beliefs. "I try to avoid end-times prophecy," Watergate felon and popular Christian leader Chuck Colson wrote in his regular *Christianity Today* column after 9/11, "that makes Christians appear irrelevant to the world." In fact, premillennialism rarely appears on the pages of this magazine anymore. But *Christianity Today*'s was not the only response to the tragedy. Chuck Smith, leader of the highly successful Calvary Chapel movement, warned his parishioners that they had better repent before time ran out. Bishop G. E. Patterson of the Church of God in Christ admonished his flock that this "could very well be the beginning of the countdown that will

This 1974 painting of Christians being raptured to heaven was used to illustrate a tract intended to explain to those who would be left behind what had happened. Evangelicals found new relevance in this illustration in the wake of the World Trade Center tragedy of September 11, 2001, since the painting features a plane crashing into a city office building.
    Courtesy of the Bible Believers' Evangelistic Association.

lead to the final world conflict." John Hagee, a Texas minister who in recent years has authored numerous best-selling apocalyptic screeds, interpreted the 9/11 attacks as the opening of World War III and the beginning of the end. In the days immediately following the attack, laypeople turned to books in search of answers, emptying stores of their stocks of evangelical prophecy manuals and apocalyptic novels. A few weeks later Americans made the new Left Behind novel—*Desecration: Antichrist Takes the Throne,* which hit store shelves that October— the best-selling hardcover novel of the year.[3]

    While many evangelicals wondered what the rising threat of Islamic radicalism forebode, the reactions of two of the nation's most famous evangelical leaders stoked even more controversy. Jerry Falwell appeared on Pat Robertson's television show just after 9/11. The Lynchburg minister told his *700 Club* host that the United States' "sins" had so angered God that he had withdrawn his protection from the country, creating the opening that Osama Bin Laden exploited. "I really believe," Falwell told Robertson, "that the pagans, and the abortionists, and the feminists, and the gays and the lesbians who are actively trying to make that an alternative lifestyle, the ACLU, People For the American Way, all of them who have tried to secularize America. I point the finger in their face and say 'you helped this happen.'" As modern-day evangelicals looked to the story of ancient Israel for patterns and precedents for God's dealings with the United States, it is no surprise that some would respond to events like 9/11 with such harsh language. For the faithful, to remove God from schools, churches, and homes was to provoke his fury. Falwell and Robertson simply tapped into a long evangelical tradition built on the model of Old Testament prophets, revived by American Puritans, and developed throughout the twentieth century. The faithful had regularly interpreted national calamities, from the sinking of the Lusitania to the stock market crash to the bombing of Pearl Harbor, as expressions of the judgments of God. What made Falwell's actions different was the advent of cable news, which guaranteed that his comments would be played over and over again. Chastened by the national outcry he provoked, Falwell apologized. Nevertheless, his words fit well within mainstream evangelical orthodoxy and the culture wars mentality that had characterized American evangelicalism for over a century.[4]

Evangelical apocalypticism once again gave Americans a language with which to make sense of the tragedy. George W. Bush's rhetoric of an axis of evil, his black-and-white, good and bad, you-are-for-us-or-against-us ultimatums and his vision for transforming the Middle East reflected the ideals of modern evangelicalism. Bush may have even invoked Ezekiel's prophecy to French president Jacques Chirac to justify the invasion of Iraq. "Gog and Magog are at work in the Middle East," the American president apparently explained. "Biblical prophecies are being fulfilled." "This confrontation," he continued, "is willed by God, who wants to use this conflict to erase His people's enemies before a new age begins." Like Reagan, Bush was not making decisions on the basis of premillennial convictions. Nevertheless, he well understood that the neoconservative ideals that shaped his foreign policy meshed almost perfectly with the ideas of evangelical apocalypticism.[5]

The 9/11 tragedies, the opening of the "war on terror," and the commencement of military action in Iraq inspired the publication of a new deluge of premillennial books. Hagee rushed into print *Attack on America: New York, Jerusalem, and the Role of Terrorism in the Last Days* (2001), which interpreted 9/11 as a sign that Armageddon was just around the corner. Hal Lindsey responded to 9/11 with *The Everlasting Hatred: The Roots of Jihad* (2002), a distorted, fear-mongering recap of the history of Islam and Islam's relationship with Jews. Just a few years later his anti-Muslim bigotry drove executives at the Trinity Broadcasting Network to cancel his weekly prophecy show, *International Intelligence Briefing.* They feared that Lindsey had gone too negative and his work was hurting the network's ministry in Arab countries. But he was soon back on the air. John Walvoord's publisher also looked to cash in on the renewed interest in prophecy with an updated, retitled edition of the deceased Dallas theologian's classic text: *Armageddon, Oil, and Terror: What the Bible Says about the Future of America, the Middle East, and the End of Western Civilization* (2007); and LaHaye and Jenkins continued to dominate best-seller lists with new Left Behind books. Meanwhile, all around the country various ministers broadcast their own low-budget local and regional prophecy shows. Others still made the most of the Internet, including the founders of the popular website raptureready.com, which tracks how close we are to Armageddon (we're really close).[6]

With an evangelical president at the helm, however, the faithful felt confident that although the world might be spiraling toward the apocalypse, the United States was in the best hands possible. Evangelicals generally supported George W. Bush, who often championed their policy priorities and who rewarded them by appointing evangelicals to important positions in his administration. Bush's rhetoric, convictions, and vision of and for the world matched their own. But the election of Barack Obama in 2008 raised new questions for the faithful. The specious theories about his place of birth, his internationalist tendencies, his measured support for Israel, and his Nobel Peace Prize echoed their long-held expectations about the coming world dictator. While a few evangelicals saw Obama as a type of the Antichrist, and the most radical evangelical critics even questioned his religious convictions and accused him of secretly practicing Islam, most of those still committed to premillennialism simply saw him as another FDR, a naive dupe of

Satan inadvertently preparing the nation to ally with the devil in the last days.[7]

Although historians, sociologists, and journalists continue to debate the future of American evangelicalism, recent surveys have reaffirmed the success and influence of evangelicals' efforts to spread their faith. Millions of Americans now believe that the time is nigh. A 2006 Pew poll revealed that 79 percent of US Christians believed in the second coming, and 20 percent expected it to happen in their lifetime. A 2010 Pew poll revealed that 41 percent of all Americans (well over one hundred million people) and 58 percent of white evangelicals believed that Jesus is "definitely" or "probably" going to return by 2050. Perhaps most illuminating, according to a 2014 survey, of the 50 percent of all Americans who have read any of the Bible in the previous year, over one-third claimed that they did so "to learn about the future." While the vast majority of the people questioned in these polls probably have little to no understanding of the complex theology undergirding their opinions, their faith in the Bible as a guidebook for the future reveals how widespread Christian apocalyptic ideas are and how thoroughly evangelical premillennialism has saturated American culture over the last 150 years. Evangelicals' conviction that Jesus is coming has become such a standard part of evangelical rhetoric that few believers ever question it. Their confidence that the time is short and God is going to hold his people accountable for their work has driven generations of believers to reclaim the seemingly secular American culture. The urgency, the absolute morals, the passion to right the world's wrongs, and the refusal to compromise, negotiate, or mediate, now defines much of American evangelicalism and a significant part of right-wing politics. We now live in a world shaped by evangelicals' apocalyptic hopes, dreams, and nightmares.[8]

As Billy Graham neared the end of his life, he both tapped into and continued to fuel modern American apocalyptic beliefs. In 2010, the elderly evangelist updated and reiterated his premillennial convictions in a new edition of *Storm Warning*. "Now at ninety-one years old," Graham explained to readers, "I believe the storm clouds are darker than they have ever been. . . . Benevolent hands reach down from heaven to offer us the most hopeful warning and remedy: 'Prepare to meet your God.' . . . The signs of His imminent return have never been greater than now." Graham's signs included the 9/11 attacks, the global economic recession, the ever-growing power of the state, the environmental crisis, the influence of godless popular culture on American society, secular school curricula, and the rise of multiculturalism. Despite his claims that he was above partisanship, he also took a swipe at Barack Obama in *Storm Warning*. In a section on the "worldly church" he wrote, "we are called to distinguish ourselves as Christ followers, not community organizers," riffing off the right-wing criticisms of the president's work as a young man in Chicago. Although Graham told *Christianity Today* that he regretted the way his political involvement had compromised his ministry, that did not stop him from taking out national newspaper ads during the 2012 campaign counseling Americans to vote for candidates "who will support the biblical definition of marriage, protect the sanctity of life and defend our religious freedoms." While he didn't explicitly say "vote Republican," his message was clear.[9]

Graham's work illustrates how premillennialists-turned-fundamentalists-turned-evangelicals since William Blackstone's *Jesus Is Coming* have masterfully linked the major issues of every generation to their reading of the coming apocalypse with the goal of transforming their culture. While the signs of the apocalypse have changed over time, they have never stopped appearing for evangelicals. Discerning their meaning has given the faithful a powerful sense of urgency, a confidence that they alone understand the world in which they are living, and a hope for a future in which they will reign supreme. They also know that their critics will soon face the wrath of the Almighty and the torments of hell. The anticipation of Armageddon has been good to Billy Graham and good to American evangelicals as a whole.

In *Storm Warning* Graham perfectly encapsulated 150 years of evangelical apocalypticism, with its blend of despair and activism. "Listen!" he preached. "The distant sounds" of the four horsemen of the apocalypse "can be heard closing in on the place you now sit reading. Above the clatter of the horses' hooves arise other sounds—the metallic thud of machine guns, the whistle of flamethrowers and mortar rounds, the crackle of burning schools, homes, and churches, the high-pitched shriek of missiles zeroing in with their nuclear warheads, the explosion of megaton bombs over our cities." But there was always room for hope. "If the human race would turn from its evil ways and return to

God," he promised, "putting behind its sins of disobedience, idolatry, pride, greed, and belligerence, and all the various aberrations that lead to war, the possibility of peace exists. But when we see society as it is, with anger and violence around us, who can anticipate such a transformation?" Who indeed.[10]

ABBREVIATIONS

NOTES

ACKNOWLEDGMENTS

INDEX

ABBREVIATIONS

Manuscript Collections

ACD	Amzi Clarence Dixon Papers, Collection 111, Southern Baptist Historical Library and Archives, Nashville.
ASM	Aimee Semple McPherson Papers, Archives, International Church of the Foursquare Gospel, Echo Park, CA.
BGCA	Billy Graham Center Archives, Wheaton, IL.
CEF	Charles E. Fuller Papers, Collection 11, Fuller Theological Seminary Archives, Pasadena, CA.
FB	Frank Bartleman Papers, Flower Pentecostal Heritage Center, Springfield, MO.
FDR	President's Personal File, Franklin D. Roosevelt Presidential Library, Hyde Park.
FDR-O	Official Papers of the President, Franklin D. Roosevelt Presidential Library, Hyde Park.
FPHC	Flower Pentecostal Heritage Center, Springfield, MO.
HJO	Harold John Ockenga Papers, Gordon Conwell Theological Seminary, South Hamilton, MA.
HS	Henry Stough Papers, Collection 106, Billy Graham Center Archives, Wheaton, IL.
ICFG	Archives, International Church of the Foursquare Gospel, Echo Park, CA.

JFN   J. Frank Norris Papers, Collection 124, Southern Baptist Histori-
          cal Library and Archives, Nashville.

JFN-M   J. Frank Norris Papers, Billy Graham Center Archives, Wheaton,
          IL (microfilm).

JMG   James M. Gray Papers, Moody Bible Institute Archives, Chicago.

JNG   J. Narver Gortner Papers, Flower Pentecostal Heritage Center,
          Springfield, MO.

JOB   J. Oliver Buswell Papers, Wheaton College Archives and Special
          Collections, Wheaton, IL.

JRS   John Roach Straton Papers, American Baptist Historical Society,
          Atlanta.

LNB   Lemuel Nelson Bell Papers, Collection 318, Billy Graham Center
          Archives, Wheaton, IL.

LS   Lyman Stewart Papers, Biola University, La Mirada, CA.

LSB   Louis S. Bauman Papers, Bob Jones University Library, Green-
          ville, SC (microfilm).

LSC   Lewis Sperry Chafer Papers, Bob Jones University Library,
          Greenville, SC (microfilm).

MAM   Mark A. Matthews Papers, Special Collections, University of
          Washington, Seattle.

MC   Records of the Moody Church, Collection 330, Billy Graham
          Center Archives, Wheaton, IL.

NAE   Papers of the National Association of Evangelicals (unprocessed),
          Collection 113, Wheaton College Archives and Special Collec-
          tions, Wheaton, IL.

RAT   Rueben Archer Torrey Papers, Moody Bible Institute Archives,
          Chicago.

RWH   Robert William and Winifred Thompson Hockman Papers,
          Collection 200, Billy Graham Center Archives, Wheaton, IL.

SHF   Stanley H. Frodsham Papers, Flower Pentecostal Heritage Center,
          Springfield, MO.

WAS   William A. Sunday Papers, Billy Graham Center Archives,
          Wheaton, IL (microfilm).

WEB   William E. Blackstone Papers, Collection 540, Billy Graham
          Center Archives, Wheaton, IL.

WMS   Wilbur M. Smith Papers, Collection 35, Fuller Theological
          Seminary Archives, Pasadena, CA.

WOHG   W. O. H. Garman Papers, Mack Library, Bob Jones University,
          Greenville, SC.

Periodicals and Newspapers

AC	Atlanta Constitution
ADW	Atlanta Daily World
AF	Apostolic Faith
AN	Amsterdam News
B&C	Baptist and Commoner
BC	Bridal Call
BG	Boston Globe
BS	Baltimore Evening Sun
BW	Biblical World
CC	Christian Century
CD	Chicago Defender
CL	Christian Life
CT	Christianity Today
CWM	Christian Workers Magazine
FC	Foursquare Crusader
KB	King's Business
LAT	Los Angeles Times
MM	Moody Monthly
NBUR	National Baptist Union-Review
NBV	National Baptist Voice
NYT	New York Times
OH	Our Hope
PC	Pittsburgh Courier
PE	Pentecostal Evangel
PM	Prophecy Monthly
REV	Revelation
SLT	Searchlight
SST	Sunday School Times
SOTL	Sword of the Lord
WP	Washington Post
WR	Western Recorder

Prologue

1 On Mauro see Gordon P. Gardiner, *Champion of the Kingdom: The Story of Philip Mauro* (Sterling, VA: Grace Abounding Ministries, n.d.).

2 Mauro letter quoted in Gordon P. Gardiner, "Champion of the Kingdom: The Story of Philip Mauro," *Bread of Life* (June 1959), 5.

3 Philip Mauro, "The 'Titanic' Catastrophe and Its Lessons," *CWM* (July 1912), 719. The story was also printed as Philip Mauro, "The Titanic Catastrophe and Its Lessons," *OH* (July 1912), 29–39. See also Philip Mauro, *The Life-Boat and the Death-Boat* (Swengel, PA: Bible Truth Depot, n.d.); on the *Titanic* see Steven Biel, *Down with the Old Canoe: A Cultural History of the Titanic Disaster* (New York: Norton, 1996).

4 The most important studies on fundamentalism that have shaped my thinking include Ernest Sandeen, *The Roots of Fundamentalism: British and American Millenarianism, 1800–1930* (Chicago: University of Chicago Press, 1970); George Marsden, *Fundamentalism and American Culture,* 2nd ed. (New York: Oxford University Press, 2006); George Marsden, *Reforming Fundamentalism: Fuller Seminary and the New Evangelicalism* (Grand Rapids, MI: Eerdmans, 1987); George Marsden, *Understanding Fundamentalism and Evangelicalism* (Grand Rapids, MI: Eerdmans, 1991); and Joel Carpenter, *Revive Us Again: The Reawaking of American Fundamentalism* (New York: Oxford University Press, 1997). I have also been influenced by forthcoming work on fundamentalism, especially Timothy

Gloege's *Guaranteed Pure: Fundamentalism, Business, and the Making of Modern Evangelicalism* (Chapel Hill: University of North Carolina Press, 2015), and Brendan Pietsch's "Dispensational Modernism" (PhD diss., Duke University, 2011). The conclusions in Michael Hamilton's excellent historiographical essay on fundamentalism generally match my own. Michael S. Hamilton, "The Interdenominational Evangelicalism of D. L. Moody and the Problem of Fundamentalism," in *American Evangelicalism: George Marsden and the State of American Religious History,* ed. Darren Dochuk, Thomas Kidd, and Kurt Peterson (Notre Dame, IN: University of Notre Dame Press, 2014).

5 In making the case for the centrality of premillennialism for fundamentalist identity, I have drawn on Paul Boyer, *When Time Shall Be No More: Prophecy Belief in Modern American Culture* (Cambridge, MA: Harvard University Press, 1992), and Timothy P. Weber, *Living in the Shadow of the Second Coming: American Premillennialism 1875–1982* (Grand Rapids, MI: Zondervan, 1983), and *On the Road to Armageddon: How Evangelicals Became Israel's Best Friend* (Grand Rapids, MI: Baker Academic, 2004).

6 On fundamentalism and gender, I have been influenced especially by Margaret Lamberts Bendroth, *Fundamentalism and Gender, 1875 to the Present* (New Haven, CT: Yale University Press, 1993), and Betty A. De-Berg, *Ungodly Women: Gender and the First Wave of American Fundamentalism* (Minneapolis: Fortress Press, 1990). There is still much work to be done on fundamentalism and race. To date the major books on white American fundamentalism and evangelicalism in the pre–civil rights period almost totally ignore issues of race. Historians of race on the other hand have done a much better job with religion. See for example Edward J. Blum, *Reforging the White Republic: Race, Religion, and American Nationalism, 1865–1898* (Baton Rouge: Louisiana State University Press, 2005); Anthea D. Butler, *Women in the Church of God in Christ: Making a Sanctified World* (Chapel Hill: University of North Carolina Press, 2007); Curtis J. Evans, "White Evangelical Protestant Responses to the Civil Rights Movement," *Harvard Theological Review* 102:2 (April 2009): 245–273; Paul Harvey, *Freedom's Coming: Religious Culture and the Shaping of the South from the Civil War through the Civil Rights Era* (Chapel Hill: University of North Carolina Press, 2005); and Miles S. Mullin II, "Neoevangelicalism and the Problem of Race in Postwar America," in *Christians and the Color Line,* ed. J. Russell Hawkins and Phillip Luke Sinitiere (New York: Oxford University Press, 2013), 15–44. On the civil rights movement see David L. Chappell, *A Stone of Hope: Prophetic Religion and the Death of Jim Crow* (Chapel Hill: University of North Carolina Press, 2004). These books demonstrate the ways that attention to race can better help us understand religion and vice versa. Historians also need to

integrate Asian American and Latinos into the history of fundamentalism—an effort beyond the scope of this project.

7 In trying to make sense of the rise of fundamentalist politics and especially the rise of the religious right, historians for the most part have focused on the post–World War II period. However, much of evangelicals'
postwar political ideology had its origins in prewar fundamentalism. On
the postwar period, see for example Randall Balmer, *Thy Kingdom Come:
How the Religious Right Distorts Faith and Threatens America, An Evangelical's
Lament* (New York: Basic Books, 2006); Seth Dowland, *Family Values: Gender, Authority, and the Rise of the Christian Right* (Philadelphia: University of
Pennsylvania Press, 2016); Jonathan P. Herzog, *The Spiritual-Industrial Complex: America's Religious Battle against Communism in the Early Cold War*
(New York: Oxford University Press, 2011); Kevin M. Kruse, *One Nation under God: The Invention of Christian America* (New York: Basic Books,
2015); Angela Lahr, *Millennial Dreams and Apocalyptic Nightmares: The
Cold War Origins of Political Evangelicalism* (New York: Oxford University
Press, 2007); William Martin, *With God on Our Side: The Rise of the Reli-
gious Right in America* (New York: Broadway Books, 1996); Jason W. Ste-
vens, *God-Fearing and Free: A Spiritual History of America's Cold War* (Cam-
bridge, MA: Harvard University Press, 2010); and Clyde Wilcox, *God's
Warriors: The Christian Right in Twentieth-Century America* (Baltimore:
Johns Hopkins University Press, 1992). However, both Darren Dochuk,
*From Bible Belt to Sunbelt: Plain-Folk Religion, Grassroots Politics, and the
Rise of Evangelical Conservatism* (New York: Norton, 2011), and Daniel K.
Williams, *God's Own Party: The Making of the Christian Right* (New York:
Oxford University Press, 2010), demonstrate that the roots of modern
evangelical political activism run deeper. The one book that specifically
focuses on fundamentalist politics in the 1930s, Leo Ribuffo's pioneering
work *The Old Christian Right,* highlights the work of three demagogues—
William Dudley Pell, Gerald B. Winrod, and Gerald L. K. Smith. Of the
three, only Winrod was tangentially associated with the larger, national
fundamentalist network. Leo P. Ribuffo, *The Old Christian Right: The
Protestant Far Right from the Great Depression to the Cold War* (Philadelphia:
Temple University Press, 1983).

1. Jesus Is Coming

1 William E. Blackstone, *Jesus Is Coming,* 2nd ed. (London: Partridge and
Co., n.d.), 99, 100, 149.

2 Blackstone, *Jesus Is Coming,* 2nd ed., 94, 95.

3 Evangelical leader and bibliophile Wilbur Smith, writing in 1966, called
Jesus Is Coming the "most widely read book in this century on our Lord's

return." Wilbur Smith, "Signs of the Times as Seen in the Early 20th Century," *MM* (July–August 1966), 57. On Blackstone see Beth Lindberg, *A God-Filled Life: The Story of William E. Blackstone* (Chicago: American Messianic Fellowship, n.d.), n.p.; see also Joel Carpenter, introduction to *The Premillennial Second Coming: Two Early Champions* (New York: Garland, 1988); and Jonathan David Moorhead, "Jesus Is Coming: The Life and Work of William E. Blackstone (1841–1935)" (PhD diss, Dallas Theological Seminary, 2008).

4 On the relationships among various Protestants in the late nineteenth century, see Grant Wacker, "The Holy Spirit and the Spirit of the Age in American Protestantism, 1880–1910," *Journal of American History* 72:1 (June 1985): 45–62.

5 On modernism see Kathryn Lofton, "The Methodology of the Modernists: Process in American Protestantism," *Church History* 75:2 (June 2006): 374–402.

6 A. T. Pierson, "The Coming of the Lord: The Doctrinal Center of the Bible," in *Addresses on the Second Coming of the Lord Delivered at The Prophetic Conference, Allegheny, PA* (Pittsburgh: Johnston and Co., 1895), 82.

7 On the tight relationship between dispensational premillennialism and modernism see Brendan Pietsch, "Dispensational Modernism" (PhD diss., Duke University, 2011).

8 J. N. Darby to Brother, October 1866, in *Letters of J. N. D.,* vol. 1, *1832–1868* (Kingston-on-Thames, England: Stow Hill Bible and Tract Depot, n.d.), 460–461. On the intellectual foundations of premillennialism see Ernest Sandeen, *The Roots of Fundamentalism: British and American Millenarianism, 1800–1930* (Chicago: University of Chicago Press, 1970).

9 All scripture quotations are from the King James version. On the varying versions of premillennialism see Timothy P. Weber, "Dispensational and Historic Premillennialism as Popular Millennialist Movements," in *A Case for Historic Premillennialism: An Alternative to "Left Behind" Eschatology,* ed. Craig Blomberg and Sung Wook Chung (Grand Rapids, MI: Baker Academic, 2009).

10 Blackstone, *Jesus Is Coming,* 2nd ed., 111; William E. Blackstone, *Jesus Is Coming,* 3rd ed. (Chicago: Revell, 1908), 234.

11 The Blackstone Memorials, 1891 and 1916, folder 6, box 6, WEB.

12 On the subject of prophecy and its relationship to the Bible conference movement, see Walter Unger, "'Earnestly Contending for the Faith': The Role of the Niagara Bible Conference in the Emergence of American Fundamentalism, 1875–1900" (PhD diss., Simon Fraser University, 1981). On the relationships between Canadian and American millennialists see Ronald George Sawatsky, "'Looking for That Blessed Hope': The

Roots of Fundamentalism in Canada, 1878–1914" (PhD diss., University of Toronto, 1985).

13 "Christ's Second Coming," *NYT,* November 1, 1878.

14 "The Prophetic Conference," *Chicago Inter Ocean,* November 8, 1878. On the men who signed the call, see Sandeen, *Roots of Fundamentalism,* 151–152.

15 "The Prophetic Conference," *Congregationalist,* November 6, 1878; "Call for the Conference," in *Second Coming of Christ: Premillennial Essays of the Prophetic Conference Held in The Church of the Holy Trinity, New York City* (Chicago: Revell, 1879), 11.

16 "Christ's Second Coming," *NYT,* November 1, 1878; the *Times* later ran a positive notice announcing the publication of the essays from the conference. "Literary Notes," *NYT,* May 6, 1879.

17 "Bible and Prophetic Conference in Chicago," *Standard,* November 25, 1886.

18 George C. Needham, preface to *Prophetic Studies of the International Prophetic Conference* (Chicago: Revell, 1886), 2; Needham, "Reasons for Holding the Bible and Prophetic Conference," in *Prophetic Studies,* 215–216.

19 E. P. Goodwin, "The Return of the Lord," in *Prophetic Studies,* 14.

20 A. J. Frost, "Condition of the Church and World at Christ's Second Advent," in *Prophetic Studies,* 174, 175; A. T. Pierson, "Premillennial Motives to Evangelism," in *Prophetic Studies,* 32, 33.

21 James H. Brookes's *Maranatha, or, The Lord Cometh* (St. Louis: E. Bredell, 1874), actually predated and helped inspire Blackstone. See also Nathaniel West, *The Thousand Years in Both Testaments* (Chicago: Revell, 1880, 1889); J. R. Graves, *The Work of Christ in the Covenant of Redemption: Developed in Seven Dispensations* (Texarkana: Baptist Sunday School Committee, 1883, 1928); L. W. Munhall, *The Lord's Return and Kindred Truth* (Philadelphia: E. and R. Munhall, 1895); Samuel Andrews, *Christianity and Anti-Christianity in Their Final Conflict,* 2nd ed. (New York: Putnam, 1899); and I. M. Haldeman, *The Signs of the Times* (New York: Charles C. Cook, 1911).

22 Joel Carpenter, *Revive Us Again: The Reawaking of American Fundamentalism* (New York: Oxford University Press, 1997), 26–27; "Our Purpose and Plan," *KB* (January 1925), n.p.; Joel Carpenter, "Moody Monthly," Warren Vinz, "SOTL," in *The Conservative Press in Twentieth-Century America,* ed. Ronald Lora and William Henry Longton (Westport, CT: Greenwood Press, 1999), 106, 130, 140; "Editorial Policy," internal memo, *Pentecostal Evangel* file, FPHC.

23 Lewis Sperry Chafer to John R. Rice, January 7, 1943, LSC. Although the Scofield Bible is certainly one of the best-selling books in the history

of Oxford University Press, the press does not have reliable statistics from the pre–World War II era, so it is impossible to determine conclusively if this is in fact its best-selling book. Donald Kraus (executive editor, Oxford University Press), e-mail to author, February 13, 2012.

24 The best book on pentecostalism, which has profoundly shaped my own thinking, is Grant Wacker's magisterial *Heaven Below: Early Pentecostals and American Culture* (Cambridge, MA: Harvard University Press, 2001). See also Randall J. Stephens's excellent book *The Fire Spreads: Holiness and Pentecostalism in the American South* (Cambridge, MA: Harvard University Press, 2008).

25 "Weird Babel of Tongues," *LAT,* April 18, 1906.

26 "A Message Concerning His Coming," *AF* (October 1906), 3; "Jesus Is Coming Soon," *AF* (January 1908), 2; W. J. S. "Behold the Bridegroom Cometh!," *AF* (January 1907), 2.

27 A. Beck, "The Warfare, the Rapture and Afterwards," *AF* (February–March 1907), 4.

28 *The Time of the End* (St. Louis: Gospel Publishing House, [1915?]), 13, 14.

29 I explore one example of the relationships of exchange and combination in Matthew Avery Sutton, "'Between the Refrigerator and the Wildfire': Aimee Semple McPherson, Pentecostalism, and the Fundamentalist-Modernist Controversy," *Church History* 72:1 (March 2003): 159–188.

30 "Should Insurance Companies Take into Account the Lord's Return?" *SST,* August 29, 1936, 566; on McPherson's cemetery see J. Narver Gortner to J. R. Evans, January 27, 1928, J. R. Evans to J. Narver Gortner, February 7, 1928, JNG. See also "Insurance Companies and the Rapture of the Church," *SST,* October 16, 1937, 724, 733.

31 S. H. Kellogg, "Premillennialism: Its Relations to Doctrine and Practice," *Biliotheca Sacra* 45 (April 1888): 272; Blackstone, *Jesus Is Coming,* 2nd ed., 149.

32 J. N. Darby, *What the World Is and How a Christian Can Live in It* (Kingston-on-Thames, England: Stow Hill Bible and Tract Depot, n.d.), 10–12.

33 C. I. Scofield, *Rightly Dividing the World of Truth* (New York: Loizeaux Brothers, 1907), 12.

34 West, *Thousand Years in Both Testaments* (1889), 448; I. M. Haldeman, *This Hour Not the Hour of the Prince of Peace* (New York: Charles Cook, 1916), 48–49. See also I. M. Haldeman, "Why I Preach the Second Coming," in *God Hath Spoken* (Philadelphia: Bible Conference Committee, 1919), 335–339; and F. C. Jennings, *The Christian and Politics* (New York: Charles C. Cook, n.d.).

35 Dwight L. Moody, "The Second Coming of Christ," in *The Second Coming of Christ* (Chicago: Revell, 1896), 28. See also "The Revival: Mr.

Moody's Sermon on the Coming of the Lord," *Chicago Tribune,* January 6, 1877.

36 "The Men and Religion Movement," *CWM* (October 1911), 76; "God and Politics," *CWM* (October 1915), 97. See also Ernest A. Bell, "How Chicago's Red Lights Were Put Out," *CWM* (March 1913), 448–449.

37 James M. Gray, "The Relation of the Christian Church to Civil Government," *Moody Bible Institute of Chicago Bulletin* (July–August 1922), n.p.; James Gray, "The Moody Bible Institute and 'Civic' Evangelism," *CWM* (February 1916), 447, 448.

38 A. C. Dixon, "Moral Issues in This Campaign," *Chicago Daily News,* October 31, 1908, clipping, folder 2, box 1, ACD; William Bell Riley, "Questions and Answers," in *Light on Prophecy* (New York: Christian Herald, 1918), 349–350; Bob Jones, "The Doctrine of the Lord's Coming as a Working Force in the Church and Community," in *The Coming and Kingdom of Christ* (Chicago: Bible Institute Colportage Association, 1914), 138; J. Wilbur Chapman, *Another Mile and Other Address,* 2nd ed. (New York: Revell, 1908), 16; George Müller, "The Second Coming of Christ," in *Second Coming of Christ* (1896), 70.

39 Lyman Stewart to Robert Speer, July 21, 1908, LS; French E. Oliver, "Signs of the Times," *KB* (September 1915), 772.

40 "The False Prophets," *NYT,* August 7, 1912; "We Stand at Armageddon and We Battle for the Lord," *OH* (November 1912), 284.

41 "The New Administration," *CWM,* March 1913, 433; Lyman Stewart to J. H. Windsor, July 1, 1913, LS. See also Lyman Stewart to Porter Phipps, July 17, 1913, LS; and "Our New President," *KB* (April 1913), 159.

42 Riley, "Questions and Answers," 344.

43 "'Striking Out' Satan," *Chicago Daily Tribune,* February 18, 1889; Billy Sunday, *Address by Billy Sunday: Americanism* (Philadelphia: Law Enforcement League of Philadelphia, April 10, 1922), 36–37; "Sunday Locked Out of His Own Meeting," *NYT,* March 10, 1914.

44 "Sunday Good—Should Be Better," *CWM* (August 1915), 768; "Law Aimed at 'Billy' Sunday," *NYT,* June 29, 1911; "The Rev. Billy Sunday," *AC,* September 22, 1907.

45 William Ashley Sunday, *The Second Coming* (Sturgis, MI: Journal Publishing Co., 1913), 5, 8; William Ashley Sunday, "The Second Coming," sermon manuscript, folder 90, box 9, WAS.

46 R. A. Torrey, *The Return of the Lord Jesus* (Los Angeles: Bible Institute of Los Angeles, 1913), 89; "Signs of the Times," *OH* (January 1913), 394; Walter Scott, "Is He Alive?" *OH* (March 1913), 554. One brief exception appeared in a 1912 *Christian Workers* article that supported the Federal Council of Churches' cry for disarmament. "The Arbitration Treaties," *CWM* (January 1912), 330.

388 NOTES TO PAGES 44-52

47 See "Appendix: List of Some Premillennialists," in *Coming and Kingdom of Christ*, 241–249.
48 Lewis Sperry Chafer to Wilbur Smith, February 24, 1941, box 9, WMS.
49 William Bell Riley, "The Significant Signs of the Times," in *Coming and Kingdom of Christ*, 98–109; Arno C. Gaebelein, "The Present-Day Apostasy," in *Coming and Kingdom of Christ*, 151.

2. Global War and Christian Nationalism

1 "8 New York City Preachers among the 25 Voted as Leaders by American Clergy," *NYT*, December 22, 1924.
2 "Political Notes and Comments," *Seattle Argus*, March 1, 1913.
3 M. A. Matthews to Woodrow Wilson, March 8, 1918, folder 12, box 4, accession 97-2, MAM.
4 Matthews advised Wilson on Mexico, "if we have to enter Mexico let us leave nothing but an evaporating odor of the decaying carcasses of an extremely offensive people and condition." M. A. Matthews to Woodrow Wilson, May 2, 1914, Secretary to the President to M. A. Matthews, May 7, 1914, folder 1, box 4, accession 97-2, MAM.
5 "War and the Shattering of Man's Empty Optimism and the Confirmation of the True Biblical Optimism," *KB* (October 1914), 493; "The Awful European Conflagration. War Has Come," *OH* (September 1914), 146; "Some Lessons for God's People," *OH* (October 1914), 201–202; "It Has Come," *OH* (October 1914), 196.
6 James M. Gray, "The Battle of Armageddon," *CWM* (October 1914), 82; Victor I. Masters, "Armageddon?," *WR*, September 10, 1914, 5. See also James M. Gray, *The Battle of Armageddon* (Chicago: Moody Bible Institute, 1914); and James M. Gray, *Prophecy and the Lord's Return* (New York: Revell, 1917), 27.
7 William E. Blackstone to William Jennings Bryan, September 25, 1914, folder 1, box 1; William E. Blackstone to Woodrow Wilson, November 4, 1914, folder 5, box 7, WEB.
8 Ford C. Ottman, "The Colossus of Gentile World-Power," *OH* (January 1915), 417; Charles G. Trumbull, *Prophecy's Light on Today* (New York: Revell, 1937), 42; "Jesus Is Coming," *SLT*, March 2, 1917, n.p.
9 Leonard Newby, "Light on the Present Crisis," *CWM* (December 1916), 277–278; William E. Blackstone to Archbishop of Canterbury, January 4, 1915, folder 2, box 4, WEB.
10 A. A. Hyde, "Religion and Government," *CWM* (November 1917), 191; French E. Oliver, "Signs of the Times," *KB* (September 1915), 775.
11 Newby, "Light on the Present Crisis," 277; "Has Christianity Failed, or Has Civilization Failed, or Has Man Failed?," *KB* (November 1914), 595;

Stanley H. Frodsham, "Our Heavenly Citizenship," *Weekly Evangel,* September 11, 1915, 3. See also "America's Present Duty," *KB* (December 1915), 1038; and James M. Gray, "The Re-gathering of Israel in Unbelief," in *Light on Prophecy* (New York: Christian Herald, 1918), 166.

12 "The World War Mad," *KB* (June 1916), 487; Henry S. Coffin, "The Preparedness of a Christian Nation," *KB* (August 1916), 694; "America's Peril," *KB* (March 1917), 196.

13 "Peace or War," *CWM* (July 1915), 666; "Regrets American Preparedness," *OH* (January 1916), 435. See also "President Hibben on Preparedness," *CWM* (July 1916), 829.

14 A. C. Dixon to Grace Dixon, March 18, 1915, A. C. Dixon to Mary Dixon, November 26, 1915, folder 4, box 7; A. C. Dixon to Dr. Saillens, December 10, 1917, folder 10, box 9, ACD.

15 William Jennings Bryan to M. A. Matthews, February 2, 1916, folder 10, box 1, accession 97-2, MAM.

16 "Dark Days Ahead," *KB* (July 1915), 557–558.

17 "The Present Political Campaign," *KB* (September 1916), 772; "The Importance of One Vote," *CWM* (November 1916), 176.

18 M. A. Matthews, "Why Mr. Hughes?," Sermonettes 1918, box 16, accession 97-2, MAM.

19 M. A. Matthews to Woodrow Wilson, November 8, 1916, Woodrow Wilson to M. A. Matthews, November 22, 1916, folder 8, box 4; William Gibbs McAdoo to M. A. Matthews, November 14, 1916, folder 12, box 2, accession 97-2, MAM. See also M. A. Matthews to Woodrow Wilson, November 10, 1916, folder 8, box 4, accession 97-2, MAM.

20 William E. Blackstone to Woodrow Wilson, April 5, 1916, William E. Blackstone to Woodrow Wilson, November 17, 1916, folder 5, box 7, WEB.

21 William E. Blackstone to Woodrow Wilson, March 29, 1917, folder 5, box 7, WEB; Woodrow Wilson, "Necessity of War against Germany (April 2, 1917)," in *Selected Addresses and Public Papers of Woodrow Wilson,* ed. Albert Bushnell Hart (New York: Boni and Liveright, 1918), 195.

22 "The United States in the World War," *OH* (June 1917), 746; William E. Blackstone to Woodrow Wilson, April 24, 1917, folder 5, box 7, WEB.

23 S. Ridout, "Should a Christian Go to War?," *OH* (September 1917), 165–169; C. I. Scofield, *The World's Approaching Crisis* (New York: OH, 1913), 12; Oswald J. Smith, *Is the Antichrist at Hand?* 5th ed. (Toronto: Tabernacle, 1926), 30; P. A. Klein, "Compulsory Military Service," *CWM* (July 1916), 836.

24 Frank Bartleman, "Christian Preparedness," *Word and Work,* clipping, FB.

25 *General Council Minutes, 1917,* 11, 12, FPHC; Minutes of a Special Meeting, May 4, 1917, Church Files, Glad Tidings, NY, FPHC.

26 "Is Patriotism a Christian Virtue?," *KB* (December 1914), 683; "Praying and Killing," *KB* (September 1916), 773. See also "Ought Christians to Go to War?," *KB* (December 1914), 683–685.

27 "Universal Military Service," *KB* (September 1917), 773.

28 "Shouldering a Gun," *CWM* (December 1915), 259; "What the Bible Teaches about War," *CWM* (November 1917), 179. See also H. F. Toews, "The Doctrine of Non-Resistance," *CWM* (July 1917), 862–863.

29 "Billy Sunday Says America Will Win," *BG,* April 8, 1917; "40,000 Cheer for War and Religion Mixed by Sunday," *NYT,* April 9, 1917.

30 Scott Anderson, "Billy Sunday, Prophet or Charlatan," *Overland Monthly and Out West Magazine* (January 1918), 77; "Calls Pacifist Judas," *WP,* February 19, 1918; "45,000 Cheer Sunday in Attacks on Kaiser," *WP,* January 7, 1918; "Billy Sunday's Prayer," *Mercury* (Australia), April 5, 1918; "When Billy Prays, Congressmen Cheer and Applaud," *Spokesman-Review,* January 27, 1918.

31 Paul Jones, "Billy's Uppercut Is Ready for Kaiser Bill's Friends," *BG,* December 8, 1917; "Hun Sympathizer Attacks Sunday on Platform," *BG,* December 21, 1917.

32 William Bell Riley, "The Last Days; The Last War and the Last King," in *Christ and Glory* (New York: Our Hope, 1919), 168; R. A. Torrey, "The Visible and Glorious Return of Christ God's Final Answer to Infidelity and All Present Form of Error," in *Christ and Glory,* 136; French Oliver, "Signs of the Times," *KB* (September 1915), 770; Cortland Myers, "War on German Theology," in *Light on Prophecy,* 176; A. C. Dixon to Mary Dixon, April 29, 1915, folder 4, box 7, ACD; "$25,000 Subscribed to Liberty Loan by Billy Sunday," *New York Tribune,* June 6, 1917.

33 T. G. Steward, *The End of the World; or, Clearing the Way for the Fullness of the Gentiles* (Philadelphia: A.M.E. Church Book Rooms, 1888), 67–68, 121. On late nineteenth-century African-American millennialism, see Timothy E. Fulop, " 'The Future Golden Day of the Race': Millennialism and Black Americans in the Nadir, 1877–1901," in *African-American Religion: Interpretive Essays in History and Culture,* ed. Timothy E. Fulop and Albert J. Raboteau (New York: Routledge, 1997), 227–254. On Steward and his differences with more typical premillennialism see Albert George Miller, *Elevating the Race: Theophilus G. Steward, Black Theology, and the Making of an African American Civil Society, 1865–1924* (Knoxville: University of Tennessee Press, 2003), 70–78.

34 Steward, *End of the World,* 71.

35 James Theodore Holly, "The Divine Plan of Human Redemption in Its Ethnological Development," *A.M.E. Church Review* (October 1884), 83, 85. On the role of Ethiopia in prophecy see Albert J. Raboteau, " 'Ethio-

pia Shall Soon Stretch Forth Her Hands': Black Destiny in Nineteenth-Century America," in *A Fire in the Bones: Reflections on African-American History* (Boston: Beacon Press, 1995), 37–56.

36 D. W. Forde, "The Near Eastern Question," *CD,* April 26, 1913; "Ebenezer A.M.E. Church, Evanston, Ill.," *CD,* March 14, 1914. See also "The Institutional Church," *CD,* April 4, 1914.

37 James Morris Webb, *A Black Man Will Be the Coming Universal King* (Chicago: published by the author, [1918?]), 3, 4.

38 "During and after the War," *NBUR,* July 6, 1918, 8; "Retrogradation," *NBUR,* May 5, 1917, 9.

39 "Safe for Democracy," *CWM* (July 1917), 852; "Will This Be the Last War?," *KB* (June 1917), 483; "What Are We Fighting For?," *KB* (October 1917), 867–868.

40 Frank Bartleman, "War and the Christian," *Word and Work,* clipping, FB.

41 M. A. Matthews, "The Morale of America in the War," Sermonettes, box 16; M. A. Matthews to Woodrow Wilson, April 27, 1918, Woodrow Wilson to M. A. Matthews, May 4, 1918, folder 13, box 4, accession 97-2, MAM.

42 Frank Bartleman, "War and the Christian," *Word and Work,* clipping, FB; Philip Mauro, *The World War—How It Is Fulfilling Prophecy* (Boston: Hamilton Bros. Scripture Truth Depot for Fleming H. Revell, 1919), 372, 373.

43 W. W. Fereday, "After the Great War," *OH* (July 1919), 37.

44 "Kaiser Nominated for Anti-christ by Billy Sunday," *BG,* December 1, 1917; G. R. Eads, "German Kaiser the Little Horn," *B&C,* November 14, 1917, 4; C. H. Mason, "The Kaiser in the Light of the Scriptures," in *The History and Life Work of Elder C. H. Mason,* ed. Mary Mason (Memphis: Church of God in Christ, 1924), 37.

45 James M. Gray, *A Text-Book on Prophecy* (New York: Revell, 1918), 183–191.

46 "Rome's Attitude," *KB* (October 1917), 874.

47 J. N. Darby to Brother, April 3, 1868, in *Letters of J. N. D.,* vol. 1, *1832–1868* (Kingston-on-Thames, England: Stow Hill Bible and Tract Depot, n.d.), 523; *The Scofield Reference Bible,* ed. C. I. Scofield (New York: Oxford University Press, 1909), 883; Gray, *Text-Book on Prophecy,* 192.

48 Ernest A. Paul, "The Great War," *Weekly Evangel,* April 6, 1918, 6–7; M. A. Matthews to Woodrow Wilson, March 22, 1920, folder 5, box 5, accession 97-2, MAM; "The Bolsheviki Movement," *OH* (February 1918), 492.

49 R. A. Torrey, "Questions and Answers," *KB* (October 1914), 528; A. C. Dixon to Susan Dixon, March 7, 1915, folder 4, box 7, ACD; R. E.,

"The Bible Says the Turk Will Come to His End," *WR,* March 11, 1915, 13. See also F. C. Jennings, *The World Conflict in the Light of the Prophetic Word,* 3rd ed. (New York: OH, 1917), 62.

50 F. Bartleman, "Passing Events," *Bridegroom's Messenger,* December 1, 1911, 3; "Billy Sunday Fires Hot Shot at Kaiser," *NYT,* February 19, 1918; "The Prostitution of German Scholarship," *KB* (April 1918), 280; H. C. Morrison, *The World War in Prophecy* (Louisville: Pentecostal Publishing Company, 1917), 57.

51 William E. Blackstone to F. M. North, February 23, 1917, folder 5, box 8, WEB.

52 Nathan Straus to William E. Blackstone, May 8, 1916, folder 6, box 7, WEB.

53 William E. Blackstone to Nathan Straus, May 22, 1917, folder 6, box 7, WEB. See also William E. Blackstone to Justice Brandeis, January 29, 1917, William E. Blackstone to Nathan Straus, January 2, 1918 and January 2, 1919, folder 6, box 7; and William E. Blackstone to Stephen Wise, July 9, 1917, folder 1, box 8, WEB.

54 William E. Blackstone to Justice Brandeis, March 19, 1917, William E. Blackstone to Justice Brandeis, April 18, 1917, folder 6, box 7, WEB.

55 On the Balfour Declaration see Donald M. Lewis, *The Origins of Christian Zionism: Lord Shaftesbury and Evangelical Support for a Jewish Homeland* (Cambridge: Cambridge University Press, 2010).

56 Stephen Wise to William E. Blackstone, March 4, 1918, Stephen Wise to William E. Blackstone, September 17, 1918, folder 6, box 7, WEB; Louis Brandeis to Jacob deHaas, May 8, 1917, Louis Brandeis to Jacob deHaas, December 6, 1917, in *Letters of Louis D. Brandeis,* vol. 4, ed. Melvin I. Urofsky and David W. Levine (Albany: State University of New York Press, 1975), 289, 327.

57 Thompson, "The Capture of Jerusalem," in *Light on Prophecy,* 144–145; Trumbull, *Prophecy's Light on Today,* 67; P. W. Philpott, "Coming Events Cast Their Shadows Before," in *Light on Prophecy,* 206; Henry Stough, "The Approaching 1936 Crisis," Lectures on Depression and National Crisis, sermon notebooks, vol. 10, folder 5, box 2, HS.

58 Thompson, "The Capture of Jerusalem," 145–147; "The Capture of Jerusalem," *OH* (February 1918), 486; "The Sick Man of Europe," *WR* (January 28, 1915), 8.

59 "The Allies' Fatal Mistake," *KB* (January 1918), 2; "The President's Call to the Nation for a Day of Humiliation, Prayer and Fasting," *KB* (July 1918), 547. In London, A. C. Dixon asked Prime Minister George David Lloyd to lead his nation in prayer and repentance as well. A. C. Dixon to Susan Dixon, October 26, 1917, folder 6, box 7, ACD.

60 "Thanksgiving Day," *KB* (December 1918), 1026–1027.

61 R. A. Torrey, *What the War Teaches or the Greatest Lessons of 1917* (Los Angeles: Biola Book Room, 1918); William E. Blackstone to Woodrow Wilson, December 6, 1918, folder 6, box 7, WEB.

62 Mauro, *World War*, 365; French E. Oliver, "The League of Nations and Prophecy's Program," *KB* (October 1920), 927; James M. Gray, "The League of Nations and the Danger of Federation," *CWM* (September 1920), 7. On the league's potential role in prophecy see also "Can a League of Nations Work?," *KB* (November 1918), 932–933; Louis Bauman, "Is the Antichrist at Hand? What of Mussolini?," *KB* (January 1926), 42; and W. W. Simpson, "The Great War and Its Results," *Weekly Evangel*, March 3, 1917, 2.

63 A. C. Dixon, "The League of Nations," *KB* (May 1919), 404; "Interview," *Sword and the Trowel* (September 1919), n.p., in folder 3, box 1, ACD; M. A. Matthews to Woodrow Wilson, March 22, 1920, folder 5, box 5, accession 97-2, MAM; M. A. Matthews, "Let the Senate Repent," *NYT*, April 25, 1920.

64 Among the sponsors was John E. Milholland, who was most likely the same John E. Milholland who helped found the National Association for the Advancement of Colored People. "New York Prophetic Conference," *OH* (January 1919), 401–403. See also "See Prophecy Fulfilled," *NYT*, November 29, 1918.

65 A. C. Gaebelein, introduction to *Christ and Glory*, 4; R. A. Torrey, "That Blessed Hope," in *Christ and Glory*, 22, 33.

3. The Birth of Fundamentalism

1 Recent scholarship has shown that liberal Protestantism has not fared as badly as scholars once thought. While the numbers and power of mainline churches have declined, liberals' ideas have penetrated much of modern American culture. On this topic see Matthew Hedstrom, *The Rise of Liberal Religion: Book Culture and American Spirituality in the Twentieth Century* (New York: Oxford University Press, 2013); and David A. Hollinger, *After Cloven Tongues of Fire: Protestant Liberalism in Modern American History* (Princeton, NJ: Princeton University Press, 2013).

2 Harry Emerson Fosdick, *Shall the Fundamentalists Win?* (n.p., 1922), 4, 10.

3 Fosdick, *Shall the Fundamentalists Win?*, 4–5, 9, 12.

4 Cecilia Rasmussen, "Oilman's Legacy Lives On in L.A.," *LAT*, March 2, 2008; "Lyman Stewart Passes," *LAT*, October 1, 1923; "Throng Mourns Union Oil Chief," *LAT*, October 2, 1923.

5 Lyman Stewart to Joseph Inazawa, April 3, 1907, Lyman Stewart to Charles Stimson, April 12, 1912, Lyman Stewart to M. Lisaner, March 11, 1910, LS.

6 Lyman Stewart to Will, May, and Fred, September 4, 1914, Lyman Stewart to Amy Saxton Fulton, June 22, 1908, Lyman Stewart to Mary Hendersen, August 19, 1909, LS.

7 Mrs. W. G. Starr to William E. Blackstone, December 8, 1927, folder 3, box 4, WEB. On his early plans for this project, see Lyman Stewart to William E. Blackstone, December 27, 1906, LS.

8 Lyman Stewart to A. C. Dixon, July 29, 1915, LS.

9 Lyman Stewart to Will, May, and Fred, September 4, 1914, LS.

10 Lyman Stewart to Arthur Hicks, July 9, 1908, LS.

11 James Orr, "Science and Christian Faith," in *The Fundamentals: A Testimony to the Truth* (Chicago: Testimony Publishing Company, 1910–1915), 4:91–104; Charles R. Erdman, "The Church and Socialism," in *Fundamentals*, 12:116, 119.

12 On Niagara and the "pre-trib"/"post-trib" divide see Walter Unger, "'Earnestly Contending for the Faith': The Role of the Niagara Bible Conference in the Emergence of American Fundamentalism, 1875–1900" (PhD diss., Simon Fraser University, 1981).

13 "Lyman Stewart," *KB* (January 1924), 3; A. C. Dixon to Lyman Stewart, December 21, 1910, A. C. Dixon to Lyman Stewart, February 2, 1911, Lyman Stewart to C. I. Scofield, January 7, 1911, LS.

14 Lyman Stewart to R. A. Torrey, December 3, 1913, Louis Meyer to Lyman Stewart, [1913?], R. A. Torrey to Lyman Stewart, November 17, 1913, R. A. Torrey to Lyman Stewart, December 8, 1913, R. A. Torrey to Lyman Stewart, December 10, 1913, LS; Charles E. Erdman, "The Coming of Christ," in *Fundamentals*, 11:87, 98. See also Lyman Stewart to Milton Stewart, September 10, 1914, LS.

15 John McNicol, "The Hope of the Church," in *Fundamentals*, 6:114; A. T. Pierson, "The Testimony of the Organic Unity of the Bible to Its Inspiration," in *Fundamentals*, 7:58; Lyman Stewart to A. C. Dixon, July 29, 1915, LS.

16 James Robert Smith, "The Fundamentals," *KB* (May 1913), 235, 258.

17 Shailer Mathews, "The Awakening of American Protestantism," *Constructive Quarterly* (March–December 1913), 102, 105, 109.

18 Mathews, "Awakening of American Protestantism," 103, 108.

19 James M. Gray, "The Awakening of American Protestantism," *Bibliotheca Sacra* 70 (October 1913), 653–668; "A Good Answer," *OH* (February 1914), 464; "Millenarianism Misrepresented," *KB* (April 1914), 183.

20 John Roach Straton, *Fighting the Devil in Modern Babylon* (Boston: Stratford, 1929), 192.

21 R. A. Torrey, "The Second Coming of Christ," *KB* (September 1918), 746; Cortland Myers, "War on German Theology," in *Light on Prophecy* (New York: Christian Herald, 1918), 176, 182; T. C. Horton, "Convention Chronicles," *KB* (August 1923), 807.

22 Shirley Jackson Case, "The Premillennial Menace," *BW* (July 1918), 17; Shirley Jackson Case, *The Millennial Hope: A Phase of War-Time Thinking* (Chicago: University of Chicago Press, 1918), 237, 240; Herbert L. Willett, "Activities and Menace of Millennialism," *CC*, August 29, 1918, 8. See also Harris Franklin Rall, "Premillennialism: III. Where Premillennialism Leads," *BW* (November 1919), 617–620.

23 Shailer Mathews, *Will Christ Come Again?* (Hyde Park: American Institute of Sacred Literature, 1917), 3, 15–16. See also "Historical Criticism and the War," *BW* (May 1918), 257.

24 I. M. Haldeman, *Professor Shailer Mathews' Burlesque on the Second Coming of Our Lord Jesus Christ* (New York: published by the author, n.d.), 1; John MacInnis, "Dr. Shailer Mathews and the Premillenarians," *KB* (January 1918), 4; R. A. Torrey, "The Second Coming of Christ," *KB* (September 1918), 745; Philip Mauro, *Dr. Shailer Mathews on Christ's Return* (New York: OH, 1918), 29–30; Daniel Bryant, "Dean Mathews Answered by a Baptist Preacher," *CWM* (June 1918), 792. See also "Will Christ Come Again?," *OH* (January 1918), 406–416; Keith L. Brooks, "What Is the Exact Situation?," *KB* (January 1921), 17–20; and "Dean Shailer Mathews and the Moody Bible Institute," *OH* (August 1917), 108–110.

25 James Allen Geissinger, "Premillennialism Tested by Its Fruits," *Sunday School Journal* (March 1916), 179, 180; Herbert L. Willett, "Millennial Hopes and the War Mood," *CC*, March 14, 1918, 4; James H. Snowden, "Summary of Objections to Premillennialism," *BW* (March 1919), 171; George Preston Mains, *Premillennialism: Non-scriptural, Non-historic, Non-scientific, Non-philosophical* (New York: Abingdon, 1920), 50, 51–52. See also James H. Snowden, *The Coming of the Lord: Will It Be Premillennial?* (New York: Macmillan, 1919); and James H. Snowden, *Is the World Growing Better?* (New York: Macmillan, 1919).

26 T. C. Horton, "Persecuting the Premillennialists," *KB* (October 1920), 917, 918.

27 Shirley Jackson Case, "The Premillennial Menace," *BW* (July 1918), 20; "Unprincipled Methods of Post-Millennialists," *KB* (April 1918), 277; see also R. A. Torrey, "Unprincipled Methods of Post-Millennialists," *OH* (May 1918), 679–681.

28 Keith L. Brooks, "Brethren Can You Beat It?," *KB* (July 1922), 649. On the issue of the Stewarts' money and their relationship to premillennialism see also Gottlieb Hafner, "Premillennialism—A Danger to the Church?," *MM* (December 1921), 712.

29 "Postmillennialism and Pacifism," *CWM* (October 1918), 83; see also James M. Gray, *Postmillennialism and Pacifism* (Chicago: Christian Workers Magazine, 1918).

30 Mark Matthews to Honorable Thomas Marshall, October 29, 1918, folder 11, box 5, accession 97-2, MAM; "Jesus Is Coming," *CWM* (February 1919), 375.

31 Report by Frank L. Turner, in re. Rev. R. A. Torrey, Alleged Violation of the Espionage Act, November 17, 1919, File 377693, Federal Bureau of Investigation, Washington, DC.

32 "Current Criticism of Premillennial Truth," *CWM* (March 1918), 548–551; "Etiquette of the Flag," *CWM* (November 1917), 197; "Penny Patriotism," *KB* (July 1917), 583; "Shall We Help the Profiteers or the Government?," *KB* (June 1918), 458.

33 *General Council Minutes, 1918,* 8, 9, FPHC; H. R. Bursell to J. W. Welch, May 13, 1917, Church Files, Spokane, WA, First Assembly of God Northwest, FPHC.

34 C. H. Mason, "The Kaiser in the Light of the Scriptures," in *The History and Life Work of Elder C. H. Mason,* ed. Mary Mason (Memphis: Church of God in Christ, 1924), 39.

35 R. A. Torrey to James Gray, December 11, 1918, RAT; Henry Stough to John Roach Straton, November 27, 1922, JRS.

36 William Bell Riley, *The Menace of Modernism* (New York: Christian Alliance Publishing Company, 1917), 155; William B. Riley, "The Great Divide, or Christ and the Present Crisis," in *God Hath Spoken* (Philadelphia: Bible Conference Committee, 1919), 27.

37 James Gray to R. A. Torrey, December 26, 1924, RAT. On the significance of MBI and its role in the making of fundamentalism see Timothy Gloege, *Guaranteed Pure: Fundamentalism, Business, and the Making of Modern Evangelicalism* (Chapel Hill: University of North Carolina Press, 2015).

38 Curtis Lee Laws, "Convention Side Lights," *Watchman-Examiner,* July 1, 1920, 834. See also Curtis Lee Laws, "Fundamentalism from the Baptist Viewpoint," *MM* (September 1922), 14–17.

39 "Where the Real Fight Is," *KB* (March 1922), 518; "No 'New Denomination,'" *Moody Monthly* (April 1921), 347. See also Keith L. Brooks, "The Real Pebble in the Critic's Shoe," *KB* (May 1919), 397.

40 J. Frank Norris, "Second Coming the Paramount Issue," *SLT,* April 20, 1923, 5. In a letter to Mordecai Ham, Norris praised Oklahoma Baptist leaders, noting that they were "one hundred per cent Fundamental and by Fundamental I mean pre-millennial." J. Frank Norris to Mordecai Ham, November 12, 1927, folder 824, box 18, JFN.

41 H. L. Mencken, "Doctor Fundamentalis," *BS,* January 18, 1937; J. Gresham Machen, *Christianity and Liberalism* (Grand Rapids, MI: Eerdmans, 1923), 49–50.

42 "Fundamentalists or Evangelicals?," *MM* (October 1923), 50; James M. Gray, *The Deadline of Doctrine around the Church* (Chicago: Moody Bible Institute, 1922), 3; Donald Grey Barnhouse, "Errors of Fundamentalism," *REV* (March 1935), 91; A. C. Dixon, *Two Addresses* (Baltimore: University Baptist Church, n.d.), 13.

43 Aimee Semple McPherson, "Trial of the Modern Liberalist College Professor versus the Lord Jesus Christ," sermon transcript, October 14, 1923, ASM.

44 Stanley Frodsham, "Dear Evangel Reader," *PE,* March 29, 1924, 15; E. N. Bell, "Questions and Answers," *PE,* December 27, 1919, 5; "Ye Are Bought with a Price," *PE,* November 26, 1921, 9; "Bible Study Course by Correspondence," *PE,* February 12, 1927, 15; Stanley H. Frodsham to Alice C. Wood, May 26, 1941, SHF.

45 "Fundamentalism and Modernism: Two Religions," *CC,* January 3, 1924, 5, 6.

46 William Bell Riley, "The Faith of the Fundamentalists," *Current History* (June 1927), 436.

47 "Still Quarreling," *WP,* December 6, 1923; "The Religious Crisis in America," *Manchester Guardian,* August 20, 1923; P. W. Wilson, "Nations Face Great Tasks as 1924 Opens," *NYT,* December 30, 1923.

48 "Is Christ Coming Soon to Rule the World by Force?," *BG,* March 26, 1922; W. P. King, "The Error of Adventism," *AC,* September 9, September 30, October 28, November 11, 1928.

49 "White Baptists," *NBUR,* April 17, 1926, 4; "He Wants to Know," *NBUR,* April 30, 1927, 2; "Among White Baptists," *NBUR,* May 7, 1927, 4; "No Time to Study Isms," *NBUR,* July 1, 1916, 9.

50 E. C. Morris, "Twenty-Seventh Annual Address of E. C. Morris, President, National Baptist Convention," *NBV,* September 17–24, 1921, 9.

51 A. B. Adams, "The Light House," *PC,* June 18, 1932; A. B. Adams, "The Light House," *PC,* September 16, 1933.

52 Ernest Rice McKinney, "This Week," *AN,* April 15, 1925; Ernest Rice McKinney, "Views and Reviews," *PC,* March 19, 1932; Lester A. Walton, "Negro, Freed from Religious Bugaboos of 'Slave' Days, Gradually Drifting from Church," *PC,* September 25, 1926.

53 Roscoe Simmons, "The Week," *CD,* February 7, 1925; December 15, December 29, 1923; January 5, September 20, 1924.

54 "The Church Caucasion," *PC,* May 31, 1924.

55 Robert C. McLeod, "What the People Say: Christianity vs. Atheism," *CD,* June 18, 1927; J. Raymond Henderson, "Sunday Sermon," *ADW,* April 22, 1934; Jesse O. Thomas, "Emory Theology Students Hear Talk by Henderson," *ADW,* October 22, 1934.

56 John M. MacInnis, "The Fundamental Principles of Christianity in the Light of Modern Thinking: X. The Immediate Outlook and Hope of the Church," *KB* (December 1914), 688, 689, 690.

4. The Culture Wars Begin

1 John Roach Straton, *Fighting the Devil in Modern Babylon* (Boston: Stratford, 1929), 85, 101, 103, 106, 111; "Straton and Brady Clash in Church over Stage Morals," *NYT,* February 13, 1922.

2 Anonymous to John Roach Straton, n.d., Harold Clausen to John Roach Straton, May 4, 1922, JRS; "Straton's Sermons Split Congregation," *NYT,* September 20, 1921; Straton, *Fighting the Devil in Modern Babylon,* 32, 149.

3 Member of a Secret Society to John Roach Straton, February 27, 1922, Mrs. Katz to John Roach Straton, September 20, 1920, Wife of a Lodge Member to John Roach Straton, April 16, 1920, A Christian Actor to John Roach Straton, September 14, 1928, JRS.

4 John Roach Straton, "The Second Coming of Christ in the Light of Present World Conditions," October 22, 1922, Sermon Manuscripts, JRS; Straton, *Fighting the Devil in Modern Babylon,* ii, 219.

5 "Signs of the Times," *KB* (July 1919), 587, 588, 590, 593.

6 Bob Jones, *The Perils of America or Where Are We Headed?* (Cleveland, TN: published by the author, 1934), 21; T. W. Callaway, "Cards, Theaters and Dancing," *CWM* (May 1915), 550; Straton, *Fighting the Devil in Modern Babylon,* 33.

7 Straton, *Fighting the Devil in Modern Babylon,* 128. See also "Fight Denounced in Many Pulpits," *NYT,* July 4, 1921; and "Pictures in Pulpit Fight as He Saw It," *NYT,* July 11, 1921.

8 Gerald Winrod, *The Great American Home* (Wichita: Defender Publishers, n.d.), 9; "Menace of the Movies," *KB* (May 1916), 389; "'Movies' and the Theater," *CWM* (January 1916), 373. See also "The Outrageous Blasphemy of the Movies," *KB* (July 1918), 550; "Let's Have Done with the Movies," *KB* (August 1918), 642; Clara Winterton, "The Morals of the Movies," *MM* (May 1923), 421–422; and L. Ray Miller, "May Christians Attend Picture Shows?," *MM* (March 1925), 317–318.

9 "Straton and Brady Clash in Church over Stage Morals," *NYT,* February 13, 1922; "Lillian Gish Speaks for Stage in Pulpit," *NYT,* February 20, 1922.

10 Roscoe Arbuckle to Rev. M. A. Matthews, September 29, 1924, folder 5, box 1, accession 97-2, MAM; "Movies and Morals," *MM* (June 1924), 496.

11 T. C. Horton, "Clean Up the Movies," *KB* (October 1922), 990; John Roach Straton to Pictorial Clubs, Inc., January 15, 1923, JRS; Harold J. Ockenga, "The Movies—or—Should Christians Boycott the Films?," n.d., 10, Sermon Manuscripts, HJO.

12 Aimee Semple McPherson, "Converting the World by Radio," *BC* (July 1923), 15.

13 On evangelicals and radio see Tona Hangen, *Redeeming the Dial: Radio, Religion, and Popular Culture in America* (Chapel Hill: University of North Carolina Press, 2002).

14 M. A. Matthews, "Interview in re Our National Duty," Sermonettes 1917, box 16, accession 97-2, MAM; Billy Sunday, *Face to Face with Satan* (Knoxville: Prudential Publishing, 1923), 75. See also "Our Immigration Problem," *CWM* (September 1914), 14–15.

15 Charles Fuller, "Prophetic Studies, Lesson Seven," Radio Bible Class, 1933, box 11, CEF.

16 D. M. Ralston, "The Latest Preparations for Antichrist," *MM* (September 1920), 14; Luke Rader, *Mystery Babylon from Which Comes the Antichrist*, 4th ed. (Minneapolis: Book Stall, n.d.); Arno C. Gaebelein, *The Conflict of the Ages* (New York: OH, 1933), 99; M. A. Matthews to Woodrow Wilson, August 20, 1919, folder 3, box 5, accession 97-2, MAM.

17 "The League of Nations and the Jewish Peril," *MM* (February 1921), 254; James M. Gray, "'The Jewish Peril' and How to Meet It," *MM* (July 1921), 469–471; A. C. Dixon, "Co-Religionists," *KB* (April 1921), 314; "Henry Ford's Confession," *MM* (September 1927), 3.

18 *"We Hold These Truths . . ."* (New York: League of American Writers, 1939), 121; "Misrepresenting 'Our Hope,'" *OH* (December 1939), 379, 382; "An Unjust, Unfair Criticism," *OH* (April 1934), 591.

19 William Bell Riley, *Protocols and Communism* (Minneapolis: L. W. Camp, [1934?]), 13; William Bell Riley, "The Blood of the Jew vs. the Blood of Jesus," *Pilot* (November 1934), 26; Gerald Winrod, *Hitler in Prophecy* (Wichita: Defender Publishers, 1933), 15. See also William Bell Riley, "Why Recognize Russia and Rag Germany?," *Pilot* (January 1934), 110.

20 William E. Blackstone to Nathan Straus, January 17, 1921, folder 6, box 7, WEB; J. Frank Norris, *Did the Jews Write the Protocols?* (Fort Worth: published by the author, n.d.); Stanley H. Frodsham to William Burton McCafferty, June 12, 1936, McCafferty Papers, FPHC; H. A. Ironside, *The Lamp of Prophecy or Signs of the Times* (Grand Rapids, MI: Zondervan, 1940), 110; Keith L. Brooks to William Burton McCafferty, August 3,

1936, McCafferty Papers, FPHC; Keith L. Brooks, "Has Oswald Smith Said the Last Word?," *PM* (November 1936), 21; Keith L. Brooks, "Who Gets Your Money When the Lord Comes?," *PM* (October 1936), 20. On Brooks's earlier prejudices, see for example Keith L. Brooks, "Did the Jews Crucify Christ?," *KB* (September 1920), 827; Keith L. Brooks, "Are the Protocols a Forgery?," *PM* (May 1932), 12–13; and "Winrod Reveals a Hidden Hand," *PM* (February 1933), 20.

21 On the nature of the Klan in this period see Leonard J. Moore, *Citizen Klansmen: The Ku Klux Klan in Indiana, 1921–1928* (Chapel Hill: University of North Carolina Press, 1991).

22 J. W. Welch to E. F. Cunningham, March 7, 1924, Ministers file— Cunningham, Eli F., FPHC.

23 "The Ku Klux Klan," *MM* (February 1923), 240; A. R. Funderburk, "The Ku Klux Klan—Is It of God?," *MM* (March 1923), 291–292.

24 John Bradbury, "Defending the Ku Klux Klan—A Reply to Mr. Funderburk," *MM* (May 1923), 420, 421.

25 "Ku Klux Klan," *MM* (June 1923), 459; "The Ku Klux Klan," *MM* (December 1923), 163; Bob Shuler, "Investigate the Ku Klux Klan," *MM* (December 1923), 182.

26 "Knights of the Ku Klux Klan to Rev. J. Frank Norris, September 10, 1922," *SLT,* September 15, 1922, 4; Mrs. W. A. Ash to J. Frank Norris, March 27, 1928, reel 14, JFN-M; William James Mahoney to John Roach Straton, November 24, 1922, JRS; Kanton Klan No. 212 to Rev. William A. Sunday, December 4, 1931, WAS; Frances Wayne, "Mrs. M'Pherson Is Kidnaped by Klan and Confers Blessing on Masked Band," *Denver Post,* June 18, 1922.

27 Paul Jones, "Good Citizenship to Solve Problem, Negroes Are Told," *BG,* November 20, 1917; "Billy Sunday as a Peacemaker between the Races," *Current Opinion* (March 1918), 201.

28 Francis J. Grimke, "Billy Sunday Cowered before Race Prejudice in Washington," *CD,* March 23, 1918; "Billy Sunday's Opportunity," *NBUR,* November 24, 1917, 1.

29 "One Token," *AP* (February–March 1907), 7; Aimee Semple McPherson, *This Is That,* 2nd rev. ed. (Los Angeles: Foursquare Publications, 1923), 118–119; Aimee Semple McPherson, "Pentecostal Camp Meeting, Key West, Florida," *BC* (March 1918), 10; Aimee Semple McPherson, "Colored Camp Meeting, Key West," *BC* (March 1918), 7; "Two Special Services Were Held for the Colored People," *BC* (July 1921), 14.

30 Donald Grey Barnhouse, "The Three Sons of Noah: The Black Man," *REV* (July 1932), 311.

31 William Bell Riley, *The Conflict of Christianity with Its Counterfeits* (Minneapolis: published by the author, [1940]), 106; William Bell Riley, "Bloodless but Red," in *New Dealism Exposed,* ed. J. Frank Norris (Fort Worth: Fundamentalist Publishing Company, n.d.), 30.

32 "The American Negro," *MM* (October 1920), 54; A. C. Dixon, "Colored Adult Suffrage," *Living Word,* January 30, 1899, in folder 3, box 5, ACD; "The American Negro," *MM* (October 1920), 54.

33 L. Nelson Bell to mother (Ruth Lee McCue Bell), December 3, 1933, folder 6, box 1, LNB; Riley, *Conflict of Christianity with Its Counterfeits,* 71; Emmett Marshall, "On Massie Case," *PC,* May 21, 1932. On condemnations of lynching, see also "Ungodly Speeches," *CWM* (December 1919), 273; "Negro Rights," *MM* (July 1921), 467; James M. Gray, "The Relation of the Christian Church to Civil Government," *Moody Bible Institute of Chicago Bulletin* (July–August 1922); and "Southern White Women Appeal for Justice," *MM* (January 1922), 748.

34 John Roach Straton, "The Reign of Lawlessness; or the Menace of the Mob in America," n.d., Sermon Manuscripts, JRS.

35 A. C. Dixon, "The Future of the Educated Negro," folder 5, box 1, ACD; John R. Rice, *The Home: Courtship, Marriage and Children* (Wheaton, IL: SOTL Publishers, 1946), 53; John R. Rice, "Relations between Christian Whites and Negroes," *SOTL,* June 8, 1945, 3; W. O. H. Garman, "America: Her Providential Past, Her Unsettled and Disturbing Present Condition, Her Only Solutions," sermon outlines [1926], WOHG; "Dr. Talbot's Question Box," *KB* (January 1946), 23.

36 Billy Sunday, *Address by Billy Sunday: Americanism* (Philadelphia: Law Enforcement League of Philadelphia, April 10, 1922), 23.

37 Donald Grey Barnhouse, "Tomorrow: Current Events in the Light of Bible Prophecy," *REV* (September 1938), 396, 399.

38 Harold J. Ockenga, "Race Prejudice," c. 1934, Harold J. Ockenga, "The Solution to the Social Question," October 10, 1943, 8, Sermon Manuscripts, HJO.

39 A Negro Mother to J. Frank Norris, n.d., reel 16, JFN-M. Another writer asked Norris: "Why pick on the negro, didn't your God make the negro to?" Anonymous to J. Frank Norris, n.d., reel 16, JFN-M.

40 Donald Grey Barnhouse, "Tomorrow: Current Events in the Light of Bible Prophecy," *REV* (September 1937), 398; Dan Gilbert, *One Minute before Midnight* (Los Angeles: Jewish Hope, 1945), 28–29; Wilbur Smith, "Paul's Final Description of the End of This Age," *OH* (February 1941), 528; Paul Rader, *The Coming World Dictator* (Chicago: World Wide Gospel Couriers, 1934), 12. Ockenga lamented that Americans tolerated "homosexuality, fornication and adultery." Harold J. Ockenga, "The

American Way of Life and Its Substitutes," May 28, 1944, 3, Sermon Manuscripts, HJO.

41 Sunday, *Address by Billy Sunday,* 42.

42 Sunday, *Address by Billy Sunday,* 42; John Roach Straton, *The Menace of Immorality in Church and State* (New York: Doran, 1920), 40; unidentified author to John Roach Straton, February 6, 1925, A. E. Holmes to John Roach Straton, April 19, 1920, JRS; Bob Jones, *The Modern Woman* (Montgomery, AL: Paragon Press, [1923]), 9–10; on additional fundamentalists blaming women for men's sexual sins, see Oswald J. Smith, *Is the Antichrist at Hand?,* 5th ed. (Toronto: Tabernacle, 1926), 51; and Elizabeth Knauss, "The Red Flag among American Young People," *SST,* May 31, 1930, 333.

43 "Bobbing the Hair," *MM* (May 1924), 471; Albert Kinzler, "What about Hair-Bobbing?," *MM* (August 1924), 605; "As to Hair Bobbing," *MM* (October 1924), 54; "If a Woman Have [*sic*] Long Hair It Is a Glory to Her," *MM* (November 1924), 101–102; Frank Bartleman, *Flapper Evangelism, Fashion's Fools, Headed for Hell* (Los Angeles: printed by the author, [1920?]), n.p.; John R. Rice, *Bobbed Hair, Bossy Wives, and Women Preachers* (Wheaton, IL: Sword of the Lord Publishers, 1941). See also A. R. Funderburk, "Serving the God of Fashion—Plain Speech from Pastor to People," *MM* (July 1925), 499–500.

44 Peter Z. Easton, "Does Woman Represent God?," *CWM* (August 1912), 785, 787.

45 "Woman Suffrage in England," *CWM* (April 1913), 499; "The Women Suffragist Movement," *OH* (September 1912), 169; Keith L. Brooks, "Woman Suffrage and the Bible," *KB* (August 1919), 701–702. For additional fundamentalist critiques of woman suffrage see "The Coming Woman," *CWM* (June 1913), 627; "Fire Losses by Suffragettes," *OH* (October 1913), 240; "The Outrageous Mrs. Pankhurst," *OH* (January 1914), 435; "Our Current Issue," *CWM* (November 1915), 169; William Parker, "True Womanhood," *CWM* (November 1915), 184–185; W. P. Wilks, "More Light on Woman's Suffrage," *WR,* March 9, 1916, 3; Margaret C. Worthington, "Woman Suffrage—A Reform, but unto What?," *CWM* (October 1916), 112–113; "Woman Suffrage," *CWM* (August 1917), 933; and "Disadvantages of Woman Suffrage," *CWM* (August 1917), 944–946. Billy Sunday and John Roach Straton favored woman suffrage. "Sunday to See Wilson," *WP,* January 8, 1915; John Roach Straton, "The Destiny of the Lost Rib," n.d., Sermon Manuscripts, JRS.

46 Paul Rader, *The End of Time* (Chicago: Chicago Gospel Tabernacle, n.d.), 6.

47 Harold L. Lundquist, "The Decline of the American Home," *MM* (November 1937), 115; "The Education of Women," *KB* (April 1916), 294; T. C. Horton, "Wanted—More Mothers," *KB* (February 1921),

107; A. C. Dixon, *Lights and Shadows of American Life* (New York: Revell, 1898), 181; M. A. Matthews, "Woman's Throne," n.d., Punchettes, folder 7, box 7, accession 97-2, MAM; M. A. Matthews, "Cowardly Husbands," Sermonettes 1923, box 17, accession 97-2, MAM.

48 Jay C. Kellogg, *Modern Women in Prophecy* (Tacoma, WA: Whole Gospel Crusaders of America, 1933), 54.

49 Henry Stough, "Is Marriage a Failure?," sermon notebooks, 3–4, folder 6, box 1, HS.

50 Straton, *Menace of Immorality,* 79; Mark Matthews, "Childlessness the Nation's Curse," *MM* (November 1929), 110; Stough, "Is Marriage a Failure?," 9.

51 Donald Grey Barnhouse, "Spank Your Children . . . !," *REV* (March 1938), 111; John R. Rice, "The Bible on Child Correction and Discipline," *SOTL,* March 22, 1940, 4; John R. Rice, "God Save the American Home!," *SOTL,* November 9, 1945, 7. See also Donald Grey Barnhouse, "Spank Your Children," *REV* (November 1932), 450.

52 "Race Suicide," *KB* (May 1918), 366–367; "Listen, America, to Mussolini," *OH* (June 1934), 740; W. Wyeth Willard, "The Christian Home," *SST,* April 23, 1949, 367. See also "World Suicide by Birth Control," *OH* (September 1932), 165.

53 "Evangelist Shows Atlanta Girls How to Catch Husbands," *BG,* December 15, 1917; Heartbroken Mother to John Roach Straton, January 13, [19??], Edwin B. Van Aken to John Roach Straton, April 12, 1920, JRS; John R. Rice, "The President's Birthday Balls," *SOTL,* January 28, 1938, 2; Rice, *Home,* 156; "Birth Control," *MM* (March 1931), 336.

54 Henry Stough, "Mysteries and Tragedies of Motherhood," sermon notebooks, n.d., folder 6, box 3, HS.

55 Henry Stough, "Highlights and Spotlights," sermon notebooks, n.d., 28, folder 3, box 1; Henry Stough, "The Scarlet Man," sermon notebooks, n.d., folder 6, box 3, HS.

56 Keith L. Brooks, "The Problem of Depression Babies," *PM* (February 1935), 16–17; Keith L. Brooks, *What Does the Bible Teach about Birth Control?* (Los Angeles: American Prophetic League, n.d.), 3–4. Brooks also addressed the question of artificial insemination, which he interpreted as a dangerous practice akin to adultery. Keith L. Brooks, "Sins Comparable to Those of Sodom and Gomorrah," *PM* (June 1937), 9–11.

5. American Education on Trial

1 William Jennings Bryan, "God and Evolution," *NYT,* February 26, 1922.

2 Harry Emerson Fosdick, "Attacks W. J. B.," *NYT,* March 12, 1922;
   Harry Emerson Fosdick, *Shall the Fundamentalists Win?* (n.p., 1922).

3 On the ramifications of this decision, see Randall J. Stephens and Karl
   Giberson, *The Anointed: Evangelical Truth in a Secular Age* (Cambridge,
   MA: Harvard University Press, 2011).

4 On MBI's origins and evolution see Timothy Gloege, *Guaranteed Pure:
   Fundamentalism, Business, and the Making of Modern Evangelicalism* (Chapel
   Hill: University of North Carolina Press, 2015).

5 James Gray to the Members of the Faculty, July 29, 1908, JMG; Wilbur
   Smith to Harold Lundquist, September 20, 1939, box 15, WMS.

6 Lyman Stewart to Dr. White, March 2, 1911, LS.

7 Lyman Stewart to Will, May, and Fred, September 4, 1914, Lyman Stewart to Henry Huntington, March 5, 1913, LS; "Old enemy" quote from
   Lyman Stewart to Porter Phipps, August 7, 1920, LS.

8 Lyman Stewart to Giles Kellogg, April 17, 1907, Lyman Stewart to Milton Stewart, July 21, 1914, LS; R. A. Torrey, "Questions and Answers,"
   KB (December 1914), 720.

9 James Gray to Mr. Fitt, May 22, 1907, JMG; Lyman Stewart to Milton
   Stewart, September 14, 1914, LS.

10 William Bell Riley, "What Manner of Persons Ought We to Be?," in
   Light on Prophecy (New York: Christian Herald, 1918), 295. On African-
   American encounters with fundamentalism see Albert G. Miller, "The
   Construction of a Black Fundamentalist Worldview," in *African Ameri-
   cans and the Bible: Sacred Texts and Social Textures,* ed. Vincent L. Wimbush
   (New York: Continuum, 2000), 712–727.

11 R. A. Torrey to James Gray, March 6, 1919, RAT. On the history of
   Bible schools see Virginia Lieson Brereton, *Training God's Army: The
   American Bible School, 1880–1940* (Bloomington: Indiana University
   Press, 1990).

12 "Concerning the Residence of Colored Students," internal memo, n.d.,
   and "Residence of Negro Students," internal memo, November 21,
   1938, Department Files, Moody Bible Institute Archives, Chicago.

13 John W. Ham, "Atheism and Suicide in Our Universities," *MM* (April
   1927), 388; Keith L. Brooks, *Prophecy and the Tottering Nations,* rev.
   and enl. ed. (Grand Rapids, MI: Zondervan, 1938), 41; William Bell
   Riley, "Sovietizing the State through the Schools," *KB* (October
   1923), 8.

14 Dan Gilbert, "Deadly Poison Gas in Tax-Supported Schools," *KB* (Feb-
   ruary 1938), 46; Dan Gilbert, "The Anti-christ Advance in the Colleges,"
   Pilot (November 1938), 40; T. C. Horton, "Pray, Brethren, Pray," *KB*
   (December 1920), 1110.

15 "U.C. Denounced as Atheistic by Militant Church Group," *LAT,* January 4, 1940; Gilbert, "Deadly Poison Gas," 47.

16 John Roach Straton, "How Rationalism in the Pulpit Makes Worldliness in the Pew," *MM* (January 1923), 193; "The Chicago Criminals," *KB* (November 1924), 685; "The Franks Case," *MM* (August 1924), 593; "The Death Penalty," *MM* (October 1924), 54.

17 Norton F. Brand, "The Bible in the Public Schools," *CWM* (July 1913), 699; William Bell Riley, *The Menace of Modernism* (New York: Christian Alliance Publishing Company, 1917), 84; Upton Sinclair to H. L. Mencken, September 24, 1926, Correspondence, box 7, Sinclair Manuscripts Collection, Lilly Library, Indiana University, Bloomington; Anonymous to FDR, October 17, 1935, Oregon file, collection 21-A, FDR.

18 "The Nation's Need," *KB* (October 1924), 612; "Cardinal Observations," *KB* (June 1912), 142; Henry Stough, "Why I Am a Protestant," Lectures on Anglo-Israel, vol. 2, folder 13, box 1; "Roman Catholic Education," *CWM* (March 1913), 434.

19 "Undue Emphasis on Sex Problems the Devil's Snare," *KB* (June 1915), 466; "Instruction in Sex Hygiene," *CWM* (January 1916), 348; Dan Gilbert, "Significance of the News," *KB* (July 1941), 258.

20 Billy Sunday, "Feed the Hungary World," *CWM* (January 1916), 353.

21 "January 5, 1913: The Creation," *CWM* (December 1912), 263; "Theistic Evolution," *CWM* (July 1915), 690–691; "Christianity and Evolution," *CWM* (January 1918), 366–368.

22 Donald Grey Barnhouse, "The Bible Says . . ." *REV* (December 1932), 498; "Dr. Talbot's Question Box," *KB* (January 1946), 22.

23 A. C. Dixon, "Why I Am Not an Evolutionist," *CWM* (November 1916), 178; R. A. Torrey, *What the War Teaches or the Greatest Lessons of 1917* (Los Angeles: Biola Book Room, 1918), 10–11; "Religious Heterodoxy and the World War," *CWM* (December 1918), 227.

24 T. C. Horton, "Rally to the Ranks!" *KB* (August 1923), 787, 788.

25 James M. Gray, *Why a Christian Cannot Be an Evolutionist* (Richmond, VA: Harvey Brown, 1925); F. C. Jennings, "Evolution? An Answer to Shailer Matthews [*sic*]," *OH* (May 1913), 668; J. W. Porter, "Can an Evolutionist Be Saved?," *WR* (February 19, 1925), 7; A. C. Dixon, *Two Addresses* (Baltimore: University Baptist Church, n.d.), 25; "No Time to Study Isms," *NBUR,* July 1, 1916, 9.

26 "Side by Side—The Deicides," *KB* (May 1925), 197.

27 "Dr. Straton Assails Museum of History," *NYT,* March 9, 1924; N. C. Nelson to John Roach Straton, April 7, 1924, JRS; James M. Warnack, "Do You Want to Start a War?," *LAT,* March 16, 1925. On the long

history of fundamentalist antievolutionism see Michael Lienesch, *In the Beginning: Fundamentalism, the Scopes Trial, and the Making of the Antievolution Movement* (Chapel Hill: University of North Carolina Press, 2007).

28 On Bryan see Michael Kazin, *A Godly Hero: The Life of William Jennings Bryan* (New York: Knopf, 2006).

29 William Jennings Bryan, *The Menace of Darwinism* (New York: Revell, 1921), 5; William Jennings Bryan, "Misrepresentations of Darwinism and Its Disciples," *MM* (April 1923), 331.

30 J. Frank Norris, "Address on Evolution before the Texas Legislature," *SLT,* February 23, 1923, 1–4; T. C. Horton, "Dr. Norris in the Texas Legislature," *KB* May 1923, 455; "Extra Copies This Issue," *B&C,* July 18, 1928, 1; B. M. B., "Help Us Put Evolution Out of Our Public Schools," *B&C,* October 10, 1928, 1; "Straton to Fight Darwin in Schools," *NYT,* February 9, 1922; Theophile Guerin to John Roach Straton, December 3, 1928, JRS; see also Keith L. Brooks, "The Coming Generation—What?," *KB* (June 1923), 570; and Mrs. Newton Wray, "The Tragedy of Religionless Public Schools and How Some Texas Communities Avoid It," *MM* (July 1924), 552–554.

31 Edward J. Larson, *Summer for the Gods: The Scopes Trial and America's Continuing Debate over Science and Religion* (New York: Basic Books, 1997), 48; *The World's Most Famous Court Trial, Tennessee Evolution Case* (Cincinnati: National Book Company, 1925), 4–5.

32 Clarence Darrow, *The Story of My Life* (New York: Scribner's, 1932), 249.

33 Frederick Lewis Allen, *Only Yesterday: An Informal History of the 1920's* (New York: Perennial Classics, 1931), 174.

34 *World's Most Famous Court Trial,* 74, 79, 87.

35 *World's Most Famous Court Trial,* 172.

36 H. L. Mencken, "Mencken Declares Strictly Fair Trial Is beyond Ken of Tennessee Fundamentalists," *BS,* 1925; H. L. Mencken, "Battle Now Over, Mencken Sees; Genesis Triumphant and Ready for New Jousts," *BS,* July 18, 1925.

37 *World's Most Famous Court Trial,* 292, 295.

38 *World's Most Famous Court Trial,* 288, 299.

39 *World's Most Famous Court Trial,* 317.

40 *World's Most Famous Court Trial,* 333.

41 H. L. Mencken, "Bryan," *BS,* July 27, 1925.

42 "William Jennings Bryan," *MM* (September 1925), 3; "Bryan the Brave," *KB* (September 1925), 379.

43 "William Jennings Bryan," *MM,* 3; Donald Grey Barnhouse, "Tennessee and Evolution," *REV* (October 1931), 334.

44 "Bryan's Last Speech Is Supreme Plea for Bible," *NBV,* August 8, 1925, 1; W. E. B. DuBois, "The Shape of Fear," *North American Review,* June 1, 1926, 296; "Dinner to Darrow on 70th Birthday," *AN,* May 4, 1927; "Ingersoll's Ashes," *CD,* April 30, 1932. On race and the Scopes trial see Jeffrey P. Moran, "Reading Race into the Scopes Trial: African American Elites, Science, and Fundamentalism," *Journal of American History* 90:3 (December 2003): 891–911.

45 Dudley Joseph Whitney, "Errors of Fundamentalist Science," *KB* (February 1928), 82.

46 "The Fight against Evolution," *MM* (April 1926), 364; "Ostrich States," *MM* (May 1926), 411.

47 Charles Trumbull, "The Los Angeles Fundamentals Convention," *SST,* July 12, 1930, 412.

48 The identification of fundamentalism with the South has been carefully documented by Mary Beth Swetnam Mathews in *Rethinking Zion: How the Print Media Placed Fundamentalism in the South* (Knoxville: University of Tennessee Press, 2006).

6. Seeking Salvation with the GOP

1 J. Frank Norris, "Salvation through Christ Versus Salvation through Romanism," in Norris, *Is America at the Crossroads? Or Roman Catholicism vs. Protestant Christianity* (Fort Worth: J. L. Rhodes, 1928), 43.

2 J. Frank Norris, "The Candidacy of Al Smith," in Norris, *Is America at the Crossroads?,* 3.

3 Shailer Mathews, "Ten Years of American Protestantism," *North American Review* (May 1923), 592.

4 James M. Gray, *"And Such Were Some of You,"* A Gospel Temperance Sermon (Chicago: Bible Institute Colportage Association, n.d.), 5, 7–8, 14.

5 "Ruthless Greed of Liquor Traffic," *KB* (July 1915), 558; Kaiser Bill and Kaiser Beer," *KB* (August 1918), 644; "Economies That Would Count," *KB* (October 1917), 872. See also "The President's Attitude on the Drink Question," *KB* (October 1917), 875.

6 Billy Sunday, *Get on the Water Wagon* (Sturgis, MI: Journal Publishing Co., 1915), 3; "Full House Hears Sunday on Jacob," *NYT,* April 12, 1917; William Jennings Bryan, "Billy Sunday and His Work," *Commoner* (December 1916), 1.

7 William E. Blackstone, *Jesus Is Coming,* 3rd revised and expanded ed. (Chicago: Revell, 1908), 234; W. H. Cossum, *Mountain Peaks of Prophecy and Sacred History* (Chicago: Evangel Publishing House, 1911), 149. On

the ways in which class divisions influenced the evolution of fundamentalism see Timothy Gloege, *Guaranteed Pure: Fundamentalism, Business, and the Making of Modern Evangelicalism* (Chapel Hill: University of North Carolina Press, 2015).

8 *Look Out! He Is Coming* (Framingham, MA: Christian Workers Union, 1919), 2; C. I. Scofield, *The World's Approaching Crisis* (New York: OH, 1913), 12, 22; "Wicked Follies of the Rich," *KB* (February 1917), 100.

9 Philip Mauro, "Discontent of the Laboring Classes," *OH* (October 1912), 229.

10 "The War in Colorado," *OH* (July 1914), 38; "Increasing Strikes and the Demands of the People," *OH* (November 1916), 292.

11 "Two Anarchists Is Norris' Theme," *SLT,* June 12, 1919, n.p.

12 Chas. J. Waehlte, "The Red Terror," *KB* (September 1922), 908; L. Nelson Bell to friends, January 21, 1927, folder 1, box 1, LNB; L. Nelson Bell to mother (Ruth Lee McCue Bell), July 21, 1929, folder 2, box 1, LNB.

13 Billy Sunday, *Address by Billy Sunday: Americanism* (Philadelphia: Law Enforcement League of Philadelphia, April 10, 1922), 18; "At High Noon of Civilization Soviet Russia Rejects God," *NBUR,* October 3, 1931, 1; "Communism Is a Threat to Our Form of Government," *NBUR,* September 4, 1937, 4; R. A. Torrey, "Our President's Colossal Blunder," *KB* (March 1919), 202; "Bolshevism and Christianity," *CWM* (October 1919), 113.

14 Louis Bauman, *God and Gog; or, The Coming Meet between Judah's Lion and Russia's Bear* (n.p.: published by the author, 1934), 5, 6; "Professor Einstein, the Scientist, Agnostic and Socialist," *OH* (May 1931), 672, 673; William Bell Riley, "Bloodless but Red," in *New Dealism Exposed,* ed. J. Frank Norris (Fort Worth: Fundamentalist Publishing Company, n.d.), 28.

15 "Bolshevism," *WR,* September 2, 1920, 8; Mark A. Matthews to J. Edgar Hoover, July 21, 1936, folder 35, box 1, accession 97-3, MAM; J. Edgar Hoover to Mark A. Matthews, July 30, 1936, J. Edgar Hoover to Mark A. Matthews, July 7, 1939, folder 11, box 1, accession 97-3, MAM. On fundamentalist support for the Red raids see "Bolshevism a Real Danger in America," *OH* (October 1919), 229–231, and "Red Propaganda," *MM* (July 1923), 507.

16 James M. Gray, *Modernism: A Revolt against Christianity, a Foe to Good Government* (Chicago: Bible Institute Colportage Association, 1924), 18; see also James M. Gray, "Modernism a Foe to Good Government," *MM* (July 1924), 545–547.

17 Sunday, *Address by Billy Sunday,* 14.

18 Walter Scott, "Signs of the Near Return of Our Lord," *OH* (August 1921), 120, 121; W. O. H. Garman, "The Gathering Force of the Spirit of Anti Christ," sermon outlines, 7–8, WOHG; M. A. Matthews to Joseph Tumulty, November 26, 1919, folder 4, box 5, accession 97-2, MAM; Sunday, *Address by Billy Sunday,* 15–16. See also "No Strikes in Russia," *KB* (October 1924), 627.

19 "At the Mercy of the Workers," *MM* (November 1922), 92; "Eugene V. Debs," *MM* (September 1922), 4; "Government Control," *MM* (December 1921), 969; "Government, Hands Off!," *MM* (November 1922), 92.

20 Sunday, *Address by Billy Sunday,* 34–35; William Ashley Sunday, sermon notebook, folder 10, box 31, WAS.

21 J. Frank Norris, "League of Nations," *SLT,* November 18, 1920, n.p.; B. M. B., "The League of Nations Foretold in the Bible," *B&C,* October 27, 1920, 1; B. M. B., "Shall Unscrupulous Politicians Control?," *B&C,* September 29, 1920, 1.

22 M. A. Matthews, "Sacrificing the World for the Presidency," 1, 4, sermonettes 1920, box 17, accession 97-2, MAM.

23 Rupert Hughes, "In Praise of Harding's Style," *NYT,* October 24, 1920.

24 Charles E. Hard to William E. Blackstone, November 16, 1920, folder 6, box 7; William E. Blackstone to Senator Warren G. Harding, December 30, 1920, folder 5, box 7, WEB; "How Did You Vote?," *MM* (December 1920), 151.

25 T. C. Horton, "The Preaching President," *KB* (September 1923), 899; "Fourth of July," *MM* (July 1921), 467; "Good Government," *MM* (November 1921), 645.

26 M. A. Matthews, "In Memoriam: Warren G. Harding," 3, 8, sermonettes 1923, box 18, accession 97-2, MAM; Lyman Stewart to Grand-daughter, August 8, 1923, LS.

27 "President Coolidge on Service," *MM* (June 1924), 496; "Smith Out of Step, Says Dry Leader," *NYT,* June 23, 1924. Silent Cal had actually been the choice of *Christian Workers* editors for the top spot on the GOP ticket in 1920 due to his commitment to "law and order," and during the campaign when Coolidge's campaign managers printed a booklet, "Law and Order—Coolidge," *Christian Workers* took credit for raising the theme. "Garfield and Coolidge," *CWM* (February 1920), 442; "Law and Order—Coolidge," *CWM* (August 1920), 925.

28 "Religion and Politics," *MM* (September 1924), 3.

29 "Catholics and Liquor Men Lining Up for Democratic Nominee for President," *B&C,* October 22, 1924, 1; "Tax Reform," *MM* (September 1924), 4; "Government Control," *MM* (September 1922), 4.

30 "President Coolidge on State Rights," *MM* (July 1926), 507.

31 Charles C. Marshall, "An Open Letter to the Honorable Alfred E. Smith," *Atlantic* (April 1927), www.theatlantic.com/magazine/archive /1927/04/an-open-letter-to-the-honorable-alfred-e-smith/6523/?single _page=true.

32 Alfred E. Smith, "Catholic and Patriot," *Atlantic* (May 1927), www.the atlantic.com/magazine/archive/1927/05/catholic-and-patriot/6522/3 /?single_page=true.

33 F. Bartleman, "Passing Events," *Bridegroom's Messenger,* December 1, 1911, 3; "Beware of Rome," *KB* (February 1917), 101; M. A. Matthews to Thomas Marshall, December 10, 1918, folder 11, box 5, accession 97-2, MAM; R. A. Torrey, "Our President's Colossal Blunder," *KB* (March 1919), 202, 204; see also Keith L. Brooks, "The Power behind the Throne," *KB* (July 1920), 640–641.

34 Lewis Sperry Chafer to Ralph Norton, June 28, 1928, LSC.

35 "Straton Reiterates Charge against Smith," *NYT,* August 27, 1928; Alfred N. Phillips, Jr., to John Roach Straton, August 30, 1928, JRS.

36 "Shall Christians Vote?," *KB* (August 1928), 462; Walter L. Lingle, "Why Hesitate at a Roman Catholic President," *MM* (June 1928), 467; J. Narver Gortner, "Fight the Good Fight of Faith," sermon manuscripts (June 1934), JNG. See also "Governor Smith's Religion," *MM* (March 1927), 324; "Don't Fail to Register," *MM* (September 1928), 4; and "Opinion Seems Solid for Hoover," *FC,* October 31, 1928.

37 John Roach Straton to J. Frank Norris, April 4, 1928, JRS.

38 Anonymous to John Roach Straton, October 10, 1928, with clipping purportedly from *Birmingham Post;* Mary Mansfield to John Roach Straton, September 13, 1928, JRS.

39 Alvin D. Covin to John Roach Straton, August 9, 1928, [illegible] to John Roach Straton, August 13, 1928, JRS.

40 A Republican and babtist [*sic*] to John Roach Straton, n.d., Anonymous to John Roach Straton, n.d., Sarah Clark Wolfe to John Roach Straton, August 27, 1928, Harry E. Goshen, Jr., to John Roach Straton, August 9, 1928, Anonymous to John Roach Straton, n.d., A 200% AMERICAN to John Roach Straton, n.d., JRS.

41 [F. C. Linders?] to John Roach Straton, August 11, 1928, Helen E. Simon to John Roach Straton, August 15, 1928, William C. Wilson to John Roach Straton, September 1, 1928, Charles E. Thompson to John Roach Straton, August 16, 1928, Al Whiton to John Roach Straton, October 3, 1928, J. H. Fletcher to John Roach Straton, August 20, 1928, JRS.

42 James Haggerty to John Roach Straton, August 10, 1928, John Gaynor to John Roach Straton, August 12, 1928, A Reader to John Roach Straton, August 11, 1928, JRS.

43 J. Frank Norris to R. B. Craeger [sic], November 25, 1927, J. Frank Nor-
    ris to R. B. Craeger [sic], March 19, 1928, reel 6, JFN-M.
44 Old Jim Anderson to J. Frank Norris, July 15, 1929, folder 2, box 1, JFN.
45 J. Frank Norris to R. B. Craeger [sic], January 23, 1928, J. Frank Norris
    to R. B. Craeger [sic], April 12, 1928, reel 6, JFN-M; Sarah Belfour to
    J. Frank Norris, October 29, 1928, folder 65, box 2, JFN.
46 William Ward Ayer to J. Frank Norris, September 12, 1928, folder 2,
    box 1, JFN; D. N. Jackson, "Political Hypocrisy," B&C, July 11, 1928, 5.
    See also "Platform Adopted by Dry Democrats," WR, August 2, 1928, 5.
47 Mordecai Ham to J. Frank Norris, March 5, 1928, J. Frank Norris to
    Mordecai Ham, May 19, 1928, folder 825, box 18; S. J. Betts to J. Frank
    Norris, August 31, 1928, folder 65, box 2, JFN.
48 "Ben M. Bogard's Speech in City Park, Little Rock," B&C, August 1,
    1928, 5.
49 "Ben M. Bogard's Speech," 6; "White Man's(?)Party," B&C, September
    5, 1928, 10; "Negro Equality and Al Smith," B&C, September 19, 1928,
    3; "Startling, Disgusting Facts, Al Smith and Tammany Hall Negro
    Equality," B&C, October 10, 1928, 2.
50 Guy Rogers to Rev. Philpott, October 1, 1928, Guy Rogers to Rev.
    Philpott, October 20, 1928, folder 6, box 1, MC; James M. Gray, "What
    Is Intolerance—And What Is Religion?," MM (December 1928), 168.
51 J. Frank Norris to Mordecai Ham, March 11, 1929, folder 826, box 18,
    JFN; J. Frank Norris to E. P. Alldredge, December 12, 1928, reel 1,
    JFN-M.
52 "Hoover and the Millennium," KB (March 1929), 116.
53 Herbert Hoover, "Full Text of Hoover's Speech Accepting Party's Nom-
    ination for the Presidency," NYT, August 12, 1928; "In the Beginning of
    Another Year," OH (January 1929), 415.
54 Paul Rader, Mystery of Mysteries (Chicago: World Wide Christian Couri-
    ers, 1931), 19, 20.

7. The Rise of the Tyrants

 1 L. Nelson Bell to mother (Ruth Lee McCue Bell), November 27, 1933,
    folder 6, box 1, LNB.
 2 Christabel Pankhurst, "Peace or War," KB (September 1924), 553, 554;
    see also "Sees Coming of Christ," NYT, September 26, 1932.
 3 "Against 'Gospel of Doom,'" NYT, February 2, 1925; A. B. Adams,
    "The Light House," PC, May 30, 1931.
 4 William E. Blackstone to O. F. Burgess, February 1, 1927, folder 14, box
    2; William E. Blackstone to O. S. Benson, October 8, 1926, folder 1, box

4; William E. Blackstone to H. Jacobs, August [29?], 1927, H. Jacobs to William E. Blackstone, September 27, 1927, folder 1, box 3, WEB. In late 1928 Blackstone arrived at a new calculation. "We shall have about five years more," he confided to a friend, "before we shall hear the shout from the sky." William E. Blackstone to O. S. Benson, December 29, 1928, folder 1, box 4, WEB.

5 William E. Blackstone to Colin Campbell Smith, April 30, 1929, folder 3, box 4, WEB. See also William E. Blackstone to S. B. Rohold, October 19, 1926, folder 7, box 4, WEB.

6 H. Robin Tourtel, "'The Day of the Lord': Christ and Antichrist," *NBUR*, March 5, 1927, 4; "Apples of Gold," *NBV*, July 25, 1931, 10. See also An Ex-Atheist, "The Beginnings of American Radicalism," *NBUR*, February 14, 1931, 3.

7 Charles H. Mason, "Storms—Storms—Storms," in *Yearbook of the Church of God in Christ, 1926* (Memphis: Church of God in Christ, n.d.), 9.

8 "Says a Black King Will Rule the World," *NYT*, September 15, 1924; R. C. Lawson, *The Anthropology of Jesus Christ Our Kinsman* (New York: n.p., [1925?]), preface.

9 William Bell Riley, "Prophecy and Present Problems," in *Unveiling the Future: Twelve Prophetic Messages,* ed. T. Richard Dunham (Findlay, OH: Fundamental Truth Publishers, 1934), 42; Arno Gaebelein, *World Prospects: How Is It All Going to End?* (New York: OH, 1934), 18.

10 Louis Bauman, "There Shall Be Signs," *KB* (March 1931), 101; Bauman to Paul Bauman, October 11, 1932, Mildred Cook to Bauman, August 7, 1933, LSB.

11 A. E. Evans and Famley to Bauman, October 2, 1932, Gladys Harper to Louis Bauman, n.d., Bauman to Harper, December 3, 1938, LSB.

12 Harry Dotson to Stanley Frodsham, January 26, 1941, SHF.

13 Donald Grey Barnhouse, "Shibboleth or Sibboleth," *REV* (January 1932), 10; Louis Bauman, "Present-Day Fulfillment of Prophecy," *KB* (March 1932), 116.

14 Louis Bauman, "The Reappearance of the Empire on the Fateful Hills of Rome," *KB* (July 1936), 257; Louis Bauman, "Is the Antichrist at Hand? What of Mussolini?," *KB* (January 1926), 15; Charles Fuller to Louis Bauman, September 14, 1926, box 11, CEF. See also Mrs. Gilbert Potter, "Will Mussolini and the Pope Join Forces?," *MM* (November 1923), 110.

15 "Pastor Attacks Parental Laxity; Mussolini Flayed," *AC*, June 14, 1926; Paul Rader, *The Coming World Dictator* (Chicago: World Wide Gospel Couriers, 1934), 40; J. Frank Norris to I. E. Gates, March 30, 1928, folder 743, box 16, JFN; L. Nelson Bell to mother (Ruth Lee McCue Bell), May 21, 1930, folder 3, box 1, LNB. See also J. Frank Norris, "The

Candidacy of Al Smith," in *Is America at the Crossroads? Or Roman Catholicism vs. Protestant Christianity* (Fort Worth: J. L. Rhodes, 1928), 15; and G. A. Griswood, "The Coming World Dictator," *OH* (January 1931), 417.

16 See for example "Premier Mussolini May Be Antichrist, Brethren Are Told," *WP*, January 24, 1927.

17 Ralph C. and Edith F. Norton, "A Personal Interview with Mussolini," *SST* August 13, 1932, 423.

18 Louis Bauman, "Present-Day Fulfillment of Prophecy," *KB* (September 1931), 389; H. A. Ironside, "The Roman Empire of the Future and the Dominating Papacy," *KB* (July 1930), 335.

19 Harold J. Ockenga, "The Ethiopian Situation—or—The Meaning of the Present World Crisis," n.d., 2, sermon manuscripts, HJO; Louis Bauman, "Socialism, Communism, and Fascism," *KB* (August 1935), 292; John R. Rice, "Is Mussolini the Anti-Christ?," *SOTL*, August 30, 1935, 1; John R. Rice, "Mussolini Restores the Roman Empire," *SOTL*, May 22, 1936, 1.

20 "Armageddon Just Ahead," *B&C*, June 16, 1926, 5; Chester Jackson to FDR, October 14, 1935, Texas file, Howard E. Oakwood to FDR, October 3, 1935, Pennsylvania file, collection 21-A, FDR.

21 Bishop Noah W. Williams, "European War Inevitable, Says Bishop Williams," *PC*, March 30, 1935; "The Present Crisis and Its Solution," *NBUR*, November 16, 1935, 3. See also Bishop Noah W. Williams, "Touring the Holy Land," *ADW*, March 30, 1935.

22 D. W. McCoy, "Ethiopia," *ADW*, March 1, 1935; Dan Burley, "Is Ethiopia Stretching Forth Her Hand?," *CD*, July 20, 1935; Dan Burley, "Sees Drastic Change in Social Order," *CD*, July 27, 1935; Mae Ida D. Solo-Billings, "The Call of Ethiopia," *CD*, September 7, 1935; Samuel A. Richardson, "Threat to Civilization," *AN*, August 24, 1935.

23 W. M. Butler, "Is Ethiopia a Type?," *CD*, June 13, 1936; "How Modernism Works to Destroy Christian Faith," *NBUR*, November 7, 1936, 4.

24 Robert (Bob) Hockman to the dear folks at home, October 20, 1933, folder 1, box 1, RWH; Robert (Bob) Hockman to everyone at home, May 12, 1935, folder 5, box 1, RWH.

25 Robert (Bob) Hockman to Dear ones, November 19, 1935, Robert (Bob) Hockman to My dearest onest atst homst [*sic*], December 3, 1935, folder 6, box 1, RWH.

26 Robert (Bob) Hockman to My dearest onest atst homst [*sic*], December 3, 1935, folder 6, box 1, RWH.

27 Donald Grey Barnhouse, "Tomorrow: Future Events in the Light of Bible Prophecy," *REV* (March 1932), 104, 134; Donald Grey Barnhouse,

"Tomorrow: Current Events in the Light of Bible Prophecy," *REV* (June 1939), 236.

28 "Spirit of the Beast Sweeps Germany," *PM* (May 1933), 1; L. Nelson Bell to mother (Ruth Lee McCue Bell), April 2, 1933, folder 6, box 1, LNB; Charles G. Trumbull, *Prophecy's Light on Today* (New York: Revell, 1937), 81.

29 Harold J. Ockenga, "The German Crisis—or—Will Hitler Save Germany?," October 10, [1933?], 13, sermon manuscripts, HJO; Charles Fuller, "The Battle of Armageddon" sermon outline, *Old Fashioned Revival Hour,* May 1, 1938, box 32, CEF; "Germany Brutally Fulfills Prophecy," *SST,* November 26, 1938, 858. See also Harold J. Ockenga, "The Jew and His Persecutors," n.d., sermon manuscripts, HJO.

30 Louis S. Bauman, *Russian Events in the Light of Bible Prophecy* (New York: Revell, 1942), 39; W. S. Hottel, "The Part Russia Will Play in the Last Days," *Pilot* (September 1932), 306.

31 "Resolutions of the Fundamentalists," *SST,* July 22, 1933, 472; L. Nelson Bell to mother (Ruth Lee McCue Bell), November 24, 1933, folder 6, box 1, LNB; William Ashley Sunday, "Sermon Notebook," folder 10, box 31, WAS; "World Conditions," *OH* (December 1934), 328. See also "Peril of Recognizing Russia," *SST,* November 25, 1933, 737.

32 Fred H. Wight to FDR, October 1, 1935, California file, Fred Z. Browne to FDR, October 15, 1935, Texas file, Ezra S. Gerig to FDR, October 11, 1935, Oregon file, collection 21-A, FDR. See also Paul J. Goodwin to FDR, November 22, 1935, Illinois file, collection 21-A, FDR.

33 Louis Bauman, *Russian Events in the Light of Bible Prophecy* (New York: Revell, 1942), 147, 151. On the "young lions" see also Gerald Winrod, *Hitler in Prophecy* (Wichita: Defender Publishers, 1933), 19; and Louis Bauman, *"Prepare War!" or Arming for Armageddon* (n.p.: published by the author, 1937), 37.

34 Gerald B. Winrod, *The Prophetic Destiny of the United States* (Wichita: Defender Publishers, 1943), 18; Canon F. E. Howitt, "Does the United States Appear in Prophecy?," *KB* (April 1931), 153; William E. Blackstone to William Jennings Bryan, September 25, 1914, folder 1, box 1, WEB; Frederick W. Childe, *Mussolini, The United States in Prophecy, Jonah and the Whale, and Other Bible Lectures* (Los Angeles: published by the author, n.d.), 99, 103.

35 John R. Rice, "Prophesied Line-up of the Nations," *SOTL,* June 28, 1940, 2; Donald Grey Barnhouse, "The Bible Says . . ." *REV* (December 1932), 498.

36 Louis T. Talbot, "The Army of the Two Hundred Million," *KB* (October 1932), 424; H. A. Ironside, "The Kings of the East," *KB* (January 1938), 9. See also H. A. Ironside, *The Lamp of Prophecy or Signs of the Times* (Grand Rapids: Zondervan, 1940), 33.

37 "America Helping Japan?," *MM* (January 1939), 244; Harold J. Ockenga, "America Pray! Or the Way Out," n.d., 5, sermon manuscripts, HJO; John R. Rice, "War—Should Christians Fight?," *SOTL,* June 14, 1940, 1; John R. Rice, "Duties of Christians Concerning Hitler and World War," *SOTL,* August 22, 1941, 1.

38 "World War between Dark, White Races of Earth Predicted by Former Windy City Minister," *CD,* April 20, 1938; Elizabeth Galley to Brother Henry, September 21, 1940, FPHC, Lewis Sperry Chafer to Louis Bauman, November 2, 1937, LSC.

39 Diary of H. A. Ironside, September Memoranda, 1938, folder 5, box 28, MC.

40 Mark A. Matthews to Neville Chamberlain, June 26, 1939, folder 32, box 1, accession 97-3, MAM; Donald Grey Barnhouse, "Tomorrow: Current Events in the Light of Bible Prophecy," *REV* (December 1938), 526; Louis S. Bauman, "The European Imbroglio," *KB* (November 1938), 368; Louis S. Bauman to Mildred Cook, March 12, 1938, LSB; John R. Rice, "Wars and Rumors of War," *SOTL,* October 14, 1938, 3; European Unrest Seen as Prelude, *NYT,* October 17, 1938. Matthews later backtracked on his criticism of Chamberlain over Munich. See Mark A. Matthews to Neville Chamberlain, September 15, 1939, folder 32, box 1, accession 97-3, MAM.

41 Alva J. McClain, "The Four Great Powers of the End-Time," *KB* (February 1938), 49.

42 Diary of H. A. Ironside, September 1, 1939, folder 1, box 29, MC; M. A. Matthews to Adolph Hitler, October 28, 1939, folder 1939, box 21, accession 97-2, MAM.

43 Louis Bauman, *Light from Bible Prophecy as Related to the Present Crisis* (New York: Revell, 1940), 29; Dan Gilbert, "Views and Reviews of Current News," *KB* (October 1939), 373; Harold J. Ockenga, *God Save America* (Boston: John W. Schaffer and Co., 1939), 14. See also L. Nelson Bell to mother (Ruth Lee McCue Bell) and Ruth (Bell), August 27, 1939, folder 3, box 2, LNB.

44 W. W. Shannon, "Evangelism and Moral Reform," *MM* (November 1943), 124; Roy L. Laurin, "Around the King's Table," *KB* (December 1939), 453; "Enlarged *King's Business*," *KB* (July 1940), 243.

45 Wilbur Smith to Will Houghton, September 24, 1938, box 14, WMS; Charles Fuller, KHJ sermon (no title), December 31, 1939, box 33, CEF; John R. Rice, "War-Signs of the Soon Coming of Christ," *SOTL,* November 1, 1940, 1. See also John Hess McComb, "Europe . . . and the Bible," *KB* (May 1940), 167.

46 Arno C. Gaebelein, "God's Hand in Prophetic Conferences," *MM* (November 1939), 117, 129; Will Houghton to J. Oliver Buswell, June 27,

1940, box 10, Houghton correspondence, JOB, Wheaton College Archives, Wheaton, IL.

47 "Statement and Call," box 10, Houghton correspondence, JOB, Wheaton College Archives, Wheaton, IL.

8. Christ's Deal versus the New Deal

1 Memorandum to Stephen Early from Stanly High, August 15, 1935, box 1, collection 857, FDR-O. On High see Dr. Stanley High, "Whose Party Is It?," *Saturday Evening Post,* February 6, 1937, 10–11, 34, 37–38.

2 L. Nelson Bell to mother (Ruth Lee McCue Bell), November 9, 1930, folder 3, box 1, LNB; H. A. Ironside to J. Oliver Buswell, September 9, 1932, box 11, JOB.

3 W. O. Carver, "Comments on the Prohibition Situation, Other Current Events," *WR,* October 27, 1932, 6; Louis Bauman to Elizabeth Bolling, November 11, 1932, LSB; Mark Matthews to J. Frank Norris, July 27, 1932, J. Frank Norris to Mark Matthews, July 30, 1932, folder 1182, box 26; Mr. and Mrs. Millard E. Pietz to J. Frank Norris, October 15, 1932, folder 1560, box 35, JFN. See also "Our Moral Slump," *MM* (November 1932), 96. For more on Norris's early opposition to FDR see also J. Frank Norris to Senator George H. Moses, August 31, 1932, folder 1183, box 26, JFN.

4 "Taxes," *MM* (July 1932), 520; "Editorial Comment on the Above," *MM* (November 1932), 106.

5 Smallwood Edmond Williams, *This Is My Story: A Significant Life Struggle* (Washington, DC: Wm. Willoughby Publishers, 1981), 90–91.

6 H. A. Ironside Diary, November 8, 1932, folder 3, box 28, MC.

7 Lewis Sperry Chafer to H. A. Ironside, November 9, 1932, LSC; Stewart P. MacLennan (guest ed.), "Crumbs from the King's Table," *KB* (January 1933), 2; Louis Bauman to Alice Evans, November 16, 1932, LSB. See also Lewis Sperry Chafer to Ralph Norton, November 10, 1932, LSC.

8 Franklin D. Roosevelt, "Address Accepting the Presidential Nomination at the Democratic National Convention in Chicago," July 2, 1932, The American Presidency Project, University of California, Santa Barbara, www.presidency.ucsb.edu/ws/index.php?pid=75174#axzz1urH9G3pf; Franklin D. Roosevelt, "Inaugural Address," March 4, 1933, The American Presidency Project, University of California, Santa Barbara, www.presidency.ucsb.edu/ws/index.php?pid=14473#axzz1urH9G3pf.

9 [Wilbur Smith], "God's Word in the Inauguration," *SST,* April 8, 1933, 241–242, 254. See also Charles Trumbull to Wilbur Smith, March 18,

1933, Wilbur Smith to Charles Trumbull, March 22, 1933, box 19, WMS.

10 "Dictatorships," *MM* (July 1933), 480; Wilbur Smith to Charles Trumbull, September 5, 1934, box 19, WMS; Louis Bauman, *N.R.A.—The Sign and Its Spiritual Significance,* in *Biblical Prophecy in an Apocalyptic Age, Selected Writings of Louis S. Bauman,* ed. Joel Carpenter (New York, 1988), 13; Harold J. Ockenga, "Famines and Earthquakes but Not the End," n.d., sermon manuscripts, HJO; William Bell Riley, *Wanted—A World Leader* (Minneapolis, [1939?]), 59; John R. Rice, "Signs of the Soon Coming of Christ," *SOTL,* June 28, 1935, 1; Loren B. Staats, *Is the Antichrist Soon to Appear?,* 3rd ed. (Blue Rock, OH: published by the author, 1931); J. N. Hoover, *When Jesus Comes* (n.p.: published by the author, n.d.), 7; E. J. Jarrell to FDR, November 7, 1935, Illinois File, collection 21-A, FDR. See also Charles Fuller, "Current Events in the Light of Prophecy," sermon manuscript, October 3, 1932, box 31, CEF; "The Coming Dictator," *SST,* September 24, 1932, 497; and L. Nelson Bell to mother (Ruth Lee McCue Bell), January 15, 1933, folder 6, box 1, LNB.

11 "About the 'Brain Trust,'" *MM* (August 1933), 528; Paul J. Goodwin to FDR, November 22, 1935, Illinois file, John G. King to FDR, October 1, 1935, Florida file, collection 21-A, FDR; Louis S. Bauman, "A Remarkable 'Horse-and-Buggy Days' Prophecy Fulfilled," *KB* (April 1937), 129; Louis S. Bauman, "1935—A Prophetic Review," *KB* (March 1936), 91. See also J. Frank Norris, "The New Deal Uncovered," in *New Dealism Exposed,* ed. J. Frank Norris (Fort Worth: Fundamentalist Publishing Company, n.d.), 12; and Henry Stough, "Franklin and Frankenstein," Lectures on Depression and National Crisis, vol. 10, folder 5, box 2, HS.

12 J. E. Redmon to FDR, November 30, 1935, Florida file, collection 21-A, FDR; Henry Stough, "Washington and the White House," Lectures on Depression and National Crisis, vol. 11, folder 1, box 3, HS. On Eleanor as a communist or socialist see L. Nelson Bell to mother (Ruth Lee McCue Bell), November 24, 1933, folder 6, box 1, LNB; and Norris, "New Deal Uncovered," 15.

13 Henry Stough, "The Drunkards of Ephraim," Lectures on Depression and National Crisis, vol. 10, folder 5, box 2, HS; Norris, "New Deal Uncovered," 16; A. V. Bradley to FDR, October 16, 1935, Texas file, Gustav Briegleb to FDR, October 4, 1935, California file, collection 21-A, FDR; Mordecai Ham to Franklin D. Roosevelt, September 28, 1935, folder 828, box 18, JFN. See also H. H. Harwell to FDR, October 24, 1935, Alabama file, collection 21-A, FDR.

14 Lightfoot Solomon Michaux to FDR, October 26, 1935, Washington, DC file, collection 21-A, FDR; M. R. Morley to J. Frank Norris, August 20, 1932, folder 1183, box 26, collection 124, JFN.

15 William Ashley Sunday, "Sermon Notebook," folder 10, box 31, WAS; Bauman, *N.R.A.,* 7, 10.

16 L. Nelson Bell to mother (Ruth Lee McCue Bell), August 27, 1933, folder 6, box 1, LNB.

17 Samuel Robert Sherman to FDR, November 12, 1935, Missouri file, R. M. Hunter to FDR, September 28, 1935, Alabama file, collection 21-A, FDR; "The Great Sin of America," *OH* (December 1934), 361; "Disaster upon Disaster," *OH* (September 1936), 189; William Ashley Sunday, "Sermon Notebook," folder 10, box 31, WAS.

18 William Dring to FDR, October 3, 1935, Colorado file, E. R. McLaughlin to FDR, September 28, 1935, New York file, collection 21-A, FDR.

19 John R. Rice, "The Townsend Plan Folly," *SOTL,* February 8, 1935, 1; John R. Rice, "The Townsend Plan Weighed by the Bible," *SOTL,* December 13, 1935, 3; Keith L. Brooks, "Can the Townsend Millennium Be Realized?," *PM* (October 1935), 7; "The Townsend Plan," *MM* (May 1935), 410; "Reviewing the Townsend Plan," *MM* (August 1935), 555; Nelson M. Good to FDR, n.d., Colorado file, collection 21-A, FDR.

20 Franklin Delano Roosevelt to Reverend and Dear Sir, September 24, 1935 (version 3), box 35, collection 21-A, FDR.

21 J. Oliver Buswell to Franklin D. Roosevelt, September 26, 1935, box 15, JOB; Lewis Sperry Chafer to Franklin Delano Roosevelt, n.d., LSC; J. Gresham Machen to FDR, September 28, 1935, Pennsylvania file, Chas. Temples to FDR, October 24, 1935, Florida file, collection 21-A, FDR. Buswell repeated the criticisms in J. Oliver Buswell, "A College President Replies," *National Prohibitionist,* November 15, 1935.

22 Dan Gilbert, *The War of the "Ages" and Other Essays* (Grand Rapids, MI: Zondervan, 1940), 15; Harold J. Ockenga, "The Events of 1936 in the Light of the Scripture," December 31, 1936, 9, sermon manuscripts, HJO; "Where Is It Going to End?," *OH* (August 1935), 83, 84.

23 L. L. Sample to FDR, October 15, 1935, Illinois file, Joe V. Baird to FDR, November 14, 1935, California file, collection 21-A, FDR.

24 Chas. E. Robinson to Stanley Frodsham, memo regarding T. L. Ward, c. April 1941, SHF; John R. Rice, "Days of Bloodshed," *SOTL,* May 29, 1936, 3.

25 Dan Gilbert, "The Rise of Beastism in America," *MM* (September 1938), 14; "Views of the News," *FC,* March 31, 1937, 1.

26 John R. Rice, "The Curse of Hidden Sins," *SOTL,* March 25, 1938, 2; "The Fear That Grips Many Nations," *PM* (March 1937), 14; L. Nelson

Bell to mother (Ruth Lee McCue Bell), June 17, 1934, folder 7, box 1, LNB. See also Harold J. Ockenga, "The European Crisis—or—Karl Marx or Jesus Christ?," n.d., 6–7, sermon manuscripts, HJO; Paul W. Rood, "Around the King's Table," *KB* (April 1937), 126; and "Views of the News," *FC,* August 18, 1937, 1.

27 F. J. Lindquist, *Where Are We Drifting?* (Minneapolis: Minneapolis Gospel Tabernacle, 1933), n.p.; William Bell Riley, *Protocols and Communism* (Minneapolis: published by the author, [1934?]), 7; Fred Z. Browne to FDR, October 15, 1935, Texas file, collection 21-A, FDR; Norris, "New Deal Uncovered," 11.

28 O. E. Tiffany to FDR, October 7, 1935, Educators file, collection 21-A, FDR.

29 A. W. Bruhn to FDR, November 14, 1935, Illinois file, collection 21-A, FDR.

30 "Aimee McPherson Thinks Roosevelt Is 'Godsend'; Predicts World Conflict," *FC,* March 21, 1934.

31 "Babson's View of Slumps," *NYT,* September 13, 1930; Percy Crawford to FDR, November 4, 1935, Pennsylvania file, Audie Ellis to FDR, November 25, 1935, Florida file, R. Rupert Flint to FDR, September 26, 1935, Florida file, Rea Andrew Warner to FDR, October 19, 1935, Pennsylvania file, H. McAllister Griffiths to FDR, October 19, 1935, Authors and Editors file, collection 21-A, FDR. See also "An Open Letter to President Roosevelt," *Presbyterian Guardian,* October 21, 1935, 23; Bob Shuler to FDR, September 27, 1935, California file, collection 21-A, FDR; and J. Frank Norris to FDR, August 17, 1934, collection 76A, FDR-O.

32 R. C. Lawson, "I Was Glad for Your Sake," *Contender for the Faith* (May 1935), 2.

33 Paul W. Rood, "Around the King's Table," *KB* (July 1936), 252; P. B. Fitzwater, "America's Predicament—Why?," *SOTL,* October 30, 1936, 3; Norris, "New Deal Uncovered," 20. See also "What Every Christian Ought to Know as Well as Every American Citizen," *OH* (August 1936), 109; Colonel E. N. Sanctuary, "Communism—Its Heart and Its Goal," *SST,* October 24, 1936, 697–698; and "How the Socialists Have Bored from Within," *PM* (June 1936), 36.

34 James Hagerty, "Hoover Assails 'Socialist March,'" *NYT,* June 11, 1936; "The Keynote Speech," *NYT,* June 10, 1936.

35 "Shall the New Deal Assassinate Our Churches and Destroy Christian Civilization?," *NBUR,* September 5, 1936, 1, 3; "The Meaning of Liberalism," *NBUR,* September 22 and 29, 1934, 6; J. G. Robinson to FDR, September 28, 1935, Authors and Editors file, collection 21-A, FDR.

36 Lightfoot Solomon Michaux to FDR, October 26, 1935, Washington, DC file, collection 21-A, FDR; Bishop C. H. Mason et. al. to the President, December 14, 1939, collection 5532, FDR; Williams, *This Is My Story,* 91; Adam Clayton Powell, Jr., "Soap Box," *AN,* October 24, 1936.

37 Paul W. Rood, "Around the King's Table," *KB* (January 1937), 4; M. H. Duncan, "Trends toward Liberalism in America," *MM* (November 1937), 118; J. Frank Norris, "The Second American Revolution," *Fundamentalist,* November 6, 1936.

38 Arno Gaebelein, "The Election Is Over," *OH* (December 1936), 403; Keith L. Brooks, "What Is Happening in the United States?," *PM* (January 1937), 10; Louis Bauman, "The National Election Viewed beneath the Searchlight of the Prophetic Word," *KB* (February 1937), 50, 71.

39 Louis S. Bauman, "1935—A Prophetic Review," *KB* (March 1936), 92; Bauman, "A Remarkable 'Horse-and-Buggy Days' Prophecy Fulfilled," 130.

40 J. E. Conant, *The Growing Menace of the "Social Gospel"* (Chicago: Bible Institute Colportage Association, 1937), 47.

41 L. Nelson Bell to mother (Ruth Lee McCue Bell), February 7, 1937, folder 10, box 1, LNB; "The Menace of Dictatorship in the United States Looms," *OH* (April 1937), 692; Harold J. Ockenga, "The Events of 1937 in the Light of Scripture," December 31, 1937, 2, sermon manuscripts, HJO; Mark A. Matthews to Burton K. Wheeler, April 16, 1937, folder 1937, box 21, accession 97-2, MAM; Keith L. Brooks, "Good Intentions and Bad Results," *PM* (May 1937), 12.

42 Theodore H. Epp, "America at the Crossroads," *SOTL,* February 14, 1941, 2.

43 Dan Gilbert, "The Antichrist Advance in America," *MM* (May 1940), 473; "New Deal's Reign Called Anti-Bible and Anti-Christian," *LAT,* July 1, 1939; Gilbert, *War of the "Ages" and Other Essays,* 18, 19, 20, 21.

44 On interwar fundamentalist businessmen, see Sarah R. Hammond, " 'God's Business Men': Entrepreneurial Evangelicals in Depression and War" (PhD diss., Yale University, 2010).

45 "Fundamentalists Warned on Communists in America," *LAT,* July 3, 1939; Epp, "America at the Crossroads," 4; Harold J. Ockenga, "Rehoboam, a Nation's Dictator—or—The Civil War of a People," n.d., 10, 15, sermon manuscripts, HJO; "Editorial Notes," *MM* (October 1940), 63. See also L. Nelson Bell to mother (Ruth Lee McCue Bell), February 19, 1939, folder 3, L. Nelson Bell to mother (Ruth Lee McCue Bell), September 22, 1940, folder 4, box 2, LNB; and "A Presidential Candidate Speaks," *OH* (November 1940), 340.

46 L. Nelson Bell to mother (Ruth Lee McCue Bell), November 11, 1938, folder 2, box 2, LNB; "Another Shadow," *OH* (December 1940), 414; Keith L. Brooks, "The Nation's Call to Prayer," *PM* (January 1941), 5.

47 Belle Daugherty to Louis Bauman, November 8, 1940, Bauman to Daugherty, November 13, 1940, Fred and Ida Benson to Louis Bauman, November 13, 1940, Bauman to Benson, December 2, 1940, Martha Nickelson to Louis Bauman, n.d., Alice C. Cary to Louis Bauman, November 9, 1940, LSB.

48 Arthur E. Phelps to Louis Bauman, November 3, 1940, LSB. See also Arthur E. Phelps to Louis Bauman, December 1, 1940, LSB.

49 John R. Rice, "Will America Get in World-Wide War?," *SOTL,* June 8, 1940, 1.

9. Reviving American Exceptionalism

1 Harold John Ockenga, *God Save America* (Boston: John W. Schaffer and Co., 1939), 15, 16, 92. See also Harold J. Ockenga, "Christians Unite against the World's Worst Threat," n.d., sermon manuscripts, HJO.

2 Andrew Preston writes, "so overwhelming and cohesive was Christian conservative support for the war, and so ambivalent were liberals, that World War II marked a decisive shift in religious attitudes toward patriotism. After two decades of being portrayed as extremists, the war offered Christian conservatives a lifeline back into the mainstream." Andrew Preston, *Sword of the Spirit, Shield of Faith: Religion in American War and Diplomacy* (New York: Knopf, 2012), 371.

3 M. A. Matthews to Franklin D. Roosevelt, November 16, 1938, folder 35, box 2, accession 97-2, MAM; L. Nelson Bell to mother (Ruth Lee McCue Bell), August 15, 1937, folder 10, box 1, L. Nelson and Virginia Bell to Friends, October 23, 1938, folder 2, box 2, LNB.

4 Harold J. Ockenga, "America Pause or Can You Read the Signs? God Save America, IV," October 1, 1939, 12, sermon manuscripts, HJO; Enoch Williams to Harold J. Ockenga, September 11, 1939, Charles P. Haseltine to Harold J. Ockenga, September 10, 1939, Jas D. Judge to Harold J. Ockenga, n.d., unprocessed correspondence, HJO. For another defense of neutrality, see John R. Rice, "World War and the End of the World," *SOTL,* September 22, 1939, 1–4.

5 J. Frank Norris to Franklin Roosevelt, October 1, 1939, reel 20, JFN-M; "Can Any Christian Be Neutral?," *PM* (November 1939), 8–9; L. Nelson Bell to mother (Ruth Lee McCue Bell), April 11, 1940, folder 4, box 2, LNB; Donald Grey Barnhouse, "Tomorrow: Current Events in the Light

of the Bible," *REV* (April 1941), 167. See also John R. Rice, "Hitler's American Friends," *SOTL,* August 29, 1941, 2.

6 John R. Rice, "War—Should Christians Fight?," *SOTL* (June 14, 1940), 4; Dan Gilbert, "Views and Reviews of Current News," *KB* (December 1938), 406.

7 Franklin D. Roosevelt, "Fireside Chat," December 29, 1940, The American Presidency Project, University of California, Santa Barbara, www .presidency.ucsb.edu/ws/?pid=15917.

8 Franklin D. Roosevelt, "Annual Message to Congress on the State of the Union," January 6, 1941, American Presidency Project, www.presidency .ucsb.edu/ws/?pid=16092; Dan Gilbert, "Premillennialism and Power Politics," *Pilot* (March 1941), 166, 190.

9 Harold John Ockenga, "America's Great Moral Decision," n.d., 3, Harold John Ockenga, "The National Crisis Hour and the National Association of Evangelicals," April 23, 1944, 8, sermon manuscripts, HJO; Donald Grey Barnhouse, "Helping Russia?," *REV* (November 1941), 510.

10 Charles Fuller, "Prophecy," sermon outline, *Old Fashioned Revival Hour,* June 16, 1940, box 34, CEF; "A Guide to Be Used after the Rapture," *SST,* March 29, 1941, 248; "The New Great World Crisis," *OH* (December 1941), 384.

11 Franklin D. Roosevelt, "Address to Congress Requesting a Declaration of War with Japan," December 8, 1941, American Presidency Project, www.presidency.ucsb.edu/ws/?pid=16053.

12 Diary of H. A. Ironside, December 8, 1941, folder 2, box 29, MC; John R. Rice, "Take Sides in the War," *SOTL,* June 5, 1942, 3; Helen Frazee-Bower, "America—Remember!" *KB* (February 1942), cover.

13 Dan Gilbert, *The Yellow Peril and Bible Prophecy,* 2nd ed. (Grand Rapids, MI: Zondervan, 1943), 19, 21, 22; John Walvoord, "The Way of the Kings of the East," *In Light for the World's Darkness,* ed. John W. Bradbury (New York: Loizeaux Brothers, 1944), 162. See also Donald Grey Barnhouse, "Tomorrow: Current Events in the Light of the Bible," *REV* (February 1942), 63.

14 Hyman Appelman, "How God Is Using Hitler (And How the Democracies Must Win)," *KB* (June 1942), 212; Clarence E. Mason, Jr., "The Pearl Harbor Disaster," *SST,* April 18, 1942, 307, 322, 323; John R. Rice, "America Gets Back Her Scrap Iron," *SOTL,* December 26, 1941, 1. See also Hyman Appelman, "Can Hitler Win the War?," *SST,* August 29, 1942, 679.

15 "Civilization Too Corrupt to Save, Churchman Says in Plea to Ministers Not to Pray for Peace," *CD,* October 21, 1939; Dan Gilbert, *One Minute before Midnight* (Los Angeles: Jewish Hope, 1945), 6–7. On abortion, see

also Albert Lindsey, "What Will Tomorrow Bring?," *MM* (September 1947), 20.

16 Louis Bauman to R. D. Barnard, October 1, 1940, LSB; Bishop C. H. Mason et. al. to the President, December 14, 1939, collection 5532, FDR; Bishop C. H. Mason, File 25–5243, Federal Bureau of Investigation, Washington, DC; John R. Rice, "Youth's Corner," *SOTL,* November 24, 1939, 2. The 1942 statement of faith for the Church of God in Christ reiterated the points in Mason's telegram. *The Sunday School Quarterly of the Church of God in Christ U.S.A.* (Kansas City, KS: Mrs. D. J. Young, Publisher, 1942).

17 John R. Rice, "Should Christians Go to War?," *SOTL,* June 12, 1942, 1–3; "Minutes of the Meeting of the Executive Council, June 19, 1942," "Minutes of a Meeting of the Corporate Session, June 26, 1942," corporate documents, ICFG; *Yearbook 1942* (Los Angeles: International Church of the Foursquare Gospel, 1942).

18 Keith L. Brooks, "The Christian in Time of War," *PM* (June 1940), 23; "Non-resisters Who Resist Government," *PM* (July 1940), 12; "Objectors to War," *OH* (February 1942), 517; "Present Responsibilities," *OH* (February 1943), 515, 516. See also "Loyalty to the Stars and Stripes," *PM* (March 1941), 3–5.

19 Grant Stroh, "Practical and Perplexing Questions," *MM* (March 1941), 420; "Because Our Sons Are in Danger," *MM* (July 1941), 627; L. Nelson Bell to mother (Ruth Lee McCue Bell), August 2, 1940, folder 4, box 2, LNB; Harold J. Ockenga, "The Christian as a Member of the State," October 20, 1940, 16, sermon manuscripts, HJO.

20 "Obliteration Raids on German Cities Protested in U.S.," *NYT,* March 6, 1944; Harold J. Ockenga, "Letters to the Times," *NYT,* March 9, 1944.

21 "Praying on Malta," *MM* (June 1945), 519; C. A. Cooper, "God Bless America? America Bless God!" *SOTL,* June 4, 1943, 4; Donald Grey Barnhouse, "Government Debauchery," *REV* (May 1944), 191; Arthur E. Phelps to Louis Bauman, November 24, 1941, LSB.

22 "A New Use for a Race Track," *KB* (July 1942), 250, 279.

23 Aimee Semple McPherson to Governor Earl Warren, Congressman John B. Costello, and Congressman Norris K. Poulson, ASM; "Aimee Protests Return of Japs," *LAT,* June 9, 1943.

24 Louis Bauman, *Russian Events in the Light of Bible Prophecy* (New York: Revell, 1942), 108; J. R. Flower to Rev. and Mrs. E. F. Cunningham, December 24, 1942, Ministers file—Cunningham, Eli F., FPHC; *Yearbook of United Holy Church of America* (1940), 7. See also Arno C. Gaebelein, "The New Great World Crisis," *OH* (January 1943), 452.

25 Donald Grey Barnhouse, "Tomorrow: Current Events in the Light of the Bible," *REV* (March 1942), 136.

26 L. Nelson Bell to mother (Ruth Lee McCue Bell), June 23, 1941, folder 5, box 2, LNB; Bauman, *Russian Events,* 84; Louis Bauman to Mr. and Mrs. John Sansom, December 17, 1941, LSB.

27 Philip Howard to Louis Bauman, December 23, 1941, LSB; "Russia and Germany," *MM* (August 1942), 714.

28 "Light from Bible Prophecy on the European War and Its Results," *SST,* October 21, 1939, 719.

29 Arno Gaebelein, "Confusion in Prophetic Interpretations," *OH* (February 1941), 521; Louis Bauman to A. Stirling Mackay, November 29, 1940, LSB; Louis S. Bauman, "Have Mussolini and His 'Resurrected Roman Empire' Both Collapsed?," *KB* (April 1941), 164; "Prelude to Prophecy," *MM* (February 1948), 397.

30 Harold J. Ockenga, "Christ for America," May 1943, 11, 13–14, sermon manuscripts, HJO.

31 Will H. Houghton, "Is America Facing Sunrise or Sunset?," *MM* (April 1944), 433; Oscar C. Hanson, "Are They Dying in Vain?," *MM* (January 1945), 274.

32 Ralph T. Davis to Will H. Houghton, J. Davis Adams, Howard W. Ferrin, Louis T. Talbot, December 11, 1940, box 67, NAE.

33 Ralph T. Davis to J. Elwin Wright, February 3, 1941, box 67, NAE; J. Elwin Wright, *Death in the Pot* (Boston: Fellowship Press, 1944), 4.

34 Ralph T. Davis to W. B. Riley, November 25, 1941, W. B. Riley to Ralph T. Davis, December 5, 1941, box 1, NAE.

35 Paul B. Fischer to Ralph T. Davis, November 27, 1941, John Brenner to Ralph T. Davis, December 19, 1941, box 1, NAE.

36 Elizabeth Morrell Evans, interview by Robert Shuster, October 8, 1984, and August 26 and 27, 1985, collection 279-Elizabeth Morrell Evans (T3 transcript), BGCA.

37 R. L. Decker, *Cooperation among Conservative Christians* (Fort Collins: published by the author, 1943), 5.

38 Harold J. Ockenga, "The Unvoiced Multitudes," sermon manuscript, April 1942, 2, 8, 9, 10, 11, 12, box 1, NAE.

39 William Ward Ayer, "Evangelical Christianity Endangered by its Fragmentized Condition," sermon manuscript, n.d. 3, box 1, NAE.

40 "Minutes of a Meeting of the Board of Directors," corporate minutes, June 21, 1943, ICFG; Ernest S. Williams to J. Roswell Flower, October 4, 1946, National Association of Evangelicals, corporate papers, FPHC.

41 Harold J. Ockenga, "The American Way of Life and Its Substitutes," May 28, 1944, 2, 3, 25, sermon manuscripts, HJO; "The Election," *MM*

(November 1944), 121; "Revolution by Scientific Technique," *PM* (March 1945), 8; John R. Rice, "Pray for Invasion Armies," *SOTL,* June 16, 1944, 3; John R. Rice, "Christian Citizenship versus the New Deal," *SOTL,* October 20, 1944, 4.

42 Diary of H. A. Ironside, November 7, 1944, folder 3, box 29, MC.

43 "Can Men Harness Basic Power?," *SST,* August 25, 1945, 658; "Editorially Speaking," *KB* (January 1946), 8; Clarence E. Benson, "The Sunday School's Place in the Atomic Age," *SST,* October 6, 1945, 767; "The Atomic Bomb," *MM* (October 1945), 57; Donald Grey Barnhouse, "Tomorrow: Current Events in the Light of the Bible," *REV* (October 1945), 407.

44 "Editorially Speaking," *KB* (January 1946), 8.

10. Becoming Cold Warriors for Christ

1 Carl F. H. Henry, *The Uneasy Conscience of Modern Fundamentalism* (Grand Rapids, MI: Eerdmans, 1947), 36, 45.

2 Henry, *Uneasy Conscience,* 26, 29, 32, 68.

3 Laurie Goodstein, "Rev. Dr. Carl F. H. Henry, 90, Brain of Evangelical Movement," *NYT,* December 13, 2003.

4 Henry Luce, "The American Century," *Life,* February 17, 1941, 63.

5 "Will the World Ever Blow Up?," *KB* (June 1929), 261.

6 "Prophetic Aspects of the Atomic Bomb," *SST,* September 1, 1945, 666; Robert B. Fischer, "The Message of the Atomic Bomb to the Church," *MM* (March 1946), 426, 450; Wilbur M. Smith, *The Atomic Bomb and the Word of God* (Chicago: Moody, 1945), 17.

7 "Russia Has It—Now What?," *KB* (November 1949), 6; Lowell Blanchard with the Valley Trio, "Jesus Hits Like an Atom Bomb," on *Atomic Platters: Cold War Music from the Golden Age of Homeland Security* (Bear Family, 2005).

8 Frank E. Lindgren, "The Atomic Bomb," *KB* (January 1946), 9; Louis S. Bauman, *The Approaching End of This Age* (Grand Rapids, MI: Zondervan, 1952), 6; Wilbur M. Smith, "World Crises and the Prophetic Scriptures," *MM* (June 1950), 679. See also Herbert Lockyer, *It Is Later Than We Think* (Grand Rapids, MI: Zondervan, 1951), 8.

9 Harris Franklin Roll, "The War and the Second Coming," *CC,* August 18, 1943, 941. On the rise of emphasis on sin, see Andrew S. Finstuen, *Original Sin and Everyday Protestants: The Theology of Reinhold Niebuhr, Billy Graham, and Paul Tillich in an Age of Anxiety* (Chapel Hill: University of North Carolina Press, 2009).

10 "Evangelist Webb Gives Views on Third World War," *CD,* April 27, 1946.

11 "World Needs," *MM* (October 1944), 62; William Bell Riley, *The Only Solution for the Sordid World Problems* (Minneapolis: published by the author), 5; R. C. Lawson, "Bird's Eye View of Things to Come, December 1958–January 1959," in *For the Defense of the Gospel,* ed. Arthur M. Anderson (New York: Church of the Lord Jesus Christ of the Apostolic Faith, Inc., 1971), 246; Bauman, *Approaching End of This Age,* 50–51.

12 "The Charter," *KB* (September 1945), 327; Dan Gilbert, *The United Nations and the Coming Antichrist* (Washington, DC: Christian Press Bureau, n.d.), 13, 28.

13 "The Muslim Menace," *CWM* (December 1918), cover; "Making a 'Shorter' Bible," *CWM* (July 1919), 795.

14 J. Frank Norris, "Palestine Restored to the Jews," *SLT,* October 21, 1920, n.p.; Keith L. Brooks, "Good Prophetic Slogan: Watch the Arab!" *PM* (May 1936), 12; Mark A. Matthews to Neville Chamberlain, June 26, 1939, folder 32, box 1, accession 97-3, MAM.

15 "Russian Eyes on the Near East," *SST,* September 14, 1946, 821; Aaron J. Kligerman, "Palestine—Jewish Homeland," *MM* (December 1946), 256; Harold J. Ockenga, "Palestine, the Arab-Jewish Problem, and the National Home for the Jews," 1946, 8, 9, sermon manuscripts, HJO; Dan Gilbert, *The Coming War over Palestine* (Washington, DC: Christian Press Bureau, 1946), 11.

16 Louis T. Talbot and William W. Orr, *The New Nation of Israel and the Word of God!* (Los Angeles: BIOLA, 1948), 4; "What Next?," *PE,* June 12, 1948, 10; "Israel Is a Nation!," *KB* (August 1948), 4.

17 Roy L. Laurin, "The Church's Greatest Service in the Nation's Greatest Crisis," *PM* (October 1950), 4; Harold J. Ockenga, "The British Experiment in Socialism," October 21, 1951, 1, 2, 3, sermon manuscripts, HJO; Carl McIntire, *The Rise of the Tyrant: Controlled Economy vs. Private Enterprise* (Collingswood, NJ: Christian Beacon Press, 1945) xiii, 218. Numerous evangelicals publically praised Hayek's *Road to Serfdom.* See for example McIntire, *Rise of the Tyrant,* 25; "Revolution by Scientific Technique," *PM* (March 1945), 11; "A Rudderless Ship on the Sea of 1951," *PM* (January 1951), 6.

18 John R. Rice, "The President Pays Off," *SOTL,* February 2, 1945, 3; McIntire, *Rise of the Tyrant,* 195; W. O. H. Garman to Dear Brethren, April 6, 1946, WOHG; "Industry and Labor," *MM* (December 1945), 190. See also Dan Gilbert, *Moscow over Hollywood* (Washington, DC: Christian Press Bureau, 1947), 52.

19 "Shall It Ring Again?," *PM* (July 1946), 3; Howard Lehn, "The Gospel and Labor Unions," *MM* (July 1946), 659, 660.

20 Maxey Jarman, "The Gospel and the Labor Problem," *MM* (October 1946), 92–93, 132.

21 R. C. Lawson, "The Greatest Evil in This World Is Race Prejudice, June 1957," 248, "Hope in a Troublesome Time, July 1948," 107, 111, "Prejudice, August 1947," 329, in Anderson, *For the Defense of the Gospel.*

22 John W. Lane, Jr., "The Young People's Prayer Meeting," *SST,* May 3, 1947, 18, 19; John W. Lane, Jr., "The Young People's Prayer Meeting," *SST,* January 29, 1949, 17.

23 "FEPC Legislation," *United Evangelical Action,* June 1, 1949, 7.

24 L. Nelson Bell, *Christian Race Relations Must Be Natural—Not Forced* (Weaverville, NC: Southern Presbyterian Journal, 1955); Dan Gilbert, *Who Will Be Elected President in 1960? A Frank and Fearless Forecast* (Los Angeles: Jewish Hope Publishing House, 1959), 14–15; the "southern evangelist" quoted in Jane Dailey, "Sex, Segregation, and the Sacred after Brown," *Journal of American History* 91:1 (June 2004): 125.

25 C. Gregg Singer, "Are We Forgetting Our Government?," *MM* (July 1947), 745, 746.

26 McIntire, *Rise of the Tyrant,* 250; Keith L. Brooks, "The Christian and Socialized Medicine," *PM* (September 1947), 8, 10; Keith L. Brooks, "Bureaucracy Entrenched through Thought-Control," *PM* (November 1948), 12.

27 Louis S. Bauman, "Prophetic Spotlight on the National Election," *PM* (February 1949), 5, 6; "Uncle Sam Is My Shepherd," *PM* (February 1949), 6–7; J. Frank Norris to M. E. Coyle, February 19, 1947, reel 6, JFN-M. On Norris's disappointment in the outcome see also J. Frank Norris to M. E. Coyle, November 19, 1948, M. E. Coyle to J. Frank Norris, November 24, 1948, reel 6, JFN-M.

28 George Kennan to James Byrnes, ["Long Telegram"], February 22, 1946, Harry S. Truman Administration file, Elsey Papers, Truman Library, Independence, MO; X [George Kennan], "The Sources of Soviet Conduct," *Foreign Affairs* 25 (July 1947): 575, 581; Winston Churchill, "The Sinews of Peace," March 5, 1946, Westminster College, Fulton, MO, The Churchill Centre, www.winstonchurchill.org/learn/speeches/speeches-of-winston-churchill/120-the-sinews-of-peace.

29 Louis T. Talbot, "Palestine, Russia and Ezekiel 38," *KB* (January 1948), 11; "Prophecy's Light on Our Times," *MM* (November 1948), 201.

30 See for example, "Mr. Truman's Precedent-Breaking Proposal," *PM* (December 1951), 8; "Liberties at Stake," *MM* (July 1947), 744; Harold J. Ockenga, "Review of Current Events," [1951?], sermon manuscripts, HJO.

31 J. Frank Norris to M. E. Coyle, February 27, 1947, M. E. Coyle to J. Frank Norris, October 14, 1947, J. Frank Norris to M. E. Coyle, November 1, 1948, M. E. Coyle to J. Frank Norris, November 4, 1948, reel 6, JFN-M; J. Frank Norris to Dwight D. Eisenhower, July 21, 1952, reel 20, JFN-M.

32 Billy Graham, *Christianity vs. Communism* (Minneapolis: Billy Graham Evangelistic Association, 1951), n.p.; Harold J. Ockenga, *The Answer to Communist Aggression* (Boston: Park Street Church, 1950), 3, copy in sermon manuscripts, HJO.

33 Keith L. Brooks, "What Can We Believe about Russia?," *PM* (February 1951), 5; J. Frank Norris, "The Four Horsemen Are Riding Fast," in *"The Four Horsemen Are Riding Fast" and Five Other Outstanding Messages* (Plano, TX: Calvary Baptist Church), 9; Ockenga, *Answer to Communist,* 5, 11.

34 Fred Schwarz, *You Can Trust the Communists* (Englewood Cliffs, NJ: Prentice Hall, 1960), 174; Billy Graham, *Labor, Christ, and the Cross* (Minneapolis: Billy Graham Evangelistic Association, 1953), n.p.; Harold J. Ockenga, "The World Challenge to the Churches," n.d., 13, sermon manuscripts, HJO. See also *What Can I Do to Combat Communism?* (Wheaton, IL: National Association of Evangelicals, n.d.).

35 William Ward Ayer, "Shall the Church Concern Itself with Society's Problems?," *MM* (January 1948), 357; William Ward Ayer, "How Wise Are Fundamentalists?," *MM* (January 1949), 331, 373; Wilbur M. Smith, *Therefore, Stand: A Plea for a Vigorous Apologetic in the Present Crisis of Evangelical Christianity* (Boston: W. A. Wilde Co., 1945), 103, 483; Harold Ockenga, "Can Fundamentalism Win America?," *CL* (June 1947), 13, 14. See also Harold J. Ockenga, "Communism and the Christian Faith," n.d., sermon manuscripts, HJO. Ockenga expanded on these ideas in an important sermon a decade later. See Harold J. Ockenga, "The New Evangelicalism," in *Park Street Spire* (Boston: Park Street Church, 1958), 2, 5–7.

36 Harold J. Ockenga, "Jesus Christ Is Coming from Heaven—So What?," April 15, 1945, 10, Harold J. Ockenga, "When the Time Is Short Turn to God," c. 1947, 3, 4, sermon manuscripts, HJO.

37 Erling C. Olsen, "Christian Politicians?," *CL* (October 1947), 49; H. A. Ironside, "Friable and Divisive," *CL* (October 1947), 98; Harold J. Ockenga, "Theological Education," n.d., 1, sermon manuscripts, HJO.

38 Billy Graham, "A Christian America," *American Mercury* (March 1955), 68–69. See also Billy Graham, *Spiritual Inventory* (Minneapolis: Billy Graham Evangelistic Association, 1955).

39 Sydney E. Ahlstrom, *A Religious History of the American People* (New Haven, CT: Yale University Press, 1972), 952. See also Robert D. Putnam

and David E. Campbell, *Amazing Grace: How Religion Divides and Unites Us* (New York: Simon and Schuster, 2010).

40 Frank Gaebelein to Wilbur Smith, December 15, 1948, box 12, WMS.

41 On Fuller Theological Seminary see George Marsden, *Reforming Fundamentalism: Fuller Seminary and the New Evangelicalism* (Grand Rapids, MI: Eerdmans, 1987).

42 Harold J. Ockenga, transcribed inaugural address, October 1, 1947, 1, 20, 23, 24, 25, Fuller Theological Seminary Archives, Pasadena, CA.

43 Billy Graham, *Just as I Am: The Autobiography of Billy Graham* (San Francisco: HarperSanFrancisco, 1997), 286, 291.

44 See for example Elton M. Eenigenburg, "The Ordination of Women," *CT,* April 27, 1959, 15, 16.

45 For 1960s subscription figures see David R. Swartz, *Moral Minority: The Evangelical Left in an Age of Conservatism* (Philadelphia: University of Pennsylvania Press, 2012), 22; for current reach see *Christianity Today*'s website, www.christianitytodayads.com/reach-your-audience/.

46 On the cozy relationship between evangelicals and business leaders in the postwar era, see Darren Grem, "The Blessings of Business: Corporate America and Conservative Evangelicalism in the Sunbelt Age, 1945–2000" (PhD diss., University of Georgia, 2010).

47 J. Howard Pew, "For several years . . ." copy of form letter, HJO.

48 Carl Henry to Nelson Bell, n.d., Nelson Bell to Harold J. Ockenga, November 10, 1965, HJO. See also Nelson Bell to Carl Henry, December 28, 1966, HJO.

49 "The Evangelical Witness in a Modern Medium," *CT,* October 15, 1956, 21; Carl Henry to Members of Christianity Today Board, June 7, 1960, HJO; L. Nelson Bell, "For Men to See," *CT,* November 23, 1959, 19; The Editor, "Has Anyone Seen 'Erape,' Part II," *CT,* January 18, 1960, 12–14.

50 William G. McLoughlin, "Is There a Third Force in Christendom?," *Daedalus* 96:2 (Winter 1967): 60, 61; "Who Are the Evangelicals?," *CT,* June 23, 1967, 22.

51 George Eldon Ladd, "The Revelation of Christ's Glory," *CT,* September 1, 1958, 13–14; John F. Walvoord, "Dispensational Premillennialism," *CT,* September 15, 1958, 11–13; Loraine Boettner, "Christian Hope and a Millennium," *CT,* September 29, 1958, 13–14; W. J. Grier, "Christian Hope and the Millennium," *CT,* October 13, 1958, 18–19; A. W. Tozer, "A Christian Looks at the Space Age," *CT,* October 13, 1958, 14; "Biblical Prophecy and World Events," *CT,* December 8, 1958, 22.

52 Clyde W. Taylor, "Behind the Scenes in Washington," in *United: A Report of the Sixth Annual Convention of the National Association of Evangelicals*

(1948), 24, NAE; "A Description of March of Freedom," collection 113, NAE.

53 Arnold W. Hearn, "Fundamentalist Renascence," *CC,* April 30, 1958, 528.

11. Apocalypse Now

1 *Revival in Our Time: The Story of the Billy Graham Evangelistic Campaigns* (Wheaton, IL: Van Kampen Press, 1950), 70.
2 *Revival in Our Time,* 71, 73.
3 Billy Graham, *Christ Is Coming* (Minneapolis: Billy Graham Evangelistic Association, 1955), n.p.
4 George L. Bernonius, "World's End Seen: Thousands Hear Billy Graham," *LAT,* September 15, 1950; Billy Graham, *Spiritual Inventory* (Minneapolis: Billy Graham Evangelistic Association, 1955), n.p.; Billy Graham, *The Ten Virgins* (Minneapolis: Billy Graham Evangelistic Association, 1957), n.p.
5 Billy Graham, *World Aflame* (New York: Doubleday, 1965), xiii, 203.
6 Graham, *World Aflame,* 216.
7 Graham, *World Aflame,* 12; Billy Graham, *Something Is Happening in America* (Minneapolis: Billy Graham Evangelistic Association, 1971), 4.
8 Harold J. Ockenga, "A Christian Looks at Vietnam," June 27, 1965, 15, sermon manuscripts, Harold J. Ockenga to the President, May 28, 1966, Harold J. Ockenga to Lt. Kenneth L. Whitehead, March 10, 1967, HJO. For *Christianity Today's* take on the war, see "Viet Nam: The Spiritual War," *CT,* September 25, 1964, 53–54; "Halting Red Aggression in Viet Nam," *CT,* April 23, 1965, 32; William K. Harrison, "Is the United States Right in Bombing North Viet Nam?," *CT,* January 7, 1966, 25–26; and "Report from Viet Nam," *CT,* March 15, 1968, 35.
9 Harold J. Ockenga, Vietnam, "World War III and the Second Coming," May 28, 1967, 6, 8, sermon manuscripts, HJO.
10 Graham, *World Aflame,* 23.
11 Billy Graham, *The Responsibilities of the Home* (Minneapolis: Billy Graham Evangelistic Association, 1955), 7, 8; Gay Pauley, "Mrs. Billy Graham Deplores Rise in Number of Working Housewives," *LAT,* May 19, 1957.
12 Ruth A. Schmidt, "Second-Class Citizenship in the Kingdom of God," *CT,* January 1, 1971, 13–14.
13 Graham, *World Aflame,* 7–8.

14 E. Earle Ellis, "Segregation and the Kingdom of God," *CT,* March 18, 1957, 7; "The Church and the Race Problem," *CT,* March 18, 1957, 21; Harold J. Ockenga, "The Christian Faces Segregation & Other Social Problems," n.d., and What's Right with America, n.d., sermon manuscripts, HJO.

15 "Race Tensions and Social Change," *CT,* January 19, 1959, 21.

16 Dan Gilbert, *Who Will Be Elected President in 1960? A Frank and Fearless Forecast* (Los Angeles: Jewish Hope Publishing House, 1959), 26.

17 "Elder Williams Helps Interracial Group to Fight Discrimination," *Bible Way News Voice,* September–October 1950; Smallwood Edmond Williams, *Significant Sermons* (Washington, DC: Bible Way Church, 1970), 81, 82.

18 Jerry Falwell, *Falwell: An Autobiography* (Lynchburg, VA: Liberty House Publishers, 1997), 312; Jerry Falwell, *Ministers and Marches* (Lynchburg, VA: Thomas Road Baptist Church, 1965), 7–8.

19 Bruce Crapuchettes, "Impressions from Selma," *Opinion* (April 1965), 1, 4; "Frank Gaebelein Dies at 83," *CT,* February 18, 1983, 28.

20 Billy Graham, *Four Great Crises* (Minneapolis: Billy Graham Evangelistic Association, 1957), n.p.; "Billy Graham Urges Restraint in Sit-Ins," *NYT,* April 18, 1963; John Herbers, "35,000 in Alabama at Biracial Rites," *NYT,* March 30, 1964.

21 William Pannell, "The Evangelical and Minority Groups," *HIS* (October 1959), 12.

22 C. Herbert Oliver, "The Christian Negro: What Should He Do?," *Eternity* (November 1960), 16, 58, 59.

23 McCandlish Phillips, "Evangelist Finds Harlem Vineyard," *NYT,* August 16, 1964; "Controversial Black Preacher Putting Stress on Social Issues," *NYT,* September 2, 1973.

24 Tom Skinner, "The U.S. Racial Crisis and World Evangelism," Urbana Address, 1970, Intervarsity Christian Fellowship, https://urbana.org/past-urbanas/urbana-70/us-racial-crisis-and-world-evangelism-1970; on Skinner see, Edward Gilbreath, "A Prophet Out of Harlem," *CT* (September 16, 1996), www.christianitytoday.com/ct/1996/september16/6ta036.html?pagingoff.

25 Andrew Young, *An Easy Burden: The Civil Rights Movement and the Transformation of America* (New York: HarperCollins, 1996), 232; John Perkins, *Let Justice Roll Down* (Ventura, CA: Regal, 1976), 103. Nevertheless, as historians have demonstrated, evangelicalism played an important role among African Americans in the civil rights movement, especially among laypeople. Paul Harvey, *Freedom's Coming: Religious*

Culture and the Shaping of the South from the Civil War through the Civil Rights Era (Chapel Hill: University of North Carolina Press, 2005). See also David L. Chappell, *A Stone of Hope: Prophetic Religion and the Death of Jim Crow* (Chapel Hill: University of North Carolina Press, 2004).

26 Chicago Declaration of Evangelical Social Concern, November 25, 1973, Evangelicals for Social Action, www.evangelicalsforsocialaction .org/chicago-declaration-of-evangelical-social-concern/.

27 Clarence Hilliard, "Down with the Honky Christ—Up with the Funky Jesus," *CT,* January 30, 1976, 430.

28 Chicago Declaration of Evangelical Social Concern, November 25, 1973.

29 Billy Graham, *The Jesus Generation* (Grand Rapids, MI: Zondervan, 1971), 21, 61. On Graham's antistatism, see also Graham, *Something Is Happening,* 7.

30 Graham, *The Jesus Generation,* 185, 186.

31 Hal Lindsey with C. C. Carlson, *The Late Great Planet Earth* (Grand Rapids, MI: Zondervan, 1970), 50–51.

32 Lindsey, *Late Great Planet Earth,* 54.

33 Hal Lindsey, *The Everlasting Hatred: The Roots of Jihad* (Murrieta, CA: Oracle House Publishing, 2002), back cover.

34 Tim LaHaye, *The Beginning of the End* (Wheaton, IL: Tyndale House, 1972), 8, 38–39, 169.

35 John F. Walvoord, *Armageddon, Oil and the Middle East Crisis* (Grand Rapids, MI: Zondervan, 1974), 20.

36 Walvoord, *Armageddon, Oil and the Middle East Crisis,* 55.

37 Dean A. Anderson, "The Original 'Left Behind,'" *CT,* March 7, 2012, www.christianitytoday.com/ct/2012/marchweb-only/originalleftbehind .html; *Finding God in the Final Days* (Des Moines: Mark IV Pictures, 1981).

38 Larry Norman, "I Wish We'd All Been Ready" (Hal Leonard Corporation, 1969). Used by permission.

39 Hal Lindsey, *The 1980's: Countdown to Armageddon* (New York: Bantam Books, 1980), xii, 8, 162.

40 Lindsey, *1980's,* 33, 63, 106, 112.

41 Lindsey, *1980's,* 141, 142, 145, 149, 154, 157.

42 Falwell, *Falwell,* 384.

43 James Mills, "The Serious Implications of a 1971 Conversation with Ronald Reagan," *San Diego Magazine* (August 1985), 141; Daniel Schorr, "Reagan Recants: His Path from Armageddon to Détente," *LAT,* Janu-

ary 3, 1988; Ronald Reagan, *The Reagan Diaries,* ed. Douglas Brinkley (New York: Harper Collins, 2007), 19, 24, 150; Wolf Blitzer, "Reagan Felt Worried before Beirut Bomb," *Jerusalem Post,* October 28, 1983. On the role of evangelicals in the Reagan election see Daniel K. Williams, *God's Own Party: The Making of the Christian Right* (New York: Oxford University Press, 2010).

44 Billy Graham, *Approaching Hoofbeats: The Four Horsemen of the Apocalypse* (Waco, TX: Word Books, 1983); Ronald Reagan, interview with Garry Clifford and Patricia Ryan of *People* Magazine, December 6, 1983, Ronald Reagan Presidential Library and Museum, www.reagan.utexas.edu /archives/speeches/1983/120683c.htm.

45 Ronald Reagan, "Remarks at the Annual Convention of the National Association of Evangelicals," March 8, 1983, The American Presidency Project, University of California, Santa Barbara, www.presidency.ucsb .edu/ws/index.php?pid41023&stNATIONALASSOCIATIONOFE VANGELICALS&st1#ixzz1KHxyOkc0.

46 "Transcript of the Reagan-Mondale Debate on Foreign Policy," *NYT,* October 22, 1984.

47 Reagan, *Reagan Diaries,* 274; "Reckoning with Armageddon," *NYT,* October 25, 1984.

48 Ed Dobson and Ed Hindson, "Apocalypse Now? What Fundamentalists Believe about the End of the World," *Policy Review* 38 (Fall 1986): 16, 21. On Falwell's apocalypticism see for example Jerry Falwell, *Armageddon and the Coming War with Russia* (n.p.: published by the author, 1980), and *Nuclear War and the Second Coming of Jesus Christ* (Lynchburg, VA: Old Time Gospel Hour, 1983). On the influence of the religious right on the GOP see Williams, *God's Own Party.*

49 Marilyn Manson and Neil Strauss, *The Long Hard Road Out of Hell* (New York: ReganBooks, 1999), 19.

50 George H. W. Bush, *All the Best, George Bush: My Life in Letters and Other Writings* (New York: Scribner, 1999), 501; John F. Walvoord, "Is Prophecy Being Fulfilled Today?," *MM* (September 1993), 64. See also Jeffery L. Sheler, "A Revelation in the Middle East," *U.S. News and World Report,* November 19, 1990, 67–68.

51 John F. Walvoord, *Armageddon, Oil and the Middle East Crisis,* rev. ed. (Grand Rapids, MI: Zondervan, 1990), 47, 127.

52 Tim LaHaye, "Twelve Reasons This Could Be the Terminal Generation," *Washington Prophecy Report* 1:4 (July–August 1991): 7.

53 Billy Graham, *Storm Warning* (Dallas: Word Publishing, 1992), 7, 244–245.

54 Graham, *Storm Warning,* 243; Billy Graham, *Storm Warning,* rev. ed. (Nashville: Thomas Nelson, 2010), 244.
55 Graham, *Storm Warning* (1992), 141, 170–171.
56 D. Brent Sandy, "Did Daniel See Mussolini? The Limits of Reading Current Events into Biblical Prophecy," *CT,* February 8, 1993, 34.
57 On the Left Behind series see Melani McAlister, "Prophecy, Politics, and the Popular: The Left Behind Series and Christian Fundamentalism's New World Order," *South Atlantic Quarterly* 102:4 (2003): 773–798; and Amy Johnson Frykholm, *Rapture Culture: Left Behind in Evangelical America* (New York: Oxford University Press, 2004).
58 "Left Behind," Tyndale House Publishers, www.leftbehind.com/06 _help_and_info/faq_general.asp; John Cloud, "Meet the Prophet," *Time,* July 1, 2002, www.time.com/time/magazine/article/0,9171,1002762,00 .html; Michael R. Smith, "Left Behind: Author LaHaye Sues Left Behind Film Producers," *CT,* April 23, 2001, www.christianitytoday.com /ct/2001/aprilweb-only/14.20.html.
59 Cloud, "Meet the Prophet"; Madeleine Albright, *The Mighty and the Almighty: Reflections on America, God, and World Affairs* (New York: HarperPerennial, 2006), 83, 134–136; on the various readings of Left Behind, see Frykholm, *Rapture Culture.*
60 Larry Eskridge, "And the Most Influential American Evangelical of the Last 25 Years Is . . . ," *Evangelical Studies Bulletin* 17:4 (Winter 2001): 4.

Epilogue

1 On the ways in which evangelicalism came to dominate American culture see Steven P. Miller, *The Age of Evangelicalism: America's Born-Again Years* (New York: Oxford University Press, 2014). On evangelical demographics see Robert D. Putnam and David E. Campbell, *Amazing Grace: How Religion Divides and Unites Us* (New York: Simon and Schuster, 2010), 17.
2 On the evangelical left see David R. Swartz, *Moral Minority: The Evangelical Left in an Age of Conservatism* (Philadelphia: University of Pennsylvania Press, 2012); on the diversity among evangelicals see Molly Worthen, *Apostles of Reason: The Crisis of Authority in American Evangelicalism* (New York: Oxford University Press, 2013).
3 Charles Colson, "Wake-up Call," *CT,* November 12, 2001, 112; William Lobdell, "Religion; In Aftermath of Attacks, Talk of 'End Days' Soars," *LAT,* September 22, 2001; Jim Remsen, "Apocalypse Now? Some Wonder They Find Parallels between the Sept. 11 Attacks and Prophecies in Scripture and Elsewhere," *Philadelphia Inquirer,* September

30, 2001; J. M. Parker, "Hagee Sees Approach of Apocalypse," *San Antonio Express-News,* September 17, 2001; Kevin Sack, "Apocalyptic Theology Revitalized by Attacks," *NYT,* November 23, 2001.

4 "Falwell Apologizes to Gays, Feminists, Lesbians," *CNN,* September 14, 2001, http://edition.cnn.com/2001/US/09/14/Falwell.apology/.

5 Bush quoted in Kurt Eichenwald, *500 Days: Secrets and Lies in the Terror Wars* (New York: Simon and Schuster, 2012), 459. See also Stephen Spector, "Gog and Magog in the White House: Did Biblical Prophecy Inspire the Invasion of Iraq?," *Journal of Church and State,* advanced access published online March 28, 2013.

6 John Hagee, *Attack on America: New York, Jerusalem, and the Role of Terrorism in the Last Days* (Nashville: Thomas Nelson, 2001); Hal Lindsey, *The Everlasting Hatred: The Roots of Jihad* (Murrieta, CA: Oracle House, 2002); John F. Walvoord and Mark Hitchcock, *Armageddon, Oil, and Terror: What the Bible Says about the Future of America, the Middle East, and the End of Western Civilization* (Carol Stream, IL: Tyndale House Publishers, 2007). The title alone of Hagee's more recent *Can America Survive? 10 Prophetic Signs That We Are the Terminal Generation* (Brentwood, TN: Howard Books, 2010), makes his convictions explicit. For an account of the Trinity Broadcasting Network story that emphasizes Lindsey's perspective see Art Moore, "TBN Admits Concern about Offending Muslims," World Net Daily, December 2, 2005, www.wnd.com/2005/12/33694/.

7 On Obama as a Muslim, see for example Hal Lindsey, *The Everlasting Hatred: The Roots of Jihad,* rev. ed. (Washington, DC: WND Books, 2011), 209; Elizabeth Tenety, "Franklin Graham Questions Obama's Christian Beliefs, Calls Santorum 'A Man of Faith,'" *WP* ("Under God" blog), February 21, 2012, www.washingtonpost.com/blogs/under-god/post/franklin-graham-questions-obamas-christian-beliefs-calls-santorum-a-man-of-faith/2012/02/21/gIQAIeElRR_blog.html.

8 Pew Research Center, "Many Americans Uneasy with Mix of Religion and Politics," August 24, 2006, www.pewforum.org/Politics-and-Elections/Many-Americans-Uneasy-with-Mix-of-Religion-and-Politics.aspx; Pew Research Center, "Jesus Christ's Return to Earth," July 14, 2010, www.pewresearch.org/daily-number/jesus-christs-return-to-earth/; Philip Goff, Arthur E. Farnsley II, and Peter J. Thuesen, *The Bible in American Life,* A National Study by the Center for the Study of Religion and American Culture, Indiana University-Purdue University Indianapolis, March 6, 2014, 22, http://www.raac.iupui.edu/files/2713/9413/8354/Bible_in_American_Life_Report_March_6_2014.pdf.

9 Billy Graham, *Storm Warning,* rev. ed. (Nashville: Thomas Nelson, 2010), 3, 130, 187; Sarah Pulliam Bailey, "Q & A: Billy Graham on Aging, Regrets, and Evangelicals," *CT* online (1/21/2011), www.christianitytoday .com/ct/2011/januaryweb-only/qabillygraham.html.

10 Graham, *Storm Warning* (2010), 205–206.

ACKNOWLEDGMENTS

I have spent the last seven years thinking about the end of the world. I am extremely grateful to the many friends and colleagues who have been willing to join me. For over a decade Jane Sherron DeHart has been a wonderful friend, incisive critic, sage counselor, and ideal mentor on whom I have relied in countless ways. She helped guide this project from the start. I am also grateful to Grant Wacker, whose wit and enthusiasm never wane. He too has advised and supported me since my career began, and he graciously critiqued a full draft of the manuscript. I met the late Paul Boyer as this research was taking shape; in addition to being a great historian, he proved to be a generous teacher and supportive colleague. I had the benefit of suggestions and criticism from both friends and peer reviewers who read drafts of the entire manuscript. Edward J. Blum, Darren Dochuk, Andrew Preston, Leigh Eric Schmidt, and Randall J. Stephens all made this a stronger book, even though we continue to debate the many issues it raises. Timothy Gloege not only carefully critiqued the entire manuscript, he generously shared ideas and documents from his own pathbreaking research on fundamentalism.

I presented elements of the research that eventually became this book at various lectures, conferences, symposia, and workshops in the United States and Europe. I am grateful for the many questions and comments I received. I am particularly indebted to those who responded to and/or read parts of the manuscript in progress. They include R. Scott Appleby, Donald T. Critchlow, Ken Fones-Wolf, Gary Gerstle, William Glass, Philip Goff, Alison Collis Greene, Paul Harvey, Kathryn Lofton, Mary Beth Mathews, Steven P. Miller, Leonard Moore, Mark Noll, Brendan Pietsch, Amanda Porterfield, Christopher Schlect, Daniel K. Williams, and the Young Scholars in American Religion class of 2007. I also appreciate the support of the *Journal of American History* and especially editor Edward T. Linenthal. The journal proved to be an ideal venue for testing an early draft of some of the material that appears in this book in a different form and context.

My editor at Harvard University Press, Joyce Seltzer, has again been a dream to work with. She continues to demonstrate why she is the best in the business. Brian Distelberg also provided enthusiastic help at HUP. I am grateful to Sandra Dijkstra for excellent advice on the business of publishing. Numerous friends have endured conversations long and short (more often long) about the end of the world. I thank Michael Moore, Jeffrey Sanders, James Seckington, and Jennifer Thigpen for their thoughts and comments over many discussions on all things fundamentalist.

Librarians and archivists have been essential to this project. I am particularly grateful to archivist Patrick Robbins at Bob Jones University. There was never a question I asked that he did not answer or a source that I needed that he could not track down. At the Billy Graham Center Archives at Wheaton College, I had consistent help over the course of many visits from the entire staff and especially Paul Ericksen and Bob Shuster. Steve Zeleny at the International Church of the Foursquare Gospel, Bill Sumners and Taffey Hall at the Southern Baptist Historical Library and Archives, Darrin Rodgers at the Flower Pentecostal Heritage Center, Robert McFadden at Gordon-Conwell Theological Seminary, and Sue Whitehead at Biola University all provided much help and support.

Little of this research and writing could have taken place without institutional assistance. At Washington State University, History Department chair Raymond Sun and senior associate dean Paul Whitney provided critical support in various ways. A WSU College of Arts and Sciences Berry Family Grant helped me complete essential early research. I am also grateful to the Southern Baptist Historical Library and Archives for a travel grant. I received a National Endowment for the Humanities fellowship for the 2011–2012 year, which allowed me to finish my research and to begin drafting chapters. I spent the following year, 2012–2013, in Dublin, Ireland, on a Fulbright U.S. Scholars Grant. I had a wonderful time at University College Dublin, where I was able to polish the manuscript while falling in love with Ireland.

Most of all, I am grateful to my family for their interminable support of my work. My sister, Sarah Nielsen, and her family and my brother, Christopher Sutton, and his family have patiently listened to the latest discoveries over many Christmas dinners and summer vacations. My father and mother-in-law, Daniel and Roxanne Coke, have been patient and enthusiastic boosters as I have dragged their grandkids all over the country and world. My parents, John and Kathleen Sutton, have always been my greatest advocates. I hope they know how much I love and appreciate them and all that they do for me and my family. My son Jackson was born around the same time that I began work on this book, and my son Nathan has never known me to be doing anything else. I love my work, but I love spending time with them far more. They remind me what matters—and it is playing with Legos, building sandcastles, and riding bikes together—not worrying about obscure sources or deconstructing Armageddon. I have dedicated this book to my wife, Kristen Coke-Sutton. She is an amazing friend on whom I depend in every way. I am so grateful to her and so appreciate the many, many ways that she made this book possible and the many sacrifices she endures for me. Kristen, thank you for everything. I love you.

INDEX